EDWARD BYRON REUTER

THE
AMERICAN
RACE
PROBLEM

Revised and with an introduction by
JITSUICHI MASUOKA

Thomas Y. Crowell Company
New York
Established 1834

CONTENTS

CONTENTS

PREFACE TO THE FIRST EDITION

The Negroes have at all times been a source of friction in American social life and the various political, economic, educational and other problems that have arisen in consequence of their presence in numbers have been endlessly discussed. All manner of men, wise and stupid, Northern and Southern, black and white, have been moved to express opinions, and the literature is singularly rich in sociological material. As in the case of other problems that come in for popular discussion, the opinions that gain currency are in major part simple rationalizations. For certain purposes these opinions may have independent value but the sociologist is not concerned to debate their validity. But he is interested in analyzing and describing them, in defining the situations to which they are inevitable responses, in tracing their mutations in a changing social order, and in defining the rôle they play in social life.

The rich variety of naïve material makes racial life and opinion a suitable point at which to introduce the student to the scientific study of concrete social reality. But the absence of any convenient organization of the material has been an obstacle in the way of its use. The very wealth of concrete data, in the absence of expert guidance, is sometimes a source of embarrassment. Discussion groups do not always distinguish between the formulation of opinion and the analysis of opinion. In this connection the present volume should be found useful. It is designed to serve as an outline and as a point of reference as well as to provide an organization and a point of view. It is not intended as a substitute for the study of the concrete material.

The bibliographical material appended to the separate chapters is not a source of reference to authoritative statements. It will introduce the student to a variety of opinions, frequently unsound and often contradictory, which he must learn to analyze if his time is not to be misspent. If he cannot learn to deal with sentiments and opinions, his own included, as objectively and dispassionately as the biologist deals with the simpler organisms, he should be directed into some field of activity where his talents will have an opportunity to function productively.

E. B. R.

The University of Iowa
1927

PREFACE TO THE THIRD EDITION

I

The first time I met Dr. Edward Byron Reuter was at the University of Hawaii in the fall of 1930. He came to the university as a visiting professor and I was then a graduate student, completing my M.A. thesis on "Racial Attitudes of the Japanese in Hawaii." I remember him as a scholar of very few words, always busy reading and writing, never wasting his time in recreational activities such as swimming in the ocean or sightseeing on the Islands. I saw him as a person of extreme personal reserve and self-restraint, almost standoffish. In those days he was busy giving the final touch to his manuscript *Race Mixture* (Whittlesey House, McGraw-Hill Book Co., 1931). As a visiting research professor Reuter gave a series of lectures on research methodology to a graduate seminar on race and culture. His lectures were carefully prepared, highly abstract, and rigorously systematic—and, I might add, much of his lecture went over our heads.

In the latter part of his stay at the university, in the spring of 1931, Reuter went around the Islands and interviewed the elite of the sugar plantations—managers and big overseers. From them he ascertained their views, public as well as private and personal, on race relations in Hawaii, the result of which, to my knowledge, has never been published in its complete form. He was viewing race relations in Hawaii from a sociological perspective—namely, social processes, social organization, and personality formation—that was broader than, and somewhat at variance with, the then popular ecological approach expressed by Andrew W. Lind in *An Island Community: Ecological Succession in Hawaii* and also more global than the approach of Romanzo Adams' *Interracial Marriage in Hawaii: A Study of the Mutually Conditioned Processes of Acculturation and Amalgamation*. To Reuter's discerning mind, it soon became

ix

clear that the first and foremost task for sociologists was to understand the Islands' social organization, if they were to comprehend manifold concrete problems stemming from the contact and association of variegated racial and cultural groups. The scientific questions of ecological and demographic transition, economic competition and the struggle for racial and ethnic survival, racial conflicts and struggle for political power, acculturation and emergence of new cultural forms, new social status, and new self-identity—these were in themselves of little value to sociological analysis of Island society. Each was the subject matter of a distinct discipline—ecology, human geography, economics, political science, social anthropology, and social psychology. But the understanding of the social organization of Hawaii on this or a higher level of abstraction could hardly come about unless more searching attention was paid to the nature of social organizations among the ruling elite of the Islands. Dispassionate descriptions and sociological analyses had to be made of this group—its role in molding of the Islands' economic, political, educational, and cultural processes and in fashioning racial attitudes and sentiments.

Upon Dr. Reuter's return to The University of Iowa I followed him to pursue my doctoral program under him. Curiously, Reuter turned his attention to the Chinese in Hawaii and left in abeyance what he had started out to do. He wrote two articles on the Chinese: "Americans of Chinese Ancestry" (Bacon Lecture, unpublished, The University of Iowa, December 1931) and "The Social Process with Special Reference to the Patterns of Personality among Chinese in Hawaii" (*Publications of the Sociological Society of America*, XXVI, 1932, 86–93). As a group, the Chinese in Hawaii were the longest in residence, the most successful of the immigrant groups, and stood, so to speak, at the terminal of the cycle of race relations in Hawaii. Why Reuter turned his attention to Chinese immigrants and their descendants rather than to the study of native Hawaiians and their mixed bloods, or to other less successful immigrant groups is not too difficult to understand in view of his theoretical position and his abiding research interest in race mixture and in American Negroes. For Reuter the Chinese represented sociologically a critical case: first, the group was well on its way to the completion of the race relations cycle; second, valid and reliable information and data were readily available in the library of the Social Laboratory at the University of Hawaii; and finally, all sociologically relevant ecological, economic, political, and cultural forces and factors have for long operated on the Chinese. A dispassionate observer like Reuter could isolate and delineate with relative ease patterns of emerging cultural forms and personality among the Chinese in Hawaii.

My first acquaintance with Reuter was not through personal contact; it was through reading his books and his articles appearing in the technical journals. As a graduate student in sociology at the University of Kansas, I read his *The Mulatto in the United States* (Boston: R. G. Badger, 1918) and *The American Race Problem* (New York: Thomas Y. Crowell Co., 1927, first edition). Donald Marsh and Professor Seba Eldridge, then the editor of Crowell's Social Science Series, were instrumental in introducing Reuter's works to me. The first book, *The Mulatto in the United States*—especially the last chapter—made a tremendous impact on my youthful mind. Reuter's hypothesis on interracial marriage can be restated: success or failure in interracial marriage is a function of the status each couple occupies. The higher the status of the couples entering into the union, the greater is their marriage success; conversely, the lower the status of the couples the greater is the probability of their marriage failure. This hypothesis interested me, since I was searching for an M.A. thesis topic. Reuter cited several cases, including that of Dr. Inazo Nitobe, the author of *Bushido*, to show the feasibility of the hypothesis. The second of Reuter's books, *The American Race Problem*, was the textbook in a course on race problems. I never got warm to it. Lacking in familiarity with American Negroes and their problems, and hampered by the fact that my knowledge of the English language was altogether inadequate, I found the book too difficult. Other books by Reuter— *Population Problems* (Philadelphia: J. B. Lippincott Co., 1923), *The Family* (with Jessie R. Runner, New York: McGraw-Hill Book Co., 1931), and *Race Mixture* (New York: McGraw-Hill Book Co., 1931)— were read after I became a graduate student at The University of Iowa, 1931–1933.

I am introducing the author of *The American Race Problem* in this manner because I know so little about the personal side of Dr. Reuter, even though I came as close to him as any of his students. Reuter was not the kind of scholar who enjoyed reminiscing; he did not buttonhole his students for chats, nor did he encourage them to tell "their personal stories." This does not mean that he was indifferent to his students— their career aspirations and their personal problems. Far from it. It was explained to me by Clyde W. Hart, Reuter's closest colleague at The University of Iowa, that beneath his stern exterior "E. B." was highly sensitive to human sufferings and their problems and that keeping his distance was one of the ways he protected his sensitivity.

II

In the early 1920's most of the students who took courses in sociology studied problems of immigration and Americanization. Within the framework of Americanization, the topics on the Negro and the Orientals received rather superficial consideration, and the focus was more political and practical than sociological and theoretical. The theoretical problem was there, to be sure, but it was stated in a rather common-sense way as the study of deculturation (discarding of Old World habits and cultural artifacts) and acculturation (gradual acquisition of new American habits and cultural artifacts), and it was related to eventual assimilation in the somewhat idyllic sense of America as a melting pot. Here the phenomenon to be investigated was the degree to which cultural affinities affected concrete adjustment problems in the New World. The more alike culturally one group was to the American prototype—white, Protestant, native-born—the easier were its adjustment problems. Focus was on cultural and national origins. Racial differences came into consideration only in a roundabout way, and nonwhite persons were viewed as inferior culturally and racially and essentially unassimilable; their admittance to the country was to be on a restricted basis, if not to be discouraged, or better still, to be wholly excluded.

Migration of people as stimulated by the demand for cheap labor was prior to, and more fundamental than, conflicts between interest groups within the American body politic. Thus, the nation already had within its fold a large body of "troublesome" peoples of different racial origins. As these people began to struggle for status, as all men do, the problem of adjustment between groups became extremely difficult. And, in this struggle for status and identity, the lines of demarcation between that which was collective and that which was personal commenced to overlap.

As racial frontiers collided with national frontiers, the principle of ordering of people by race or by national origin simply collapsed: there was no mutually satisfactory arrangement between diverse groups, since there was no stable social structure or mechanism to legitimatize politically espoused principles of ordering of peoples. It was here that the demand for clarification of old concepts, as well as a claim for new concepts, made itself felt upon the students of race relations. In the late 1920's challenge was there, and some had accepted it and made significant contribution in this area. Among the few whose contribution toward understanding of race problems has stood the test of time are F. H. Hankins, Robert E. Park, E. B. Reuter, W. E. B. DuBois, E. Franklin Frazier, and Charles S. Johnson.

Unlike students of Americanization, the students of race relations were entering into a quest for new knowledge. The study of race and culture contact had from its inception a theoretical interest that was distinguished from the practical. Sociological interest became one of understanding the nature of society; human nature and struggles for status rather than racial survival became phenomena to be investigated and eventually to be better understood.

Of all American minority groups the Negro constituted the largest in number, the most highly visible, and the most difficult one to assimilate.

Negroes did not come as other immigrants did—either voluntarily in search of greater opportunity or freedom, or to escape from sheer starvation; they did not come with a vision of eventually carving out a niche in a new society because the old had no place for them. Negroes were brought to America literally in chains: they came as slaves. They were assigned the lowest station in the social order: they were dehumanized or depersonalized as ties of kinship were severed and they were deprived of any reminders of tribal identities. Labeled as soulless, they came to be treated as chattels, a mere component in the accounting system of the plantation economy. In spite of this label—a man without soul—the label and the substance were at odds. Slaves were human. During a long, continuous contact and association, slave and master each came to see in the other the qualities of being human. The very process of attributing human qualities to slaves indubitably changed the quality of the attributor himself—a master became a new master, a slave a new slave. Thus the slave was no longer a mere chattel but a person who occupied an inferior position vis-a-vis his master. It was this "sense of position"—superior and inferior—that became preeminent in the conduct of the master vis-a-vis the slave. The plantation was more than an economic institution; it was political as much as economic. It was more than these: it was a total institution within which the preservation of the sense of position became the central problem in the mind of the planters and other whites. The plantation was the dominant institution in the antebellum South, and the sense of position so characteristic of the plantation diffused from it to mold norms of conduct in all the other institutions of the South. The question of color or race, as it became the matter of status, became indeed the hub of the mind of the South.

The decade from roughly 1925 to 1935 marked a period of great intellectual ferments in American sociology, particularly in that area of study then called Race and Culture. Having successfully emerged from the shackles of Social Darwinism and trait sociology—the sociology of instincts, needs, and interests—the students of race relations turned their attention to studying social attitude, social interaction, and social process. Sociology at the University of Chicago was at its height—Robert E. Park and E. W. Burgess had just published their *Introduction to the Science of Sociology* (University of Chicago Press, 1922), and under Park's dynamic leadership a group of capable and enthusiastic students began to investigate sociologically the city of Chicago. The city became a laboratory, and the group's findings were published in a series of monographs. (See E. W. Burgess and Donald Bogue, *Contributions to Urban Sociology*, University of Chicago Press, 1964, Ch. 1.)

Immigration as a political issue subsided with World War I, and the final blow came with the passage of the Exclusion Act of 1924, but the residual problem of cultural adjustment was there on the Pacific Coast. Here Park and his students carried out social surveys among Orientals, and for the first time a comprehensive analysis was made of the Chinese and Japanese immigrants and their descendants on the Coast. Park's notion of community as a constellation of institutions logically led to the investigation of the transplanted Old World institutions—their structural change accompanied by institutionalization of new values and norms in the New World setting. His interest in social attitudes led him also to the collection of human documents revealing the attitudes and experience of tl.e immigrants and their descendants in race relations. On the frontiers, relations of races rarely begin at the political level—marked by conflict and race consciousness; initially race relations are often geographic, ecological, and economic. But they do become political and eventually cultural and moral. Park contended that race-relational phenomena can be discovered and observed scientifically whenever and wherever races and people come together. He suggested that we might study race relations in a fishing village, in a lumber camp, on a farm, in a small town, on an island, in a prison, in industry—as much as in a big city. Race contact situations are found not only in America but in many other parts of the world. Park was particularly interested in having his students study the oceans' main highways, the ports of entry—such as Hong Kong, Honolulu, Singapore, San Francisco, Seattle, Macao, and Bahia in Brazil. It was in this period of his life that Park developed numerous concepts—racial frontiers, social distance, marginal man, race relations cycle—and they stimulated empirical researches of the first order in many parts of the world.

An oft-quoted passage of Dr. Park is an example of the way he conceptualized the problem:

The new economic organization . . . inevitably becomes the basis for a new political order. The relations of races and people are never for very long merely economic and utilitarian, and no efforts to conceive them in this way have ever been permanently successful. We have imported labor as if it were mere commodity, and sometimes we have been disappointed to find, as we invariably do, that the laborers were human like ourselves. In this way it comes about that race relations which were economic become later political and cultural. The struggle for existence terminates in a struggle for status, for recognition, for position and prestige, within an existing political and moral order. (*Survey Graphic*, LVI, May 1926, 196.)

How does this transition come about in a society? And what does it mean in terms of human experience? How are we to reckon with the inevitable emergence of primary relations—friendship, comradeship, neighborliness? What effects do they have on the preexisting formal and secondary relations between races? How is spatial order related to moral order; physical proximity to social nearness and the degree of understanding (social distance)? Why do patterns of segregation show considerable variation from one area to another within or between states, even though laws separating the races are the same? How can authority be maintained in the face of growing intimacy? What, then, is the function of racial etiquette? There were also conceptual problems of a different order that needed clarification. What is race, biologically speaking? What is race sociologically? What is the nature of race prejudice? How is prejudice related to discrimination? How and in what ways are social processes affected by the contact and association of diverse races and cultures? How is education as a cultural process affected by the presence of diverse races? These, in short, were the kinds of questions raised by Park and his students, who carried out research to gain richer understanding.

Such broad questions transcended any particular group. Students sought to understand society and human personality in general. The study of the Negroes, the Chinese, the Japanese, the Mexicans, from this broad perspective became respectable subject matter for sociologists. Using this approach, a Negro sociologist could hardly write about his own group without first "getting outside" it and eventually returning to it; likewise, a white sociologist could hardly write about Negro problems without first "getting inside" the Negro, so to speak, and eventually returning to the group of his origin. This process of taking the viewpoint of another individual or collectivity in order to understand one's own is a prerequisite for gaining sociological perspectives. Simply stated, this is what we mean by taking a point of view of a larger society constituted of diverse races and people. Those who left behind them work worthy of republishing in a series which one might name "Sociological Heritage of Race Relations Studies" might well include the published and unpublished works of men like Robert E. Park, E. B. Reuter, Charles S. Johnson, E. Franklin Frazier, W. E. B. DuBois, and Louis Wirth. These were the men who were successful in addressing themselves to an understanding of humanity and its problems. They subordinated facts to understanding and avoided needless minute description of the obvious—for them the understanding of the nature of society and human personality was the sociological objective.

III

What manner of man was E. B. Reuter, the author of *The American Race Problem*? Edward Byron Reuter was born on a farm near Holden, Missouri. He grew to manhood in the rural community and finished his elementary education in a nearby country school. At the age of nineteen he completed a two-year course at the State Normal School in Warrensburg, Missouri, taught a year, then returned for two more years as a student in the "English Course of Instruction" at Warrensburg. He was an instructor in the Booneville, Missouri, Reform School from 1902 to 1906. He entered the University of Missouri in 1906, where he turned his interest to the study of social science, majoring in sociology. He stayed on for a year of graduate work at Missouri, receiving his Master of Arts degree in 1911. After three years as principal of the Tuolumne High School in California, he continued his graduate study in sociology at the University of Chicago (1914–17). He studied under Albion W. Small, W. I. Thomas, Park, and George H. Mead, and under their tutelage he "discovered a conception of sociology that to his critical mind appeared to be logically defensible and practically useful" (Clyde W. Hart, "Edward Byron Reuter, 1880–1946," *American Journal of Sociology,* LII:2, September 1946, 102). In 1919 he submitted as a doctoral dissertation his study "The Mulatto in the United States," and he was awarded the Ph.D. degree, *magna cum laude.*

Reuter's college teaching began in 1918, as an instructor at the University of Illinois (1918–19); as a professor of sociology at Goucher College (1919–20); and as a professor of sociology and director of the Red Cross School of Social Work at Tulane University (1920–21). The following year he began his long tenure (1921–44) at The University of Iowa. For more than twenty years he was chairman of the Sociology Division of the Department of Economics and Sociology. During these long years of teaching he was granted leave on three occasions. He was visiting research professor at the University of Hawaii (1930–31), visiting professor at the University of Chicago (spring quarter, 1935), and exchange professor at the University of Puerto Rico (1941–42). He taught summer school at the University of Colorado (1928), Cornell University (1930), the University of Michigan (1939), and Stanford University (1941). He resigned from the staff of The University of Iowa in the summer of 1944 and joined the Department of Social Sciences at Fisk University as professor of sociology to succeed the late Robert E. Park. He served as consultant to students and colleagues until his death on May 28, 1946.

Reuter was president of the American Sociological Society in 1933, secretary-treasurer of the Sociological Research Association from 1936 to 1938, and its president in 1939. He was a fellow of the American Association for the Advancement of Science. He was consulting editor of the McGraw-Hill Publications in Sociology Series from 1928 until failing health compelled him to resign only a few months before his death in 1946. He was for several years an advisory editor of the *American Journal of Sociology.* In May 1936 Reuter suffered a severe heart attack, but this did not deter him from carrying out with the same vigor his teaching and other academic duties. He carried on his research and writing, as well as his editorial work. During ten years of ill health he produced two published books, three unpublished manuscripts, nearly thirty published and unpublished scholarly papers, and fifty-eight book reviews. (See Donald G. Reuter, "Bibliography of Edward Byron Reuter, 1880–1946," *American Journal of Sociology*, LII:2, September 1946, 106–111.)

One evening, after I had come to Fisk University as an instructor in sociology, I was taking my usual after-supper stroll about the campus with Dr. Robert E. Park, who was professor of sociology there following his retirement from the University of Chicago until his death in 1944. Dr. Park began talking about good scientific writing. I remember well what he said: "I know two who write beautifully and write with ease— E. B. Reuter and Robert Redfield." And he proceeded to elaborate on what he regarded as good writing in sociology. There was a tender affection in his tone, as was the case whenever he spoke of Reuter, Redfield, and Everett and Helen Hughes.

In his flawless English Reuter wrote concisely and clearly, wasting no words in needless adjectives and phrases. Reuter wrote without fear and without hesitation; he incessantly attacked the pretentions of those who paraded their work as being "objective" when their observations were, in fact, subjective. Reuter wrote objectively, basing his conclusions on the "cold facts," linking data and weaving the patterns of relationships with the aid of his clear, logical mind. He wrote and said what scientific logic led him to write and say. For Reuter writing came easily; he did not have to struggle with ideas nor with their precise expressions. Since he did not seek to please the general public or the novice—he might value the opinion of the few outstanding sociologists of the time—he wrote straightforwardly. As one reads his books (eight in all) and his book reviews (117 in all), one sees that Reuter was quick to praise good work (which was infrequent); he was equally quick (I might add, far more vehement) in pointing out shortcomings: faulty logic, pretentiousness, and sheer rhetoric. He was extremely impatient of a sociologist—"who ought to know better," as he used to say—writing in a popular vein to achieve his own selfish end. Sociology, to him, was a discipline, and it was to be taught as one would teach plane or solid geometry. The learner had to begin afresh. Thus, one of the important functions of a teacher of sociology was that of exposing so-called experts and popular practitioners; of debunking popular sentiments, beliefs, and attitudes about race relations; and of criticizing the acceptance of economic, political, or religious ideology as justifications for keeping the *status quo* or for initiating changes.

In his classes he played the role of debunker extremely well, and many students found his lectures shocking to their jaundiced views of the world

that had been nurtured in the conservative climate of the Midwest. However, debunking was not used by Reuter as an end in itself: he employed
it to shock students loose from their apathy, indifference, and naiveté, or
from their "know-it-all" attitude about society in general and race relations in particular. Then, too, common sense as a guide in the solutions
of concrete social problems came under frequent frontal assault: prediction and control of human behavior, he contended, should grow out of
rigorous empirical research of the first order.

The area of "race and culture contact," particularly the study of Negro
problems in America, interested Dr. Reuter the most. Here he found folk
sociology, masking itself as scientific, receiving a wide recognition and
a ready audience. He found that in innumerable ways folk knowledge
was confused with the scientific; jaundiced evaluation of the situation
with the rational and objective; adolescent enthusiasm with the tempered
and mature concern for the well-being of a society; practical problems
with the sociological; and practical or technological programs of action
with the scientific. So Reuter often began his class, as he does also in *The
American Race Problem*, with popular views of Negro problems, and he
was quick to show how certain views had no legs to stand on save that
of individual prejudice.

Reuter's cunning skill and his ability to make explicit popular views on
the question of race evoked varied emotional responses from students in
the class: soon the questions came from all directions, each representing
unique social and personal experience, and later the questions became
merely strident. Some students remained shocked and voiceless. Reuter
would entertain a few eager challengers in the class, but he would soon
terminate the asking of trivial questions by saying: "Any other questions?" He then proceeded to dispel popular misconceptions by con-
fronting students with cold facts—data assembled with care and but-
tressed with theory. To him teaching was dialectic, and learning, at its
best, was an inner dialogue. Students learned quickly that the viability
of a classroom could not be measured by the sound of the teacher's voice
stimulated by his own echoes or by the amount of "discussion." There
could be a lively class as long as its members read widely (Reuter would
say, "Civilized people read, the folk people talk") and discovered within
themselves important questions about social organization and personality
formation.

Most of us students at Iowa found it very difficult to follow Reuter all
the way. He demanded of us rigorous self-discipline, intellectual honesty,
clarity of thinking, and above all hard work and undivided devotion to
the science of sociology—all of which he also demanded of himself. He
used to encourage me to do research: "There is not much reward in just
teaching. I count on the fingers of one hand the number of students whom

I produced over the years of teaching whose accomplishments can be said to justify my long years of teaching. You must engage in research and publish your findings." He was extremely critical without being totally skeptical of the institutions of higher learning, with their medieval rituals and paraphernalia—as Thorstein Veblen was—where lively learning was as scarce as productive Ph.D.'s. At times he was even contemptuous of important academic administrators: heads of departments, deans of colleges, even the president.

IV

It has been alluded to on several occasions that a study of a concrete group as such was not Reuter's chief interest. This, to him, was a task for social historians but not for sociologists. A study of a concrete group and its problems—be it the American Negroes, the Chinese, the Japanese, the Puerto Ricans, or the American Indians—was always secondary to his primary concern: to increase our understanding of human society and human personality. Facts were necessary, but were to be subordinated to theory; as for scientific method, there was only one—observation, collection, organization, and explanation of phenomena. The techniques of research—historical, statistical, interview, and case-history, among others—were always to be subordinate to the theoretical problem under investigation. And, as for the subject matter of the science of sociology, Reuter contended that it was not social structure or the end product of concerted collective action and activities, but the social process.

According to Reuter, the tasks the science of sociology sets forth for itself are twofold: (1) to define the social heritage as a product of human activity and as an influence in subsequent behavior and relations, and (2) to understand human personality as defined by the individual's milieu and social heritage. Emphasis may be placed on either aspect of the problem. The general problem of sociology was, for Reuter, a description of the social process, and for him process was the key concept. By the process, he meant "the sequence of occurrences by means of which transition is made from one condition to another." A social process, to Reuter, was "the sequence of steps by which transition is made from one social condition to another." Sociology thus seeks to discover the mechanisms of social interaction that account for the development of personality and the changes in culture. (See E. B. Reuter and C. W. Hart, *Introduction to Sociology*, New York: McGraw-Hill Book Co., 1933, Chapter 1.) To Reuter, the fundamental object of attention was always the abstract social process, and it was in terms of this social process that Reuter made a distinction between sociology and history, sociology and general science, sociology and social sciences, sociology and social practice. The sociological point of view or reference is the human group, and the attention is on the general process of human interaction as manifested in all phases of collective life. Reuter was always in search of a critical case— a case that would demonstrate the soundness of his theory—and each case was always subordinated to his interest in understanding society. The American Negro was such a case.

In the area of race relations, Reuter felt that the most important thing to study was the natural history of race and culture contact. (It is well that the reader carefully read Reuter's paper on "The Natural History of Race Relations," in the Appendix.)

It has been suggested by some that the fathers of science should be buried so that the younger generation may gain new sociological perspective. Should this be necessary, we will do this, I hope, in order to rediscover these pioneers and to increase our appreciation of their contribution to the advancement of sociology, particularly a sociology of race and race relations. It is well that we pause and reflect on this question: How much progress have we made in sociological scholarship on "racial realities" since the time of Park, Reuter, Johnson, and Wirth?

V

In order to avoid misunderstanding it should be made clear that this third edition of *The American Race Problem* is not a revision of the 1938 edition. With some minor deletions of words suggestive of racial stereotypes, Chapters 1, 2, 4, 5, 6, 7, 8, 9, 13, 14, 17, 18, and 19 remain as in the 1938 edition. Whenever possible, I have brought statistical material up to 1960 or later. In updating statistical data, I have endeavored to make their presentation comparable to Reuter's original work. The following chapters have revisions—mostly minor—involving statistical data and their interpretation: 3, 10, 11, 12, 15, and 16. Recent bibliographical references have been added to all chapters.

Throughout, the interpretations of the American race problem are Reuter's. My role in the updating of this book does not mean that I share fully Reuter's views on and interpretations of the question of race.

I wish to acknowledge the helpful editing done by Barbara E. Smith. Her labors are deeply appreciated. The assistance of my wife, Dr. Edna C. Masuoka, in assembling statistical data and typing and editing chapters to which new statistical data were added, is greatly appreciated.

JITSUICHI MASUOKA

Fisk University
Nashville, Tennessee
1969

THE
AMERICAN
RACE
PROBLEM

I

INTRODUCTION*

The racial situation resulting from the presence in 1960 of roughly 20 million Negroes in a population preponderantly white is commonly accepted as America's greatest social problem. Whether or not it be given first position, it certainly occupies a prominent place among the serious problems of the national life. It touches the social organization at all points and directly or indirectly exercises an influence in determining the present order and the future development. The character of the population is modified by the presence of this divergent stock; the health and living standards of the country are profoundly affected by its presence; the economic structure of the society is changed and its evolution in part determined by the fact of its presence; the processes of political life, at least in certain parts of the country, have been so perverted because of the presence of the Negroes that political democracy has become little more than an empty form. In every phase of life, political, economic, intellectual, moral, and social, the Negro enters either directly as a factor or indirectly as a condition determining personal and group behavior. The direction and the degree of development of American life has been in part determined by the presence of the Negro people, and their significance for the future is no less important than their significance in the past.

The Negro people and the problems that center in or revolve about their presence and place in American life have been the theme of much discussion. The literature bearing upon the so-called race problem is voluminous and continually increasing. Various phases of the problem have been made the subject of official and unofficial investigation and report. It is a theme for poetry and fiction as well as a subject for popular and scholarly books. Few subjects have claimed a larger amount of space in the maga-

* Except for minor editorial changes and deletions, this chapter is the same as in the second edition.

3

zines of general circulation. Above a dozen periodicals and several hundred newspapers are devoted exclusively or in larger part to problems of race and race relations. The problem is a periodic subject for debate in legislative halls. It is a favorite topic for lectures and for discussion before church audiences, women's clubs, and other semi-intellectual groups. Hundreds of organizations have been formed for the purpose of giving individuals opportunity to express their opinions and advocate their solutions. The interest in the problem is general and people derive great satisfaction from its discussion.

The discussion discloses a wide diversity of points of view. To the Negro, the problem normally presents itself as the practical one of finding a way by which life may be made tolerable in a community the major part of which is neither friendly nor sympathetic. To the white man the problem is likely to appear as one of finding means to prevent the cultural advance of a traditionally servile group, or to prevent a culturally backward racial minority from corrupting the population stock and debasing the social and institutional standards. Whether the particular angle of approach be political, economic, educational, eugenic, sentimental, or whatever, and whether the discussion be by white man or Negro, the point of view is prevailingly doctrinaire and the discussion impressionistic. Aside from the value that always inheres in discussion in a democracy, the writing on the Negro problem, in spite of its volume and the numerous points of view presented, has resulted in remarkably little of practical significance or scientific value.

The popular attitudes of and toward the Negro people are a function of their past and present social status. Consequently, the problem has a natural history in the light of which the prevailing attitudes must be interpreted and understood. And the social status and mental attitudes of the Negro people themselves may be understood only in the light of their history as a racial minority and as a culturally excluded group. The basic conditions of American life have undergone great and rapid changes, the character of the population has undergone changes perhaps equally as great, and the culture of the Negro element of the population has been different at different periods. The problem has always existed but the form it has taken has changed with the changing conditions of life and the changing nature of the people and their stage of development. The social attitudes that come to prevail reflect the present conditions modified by the pre-existing attitudes. In the situation a racial philosophy changes with changes in the attitudes growing out of the practical situation.

THE NEGRO IN AMERICA

The status of slavery lies well within the mores of the Negro races. In the ancient world they appear to have been reduced to slavery by every people with whom they came into contact, and the institution was usual in many of the African tribes. At the time of the African exploration it was generally prevalent except among the hunting tribes, and there was a general inheritance of the slave status. The extent and nature of the system varied with different regions but the demand for slaves was active and the native economy and social order were kept more or less chronically deranged by the trading in captives and the raiding expeditions incident thereto. From the eighth century, the Arabs, incident to their trade relations with Africa, engaged in the capture, purchase, and distribution of African slaves.

In the latter half of the fifteenth century the Spanish and Portuguese merchants developed an active trade in African slaves. The first shipload, 225 Negroes captured on the African West Coast, was taken to Portugal in 1444. There proved to be a demand for them as domestic servants in the towns and as laborers on the estates from which the Moors had been recently expelled. Others were sold into Spain, where they were similarly employed. The Spanish merchants also engaged in the traffic and at the time of the discovery of America there was a considerable Negro population on the Iberian Peninsula and the system of Negro slavery was well established in both Spain and Portugal.

In the Spanish colonies in America slavery existed from the beginning. The Island Indians were converted and presently put to work on the plantations and in the mines on the mainland. But they proved ill-adapted to servile labor; under the rigors of a slave régime the native population rapidly declined. Smallpox and other European diseases with which the native peoples had had no previous racial experience further decimated the population. In a very few years after they were settled, Cuba and the neighboring islands were almost without a labor supply. Christianized Negroes were shipped from Europe to take the place of the disappearing native. Direct traffic with Africa was at first prohibited in an effort to keep the colonies free from non-Catholic influences but the demand for Negro slaves soon exceeded the available supply of Christianized blacks. Consequently the pagan blacks came to be looked upon as having no religion, and after 1510 their importation direct from Africa was allowed.

In the latter part of the sixteenth and all during the seventeenth and eighteenth centuries, the slave trade bulked large and all the important maritime powers sought an active share in it. The Dutch engaged extensively in the traffic, particularly after about 1600. England chartered the Royal African Company in 1672, though English merchants had been engaged in the traffic a hundred years earlier. During the period of the settlement of the North American colonies the traffic in African slaves was carried on with the sanction and under the patronage of the chief European nations.

For a century after the introduction of Negroes into the Virginia Colony in 1619 the growth in numbers was very slow. The importations were inconsiderable. Probably not above 25,000 were imported prior to 1700 and it was the middle of the century before the slave trade to the North American Colonies became sufficiently large to attract attention. Subsequently, the numbers grew more rapidly. The natural increase was high, and this was supplemented by ever-increasing importations. In the first half of the eighteenth century the importations numbered in the neighborhood of 100,000, perhaps four times the total of all previous importations. In the following decade, 1751–1760, the number imported is estimated at 35,000. An additional 100,000 had been imported by the end of the century. In 1790 the slave population number 697,624.

As slavery became an established and a socially and legally sanctioned institution, there grew up and flourished an active domestic trade in Negroes. This trade became particularly important after the system became characteristically Southern. The rise in the market price of slaves furnished an incentive to Northern owners to dispose of their relatively unprofitable holdings in the Southern market. The tendency was accentuated by the later action of the Northern states in abolishing slavery.

The abduction and sale of free Negroes was an element of some importance in the domestic trade. Kidnapping gangs flourished. Free Negro children were frequently kidnapped and sold into slavery. In some cases whole families were carried away. White children were sometimes stolen and sold. There is very little basis for estimating the number of legally free persons thus sold into slavery but the number was considerable; it was probably equal to and possibly exceeded the number of Negroes who escaped from bondage.

Another element of some importance in the latter days of the institution was slave breeding. The extent to which this was carried on as a stock-breeding business in Virginia, Maryland, and other border states has probably been at times exaggerated; but that certain owners did encourage the multiplication of their slaves in order to profit by the sale of the children there is no reason to question. In general the numbers increased rapidly without regard for the master's wishes. In the border states the plantations were frequently overstocked by the natural increase, and the surplus sold South where the system was more profitable, the demand active, and the prices high.

The emancipation of the slaves came as an emergency war measure and without provision having been made to mediate the transition from slavery to freedom. The result was an unnecessarily large amount of social and economic disorganization and personal demoralization. The haste with which the franchise was thrust into the hands of the freedmen added political to social and economic disorganization and intensified Southern feeling against the advance of the Negroes. The effort to resolve the sectional differences by the resort to major force, without an adequately ruthless exercise of this force, created problems more delicate and difficult than those it undertook to solve.

The Formation of Racial Attitudes

The Negroes brought into the New World situation and presently reduced to a perpetual servitude became very rapidly accommodated to the environment and the status. One factor in the initial adjustment of the Negroes to the New World was a certain degree of domestication on the part of the slave group. It is impossible to determine in how far the slave system operated as a selective force, but that there was a selective tendency is certain. It has been claimed, for example, that the slave trade itself was in a measure selective in that the more vigorous and intelligent of the Africans escaped the slavers, were themselves slavers, and that the more stupid were captured and sold into servitude. The frightful death rate in the ocean voyage probably operated selectively to increase the proportion of the physically vigorous and the mentally placid. In the American situation it is probable that the slaves who escaped into free territory or joined the Indian tribes were active types in larger measure than the average of the slave population. In the later slavery days the custom of selling the unruly and vicious Negroes to the far South, where the term of life was short and the opportunity to reproduce less than in the easier conditions farther north, may have had some influence on the temperamental type of the American Negro people. But certainly no great change could have been wrought in the relatively short period of American slavery.

Aside from any process of domestication, selection operating through the biological processes to preserve certain types rather than others, the Negroes became easily and rapidly habituated to the American life. They assimilated the culture facts of the white group with ease and rapidity. The tribal dispersion made the perpetuation of the native dialects impossible and the Negroes everywhere acquired some command of the English language. The native religious ideas rapidly took on the forms and symbols of Christianity. As rapidly as opportunity and example offered, the Negroes learned the manners and customs of the master class. And so in regard to other elements of the culture: the slaves lost their own social heritage and adopted that of the whites at a stroke. This cultural transformation was the more easily accomplished because of the absence of any spirit of nationality among the captives, and because of the deliberate or accidental mixture of types in America.

In the process of assimilating American culture they were at the same time habituated to the slave régime. The second and subsequent generations were born into and lived among a group of white superiors. Their habits of thought and action were molded by this fact. They accepted the white as the superior and the master; they came to expect mastery and superiority from the white. They developed the type of behavior that enabled them to live in the inferior status, the type of behavior expected from them in the situation. They accepted their own inferior status as a part of the order of nature and developed the whole body of sentiments, attitudes, loyalties, and beliefs that follow inevitably from the inferior status. The Negro was thus not alone a slave in body; he came to be a slave in mind as well. Without the appropriate mental attitudes no people could be kept in such servitude as characterized the American situation; no slave system can rest alone on the basis of physical force.

The accommodation of the white to the slave status was no less marked than that of the Negro. The existence of the slave implied the existence of the master. The exercise of control developed the attitudes of mind essential to and characteristic of a ruling caste. Thus a slave-owning aristocracy developed as a physical reality and as a state of mind. The existence of the inferior implied and made necessary the existence of the superior.

The emancipation of the slaves changed in a moment the whole economic and legal system. The Negroes became legally free with formal rights and privileges identical with those of other persons in the society. But they became freedmen rather than free men. The fundamental realities, developed through generations of master-slave contacts, were not modified by the political proclamation.

The reciprocal attitudes of the Negroes and the whites, the sentimental body of reality on which the institution of slavery in reality rested, did not and could not suddenly change to make possible a realization of the new political order. Habituated to an inferior status, the Negro retained the mental attitudes and behavior responses appropriate to that status. He had the feeling of dependence of the man upon the master. The white man had made it possible for him to survive in America and the Negro largely thought of himself and his development as for the white man's use. He was subservient in his attitudes, as he was inferior in his economic and social status. He looked upon the white man as superior by nature, as he had in reality been by law and custom. Nor did the legal edict change in any way the attitude of the white man. The type of mentality appropriate to an aristocratic and dominating group remained. To him the freedman as the slave was a being somewhat between a child and an animal. He considered and treated the Negro as an inferior, never as an equal. The reciprocal attitudes of the former master and of the former slave persisted and controlled the mutual behavior; the legal status existed as a potential rather than as an actual status.

It was only gradually, and with the passing of time and the change of generations, that the Negroes developed attitudes appropriate to their legal status. In the transition they conducted themselves with surprising moderation. The older generation, schooled in the restraints of slavery, retained the sentiments and attitudes determined by the past relation. But as the Negroes became habituated to freedom and responsibility for their own support, there developed gradually new types of mental and social attitudes. Gradually they acquired a sense of group separateness and the beginnings of a racial consciousness. Especially as a new generation which had never known the restraints enforced by a slave régime appeared, the attitude of loyalty to and acquiescence in any and all desires and wishes of the whites changed to one of restlessness under oppression and sometimes to one of secret and bitter hatred for the dominant whites.

The changing social, economic, and educational status of the Negroes tended to bring new contacts between the races. With the existing racial attitudes of the whites, these new contacts and relations were galling. They were in a way a challenge to white superiority and frequently resulted in friction and conflict. The Negro, in the Southern phrase, was acceptable "in his place," that is, in the position of an inferior and a subordinate. As a man, he was, in the attitude of the whites, intolerable, and association with him, on a plane of equality, was unbearable. This emotional reaction, not to the Negro but to the Negro in a new relation, presently came to dominate the thinking of large groups. In the thinking of the white man, the attitude was not recognized as a narrow prejudice; it was conceived of as a vital necessity if the white race and its culture were to be preserved. Having accepted the doctrine that the white is superior by nature, the conclusion followed that to give the Negro of any social class any sort of social equality was to doom the whites. To the support of this doctrine racial prejudice was a necessary attitude, the enforcement of racial exclusion a necessary practice. Thus the white man was always ready to push the ambitious Negro back among the masses from which he attempted to rise. This was particularly true as the lower classes—descendants of the non-slave-holding "poor whites"—came to exercise more influence in economic life and industrial occupations and to have a larger voice in civic and political matters.

The opposition to the Negro in the new relation, in a relation that accepted him as a man and an equal rather than as a Negro and an inferior, found expression in various and diverse efforts to retard the progress of the race. The whites desired to keep the Negroes "in their place" as laborers and inferiors; and to this end there grew up various legal and extra-legal, various legislative, administrative, and mob devices, to retard the progress of the Negro and to maintain the cultural distance between the groups. Laws were passed designed to abridge in various ways the liberties of the freedman, to control his contacts, and fix his status as near as possible to that of servitude. There grew up the habit of dealing by repression and terrorism with friction and disorder resulting from the increased individual competition of the races and the conflict of interest whenever the behavior or interests of the Negroes ran counter to the white man's desires. By intimidation and physical force the Negroes were compelled to modify their behavior to please the dominant caste. The repressive measures used by the whites operated to retard the cultural advance of the Negroes and to maintain and perpetuate the traditional racial inequality.

The racial sentiments and attitudes of the whites in the presence of the rapidly changing economic, educational, and industrial conditions of the Negroes gradually crystallized into an intolerant racial creed. In practice this creed operated to guarantee the economic and political domination of the whites and to maintain a strict social color line. The system in theory and practice was a caste separation on the basis of race, a white aristocracy and a Negro peasantry. The idea of race integrity became an obsession of a large segment of the white population; the supposed aspirations of the Negroes were used by the social and political demagogues and economic exploiters to stimulate the fears of the whites. To keep the Negro in his place assumed an importance transcending all other things and operated to the detriment of both the Negro and the white.

Meanwhile, the Negroes continued to progress, gaining in education and wealth and becoming an increasingly important factor in the political and cultural life of the nation. To the extent that they advanced, the fear of Negro domination increased, and with their increase there came a more bitter and determined effort to retard their progress. And the Negroes, in proportion to their advance, became restless under restriction, limitation, and racial discrimination; a spirit of resistance to injustice and mistreatment developed among all classes of the race. The races tended to draw apart, to form separate communities, and to have no contacts except the secondary and impersonal relations of business and industry. The sympathetic attitudes that often characterized the earlier relations tended to disappear and the races came to know each other only in the impersonal relations of life.

A STATEMENT OF THE RACE PROBLEM

It is out of this situation that the race problem of the present day arises. Both racial groups live and of necessity must continue to live within the same political and industrial areas. It is inevitable, therefore, that they come and will continue to come into competition, either as individuals or as racial groups. But the races in general do not know each other. The behavior of the white man is determined by a complex of deep-seated prejudices toward the Negro and by a fixed conception of the proper place of the Negro in the social and industrial order. In the meanwhile, as the Negroes advance in culture and become racially self-conscious, they become more and more prone to challenge the white man's assumption of a social superiority and his racial dogmas in regard to the fixity and natural basis of the existing caste order of society. The race problem as a practical problem of the social order is thus a heritage from an earlier social order. It is the problem of maintaining some sort of harmonious and mutually satisfactory working relations between the two racial groups in the population.

The situation also involves certain important questions of the social heritage. To the extent that the Negro people differ from the white people in their temperamental characteristics, the differences will express themselves in a modification of the cultural characteristics of the society to the extent that the members of the divergent group are permitted to participate freely in the group life. The social values and institutional arrangements will undergo evolutionary change fitting them more adequately to serve the fundamental needs of the Negro people. The perpetuation of the existing culture complex, many persons believe, depends upon the exclusion of the Negro peoples from full cultural participation. They oppose such participation on the ground that it would inevitably mean an Africanization of American culture.

The political situation involves a similar question. The essential meaning of political democracy is a political order in which all members of the group participate. To the extent that such participation is restricted, to that extent the order fails to be a democratic one. But participation in political affairs is assumed to involve an intelligent appreciation, if not an understanding, of the questions involved. If such understanding does not exist, an effective political order cannot be maintained on a democratic basis. It is said that the Negroes are wholly without comprehension of a democratic political order; they are a culturally backward, educationally retarded, and socially excluded group, only a few decades removed from slavery. To permit their full participation in the political life would be to put a strain on the social order which it would be unable to bear. To exclude them from full participation is to that extent to discard democracy for some type of political control that does not require the consent or participation of the governed.

Any acceptable solution of the practical aspects of the racial problem must necessarily be an arrangement that will insure the Negroes justice before the law. They are and in all probability will remain a minority group in the population. It is necessary that means be found that will permit the Negroes to be men and to be Americans. If they are to be men and take their place as citizens in American life and advance with the advancing culture, they must participate in that culture. But the habits and attitudes of a large part of the white world are antagonistic to the cultural progress of Negroes. As a numerically weaker group in the population they must be guaranteed certain essential economic, educational, political, and social rights. The problem of securing opportunity and social justice for the minority group is an important phase of the Negro problem.

If the Negroes are to be an efficient and socially productive element in the population, their educational status must be made to conform more nearly to that of the modern peoples. The problem involves, therefore, the task of enlightening the masses to a point where they can participate in the American culture and make to it such contributions as their latent genius is capable of making. There is also the problem of raising the industrial efficiency of the group in order that it may not be a handicap to the economic evolution. The social status of the race must be raised. The health standards must be improved. The home life must be purified. The moral standards must be brought into conformity with the prevailing standards of the time. All these are elements of the Negro problem, not because the Negro is black and of a different race but because the group is culturally backward in the midst of a foreign culture.

The existence of a policy of exclusion and segregation inevitably leads to the development of a racially self-conscious group. The existence of a nationalistic sentiment, in turn, leads to the voluntary withdrawal of the racially conscious individuals. Such segregated groups must, as the result of the cultural isolation, become or remain culturally retarded. Such groups inevitably come into competition with other groups in society. When such competition becomes keen it becomes conscious and results on slight provocation in racial conflict. If such segregated, self-conscious groups are to be created in the community, it is necessary that some machinery be developed to mediate the relations with other groups in order to avoid open hostilities. The existence of such groups means the restriction of individual competition with all that such restriction means in the limitation of individual success and development.

The problem also involves questions as to the future status of this element in the population. Are the Negroes to remain a retarded and excluded group—a black peasantry and a labor proletariat—or are they to be raised, or be allowed to rise, to the cultural and educational level of the white population? Is it possible that they can receive education, acquire wealth, and otherwise advance while white America still maintains her cherished prejudices? Can this element of the population be kept ignorant and backward without retarding the cultural advance of the society? Is it possible to avoid racial conflict if the Negroes are allowed to advance in wealth and education? To what extent may tolerance, good will, and mutual understanding replace the spirit of hatred, suspicion, intolerance, and misunderstanding that now so largely prevails? Will discussion or brute force determine the racial policies?

Finally, it should be remarked that the race problem in America is not a unique phenomenon in the affairs of men. A similar problem seems to have arisen wherever races of divergent appearance and different culture have come into contact in the modern world. The racial problems of South Africa, Brazil, Hawaii, and elsewhere differ in details but involve the same essential elements and raise the same type of question.

THE PRACTICAL IMPORTANCE OF THE RACE PROBLEM

Something of the nature of the problem created by the presence of the Negroes in the American situation has been suggested. From a practical point of view the importance of the problem is not easy to exaggerate. The group includes practically one-tenth of the total population of the country, and anything that concerns so large a segment of a country's population is a matter of general social interest. A backward group of smaller dimensions might perhaps be ignored without serious notable harm to the country as a whole. But to neglect the welfare of a group comprising ten per cent of the population and to ignore the problems that their presence creates is neither a wise nor practical public policy. The cultural status of the Negro people is a matter of vital concern to the entire country.

But the Negro group and the race problem have a special interest and social importance. The group is not only a numerically important part of the population; it has particular significance because of its conspicuous cultural retardation. The masses of the Negroes are uneducated and a high percentage entirely illiterate. The sickness and death rates are high and the health standards are low. The standards of family life of a large proportion of the group are low. The percentage of economic inefficiency is high. The planes and standards of living are inferior. The Negroes are prone to a varied assortment of vices characteristic of a poor and ignorant people. It is part of a wise public policy to advance the cultural status of the backward groups and otherwise provide for their welfare.

But the welfare of other elements of the population is equally at stake; the condition of the Negroes is of no less importance to the whites than it is to the Negroes themselves. The welfare of every group in a population is directly or indirectly affected by the social condition of other groups; there can be no movement or change in one race that will not have an effect upon the other. The whites are and will continue to be retarded where the Negro element of the population is retarded. In the present situation the white South is the most direct and immediate sufferer. It is not possible for a population handicapped by a large backward and in-efficient group to make the same cultural advance as could be made by the same group without such handicap. The general social, economic, educa-tional, and political backwardness of the Southern sections of the country is, in large part, the outcome of policies that have not only failed to utilize the creative power of the colored element but have also diverted much of the energy of other elements of the section into negative and futile en-deavor. And the entire nation suffers from the backwardness of a section and of a racial group.

The problem takes on an added importance because it is one of the rela-tively permanent facts of American life. There is no present evidence to indicate that the problem will pass or become of less importance in the near future. On the contrary, there is every indication that it will become a more acute and more important problem. As people become increasingly conscious of population welfare and more desirous to control the factors that accelerate or retard social advance, more attention will be given to the population stock and to the Negro element as the important group lying on the outside and acting as a drag on the social and cultural welfare of the group.

RACE AND SOCIAL SCIENCE

Aside from any political or reform interest, the Negroes in America offer one of the best and one of the most neglected opportunities for sci-entific study of any group in the modern world. The reformer and the administrator are interested in the Negro people because of the problem which they introduce into the social and political life. But the student of social life is little concerned with the problem in the form in which it interests the reformer and the administrator except as this form of the problem throws light upon the facts and processes of the human social order which he is concerned to understand. His interest is the scientific and only ultimately practical one, the effort to discover the mechanisms, the causal relations, in social phenomena and so provide a basis for social and administrative technique.

For this scientific study the Negroes in America are valuable above most other social groups. They represent various stages of culture devel-opment. In the group are men and women highly and fully educated and refined, persons who have thoroughly assimilated the European culture heritage and have in some respects added to it. At the opposite extreme are persons but slightly removed from the African culture level. There are other groups of longer time in America but whose residence in the isolated regions of the hinterland has so retarded the assimilative process that they are still, in many respects, outside the modern culture. There are Negroes in America who speak dialects hardly intelligible to outsiders.

There is no better laboratory than that provided by the Negroes for the study of personality development. The processes of accommodation and assimilation, the growth of nationality sentiments, the fluctuation in racial attitudes, and the other phenomena of racial and cultural contacts are present and open to observation.

In the group it is possible to study the evolution of human and social institutions in process. Almost every stage in culture evolution may be seen as it is actually developing. What must usually be studied by a historic method may here be studied by an observational and scientific procedure.

On the physical side the race includes every variation of amalgamated stock from the Negroes of unmixed African ancestry to those with the merest trace of Negro blood. Between these extremes are to be found every degree and type of racial intermixture. In this mixed population it is possible to study the effects of race crossing in a way not possible elsewhere. The race offers a laboratory for the student interested in human biology as it does to the sociologist interested in the social and cultural and human facts.

THE PRESENT VOLUME

It is the purpose of the present volume to state in a simple way the problem created by the presence in the population of this racially divergent minority. It is no part of the task to seek a solution for the problem; in the very nature of the case, there is no solution. The intention here is, rather, briefly to present the minimum body of information essential to intelligent discussion and understanding of the racial problems. To this end the present situation and condition of the Negro people will be presented from different important angles, attention will be given to answering the question as to why the present situation is what it is, and the present tendencies in race development and racial relations will be indicated.

The body of literature concerned with the Negro in America is very large but its quality is not high: in large measure it is polemic, and for the most part it proceeds from unanalyzed assumptions. It has value chiefly as an exemplification of the historic and current attitudes. For the purposes immediately in hand, this controversial writing may be ignored; the attention of the students is directed to a limited number of pertinent titles. For an extensive and classified list of references to the literature, the student should consult *A Bibliography of the Negro in Africa and America* by Monroe N. Work. The volume by W. D. Weatherford and Charles S. Johnson on *Race Relations* contains a brief list of titles, pp. 556–576. *The Monthly Labor Review*, 22 (1926), 216–244, has a selected annotated bibliography. There is a brief classified bibliography in Alain Locke, editor, *The New Negro*, pp. 421–446.

The references given here and at the close of the following chapters are selected in the interests of profitable discussion. The lists contain some of the better titles but they are not inclusive; they are designed to introduce various points of view rather than to support a particular position. The beginning student will do well to consult John P. Davis, ed., *The American Negro Reference Book*, and the *Encyclopaedia of the Social Sciences* and *International Encyclopedia of the Social Sciences* on the various points of discussion and to continue his reading in the titles cited in the reference lists.

Boas, Franz, "Race," *Encyclopaedia of the Social Sciences.*
Bogardus, E. S., "A Race-Relation Cycle," *American Journal of Sociology*, 35(1930), 612–617.
Brown, F. J., and Roucek, J. S., *Our Racial and National Minorities*, pp. 56–66.
Buell, R. L., *The Native Problem in Africa.*
Chicago Commission on Race Relations, *The Negro in Chicago: A Study of Race Relations and a Race Riot.*
Embree, E. R., *Brown America*, "The New Race," pp. 3–24.
Herskovits, M. J., "The Negro in the New World: The Statement of a Problem," *American Anthropologist*, 32(1930), 145–155.
House, F. M., "Viewpoints and Methods in the Study of Race Relations," *American Journal of Sociology*, 40(1935), 440–452.
Johnson, C. S., *The Negro in American Civilization*, "The Seven Labors in the World," pp. 3–15.
Keyserling, H., "What the Negro Means to America," *Atlantic*, 144(1929), 444–447.
Locke, Alain, *The New Negro*, "The New Negro," pp. 3–16.
Reuter, E. B., ed., *Race and Culture Contacts.*
Schrieke, B., *Alien Americans*, "The South and the Negro," pp. 104–157.
Weatherford, W. D., and Johnson, C. S., *Race Relations*, "The Origins of Race and Theories of Race," pp. 3–20.

Woofter, T. J., *Races and Ethnic Groups in American Life,* "The Ethnic Pattern," pp. 1–11.
Young, Donald, ed., *The American Negro.*
——, *American Minority Peoples,* "Racial Prejudices," pp. 1–20.

FURTHER READINGS

Additional Classified Bibliographies

Miller, Elizabeth W., *The Negro in America: A Bibliography.* Cambridge, Mass.: Harvard University Press, 1966.
Thompson, Edgar T., and Thompson, Alma Macy, *Race and Region: A Descriptive Bibliography Compiled with Special Reference to the Relations Between Whites and Negroes in the United States.* Chapel Hill: University of North Carolina Press, 1949.

Books and Articles

Allport, G. W., *The Nature of Prejudice.* Cambridge, Mass.: Addison-Wesley, 1954.
Berry, Brewton, *Race and Ethnic Relations.* Boston: Houghton Mifflin, 1958.
Bettelheim, B., and Janowitz, M., *Dynamics of Prejudice: A Psychological and Sociological Study of Veterans.* New York: Harper, 1950.
Blumer, H., "Recent Research on Racial Relations in the United States of America," *UNESCO International Social Science Bulletin,* 10(1958), 403–447.
Broom, Leonard, and Glenn, Norval, *Transformation of the Negro American.* New York: Harper & Row, 1965.
Edwards, G. Franklin, ed., *E. Franklin Frazier on Race Relations.* Chicago: University of Chicago Press, 1968.
Franklin, John Hope, *From Slavery to Freedom.* New York: Alfred A. Knopf, 1956, 3rd ed. 1967.
Frazier, E. Franklin, *The Negro in the United States,* rev. ed. New York: Macmillan, 1957.
Gordon, Milton M., *Assimilation in American Life: The Role of Race, Religion, and National Origins.* New York: Oxford University Press, 1964.
Hughes, Everett C., and Hughes, Helen M., *Where Peoples Meet: Racial and Ethnic Frontiers.* Glencoe, Ill.: Free Press, 1952.
MacIver, Robert M., *The More Perfect Union.* New York: Macmillan, 1948.
Marden, Charles F., and Meyer, Gladys, *Minorities in American Society,* 2nd ed. New York: American Book Co., 1962.
Masuoka, Jitsuichi, and Valien, Preston, *Race Relations: Problems and Theory.* Chapel Hill: University of North Carolina Press, 1961.
Myrdal, Gunnar, *An American Dilemma: The Negro Problem and Modern Democracy,* 2 vols. New York: Harper, 1944.
Park, Robert E., *Collected Papers of Robert Ezra Park.* Vol. 1, *Race and Culture.* Glencoe, Ill.: Free Press, 1950.
Parsons, Talcott, and Clark, Kenneth, eds., *The Negro American.* Boston: Beacon, 1967.

Pettigrew, Thomas F., *A Profile of the Negro American*. Princeton, N.J.: Van Nostrand, 1964.

Pinkney, Alphonso, *Black Americans*. Englewood Cliffs, N.J.: Prentice-Hall, 1969.

Simpson, George Eaton, and Yinger, J. M., *Racial and Cultural Minorities: An Analysis of Prejudice and Discrimination*, 3rd ed. New York: Harper & Row, 1965.

Thompson, Edgar T., and Hughes, Everett C., *Race: Individual and Collective Behavior*. New York: Free Press, 1958.

Vander Zanden, James W., *American Minority Relations*. New York: Ronald Press, 1963.

Williams, Robin M., Jr., *Strangers Next Door: Ethnic Relations in American Communities*. Englewood Cliffs, N.J.: Prentice-Hall, 1964.

I I

RACE AS A SOCIOLOGICAL CONCEPT*

In strict anthropological usage, race is a species subdivision, or possibly a division of a sub-species. It has the same general connotation as the term breed, which is used to designate a species subdivision of cultivated plants or domestic animals. Applied to human beings, the term race implies a blood related group with characteristic and common hereditary traits. In the strict use of this terminology human beings constitute a distinct species division of the genus homo, the various existing and extinct types of mankind being varieties or races. In a slightly different usage the human animal is treated as a distinct species with three or more sub-species—Caucasian, Mongoloid, and Negroid—the divisions of which are races. Thus the Caucasian is a sub-species while the divisions of the Caucasian—the Nordic, the Alpine, the Mediterranean, and the Hindu—are races.

A race in this sense ordinarily owes its origin to the fact that a biological mutation or series of mutations produced an individual or series of individuals possessed of distinctive characters, and to the fact that a physical isolation of these divergent types resulted in their inbreeding and, consequently, in the fixation of the distinctive characters by environmental selection. The conditions that give rise to mutant types are not yet established, but once the mutant form has appeared the subsequent process is clear. The new character may be swamped by a crossing with non-mutant types or, if unfitted to the existing conditions of life, it may disappear in the competitive process of natural selection. On the other hand, the divergent type, by some happy chance or because of some peculiar fitness in the existing situation, may survive and transmit its divergent characters. In succeeding generations, assuming a superior survival value to inhere in the mutant form, the race may be changed by the selective process and

* This chapter is the same as in the second edition.

come to be characterized by what in its origin was a divergent character. In this case the race undergoes an evolutionary change better fitting it to meet the exigencies of life. It may happen that, through accident or choice or because of expulsion from the normal group, the mutant individuals, or offspring carrying the germinal determinants for the divergent characters, may become segregated and interbred. In such case the mutant characters become fixed and characterize a new race or variety of the species. It is, perhaps, also possible for new types to appear and become fixed as races in the absence of mutational change. Crossbreeding may produce hybrid types with intermediate characters and these hybrids may by inbreeding establish a type which will breed true to the hybrid character. It seems to be genetically possible, for example, for a human race characterized by a brown skin to be produced, without mutation, through the crossing of Negroid and Caucasian individuals, followed by a selective breeding of the hybrid types.

The problem of racial classification is beset with very great, possibly unsurmountable, difficulties. Existing racial types are not distinct and clear cut and there is no single criterion nor any group of criteria by means of which definite and logical lines of division may be drawn. Stature, perhaps the most striking of all human traits, is of relatively slight value since racial differences are generally slight and individual variations relatively large, and because it is subject to considerable variation through environmental influence. Skin color, another conspicuous racial mark, is by itself of little value for purposes of race identification or classification: skin color is a question of degree, all races being colored and the pigment being the same in all. It varies almost continuously through all the shades from pink to black, shows great individual variation among members of the same race, and is markedly influenced by environmental conditions, particularly by exposure to light. Hair color is a character apparently without adaptive significance and consequently more stable and so more important for purposes of racial classification but it shows a relatively small range of variation. With the exception of a single racial stock all peoples have "black" hair. Eye color has the same limitation on its value as a criterion of classification. Skull capacity is dependent among other things upon body stature and the cephalic index, and shows two or three times more individual than average racial variation. The cephalic index itself, the color of the eye, the nasal index, prognathism, hairiness of body, texture of hair, and other criteria have some diagnostic value. The results of attempts to classify races differ according to the criteria selected. The effort to take into account all criteria and to weight them according to their importance for classificatory purposes results in the concept of a race as a sort of average of a group of individuals showing a rather wide range of individual variation. Race ceases to be an empirical reality; it becomes a statistical concept. Between the Chinese and the North European or between other extreme types there is no confusion. But the degree of variation among the type forms is generally less than the individual variations within the types so there is a consequent overlapping which, in the less divergent racial types, tends to be continuous.

The minute study and comparison of the different racial types has led to a pretty general acceptance of a threefold major classification as capable of including all but a fraction of the world's people. But these primary races or sub-species—the Caucasian, the Mongoloid, and the Negroid—are generalized racial types, hypothetical stocks, rather than living races.

RACES AND PEOPLES

After the original human form had become differentiated into the three or four primary stocks the sub-species underwent further evolutionary change. New types appeared and gradually established themselves as independent racial divisions beside the parent stock or perhaps displaced the parent group. The original Caucasian stock split up into three or four distinct sub-types. To the North appeared a tall, light-skinned, blue-eyed type with dolichocephalic head, narrow nose, and straight face. This Nordic type survived and presently established itself as the sole possessor of the region, possibly because of a peculiar fitness to the climatic conditions, possibly because its divergent appearance gave an advantage in the process of sexual selection. Farther to the South the broad-headed, brown-haired, Alpine race became differentiated from the parent stock. Elsewhere and under appropriate conditions for survival appeared the Mediterranean and Hindu racial branches of this primary stock. Thus the hypothetical Caucasian stock came to be represented on the European continent by the Nordic, the Alpine, and the Mediterranean, and perhaps other divisions. The other primary stocks underwent similar differentiation as the result of peculiar selective forces operating on the basis of mutational changes. The process of racial differentiation, resulting in hundreds of minor races and racial types, is still in active operation; every isolated human group comes to be characterized by physical traits that are in reality racial.

But the opposite type of influence was also active. Migration has been one of the most universal of human tendencies. Whenever the isolating barriers were broken down, the races met and intermixed with the consequent production of hybrid types. The mating of these hybrid stocks as well as their intermixture with the parent stocks led to the blending of characters as well as to the mixture of segregating characters and so to the establishment of mixed types intermediate between the various parent races.

The whole series of related questions concerning the origin of man, his place in the animal series, the evolutionary steps in the appearance of the human form, the fossil and extinct human and prehuman types and their relationship to present or past anthropoid types and to the living forms of man, the classification of present and earlier forms, and various other questions of man's origin and place in nature fall outside the sociological field of research. The questions are physical and biological; they are not sociological in any accurate usage and generally are not even social questions. They engage the attention of specialized groups of scholars who have developed and perfected a methodological procedure for their study. The sociological problem of race is in a way related but is at the same time quite distinct from that of anthropology or human biology. It involves a distinct methodology and has a different scientific objective. The racial problems that concern the anthropologist come within the sociologist's sphere of interest only when and to the extent that they condition or determine social contacts and so determine or condition human and social behavior.

Peoples as a Social Concept

The age-long process of racial differentiation and blending of racial stocks bears little relation to the modern aggregations of peoples. The modern and existing nationalistic groupings are historic products; the world populations are not homogeneous racial groups. Political boundaries are run with little or no attention to the ethnic character of the groups included or excluded. The modern nationalistic unity is one of culture and not of race. The other form of tribal unity, based upon kinship, has been replaced by a unity dependent upon language, religion, political memories, and other facts of a common social heritage.

The bulk of the population of the British Isles is Nordic but modified and intermixed with Alpine, Iberian, Mediterranean, and other racial types. The population of France is Nordic in the North and Alpine in the South and this is also true of Germany. A greater racial affinity exists between the Nordic stock in the northern parts of these countries or between the Alpine stocks in the southern parts than between the northern and southern parts of either country. Italy, Alpine in the North and Mediterranean in the South, is bi-racial. Spain is a medley of racial stocks, a mixture of races resulting from the various invasions of the region within historic times. The peninsula was overrun by the Phoenicians, who intermixed with the previously hybridized Iberians and Scots, and later by the Carthaginians, Romans, Visigoths, Vandals, Arabs, and Moors. Other divergent racial types were introduced by the immigration of the Jews and by the introduction of black slaves from the continent of Africa. Every European nation is a mosaic of mixed and imperfectly blended racial types. The United States, with its original inhabitants of Mongolian racial stock, was settled by the mixed Caucasian racial stock of the British Isles. Additional Nordic stock was introduced by immigration from Scandinavia and North Germany; Alpine strains were introduced by the immigration from South Germany, Austria, Hungaria, and Russia; Mediterranean stocks came with the Italian and other South European immigration; and non-Caucasian racial stocks came with the importation of the Negroes and the immigration of the Orientals.

Nationality is thus not an ethnic concept. The unity of political groups is in no sense dependent upon racial homogeneity and may exist in spite of the greatest ethnic diversity. The unity of nationality is political, cultural, and historical. It is based upon a common language, on customs, memories, and political traditions, not upon the biological fact of common racial origin.

THE NEGROES AS A RACE

The African Negro, of which the American Negro population is an offshoot, is one of the three fairly well-marked divisions of the Negroid stock.

The origin of this racial group is unknown. The first evidence of a Negroid stock is certain skeletal remains of the so-called Grimaldi race which date from the Aurignacian period of the Old Stone Age. Neither the ancestors nor the descendants of this form have been traced but the discovery of the remains indicates a differentiation of the type at a period antedating the birth of Christ by some twenty to twenty-five thousand years. It is, therefore, so far as known, of very recent origin. The relationship of this form to the other races has not been made out. It was possibly the ancestral type from which the modern Negro races are descended but if so the connecting links are not known.

The African branch of the Negroid races with which we are alone concerned does not present a single type. The African Negroes are typically tall of stature, with narrow head, dark skin, broad nose, prognathous jaw, woolly hair, and slight hairiness of face and body. But in the rich variety of their native environment the type has undergone disintegration into partially differentiated stocks and races differing widely in characteristics. It is also probable that there was a considerable intermixture of racial stocks in Africa in periods antedating historic records; some of the divergence between the historic types seems to be an expression of these prehistoric contacts. Certainly all through the historic period there have been numerous contacts with the African peoples and other racial groups. From the earliest historic periods Negroes from Central Africa and from the East Coast were used as slaves by the Egyptians and gradually disappeared into the Egyptian population. The admixture of Egyptian blood also modified the Negro type in all regions where the races came into contact. In the North the contact of the Arabs modified the Negro type, and the various tribal stocks throughout the continent have been modified through the immigration and mixing of peoples incident to the domestic African slave trade.

The modern Negroes are consequently mixed races. They represent a large number of tribes and tribal stocks partly segregated and so partly individualized racially. But these tribal stocks are racially impure; perhaps only the Congo-Pigmies, the Bushmen, and a few tribes of forest Negroes are without more or less trace of an ancient white intermixture. The population divisions of Africa, like the population divisions of other countries, are political and lingual as well as geographic and ethnic.

The Importance of Racial Traits

The various biological marks of race such as stature, skin color, cephalic index, and the like have a meaning and a value for purposes of classification and for attacking the problems of racial origins and relationships, for problems of evolutionary change and development, and for other problems of interest from an anthropological point of view.

These racial characteristics seem in some cases to have adaptive significance. Individuals with characters of value in a given environment would survive in a larger percentage of cases than would other individuals not so marked and would, therefore, tend to exclude by selection all other types. Such survival value may inhere, for example, in skin color. It appears that a dark skin, being an excellent protection against injurious light rays, has a survival value in the tropics and in other regions of intense light. It is frequently asserted that the white race is ill-adapted to the climatic conditions in America and that the operation of natural selective processes will ultimately change the skin color of the population to a darker shade.

In other cases the racial marks appear to have no adaptive significance. It has not been shown for example that the texture of the hair, the facial angle, or the nasal index have any survival value. These and other marks of race appear to persist because they are selectively indifferent—they are neither valuable nor injurious to the individual. Some of these biologically indifferent traits may, however, have a significance and survival value in the processes of sexual selection. It is possible, for example, that the establishment of the Nordic race in the Baltic regions was due to the fact that the striking appearance of the blond type gave an advantage in the struggle for mates. At any rate it does not appear that blondness has any climatically adaptive value.

Whatever value may inhere in these race characters as physical and biological determinants of survival, they appear to be without direct culture significance. Racial stocks are mixed in all nationalistic groups, and groups of similar ethnic composition have made very different degrees of advancement. It does not appear to be possible to interpret culture racially.

Race is a physical concept; the problems involved are physical and biological. This fact must be clearly understood and definitely recognized in order to avoid the endless confusion that has characterized discussions of both theoretical and practical problems of race and culture.

THE SOCIOLOGICAL SIGNIFICANCE OF RACE MARKS

The recognition of race as a biological concept does not, however, lessen its significance for problems of social reality. It changes the statement of the problem and makes it possible to understand certain types of social reality in a way that is not possible so long as such distinctions are not made. There are problems of race that are distinctly and exclusively sociological just as there are others that are definitely and exclusively biological. A first step in clear thinking is the rigid separation of the two, and the establishment of the relation that exists between them.

In the contacts of peoples the external marks play an important role. They are the visible and obvious signs of group membership. In the primitive situation they are the danger signals that distinguish friend from enemy. So important are they that, in the absence of natural marks that readily distinguish tribal groups, primitive peoples and others have found it advantageous to provide artificial signs for purposes of easy identification. A scarified skin, a painted body, a distinctive dress, and the like serve, especially in times of war and group danger, other than ornamental purposes; they are the visible symbols of the friend and tribal member.

In the slave type of social organization, obvious advantages inhere in the fact of racial differences. As a rational and social being, man is obliged to justify his behavior before the social consciousness of his age, and justification of slavery is easy in proportion as race or other difference makes possible the exclusion of the slave from the human category. In primitive morality, the man of alien blood has no rights. Any native repugnance to the system of human exploitation is more easily overcome when the members of the servile group are a physically divergent type; they seem less human, and sympathetic feelings that would interfere with the effective working of the system are less easily and less frequently aroused by the sufferings of racially contrasted persons. Discipline is easier. Escape is more difficult. The dangers of insurrection are less. The racial marks, if not sufficiently striking, may be supplemented by branding or by other forms of mutilation and by the imposition of a distinctive dress.

When an invading horde has conquered a foreign group and imposed itself as a ruling class, a difference in racial appearance is a factor of importance in the resulting political and social organization. The external marks of the conquered group become a convenient badge of servitude, or determine the individual social status. They serve also to justify the exploitation of the subject group, the conquered group being always looked upon as of inferior race. The lower and more miserable the subject group becomes as a result of the political order, the greater becomes the difference between the ruling and subject classes, and the clearer becomes the justification of the system. In every order of society, the ruling groups and classes justify the order by the same type of reasoning—by an inverted logic. The exploited classes or subject races are thought to be inherently inferior—the status being assumed to be the result of an essential inferiority. If race differences exist in such a political order they reinforce the plausibility of the theory on which the political oppression rests. These class and race discriminations remain as a part of the social order until the fusion of the contrasted cultures and the amalgamation of the conquered and conquerors blur and finally obliterate the distinguishing marks of race and culture.

In the contact of peoples of different cultures or on different culture levels, racial differences are immediately important. Skin color or another obvious mark becomes a symbol to designate cultural as well as racial and nationalistic differences. The concept of race is associated with the type of culture and the latter interpreted in terms of race. In virtually every country of the modern colonial world, slavery of the natives is more or less openly at the basis of the economic order and is justified in terms of an anthropological doctrine which colonial administration has everywhere endorsed. The racial inferiority of the culturally retarded natives is assumed; slavery under white domination is asserted to operate to their welfare, to be preferable to the alternative and prior social conditions.

In any such bi-racial situation the physical and racial marks of the individual determine the type of treatment. One racial group is characterized by a backward culture, and the status of the individual is determined by the fact of race. The characteristics of the individuals of the race are assumed to be those common to the racial group to which they belong. The external marks serve to classify the individuals, to put them in a certain category. Their place and role in the society are determined not by their personal worth, intelligence, or other individual or personal traits but by the fact that the external signs serve the purposes of easy classification.

The individual in the situation is thus an unfree person. The external racial marks serve as a basis for social distinctions; consequently they determine the type and number of social contacts. The individual of the exploited race is restricted in his educational and industrial opportunities, in his associations, and in his place and manner of life. By virtue of a distinctive appearance, he is more or less completely isolated from cultural contacts and a certain, usually a profound, cultural retardation is inevitable.

Race thus has a profound sociological significance. Aside from all questions of a biological nature, it is made the symbol of cultural status and thus serves to justify the exploitation of the weaker group with the inevitable political and cultural consequences. Being a symbol of cultural status it serves automatically to classify individuals, so to retard their advance by limiting their freedom and determining the cultural values to which they have access. In this sense the facts of culture may depend upon the facts of race.

The sociological problems exist apart from the questions of racial origins, racial classifications, the biological effects of amalgamation, and other problems of importance and of interest to biological and anthropological students. The social and sociological problems that arise in consequence of racial differences—educational and cultural retardation, personality, race consciousness, nationality, and the like—are problems which concern the students of social phenomena. They do not fall within the orbit of interest of the biological student and the biologist has no methodological technique by means of which he may approach them.

THE SOCIOLOGICAL NATURE OF THE PRESENT STUDY

In the present volume we are not concerned with race as a physical and biological fact. These facts are of interest and receive attention only when and to the extent that they condition or determine social contacts and so determine the status of the individual and the role that he plays in the social situation. We are thus concerned with race as a sociological and as a social problem, with the results of racial differences as they find expression in culture, and with the personal and cultural effects of the peculiar contacts determined by the fact of race.

The American Negroes are not a race in the anthropological sense; they are a population group, highly mixed in racial stock and ancestry. But by virtue of a distinctive appearance they tend to occupy a definite and restricted social status. As a result of this status they possess certain characteristic mental attitudes and social traits. Because of their status and the consequent social characteristics, they create in the American situation a group of social problems that are subject to independent study. These problems and characteristics are social, not biological. It is with these social and sociological race problems that we are here concerned.

Boas, Franz, *Anthropology and Modern Life*, pp. 18–61.

Bond, H. M., "Two Racial Islands in Alabama," *American Journal of Sociology*, 36(1931), 552–567.

Case, C. M., *Outlines of Introductory Sociology*, "Race and Culture," pp. 89–105.

Faris, Ellsworth, *The Nature of Human Nature*, "Attitudes and Sentiments," pp. 317–328.

Fouillée, A., "Race from the Sociological Standpoint," G. Spiller, ed., *Inter-Racial Problems*, pp. 24–29.

Frazier, E. F., "The Negro Community, A Cultural Phenomenon," *Social Forces*, 7(1929), 415–420.

Hankins, F. H., *The Racial Basis of Civilization*, pp. 3–13.

Kantor, J. R., "Anthropology, Race, Psychology, and Culture," *American Anthropologist*, 27(1925), 267–283.

Nathan, G. J., "The Wail of the Negro," *American Mercury*, 18(1929), 114–116.

Reuter, E. B., *The Mulatto in the United States*, "Introduction," pp. 11–20.

———, "The Relation of Biology to Sociology," *American Journal of Sociology*, 32(1926–1927), 705–718.

———, ed., *Race and Culture Contacts*.

Stephenson, G. T., *Race Distinction in American Law*, "What Is a Negro?" pp. 12–25.

Stonequist, E. V., "The Problem of the Marginal Man," *American Journal of Sociology*, 41(1935), 1–12.

———, *The Marginal Man*.

Thomas, W. I., "Race Psychology," *American Journal of Sociology*, 17(1912), 725–775.

Benedict, Ruth, *Race: Science and Politics*. New York: Modern Age, 1940.

Boyd, W. C., *Genetics and the Races of Man*. Boston: Boston University Press, 1958.

Comas, Juan, " 'Scientific' Racism Again?", *Current Anthropology*, 2(1961), 303–340.

———, "More on 'Scientific' Racism," *Current Anthropology*, 3(1962), 284 ff.

Dunn, L. C., *Heredity and Evolution in Human Populations*. Cambridge: Harvard University Press, 1960.

Garn, Stanley, *Human Races*. Springfield, Ill.: Charles C. Thomas, 1961, 2nd ed. 1968.

Mack, Raymond W., *Race, Class, and Power*. New York: American Book Company, 1968.

Mead, Margaret; Dobzhansky, T.; et al., *Science and the Concept of Race.* New York: Columbia University Press, 1968.

Montagu, Ashley, ed., *The Concept of Race.* New York: Free Press, 1964.

——, *Man's Most Dangerous Myth: The Fallacy of Race*, 3rd ed. New York: Harper & Row, 1953.

Redfield, Robert, "What We Do Know About Race," *Scientific Monthly* (September 1943), 193–201.

Thompson, Edgar T., and Hughes, Everett C., eds., *Race: Individual and Collective Behavior.* New York: Free Press, 1958.

UNESCO, *Race and Science: The Race Question in Modern Science.* New York: Columbia University Press, 1961.

"Unesco Statement on Race and Racial Prejudice," *Current Anthropology*, 9(October 1968), 270–272.

I I I

THE NEGRO POPULATION

As enumerated in the 1960 census, the Negro population of the United States—including persons of mixed white and Negro parentage as well as persons of unmixed Negro blood—numbered nearly 18.9 million persons. This number was somewhat less than twice the number of such persons in 1910, more than four times the number counted in 1860, and nearly twenty-five times the total number of Negroes at the time of the first enumeration in 1790. Previous to 1790 the numbers are known only for certain regions and then chiefly from estimates made at irregular intervals.

The rate of growth of the Negro population in the early census periods was in part attributable to the continued importation of slaves. Since about the first decade of the nineteenth century, however, the net immigration or emigration of Negroes has been inconsiderable. The population has grown by natural increase—that is, by an excess of births over deaths—and consequently the rate of growth has not been subject to violent fluctuations. It is possible, therefore, in the light of subsequent enumerations to discover and discount certain inaccuracies in the earlier enumerations.

When such revisions have been made, the increase is seen to have been a regular and consistent growth. The additions in each decade have been greater than in the preceding. Where such appears not to be the case, the explanation is in the inaccuracies of the enumeration. A growth in numbers is seen, for example, in the decade from 1950 to 1960, when the natural increase of the Negroes was slightly more than five times the total Negro population at the time of the first enumeration. Table 1-1 gives the total number of Negroes, according to the revised figures, in the population of the United States at each of the eighteen decennial censuses, and the net increase each decade.

As may be seen from this table, the growth of the Negro population has been continuous and, for the entire period, very rapid, but the rate of in-

Table 1-1: NEGRO POPULATION OF THE UNITED STATES, AND THE
NET DECENNIAL INCREASE, 1790–1960

Year	Number	Increase
1790	757,208	......
1800	1,002,037	244,829
1810	1,377,808	375,771
1820	1,771,656	393,848
1830	2,328,642	556,986
1840	2,873,648	545,006
1850	3,638,808	765,160
1860	4,441,830	803,022
1870[a]	5,392,172	950,342[c]
1880	6,580,793	1,188,621[c]
1890[b]	7,760,000	1,179,207[c]
1900	8,833,994	1,073,994[c]
1910	9,827,763	993,769
1920	10,463,131	635,368
1930	11,891,143	1,428,012
1940	12,865,518	974,375
1950	15,042,286	2,176,768
1960[d]	18,871,831	3,829,545

[a] Estimated enumeration figure: 4,880,009
[b] Estimated enumeration figure: 7,488,676
[c] Revised figure
[d] Includes Alaska and Hawaii; exclusive of these two states, the number of Negroes is 18,860,117

crease has declined with much consistency up to around 1950. Since then, there has been a reversal of the trend in the rate of growth. The rate of increase was particularly high in the earlier decades of the nineteenth century. The numbers approximately doubled in the first twenty-five-year period and quadrupled in a little over half a century. Following 1840 the numbers doubled in the space of approximately thirty-five years. In the half century between 1880 and 1930, the numbers less than doubled; but in a short span of thirty years, since 1930, the numbers of Negroes increased 1.6 times.

RELATIVE NEGRO AND WHITE INCREASE

Rapid as has been the growth of the Negro population it has at all times been less rapid than that of the whites up until 1950. In the earlier decades the native white stock had a very high rate of natural increase. There has, however, been a rapid decline in the white rate of increase, and in the later decades it has possibly fallen below the rate of increase of the Negro people. But the natural increase of the white population has been supplemented by an immigration that has at times been very large. It is this influx of foreign stocks and their natural increase in America that accounts in major part for the more rapid growth of the white population. Until about 1950 the total rate of increase of the whites has at all times exceeded that of the Negroes; since then, for the first time, the rate of increase of the Negroes exceeded that of whites.

Table 1-2: RELATIVE INCREASE OF THE NEGRO AND WHITE
POPULATIONS (REVISED FIGURES), 1790–1960

Year	Per Cent Increase of White Population	Per Cent Increase of Negro Population	Per Cent of Population Negro	Negroes per 1,000 White
1790	....	....	19.3	239
1800	34.0	32.3	18.9	233
1810	34.9	37.5	19.0	235
1820	34.2	28.6	18.4	225
1830	33.7	31.4	18.1	221
1840	34.3	23.4	16.8	202
1850	35.4	26.6	15.7	186
1860	36.8	22.0	14.1	165
1870	27.5	21.4	13.5	161
1880	26.4	22.0	13.1	152
1890	26.7	17.9	12.3	142
1900	21.2	13.8	11.6	132
1910	22.3	11.2	10.7	120
1920	15.7	6.5	9.9	110
1930	15.7	13.6	9.7	109
1940	7.2	8.2	9.8	109
1950	14.1	16.9	10.0	111
1960*	17.7	25.5	10.5*	119

* Including Alaska and Hawaii

It is evident from Table 1-2 that while the number of Negroes in the population has increased, their relative numerical importance declined up to World War I. At the first enumeration they comprised 19.3 per cent of the population; at the fifteenth census this per cent had fallen to 9.7. But since then their numerical importance has been on the increase at each census year, and by the last enumeration it had increased to 10.5. The facts as to number and increase of the two races are illustrated in the accompanying chart, which gives, absolutely and relatively, the facts for each. It can be readily seen from the chart that since 1900 both the whites and Negroes in the United States have more than doubled their numbers, albeit the former by 2.4 and the latter by 2.1 times.

The future growth of the Negro population in the United States has been a favorite field of speculation. Certain persons, under the impression that the Negroes were increasing more rapidly than the whites, have foretold a time when the whites would be outnumbered and displaced. Others with equal confidence have declared the Negro group to be declining and

NEGRO AND WHITE POPULATION AT EACH CENSUS 1790-1930

MILLIONS

NEGRO POPULATION

WHITE POPULATION

1930 1920 1910 1900 1890 1880 1870 1860 1850 1840 1830 1820 1810 1800 1790

have predicted its eventual extinction or absorption. Such predictions are seldom more than the expression of a fear or the voicing of a hope. In the present absence of fundamental analysis of the factors controlling population growth, there is no basis for prediction. The statistical data are not adequate for the usual type of population forecast on the basis of age distribution and the birth rate and death rate trends. In the 1930's most competent students of population predicted that there would be 20 million Negroes by A.D. 2000.

This number—20 million Negroes by the year 2000—was a widely held estimate among competent students of population in the 1930's. But World War II, followed by unprecedented economic prosperity and "baby boom" years of the 40's, affected fertility rates for both the races. The Negro birth rate has not shown a downward trend—instead it has shown a slight upward trend; the Negro death rate has not remained high, but has declined with the general improvement in the health of the people. The result has been that the estimate of 20 million Negro persons originally projected for A.D. 2000 has already been reached. It is generally agreed that the relative numerical position of the Negro will be 10 to 10.5 per cent of the population in A.D. 2000. On the basis of this assumption—and by using projected estimates for the United States as a whole—the total population by the beginning of the next century will be 312 million; at the beginning of the twenty-first century the number of Negroes in the population will be somewhere between 30 and 33 million.

The Geographic Distribution of the Negro

The geographic distribution of the Negro population is and has been at all times extremely irregular. The original centers of the population within the United States were the states of Virginia, Maryland, North Carolina, and South Carolina. At the time of the first census enumeration approximately eighty-three per cent of the total Negro population was in these four states. Subsequently the slave population of the Lower South increased, and by the time of the Civil War this region—the South Atlantic, the East South Central, and the West South Central divisions—contained ninety-two per cent of all the Negroes in the United States.

Although the Civil War freed the Negroes from the necessity of remaining in any particular section of the country, it had, in fact, no appreciable influence on their geographic distribution. Indeed, the tendency was toward a greater concentration in the South. The center of the Negro population in 1790—the point through which a north-south line would divide the population equally east and west, and through which an east-west line would divide the population equally north and south—was near Petersburg, Virginia. For 120 years this center moved south and west, at first rapidly and in the later decades slowly, until in 1910 it was located in the northeastern part of Alabama, 478 miles southwest of the original location. At that time, fifty years after the Emancipation, eighty-nine per cent of the Negroes resided in the South.

The demand for unskilled labor in the industrial centers of the North during and following World War I gave rise to a considerable long-distance migration and to some redistribution of the Negro population. The center of population for the first time moved north and east. In 1920 it was located nine and a half miles east and nineteen and a half miles north of its location in 1910. But even after this migration, 85.2 per cent of the Negro population was still in the Southern states. In 1920 the location of the center of the Negro population was 34° 46′ 52″ North Latitude and 85° 30′ 48″ West Longitude, approximately 1.8 miles north-northeast of Rising Fawn, Georgia. The Bureau of the Census has not computed the location of the center of the Negro population since 1920.

In the decades since 1920 the Negro population has increased in all sections of the country except the mountain areas of the West. The greatest increases in total numbers and in percentages have been in the Middle Atlantic and East North Central areas. In these two geographic divisions there was an increase of 868,000 Negroes, or 77.8 per cent, in a single decade, 1920–30. The Depression years of the 30's slowed down the migration considerably, but the renewed expansion of the war industries and national governmental functions during and after World War II stimulated greatly the emigration of Negroes from rural areas of the South. Consequently, these two areas—the Middle Atlantic and the East North Central —contain one-third of the total Negro population, and this segment comprises roughly 5.7 million Negro persons. In fact, during the decade 1950–60, these regions experienced an increase of nearly 2 million Negroes. The greatest loss was in the South.

World War II was also a great stimulant to the mass migration of Negroes toward the Pacific Coast. There were in 1930 only 90,000 Negroes in the Pacific Area. By 1950 this number had reached the half-million mark and a decade later it neared the million mark; over a short period of thirty years the number of Negroes in the Pacific Coast increased tenfold. The distribution of the Negro population by geographic divisions is shown in Table 2-1.

As can be seen from Table 2-1, in spite of their increase in mobility Negroes are found predominantly in the South. For whatever the reasons, Negroes are as yet disproportionately highly concentrated in the South. As late as 1930, about seventy years after the Emancipation, well over three-fourths of the Negroes were resident in the three southern divisions —namely, the South Atlantic, East South Central, and West South Central. In 1960, thirty years later, sixty per cent of all Negroes in the United States were still living in these three areas. But the concentration of the

Table 2-1: DISTRIBUTION OF THE NEGRO POPULATION OF THE UNITED STATES, 1920–1960

Division	1920		1930		1940		1950		1960	
	Number*	Per Cent	Number*	Per Cent	Number*	Per Cent	Number*	Per Cent	Number*	Per Cent
New England	79	0.8	94	0.7	102	0.8	143	0.9	243	1.3
Middle Atlantic	600	5.7	1,053	8.9	1,268	9.9	1,875	12.5	2,785	14.8
East North Central	515	4.9	930	7.8	1,069	8.3	1,804	12.0	2,885	15.3
West North Central	278	2.7	332	2.8	351	2.7	424	2.8	561	3.0
South Atlantic	4,325	41.3	4,421	37.2	4,699	36.7	5,095	33.9	5,845	31.0
East South Central	2,524	24.1	2,658	22.4	2,781	21.6	2,699	17.9	2,699	14.3
West South Central	2,064	19.7	2,282	19.2	2,425	18.9	2,432	16.2	2,768	14.7
Mountain	31	0.3	30	0.2	36	0.3	66	0.4	123	0.6
Pacific	48	0.5	90	0.8	135	1.0	507	3.4	962	5.1

* In thousands

Negro population is not adequately appreciated until it is examined in terms of smaller units and in terms of the percentages of Negroes in the areas. In 1930 there were as many as sixteen states with Negroes constituting less than one per cent of the population; and in fourteen additional states Negroes comprised less than five per cent of the population. But by 1960 the number of states having from five to less than twenty-five per cent Negroes greatly increased from nine to nineteen; conversely, those states with Negroes constituting twenty-five per cent and more decreased from nine to five. In the District of Columbia in 1960 as much as 53.9 per cent of the population was Negro. The state of Mississippi, whose population was well over fifty per cent Negro in 1930, had forty-two per cent in 1960.

The states with high percentages of Negroes in the population, and the per cent the Negroes constituted of the total populations of these states at the more recent enumerations, are given in Table 2-2.

Table 2-2: STATES WITH LARGE NEGRO POPULATIONS, PERCENTAGES FOR 1910–1960

States	1910	1920	1930	1940	1950	1960
Alabama	42.5	38.4	35.7	34.7	32.0	30.0
Arkansas	28.1	27.0	25.8	24.8	22.3	21.8
Delaware	15.4	13.6	13.7	13.5	13.7	13.6
District of Columbia	28.5	25.1	27.1	28.2	35.0	53.9
Florida	41.0	34.0	29.4	27.1	21.7	17.8
Georgia	45.1	41.7	36.8	34.7	30.9	28.5
Louisiana	43.1	38.9	36.9	35.9	32.9	31.9
Maryland	17.9	16.9	16.9	16.6	16.5	16.7
Mississippi	56.2	52.2	50.2	49.2	45.3	42.0
North Carolina	31.6	29.8	29.0	27.5	25.8	24.5
South Carolina	55.2	51.4	45.6	42.9	38.8	34.8
Tennessee	21.7	19.3	18.3	17.4	16.1	16.5
Texas	17.7	15.9	14.7	14.4	12.7	12.4
Virginia	32.6	29.9	26.8	24.7	22.1	20.6

In certain counties of states in the South the percentage of Negroes is much higher than in any of the states as a whole. The so-called Black Belt, the area whose population is more than fifty per cent Negro, consists of a belt of counties along the Atlantic coast through South Carolina, Central Georgia, and Alabama, and a portion of the lower Mississippi Valley. In 1960 there were 140 Black Belt counties, and they had a Negro population of 1.68 million, which was slightly less than fifteen per cent of the total Negro population of the South (excluding Delaware, Maryland, and West Virginia). However, in 1930 there were 191 such counties, which all told had 2.7 million Negroes, or 29.3 per cent of the total Negro population of the South. In 1920 there were 221 such counties, and in 1910 there were

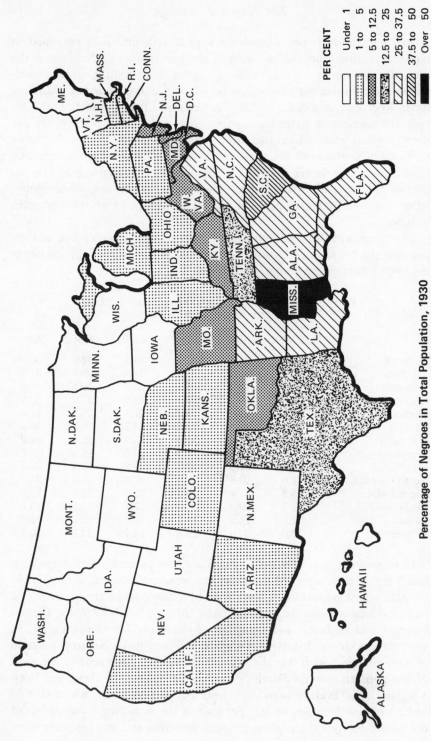

PER CENT

	Under 1
	1 to 5
	5 to 12.5
	12.5 to 25
	25 to 37.5
	37.5 to 50
	Over 50

Percentage of Negroes in Total Population, 1930

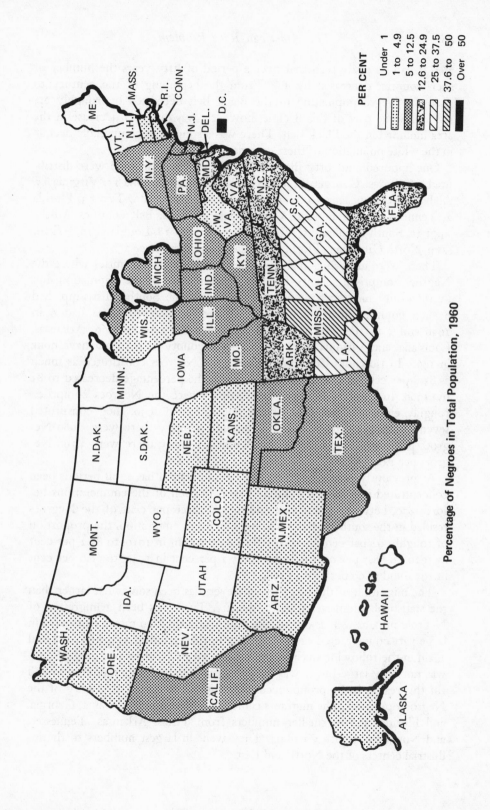

PER CENT

	Under 1
	1 to 4.9
	5 to 12.5
	12.6 to 24.9
	25 to 37.5
	37.6 to 50
	Over 50

Percentage of Negroes in Total Population, 1960

264. It can be easily seen that over a period of fifty years the number of such counties decreased by 124. From the beginning of the century to 1960 the Negro population of the Black Belt decreased by roughly 2.3 million. Some part of this decline, however, was due to a decrease in the area included in the Black Belt. There was a somewhat comparable decline in the white population of these counties.

One hundred and forty Black Belt counties found in 1960 were distributed as follows: Georgia 34, Mississippi 29, South Carolina 15, Virginia 15, Alabama 15, Louisiana 10, North Carolina 9, Arkansas 6, Texas 3, Florida 2, Tennessee 2. But in 1930, Georgia had 48 Black Belt counties, Mississippi 35, South Carolina 25, Virginia 21, Alabama 18, Louisiana 16, Arkansas 9, North Carolina 9, Florida 4, Texas 4, and Tennessee 2.

There were in 1930 as many as nineteen Black Belt counties where the Negroes comprised seventy-five per cent or more of the population, but in 1960 only nine such counties remained in the South. Mississippi had 8 such counties in 1930, but only 3 left in 1960. Alabama had 6 in 1930 and 5 in 1960. Georgia had 2 in 1930 but one in 1960. Arkansas, Louisiana, and Virginia each had one such county in 1930 but have none in 1960. In Lowndes County, Alabama, the Negroes constituted as much as 85.8 per cent of the population in 1930; the percentage decreased to 81 by 1960. In Tunicia County, Mississippi, where the Negroes comprised roughly eighty-six per cent of the population in 1930, they constituted seventy-nine per cent in 1960. In Lowndes County there were 5,060 Negroes per 1,000 whites in 1960; in Tunicia County there were 3,799 Negroes per 1,000 whites.

As previously pointed out, the Negro population has at all periods been concentrated in a relatively limited area. In each of the enumerations before 1870, between ninety-one and ninety-three per cent of the Negroes resided in the southern states. Owing chiefly to emigration, the proportion of roughly 92 per cent in 1900 fell to 89 per cent in 1910, to 85.2 per cent in 1920, to 78.7 per cent in 1930, to 77.2 per cent in 1940, to 68.0 per cent in 1950, and to 60 per cent in 1960.

The migration of the Negroes, however, has been somewhat larger than the statistical summaries usually indicate. There has been a migration of Negroes into, as well as out of, the South, and the two movements have in large part counteracted each other. But in the period of World War I and again in the following decade, the movement of Negroes out of the South was not only large but it was in large part a long-distance migration and for this reason had a pronounced effect upon the center of gravity of the Negro population. The migrants came from Mississippi, Alabama, Georgia, and Florida, and in smaller numbers from Texas, Arkansas, Tennessee, and North and South Carolina. They went in largest numbers to the industrial centers of the North and East.

But in spite of the large migration of this period, the great majority of Negroes in the South continued to live in the state of their birth. The percentages living in states other than those of their birth has changed only slightly in the recent enumerations. In 1900 some 15.6 per cent of the Negroes were living in other states than those in which they were born; in 1910 the per cent was 16.4; in 1920 it was 19.6; in 1930 it was 24.9, in 1940 it was 23.5, and in 1950 it was 28.8.

The exodus of Negroes from the South during and following World War I took on the form of a somewhat spectacular mass movement and so attracted a widespread popular interest. The significance of the movement has aroused much discussion and difference of opinion. On the one hand it has been rather emphatically asserted that the movement is merely a temporary dislocation and indicative of no general redistribution of the Negro peoples. On the other hand it has been asserted, with perhaps equal dogmatism, that the movement is symptomatic—the forerunner of a migration that will tend to equalize the Negroes' numbers in various states. The factors involved are such as to make prediction hazardous. It is to be anticipated that as the Negroes become more literate they will become more mobile. The migration itself will in general operate to attract or repel more migrants to the extent of their success in the new situations. In turn, the success of these migrants, for the most part unskilled laborers, will depend in large part upon the immigration policy of the national government. In any long-term view of the case, the development of the South must be included as a factor.

THE URBANIZATION OF THE NEGRO PEOPLE

Of more significance than the interstate migration is the movement of Negroes to cities. This, like the interstate movement, is a development of recent decades. The Negroes, and particularly the southern Negroes, have been essentially a rural population. But the demand for unskilled laborers in industry during and following World War I attracted large numbers of southern rural Negroes to the cities in the North and East. Emigration of the southern rural Negroes to these cities came to a virtual halt during the Depression years of the 1930's. But the cities of the South continued to be attractive to these rural migrants. Long-distance migration of the southern rural Negroes, initiated by World War I, was renewed by the event of World War II and the subsequent industrial and commercial expansion that followed with America's new role in world politics. In consequence, the Negro population of urban communities increased rapidly while the rural Negro population steadily declined. During the past fifty years the urban Negro population has increased at a greater rate than the white population. By 1960, 73.2 per cent of Negroes were classified as urban.

The degree to which urbanization has progressed varies with the section of the country and with the racial elements in the population. The distribution in 1930 and 1960 is shown in Table 3-1.

Table 3-1: PERCENTAGE OF POPULATIONS, URBAN AND RURAL,
BY SECTIONS AND RACIAL CLASSES, 1930 AND 1960

Class	United States		South		North		West	
	1930	1960	1930	1960	1930	1960	1930	1960
Urban								
All Classes	56.2	69.9	34.1	58.5	67.2	74.1	58.8	78.0
Negro	43.7	73.2	31.7	58.4	88.3	95.7	82.5	92.5
White	57.7	69.5	34.7	58.5	66.5	72.8	59.6	74.2
Rural								
All Classes	43.8	30.1	65.9	41.5	32.8	25.9	41.2	22.0
Negro	56.3	26.8	68.3	41.6	11.7	4.3	17.5	7.5
White	42.3	30.5	65.3	41.5	33.5	27.2	40.4	25.8

The urbanization movement has progressed less rapidly in the South than in other sections of the country. This is true of both the white and the Negro elements. Inasmuch as the Negroes are in major part a southern population, they have been influenced by the regional trend. But the rapidity with which the Negro population is becoming urbanized may be seen in Table 3-2, which shows, separately for the United States and the southern regions, the percentages of urban and rural Negroes at the different enumerations.

Table 3-2: THE URBAN AND RURAL DISTRIBUTION OF NEGROES IN THE
UNITED STATES AND IN THE SOUTH, 1890–1960

Year	United States		The South	
	Per Cent Urban	Per Cent Rural	Per Cent Urban	Per Cent Rural
1890	19.4	80.6	15.3	84.7
1900	22.7	77.3	17.2	82.8
1910	27.3	72.7	21.2	78.8
1920	34.0	66.0	25.3	74.7
1930	43.7	56.3	31.7	68.3
1940	48.6	57.4	36.2	63.8
1950	62.4	37.6	47.6	52.4
1960	73.2	26.8	58.4	41.6

The white population of the United States has for some decades been predominantly urban; the Negro population has been chiefly rural. But by 1960 the Negro population was more urbanized than the white. The percentage distribution of the population elements is shown in Table 3-3.

It is here obvious that the urbanization includes both whites and Negroes. The chief difference appears to be a matter of time; the urban

Table 3-3: PERCENTAGE DISTRIBUTION OF THE RURAL AND URBAN
POPULATION OF THE UNITED STATES, BY RACE, 1910–1960

Year	Total		White		Negro	
	Urban	Rural	Urban	Rural	Urban	Rural
1910	45.8	54.2	48.2	51.8	27.3	72.7
1920	51.4	48.6	53.4	46.6	34.0	66.0
1930	56.2	43.8	57.7	42.3	43.7	56.3
1940	56.5	43.5	57.5	42.5	48.0	52.0
1950	64.0	36.0	64.3	35.7	61.6	38.4
1960	69.9	30.1	69.5	30.5	73.2	26.8

growth began earlier in the case of the whites than in the case of the Negroes. But once the process took hold, the Negroes participated in the urbanization movement at a much faster rate than the whites.

The relative increase of the two types of communities in the recent decades is striking. The increase of the urban population has been constant and rapid; the rate of rural increase in the past two decades has become negative, not only in the South but in the country as a whole. The percentage increases and decreases of the Negro urban and rural population in the last seven decades are shown in Table 3-4.

Table 3-4: PERCENTAGE INCREASES AND DECREASES OF THE
URBAN AND RURAL NEGRO POPULATION, 1890–1960

Decades	Per Cent Urban	Per Cent Rural
1890–1900	35.4	13.6
1900–1910	34.0	4.5
1910–1920	32.6	−3.4
1920–1930	45.9	−3.0
1930–1940	20.4	−1.3
1940–1950	43.2	−14.5
1950–1960	46.8	−10.5

In 1920 the Negroes constituted 9.9 per cent of the total population of the country; in 1930, 9.7 per cent; in 1940, 9.8 per cent; in 1950, 10.0 per cent; and in 1960, 10.5 per cent. Of the urban population, they constituted 6.6 per cent in 1920; 7.5 per cent in 1930; 8.4 per cent in 1940; 9.7 per cent in 1950; and 11.0 per cent in 1960. Of the rural population, they constituted 13.4 per cent in 1920; 12.4 per cent in 1930; 11.6 per cent in 1940; 10.4 per cent in 1950, and 9.4 per cent in 1960. The per cent they comprised of the urban population in 1920 was practically the same as in the two preceding enumerations. But the per cent of the total rural population declined from one decade to the next, whereas the per cent of the urban population increased steadily from 1930 on.

The distribution of the two racial elements in the rural and urban populations of the different sections of the country (see Table 3-5) shows how

Table 3-5: NEGRO POPULATION OF THE UNITED STATES,
BY URBAN AND RURAL RESIDENCE, 1900–1960

Year	Total*	Urban*	Rural*	Total	Per Cent Urban	Rural
1900	8,834	2,002	6,832	11.6	6.6	15.0
1910	9,828	2,685	7,143	10.7	6.4	14.3
1920	10,463	3,559	6,904	9.9	6.6	13.4
1930	11,891	5,194	6,697	9.7	7.5	12.4
1940	12,866	6,254	6,612	9.8	8.4	11.6
1950	15,042	9,393	5,650	10.0	9.7	10.4
1960	18,849	13,792	5,057	10.5	11.0	9.4

* Number in thousands

far urbanization has progressed. In the North and West the Negroes are well over ninety per cent urban dwellers; the bulk of the Negro rural population is in the South. The distribution of the white population, while more urbanized in the North and West than in the South, does not show such extreme contrasts. Table 3-6 gives the comparative racial distribution for 1920, 1930, and 1960.

Table 3-6: PERCENTAGE DISTRIBUTION OF THE NEGRO AND WHITE
POPULATIONS, BY SECTIONS AND BY URBAN AND
RURAL RESIDENCE, 1920, 1930, AND 1960

Section	White 1920	1930	1960	Negro 1920	1930	1960
Urban						
South	13.9	15.3	24.5	63.2	57.1	47.8
North	77.1	74.5	62.4	35.1	41.0	44.9
West	9.0	10.3	13.1	1.6	1.9	7.2
Rural						
South	38.7	39.3	38.6	96.5	95.5	93.0
North	52.2	51.2	51.3	3.2	4.2	5.5
West	9.1	9.5	10.1	.3	.3	1.5

In practically all the large cities of the United States there has been an increase in the Negro element. This increase in the decade ending in 1910 was in harmony with a similar tendency of the white population. But the increases during the decade of World War I and in the following decade were far in excess of any tendency toward urbanization previously manifested by this element of the population. The growth was particularly rapid in certain of the large industrial centers of the North and East. The trend has continued well into the present decade (Depression years of the 30's slowed it down, but it was renewed by the event of World War II).

In the ninety-three cities with a population of 100,000 or over in 1930, there were 2,881,790 Negroes: each of seven cities had a Negro population of over 100,000. In 1960 there were 8,684,357 Negroes residing in 127 cities of 100,000 or over. Out of the total of roughly 8.7 million, 5.9 million Negroes were concentrated in eighteen of these large cities. The seven cities in 1930 and eighteen cities in 1960, with their Negro populations and the percentages the Negroes constituted of the total populations, are given in Table 3-7.

Table 3-7: CITIES IN THE UNITED STATES WITH 100,000 OR MORE
NEGROES, 1930 AND 1960

	1930		1960	
	Negro	Percentage of	Negro	Percentage of
	Population	Population	Population	Population
Cities		Negro		Negro
New York	327,706	4.7	1,087,931	14.0
Chicago	233,903	6.9	812,637	22.9
Philadelphia	219,599	11.3	529,240	26.4
Baltimore	142,106	17.7	325,589	34.7
Washington, D.C.	132,068	27.1	411,737	53.9
New Orleans	129,632	28.3	236,514	37.2
Detroit	120,066	7.7	482,223	28.9
Los Angeles			334,916	13.5
Cleveland			250,818	28.6
Houston			215,037	22.9
St. Louis			214,377	28.6
Atlanta			186,464	38.3
Memphis			184,084	37.1
Newark			138,035	34.1
Birmingham			135,113	39.6
Dallas			129,242	19.0
Cincinnati			108,754	21.6
Pittsburgh			100,692	16.7

The northern Negroes are not only an urbanized population but they are found for the most part in the larger cities. Over one-third of the Negroes in the North are concentrated in four cities having over 100,000 Negroes each, and over two-thirds of the northern Negroes are in cities with populations of 100,000 or more inhabitants. In 1930 there were eighty cities in the United States with Negro populations of 10,000 or more; in 1960, there were sixty-eight such cities (population of Negroes 4,279,835). In general the proportion of Negroes is increasing in the northern cities, particularly in the central cities.

The recent increase in the number of Negroes in northern cities with large Negro populations is shown in Table 3-8, which gives the percentage increase of the Negro populations during the five decades 1910–20, 1920–30, 1930–40, 1940–50, and 1950–60.

Table 3-8: AMOUNT AND PERCENT CHANGE IN NEGRO POPULATIONS OF NORTHERN CITIES
WITH OVER 100,000 NEGROES, 1910–1960*

Cities	1910–20		1920–30		1930–40		1940–50		1950–60	
	Number†	Per Cent	Number†	Per Cent	Number†	Per Cent	Number†	Per Cent	Number†	Per Cent
New York	61	66.3	175	114.9	131	39.9	289	63.1	340	45.5
Chicago	65	148.2	124	113.7	44	18.7	215	77.2	320	65.1
Philadelphia	50	58.9	85	63.6	31	14.2	125	49.9	153	40.7
Detroit	35	611.3	79	194.0	29	24.2	151	101.5	182	60.5

* Source: U.S. Census of Population, 1960, *Standard Metropolitan Statistical Areas,* PC(3)-1D, Table 1
† In thousands

Despite the movement of large numbers to the cities since 1910, the mass of the Negro population still lives in the rural districts. In most of the large industrial cities of the North the Negroes constitute a relatively minor part of the population. But in many of the southern cities, while the actual number of Negroes is less, they constitute a larger percentage of the total population. In some of the smaller cities over half the population is Negro. During the decade 1930–1940 it was the large southern cities that attracted a large number of rural Negroes. Table 3-9 shows large southern cities that have a relatively high percentage of Negroes.

Table 3-9: PERCENTAGE OF NEGROES IN THE TOTAL POPULATIONS OF SELECTED SOUTHERN CITIES, 1920–1960*

Cities	1920	1930	1940	1950	1960
Bessemer, Ala.	56.6	56.4	58.2	60.7	57.5
Savannah, Ga.	47.1	45.7	45.0	40.4	35.5
Montgomery, Ala.	45.6	45.4	44.2	39.9	35.1
Charleston, S.C.	47.6	45.1	44.6	44.0	50.8
Petersburg, Va.	43.9	44.1	43.9	....	47.2
Winston-Salem, N.C.	42.8	43.3	45.1	41.8	37.1
Macon, Ga.	43.6	43.0	44.2	42.0	44.3
Jackson, Miss.	43.5	40.2	39.1	40.9	35.7
Augusta, Ga.	43.0	40.1	41.0	41.0	45.0
Birmingham, Ala.	39.3	38.2	40.7	39.9	39.6
Memphis, Tenn.	37.7	38.1	41.5	38.0	37.0
Jacksonville, Fla.	45.3	37.2	35.7	35.4	41.1
Mobile, Ala.	39.3	35.9	36.9	35.5	32.4
Newport News-Hampton, Va. (central city)	38.9	39.4	39.6	42.3	28.4
Richmond, Va.	31.5	29.0	31.7	31.7	41.8

* Source: U.S. Census of Population, 1960, *Standard Metropolitan Statistical Areas*, PC(3)-1D, Table 1

In general the proportion of Negroes is decreasing in the southern cities, but this is by no means true of all. In certain cities in the South as well as in the North the recent rates of increase have been extremely rapid. In the cities of small population the percentage increase of Negroes has been larger than in cities receiving a larger total number of migrants.

The cities shown in Table 3-10 are notable for the number of Negroes they have attracted in the recent decades relative to their Negro populations in 1910.

THE SEX DISTRIBUTION

The sex distribution of the Negro people in America is irregular and shows some peculiar characteristics. The figure for the total Negro population in 1960 was 97.1 males per 100 females. The sex ratio was 94.3 in

Table 3-10: CITIES SHOWING A HIGH PERCENTAGE INCREASE IN
NEGRO POPULATION, 1910–1960* †

Cities	1910	1920	1930	1940	1950	1960
Akron, Ohio	..	6	11	12	24	38
Chattanooga, Tenn.	18	19	33	36	39	43
Detroit, Mich.	6	41	120	149	301	482
Durham, N.C.	7	8	19	23	26	28
Gary-Hammond-E. Chicago, Ind.	..	7	24	27	50	85
Greensboro-High Point, N.C.	8	9	21	24	27	42
Houston, Tex.	24	34	63	86	135	215
Jackson, Miss.	11	10	19	24	64	52
Knoxville, Tenn.	8	11	17	16	19	21
Los Angeles-Long Beach, Calif.	8	16	39	64	175	344
Miami, Fla.	2	9	25	37	40	65
Monroe, La.	5	6	10	12	17	23
Oklahoma City, Okla.	7	8	15	19	21	38
Port Arthur-Beaumont, Tex.	8	17	29	28	17	22
Tulsa, Okla.	2	9	15	15	17	22
Winston-Salem, N.C.	9	21	33	36	37	41

* Source: U.S. Census of Population, 1960, *Standard Metropolitan Statistical Areas*, PC(3)-1D, Table 1
† Numbers in thousands of persons

1950; 95.0 in 1940; 97.0 in 1930; 99.2 in 1920; 98.9 in 1910; and 98.6 in 1900. A similar excess of females has appeared in each enumeration beginning with that of 1840. This excess of females is, of course, an exception to the rule and, perhaps, reflected the under-enumeration of Negro males. In the white population of the United States men were in excess of women in the ratio of 1,029 to 1,000 in 1930; however, in the last two decades females exceeded the males. Each of the other elements of the population, with the exception of the native white group of foreign or mixed parentage, shows a considerable masculine plurality. And in the case of the group of foreign and mixed parentage the feminine plurality is to be readily accounted for in terms of errors in classification.

The sex ratios of the Negro and white populations from 1840 to 1960 are given in Table 4-1.

The Negro sex ratios vary with geographic regions. In the South there is a paucity of Negro males; the sex ratio in the South in 1930 was 95.9, and it was 93.4 in 1960. In the North and West men were in excess in 1930: the Negro sex ratio was 101.0 in the North but it came down to 92.1 in 1960, and it was 104.1 in the West in 1930 but 99.4 in 1960. These differences around 1930 are perhaps adequately understood as a result of migration: men more frequently than women undertook long-distance migra-

Table 4-1: SEX RATIOS OF THE NEGRO AND WHITE POPULATIONS
OF THE UNITED STATES, 1840–1960

Year	Negro Population	Total White Population
1840	99.5	104.5
1850	99.1	105.2
1860	99.6	105.3
1870	96.2	102.8
1880	97.8	104.0
1890	99.5	105.4
1900	98.6	104.9
1910	98.9	106.6
1920	99.2	104.4
1930	97.0	102.9
1940	95.0	101.2
1950	94.3	99.0
1960	93.4	97.4

tion, and the Negro populations of the North and West at that time contained many recent migrants.

As between the rural and urban elements of the Negro population, women are in excess in the urban and men in the rural areas. This is similar to the urban-rural sex distribution of the white population and is explained by the greater short-distance migration of women. But the excess of white men in the rural population is very much greater than is the excess of Negro men—109.0 for the whites, 101.7 for the Negroes. The sex ratios for the urban and rural elements of the population are shown, since the beginning of the present century, in Table 4-2.

Table 4-2: NEGRO MALES PER 100 NEGRO FEMALES, BY URBAN AND
RURAL RESIDENCE, 1900–1960

Year	Total	Urban	Rural Nonfarm	Rural Farm
1900	98.6	87.8	102.1	
1910	98.9	90.8	102.1	
1920	99.2	95.4		
1930	97.0	91.3	103.7	100.3
1940	95.0	88.1	102.8	101.2
1950	94.3	90.0	99.8	103.1
1960	93.3	90.3	101.7	101.9

The Negro sex distribution by age is strikingly irregular. There is an excess of females in all age groups under 45 years. The excess of females is greatest in years of early maturity—15 to 35 years. In 1930 the excess of females was greatest in the age group of 20–24; in 1960 the excess was greatest in the age-group of 30–34 years.

The excess of females is a characteristic of the mixed-blood segment of the Negro population. At the 1930 enumeration no data were assembled in regard to the status of racial intermixture. At the previous enumeration the Negroes classed as being of full blood had a slight excess of males in all sections of the country. But in the mulatto division the females were in excess in all sections except the West, where long-distance migration had led to a slight masculine plurality, the excess being almost ten to eight. The tabulation in Table 4-3 shows the contrast in a striking way.

Table 4-3: NEGRO AND MULATTO MALES PER 1,000 FEMALES IN THE
URBAN AND RURAL POPULATIONS, 1920

Classification	Urban	Rural
Total Negro Population	908	1,021
Full-blood Negroes	947	1,043
Mixed-blood Negroes	810	931

In explanation of this somewhat remarkable sex distribution it is possible to resort to the idea that crossbreeding produces an excess of females. But it seems unnecessary to advance this order of explanation. The reasons for the facts seem to lie in part in accidental omissions from the count, which would be greater in the case of men than of women, and in inaccuracies resulting from an imperfect classification. But of more importance than either, perhaps, is the annual loss to the race that results from light-colored mulattoes changing their racial status and passing as white men. A considerable number of light-colored individuals, as they come to early manhood, move to new localities and report themselves as white. The number of light mulattoes who pass temporarily or permanently into the white race is much larger in the case of men than of women.

THE AGE COMPOSITION

The age composition of a population is important. The age ratios are normally determined by the birth and death rates; a high percentage of the population in the early age groups suggests either a rapid natural increase or a short average duration of life. Also, the social and psychological characteristics of the group are in part dependent upon the age factor.

Table 5-1 allows a comparison of the age composition of the Negro population with that of the white population of native parentage from 1910 to 1960, and a comparison of the distribution for each group at the six enumerations.

The median age of the Negro population—that is, the age at which the population divides into two equal groups, the number younger being exactly the same as the number older—is lower than that of the white population. Prior to 1930 the median age of the whites was, of course, affected

Table 5-1: PERCENTAGE COMPOSITION OF THE POPULATIONS BY AGE GROUPS, 1910–1960

Age Groups	Negro						Native White of Native Parentage					
	1910	1920	1930	1940	1950	1960	1910	1920	1930	1940	1950	1960
Under 5 Years	12.9	10.9	10.3	9.7	12.5	14.4	13.2	12.6	11.3	7.8	10.5	10.9
5 to 9 Years	12.7	12.1	11.5	10.1	10.2	12.7	11.8	11.9	11.9	7.9	8.6	10.1
10 to 14 Years	11.8	11.8	10.5	10.3	9.1	10.5	10.8	11.1	10.7	8.7	7.2	9.2
15 to 19 Years	10.8	10.4	10.5	10.1	8.1	7.9	10.3	9.6	9.9	9.3	6.9	7.3
20 to 44 Years	37.3	38.2	39.7	39.9	38.0	31.5	35.6	35.9	36.3	38.8	37.6	32.3
45 Years and Over	14.5	16.4	17.3	19.9	22.1	23.0	18.1	18.8	19.9	27.5	29.2	30.2

by the age distribution of the foreign-born, relatively few of whom were in their younger years. In 1910 the median age of the native whites was 21.4 years, as against 24.4 years for the total white population; in 1930 the median age of the native whites was 23.8 as against 26.9 for the total white population. In the case of both the Negroes and the whites there has been a slight increase in the median age. The increase has been greater since 1940. The increase in each case is probably due in some part to a decline in the mortality rates, but certainly in part also to the decline in the birth rates. Each tends to raise the median age—the declining death rates, by increasing the number in the upper age groups; the declining birth rates, by reducing the number in the younger age groups. Table 5-2 shows the significant facts in regard to the median age of the Negro and the white populations.

Table 5-2: MEDIAN AGE OF NEGRO AND WHITE POPULATIONS, 1900–1960

Year and Race		Both Sexes	Males	Females
1900	Negro	19.6	19.5	19.4
	White	23.4	23.8	22.9
1910	Negro	20.9	21.1	20.6
	White	24.4	24.9	23.9
1920	Negro	22.4	22.8	22.0
	White	25.6	26.1	25.1
1930	Negro	23.6	23.7	23.2
	White	26.9	27.1	26.6
1940	Negro	25.4	25.3	25.3
	White	29.5	29.5	29.5
1950	Negro	26.1	25.9	26.2
	White	30.8	30.4	31.1
1960	Negro	23.5	22.3	24.5
	White	30.3	29.4	31.1

The age distribution of the Negro population shows a considerable range of variation in different sections of the country. The number of children under 20 years in 1930 comprised 46.0 per cent of the Negro population in the South, 31.8 per cent in the North, and 27.2 per cent in the West. The proportion in the South is slightly above that in the North and West, markedly below that of the Negro population as a whole. In the middle age group, 35 to 44 years, in 1930 the percentage for the total Negro population was 13.3, for the South 12.0, for the North 17.7, and for the West 20.1; whereas in 1960 the corresponding percentages were 12.2, 11.0, 14.0, and 14.5. Some of the variations observed may be due to sectional differences in the birth and death rates, but the chief explanation doubtless lies in the facts of Negro migration. The effects of changes in residence are chiefly to be seen in the regions where the number of Negroes is small, since in these regions the migrants are most important relative to the total population. Consequently in 1930, the age disturbances appear chiefly in the North and West, where the numbers of the race are comparatively small. By 1960 regional variations are becoming less noticeable as seen in Table 5-3.

Table 5-3: AGE COMPOSITION OF THE NEGRO POPULATION, 1930 AND 1960

Age Period	United States 1930	United States 1960	South 1930	South 1960	North 1930	North 1960	West 1930	West 1960
Under 5 years	10.3	14.4	10.9	14.6	8.5	14.2	6.5	14.9
5 to 9 years	11.5	12.7	12.3	13.3	8.7	11.7	7.3	12.1
10 to 14 years	10.5	10.5	11.4	11.4	7.2	9.1	6.6	9.2
15 to 19 years	10.5	7.9	11.4	8.8	7.4	6.7	6.8	6.7
20 to 24 years	10.1	6.4	10.2	6.2	9.9	6.6	8.2	7.5
25 to 29 years	9.0	6.3	8.3	5.6	11.9	7.2	9.6	7.6
30 to 34 years	7.3	6.5	6.4	5.7	10.5	7.7	9.9	7.6
35 to 44 years	13.3	12.2	12.0	11.0	17.7	14.0	20.1	14.5
45 to 54 years	9.5	9.9	9.2	9.7	10.7	10.2	14.3	9.9
55 to 64 years	4.6	6.9	4.7	6.9	4.5	7.2	6.5	5.7
65 years and over	3.1	6.2	3.2	6.8	2.7	5.4	3.8	4.1
Age unknown	0.1		0.1		0.2			

A similar variation in age composition appears from state to state. Where the total Negro population is small the entrance or departure of a small number of persons of a certain age group may profoundly disturb the normal age distribution. The median age is lower in the southern than in any of the northern states. The states with a high median age are those where the proportion of migrants is high. The range in 1920 was from 17.5 years (18.1 years in 1960) as the median age in South Carolina to 33.1 years (24.2 years in 1960) as the median age in the state of Oregon.

The age distribution is likewise affected by the cityward migration. This movement chiefly involves persons in the middle years of life; members of both the younger and the older age groups remain behind. Consequently, the urban population is made up in much larger part than is the rural of persons in the productive years of life. In 1930, 37.8 per cent of the urban Negroes and 23.2 per cent of the rural Negroes were in the group aged 25–44. One was above and the other below the average of the Negro population as a whole, which was 29.6 per cent. The more disturbed ratios of the urban populations are due to the fact that the total number of urban Negroes is less than the total number of rural Negroes; the migration to the cities upsets the ratios more profoundly there than in the rural regions. The differences in birth and death rates between the Negro urban and rural communities also affect the ratios, at least slightly.

THE ETHNIC COMPOSITION

The enumeration statistics suggest rather than measure the degree of racial amalgamation. The terms "black" and "mulatto" do not correspond with any nicety to differences in physical characters. Rather few of the American Negroes are black and by no means all the dark-skinned individuals are pure-blood Negroes. The term mulatto is used in a generic sense to include all persons, except full-blood Negroes, with any perceptible trace of Negro blood. It comprehends all grades and degrees of intermixture from the Negro with the smallest perceptible trace of white admixture to the white person with any perceptible trace of Negro admixture. The number of mulattoes is not, therefore, a measure of the extent to which the races have mingled. The one effort on the part of the Census Bureau to measure more accurately the extent of the racial intermixture was admittedly not a success. Equal traces of Negro and white blood do not show equally in different individuals. Moreover, the definitions of the terms black and mulatto have not been the same at the different enumerations.

Table 6-1 gives the census data available in regard to the numbers and percentages of black and mulatto elements in the population at the different enumerations when the distinction was made.

Table 6-1: THE NEGRO POPULATION, BLACK AND MULATTO ELEMENTS

Census Year	Total	Black	Mulatto Number	Per Cent	Mulattoes to 1,000 Blacks
1850	3,638,808	3,233,057	405,751	11.2	126
1860	4,441,830	3,853,467	588,363	13.2	153
1870	4,880,009	4,295,960	584,049	12.0	136
1890	7,488,676*	6,337,980	1,132,060	15.2	179
1910	9,827,763	7,777,077	2,050,686	20.9	264
1920	10,463,131	8,802,577	1,660,554	15.9	189

* Includes 18,636 Negroes enumerated in Indian territory, not distinguished as black and mulatto

Owing to enumeration difficulties and inaccuracies the increase of the mixed-blood element of the population appears to be highly irregular. But aside from the irregularity the table shows an increase in the percentage of mulattoes. This would naturally be the case inasmuch as the group grows by natural increase resulting from the union of mulattoes with mulattoes as well as by the increase that results from the union of whites with both the black and the mulatto members of the Negro group. The increase of the full-blood Negroes is restricted to the natural increase resulting from the union of blacks with blacks and to the offspring of black and mulatto unions where the trace of white blood in the offspring is too small to be perceptible. The immigration of full-blood Negroes is a negligible factor in the numerical increase. The increasing proportion of mulattoes may and at least in part does show the dissemination of the white blood already within the race rather than a continuous infusion of white blood.

The physical characters of the Negro population are thus being changed by the gradual diffusion of the white blood already in the race. As this process goes on, the increase of the mixed-blood group at the expense of the full-blood group, the Negro population becomes more and more a mulatto population. It is variously estimated that one-third, one-half, or even three-fourths of the American Negroes already show some larger or smaller trace of intermixture but which is in many cases so slight as to escape the notice of enumerators. As this intermixture becomes more widespread, as the Negro type is modified by traces of white blood imperceptible to common observation, there is a shift in the basis on which comparison is made. The standard of comparison is the full-blood Negro. But as the type becomes modified by the spread of the white intermixture, there ceases to be a full-blood type. The darker members of the mixed-blood population become the basis for comparison and the contrast between the black and the mulatto becomes less sharp.

There is also an opposite force at work. Each year the mulatto group loses a larger or smaller number of its members through their disappearance into the white population. Many individuals whose percentage of Negro blood is only one-eighth or less are to all appearances white persons. In any region where the person and his ancestry are not known he may pass as a person of pure white ancestry. This matter of loss from the lighter end of the racial group has gone on for a very long time. Also, it tends to increase to the extent that the white blood becomes more general in the race by the intermixture of the whites and the mulattoes. It also becomes easier for light colored mulattoes to pass as white men as the fundamental characters of the white stock are modified by the tinge of Negro blood thus entering and by the immigration and amalgamation of stocks less sharply contrasted in physical type than were the older American type and the Negro peoples.

At each of the enumerations, the proportion of mulattoes has been lowest in the South and, except in 1850, highest in the West. The essential facts for the five mulatto enumerations are shown in Table 6-2.

In actual numbers, the great majority of the mixed-bloods are, and at all times have been, in the South. The rate of increase of this element of the population has been far more rapid in the southern regions. From 1850 to 1920 the mulatto population increased 1,254,803; the mulatto population of the South increased 1,062,799, that of the North 173,709, and that of the West 19,295.

Table 6-2: MULATTOES IN THE NEGRO POPULATION, BY GEOGRAPHIC AREAS, 1850, 1860, 1890, 1900, AND 1920

	United States	South	North	West
1850				
Per Cent Mulatto	11.2	10.0	24.8	23.4
Mulattoes to 1,000 Blacks	126	111	329	306
1870				
Per Cent Mulatto	12.0	11.1	20.3	35.6
Mulattoes to 1,000 Blacks	136	125	255	553
1890				
Per Cent Mulatto	15.2	13.7	28.0	39.2
Mulattoes to 1,000 Blacks	179	159	390	644
1900				
Per Cent Mulatto	20.9	20.1	26.6	32.1
Mulattoes to 1,000 Blacks	264	252	363	473
1920				
Per Cent Mulatto	15.9	15.7	16.5	24.9
Mulattoes to 1,000 Blacks	189	186	198	366

The percentages of the Negro population reported as of mixed blood in the enumerations of 1910 and 1920 are given in Table 6-3 by geographic divisions.

The changing proportions may be accounted for at least in part in terms of migration. Among the migrants the percentage of mulattoes is probably higher than is their percentage in the South but lower than their percentage in the North and West. The net result of the migration was thus in some cases to lower the percentage of mulattoes in the North and West. The increase of the two elements was unequal. From 1850 to 1910 the blacks increased 140.5 per cent and the mulattoes increased 405.4 per cent. In 1910 the number of blacks was less than two and one-half times as great as in 1850. The number of mulattoes, however, was more than five times as great in 1910 as in 1850.

Table 6-3: PER CENT MULATTO IN TOTAL NEGRO POPULATION, 1910, 1920

Division	1910	1920
United States	15.9	20.9
New England	19.4	33.4
Middle Atlantic	11.6	19.6
East North Central	20.7	33.2
West North Central	18.7	28.7
South Atlantic	16.1	20.8
East South Central	15.0	19.1
West South Central	15.5	20.1
Mountain	18.1	28.6
Pacific	29.3	34.7

In the South the relative increase of the two elements was about the same. In the North and West the increase of mulattoes was less than in the South and the increase of blacks was greater than in the South. In the 60-year period the black element in the North and West increased 265.8 per cent while the mulatto element in the same regions increased 308 per cent. In the South the mulattoes increased 426.1 per cent between 1850 and 1910, while the black element increased only 131.6 per cent. In the period from 1890 to 1910 the increase of the black element in the South was 20.1 per cent; the increase in the mulatto element was 90.4 per cent. In the North during the same period the blacks increased 49.5 per cent and the mulattoes 39.2 per cent. In the West the increase of the blacks during the same period was 108.7 per cent and the increase of the mulattoes was 53.4 per cent.

The migration of the Negroes from the South into the North and West accounts for the relatively more rapid increase of the black element as compared with the increase of the mulatto element in these sections from 1890 to 1910. In 1890 the proportion of mulattoes in the Negro population of the South was 13.7 per cent; in the North it was 28.0 per cent—more than twice as great. If the blacks and the mulattoes among the migrants were in the same proportion as in the southern Negro population, the effect of the migration would be to add relatively larger numbers to the black than to the mulatto elements of the North and West. As a matter of fact, it is probable that the percentage of mulattoes was somewhat larger among the migrants than in the general Negro population of the South but less than the ratio existing in the North and West, and hence operated to reduce the proportion of mulattoes in these regions.

In the earlier decades the selective nature of the migration on the basis of intermixture was greater than in the later. In the decades following the Civil War the mulatto element of the North increased more rapidly than the black. For the black it was 39.9 per cent; for the mulatto it was 113.4 per cent. In these decades the migration of the mulattoes out of the South was pronounced. This mulatto exodus later declined. In the period from 1890 to 1910 the mulattoes in the North increased 39.2 per cent as against an increase of 113.4 per cent in the period from 1870 to 1890. The migration of mulattoes became less and the migration of the black Negroes greater.

Census Bureau, *Negro Population in the United States, 1790–1915.*
———, *Negroes in the United States, 1920–1932.*
Holmes, S. J., "Increasing Growth Rate of the Negro Population," *American Journal of Sociology,* 42(1936), 202–214.
———, *The Negro's Struggle for Survival.*
———, and Parker, S. L., "Stabilized Natural Increase of the Negro," *Journal of the American Statistical Association,* 26(1931), 159–171.
"Interstate Migration of Negroes," *Monthly Labor Review,* 42(1936), 976–978.
Johnson, C. S., *The Negro in American Civilization,* "Migration," pp. 16–28.
Kennedy, L. V., *The Negro Peasant Turns Cityward.*
Reuter, E. B., *Population Problems,* 2nd ed., pp. 61–63, 78–79.
———, "The Sex Distribution of the Negro and Mulatto Population of the United States," *Journal of Applied Sociology,* 7(1923), 130–138.
———, "Population Growth in the United States," L. I. Dublin, ed., *Population Problems,* 19–32.
Ross, F. A., *The Urbanization of the Negro.*
Thompson, W. S., *Population Problems,* 2nd ed., "The Negro in the United States," pp. 275–295.
Thompson, W. S., and Whelpton, P. K., *Population Trends in the United States,* Index.
Woofter, T. J., *Negro Migration: Changes in Rural Organization and Population of the Cotton Belt.*
———, *Races and Ethnic Groups in American Life,* pp. 71–79.

FURTHER READINGS

Bogue, Donald J., *The Population of the United States.* Glencoe, Ill.: Free Press, 1959.
Broom, Leonard, and Glenn, Norval D., *Transformation of the Negro American,* Ch. 8. New York: Harper & Row, 1965.
Campbell, Arthur, "White-Nonwhite Difference in Family Planning in the United States," *Health, Education, and Welfare Indicators,* February 1966.
Carter, Hugh, and Glick, Paul C., "Trends and Current Patterns of Marital Status Among Nonwhite Persons," *Demography,* 3:1(1966), 276–288.
Division of Vital Statistics, National Center for Health Statistics, *Natality Statistics Analysis: United States, 1963.* Washington, D.C.: U.S. Department of Health, Education, and Welfare, 1966.
Farley, Reynolds, "The Demographic Rates and Social Institutions of the Nineteenth-Century Negro Population: A Stable Population Analysis," *Demography,* 2 (1965), 386–398.
———, "Recent Changes in Negro Fertility," *Demography,* 3:1(1966), 188–203.

Frazier, E. Franklin, "The Negro in the United States," in Lind, Andrew F., ed., *Race Relations in World Perspective*. Honolulu: University of Hawaii Press, 1955.

Hamilton, C. Horace, "Continuity and Change in Southern Migration," in McKinney, John C., and Thompson, Edgar T., eds., *The South in Continuity and Change*. Durham, N.C.: Duke University Press, 1965.

———, "The Negro Leaves the South," *Demography*, 1:1 (1964), 273–295.

Hauser, Philip M., "Demographic Factors in the Integration of the Negro," *Daedalus*, 94(Fall 1965), 847–877.

Kiser, Clyde V., and Frank, Myrna E., "Factors Associated with the Low Fertility of Nonwhite Women of College Attainment," *Milbank Memorial Fund Quarterly*, 45:4 (October 1967), 427–499.

Lunde, Anders S., "White-nonwhite Fertility Differentials in the United States," *Health, Education, and Welfare Indicators* (September 1965), 23–38.

———, Misra, Bhaskar D., and Dandekar, D. P., "A New Estimate of the Negro Population and Negro Vital Rates in the United States, 1930–1960," *Demography*, 1:1 (1964).

Roach, J. L., et al., "The Effects of Race and Socio-Economic Status on Family Planning," *Journal of Health and Human Behavior*, 8:1(1967), 40–45.

Taeuber, Conrad, and Taeuber, Irene B., *The Changing Population of the United States*. New York: Wiley, 1958.

Taeuber, Karl E., and Taeuber, Alma F., "The Changing Character of Negro Migration," *American Journal of Sociology*, 70(January 1965), 429–441.

U.S. Bureau of the Census, U.S. Census of Population, 1960, *The Negro Population*. Washington, D.C.: U.S. Government Printing Office, 1965.

Whelpton, Pascal K.; Campbell, Arthur A.; and Patterson, John E., *Fertility and Family Planning in the United States*. Princeton, N.J.: Princeton University Press, 1966.

I V

RACIAL DIFFERENCES*

It becomes necessary at this point to raise the question of comparative racial worth. If the races are substantially equal in native capacity, such differences as appear in their history or in their present status are evidently the result of causes that lie outside the hereditary equipment of the race and an analysis of the environmental circumstances is essential to an understanding of the historic achievement or of the present cultural position. If hereditary racial inequalities exist, they would be reinforced by social factors, and the cultural differences that have appeared would be a resultant of heredity and overlying cultural forces operating on the whole in the same direction; consequently an analysis of environmental circumstances is an essential prerequisite to any estimate of the strength of the hereditary factor.

There is need for great care and guarded statement. The question is beset with peculiar difficulties since both the hereditary and the cultural factors are unknown quantities. The historical achievement or the present cultural status of any group—the thing objectively before us—is the end product of two interacting sets of causal factors both of which are indeterminate variables.

The question is also pregnant with immediate practical implications. Any policy in regard to culturally backward racial groups, that is to rise above the ethical level of the exploitation of their vital power, hinges upon this point. If certain races and groups of men are inferior in inherited capacity to other more cultured races and groups, social policy demands that they be treated in considerable degree apart. In a political democracy, for example, they would of necessity be excluded permanently from many important governmental functions. Any comprehen-

* Except for minor deletions, this chapter remains the same as in the second edition.

sive population policy will turn upon this point. Any governmental practice in regard to foreign immigration implies a decision in regard to the comparative racial worth of those who would come. Every educational régime operates consciously or naïvely upon some theory of relative racial and individual capacity. Any theory of racial inferiority provides a basis and a justification for the cultural exclusion and exploitation of the inferior, just as any theory of racial identity justifies their cultural inclusion in the body politic and their incorporation into the population stock. Error in either direction is fraught with human consequences of such magnitude that extreme caution becomes an imperative moral obligation of the scientist who approaches the problem.

In spite of the obvious difficulty of arriving at an objectively valid judgment, and of the practical consequences that may result from premature pronouncement, there is an almost unanimous prejudging of the problem. The general popular opinion is doubtless to the effect that innate racial differences—physical, temperamental, mental, and moral—not only exist but are so marked as to make possible a hierarchy of races in terms of development along the scale of organic evolution. Certain racial groups are believed not only to be backward in culture but also to be so lacking in natural capacity that they are predestined to remain culturally inferior to the final extermination of the stock. In America this doctrine has taken the extreme form of a belief in the innate superiority of the native-born American and especially in the mental superiority of the Nordic stock—the so-called North European blond.

The popular bias is of course more or less inevitable. Like most problems of social reality, the gross phenomena are matters of direct observation and the naïve person is prone to assume an understanding on the basis of a certain degree of acquaintanceship and familiarity. But there is nothing so misleading as direct observation; for numberless generations people believed that the earth was flat and stationary and that the sun revolved about it. This was a common-sense generalization based on direct observation. It was a self-evident truth; everyone could see that it was so. In a somewhat similar way persons observe certain facts of race and it seems obvious common sense to recognize the superiority of some to others. There has come to be a very large body of this folk-lore—that is, common-sense generalization—which gets into the non-rational mental habits of persons and thus reinforces the natural fallacy inherent in all folk-reasoning. If we avoid the common-sense illusion, racial superiority and inferiority are by no means self-evident. But such avoidance is not usual. Many persons who would frankly recognize their inability to deal with a simple thing, like the adjustment of a gas engine, and call in an expert, assume their entire competence in the field of social phenomena. Matters that engage the attention of the scholar in the social field frequently present no problem to the untrained person: the facts and their meaning appear to be obvious. The tendency to common-sense generalization on the basis of limited personal observation of the gross phenomena is not wholly confined to the untrained. The literature contains numberless examples of scholars, presumably competent in other fields, who have apparently lost all sense of scientific caution and regard for evidence when they have gone aside to discuss problems in the racial field. When the patter of folk-lore is repeated by men of standing in other fields, the prestige of scholarship becomes a reinforcement of common-sense inaccuracy.

Another important source of error lies in the paradox that familiarity with the phenomenal matter is frequently a hindrance to logical thought. An emotional attitude arises out of the activity and decisions consequent upon a practical situation; opinion is then based upon this emotion-activity complex rather than upon an impartial examination and verification of the facts. By the familiar process of rationalization, a reasoned support for the opinion is subsequently found. That the belief in racial inequality frequently is a rationalization is evidenced by the profound feeling of certitude that accompanies the belief and by the emotional resistance to inquiry concerning its basis. Opinions which are held because they are true in the sense that they are verifiable do not arouse, when questioned, the emotional reactions that characteristically appear when religious ideas, family institutions, and other non-rationally founded practices and beliefs are under criticism. In such cases there is an uneasy sense that a critical examination may destroy the basis of a belief which the individuals do not desire to have disturbed. It must be recognized, of course, that the fact that a belief is emotionally and not critically founded does not prove the belief to be untrue. A profound and passionate belief tells much about the person who holds the belief but it tells nothing concerning the truth or falsity of the belief that is held.

It is the belief in the innate and unalterable racial inferiority of the Negro to the white racial stocks that we propose to examine in some detail in the present chapter. The whole body of concrete material presented in the volume has of course a direct bearing upon the point, but the immediate interest centers on the present state of scientific opinion.

RACIAL DIFFERENCES IN PHYSICAL TRAITS

The biological aspect of the problem has two phases: first, the physical structure of the races with respect to their relative anatomical resemblance to the anthropoids; second, the comparative nature of racial brain structure.

The generalized Negro type is distinguished by a number of well-marked physical characteristics. In stature the type is tall and, owing to the dolichocephalic head and the inward curvature of the lumbar verte-brae, somewhat out of perpendicular. The arms, especially the forearms, are long and the legs slender and weak with relatively undeveloped calves. The foot is broad and flat, occasionally with larkspur heel. The head is dolichocephalic, the jaw prognathous, and the nasal index high. The skin color is dark; the hair is short, black, and spirally coiled.

A number of other physical characteristics are commonly noted. The knees frequently bend outward. The cranium is thick and massive, the forehead is receding. The zygomatic arches are large; the cheek bones are small. The cranial sutures are said to close somewhat earlier in the Negro than in other races. The lips are thick, tumid, everted. The nose is short and flat, broad at the extremity and depressed at the base, with wide nostrils and concave ridge. The great toe is protruding and some-what prehensile. The skin is thick, soft and velvety, and mostly hairless. The eyes are large, round, and prominent with black iris and yellowish cornea. The brain weight is somewhat less than that of other races. The venous system is more highly developed.

The physical peculiarities of the Negro people are thus seen to be nu-merous and in some respects highly contrasted to those of other racial types. The question at once arises as to the evolutionary meaning of the characteristic morphological characters. If the Negro in his anatomical features is more closely akin to the apes than is the white man there may be reason to believe that he represents a lower state in organic develop-ment. This was the usual position of the physical anthropologists of the older school and, among non-scientific men, it is very commonly held today. The prognathous jaw, the cranial massiveness, the arm length, and the like are advanced as evidence that the Negro is a less highly developed form than is the white man and, on the evolutionary scale, stands some-what more nearly related to the higher anthropoids.

In regard to this position several things may be said. In the first place, the general contention seems to show a somewhat inadequate and inaccu-rate conception of the evolutionary hypothesis as applied to man. That hypothesis does not hold the anthropoid apes, either the fossil or the living forms, to be the ancestral type from which man descended. There is, of course, a genetic relationship: the ancestry of each traces back to some pre-existing form that probably was neither man nor ape. Each of the living species represents a specialized divergent development. But there is inadequate evidence in which to anchor a belief that the general ancestral form was of ape-like rather than of human type; and consequently there is an absence of evidence to support a belief that one race, because of its anatomical structure, is genetically closer than another to the common precursor of each.

But if this point be conceded, the things commonly presented as characterizing the Negro and placing him lower in the evolutionary scale do not seem to bear critical examination. The morphological characters do not appear to possess any deep meaning: they do not in general connote vitality nor a high or low place in the normal scale of development. Many of the characters most useful in distinguishing types of physical race are non-adaptive and apparently useless. The nasal index, for example, is a very valuable racial mark but it has no zoonomic explanation. The hair formation, perhaps the most valuable single racial mark, appears to be wholly devoid of adaptive significance; hence its persistence and hence its value in racial classification.

But if this evidence be admitted as significant it immediately appears that it is not consistent. The so-called morphological marks of inferiority are not the exclusive possession of any one race. In prognathism, cranial massiveness, receding forehead, arm length, slight development of the lower body, and in some other respects the Negro appears to be more nearly related than the white man to the higher anthropoids. But in other respects the white man appears to occupy a lower place on the developmental scale. Hairiness of body is an ape-like character and in this respect the white man is nearest to the apes and the Negro farthest removed. In the woolly character of his hair the Negro of all the races is least ape-like. The full, red, everted lips of the Negro are perhaps the most human of all physical characters in the sense that they stand most markedly contrasted to the thin, bloodless lips of the anthropoids.

Thus in some respects the Negro shows less development, when measured by the degree of similarity to the anthropoids, than does the white man; in other respects the peculiarly human characteristics show a higher degree of development in the Negro. The only conclusion that is at present possible is that the persistent tendency to point to morphological characters as evidence of a lower position on the organic scale of evolutionary development is not well grounded. The possession of so-called simian characters is not an evidence of inferiority or of a transition stage from beast to man. The possession of them does not correspond with any effort to classify races on a scale ascending from the ape-like progenitor. Races differ in physical type, but it may not, with our present knowledge, be asserted that one race is physically inferior or less advanced than another. Superiority and inferiority may be asserted only in regard to a specific peculiarity in a specified situation. This is not to be interpreted as asserting the physical equality of the races. What it does assert is that with regard to certain specific things the Negro is inferior to the white man, and in other specific things he is superior to the white man. Any general inferiority of one race to the other, if it exists at all, is simply a statistical average of the various specific superiorities and inferiorities of the two races. That a balancing of the peculiarities would show the Negro to be inferior is possible, but inferiority in this statistical sense, if it should be demonstrated, would seem to have no particular significance.

RACIAL DIFFERENCES IN BRAIN WEIGHT AND STRUCTURE

The comparative nature of racial brains, gross and microscopic, is the phase of the physical problem that is most directly significant. Any anatomical differences of this sort are generally assumed to bear some very direct relation to mental ability and capacity for civilization. The problem of comparative structure is difficult, the amount of data is limited, and any conclusions at the present time must be tentative. The classic papers by Mall and Bean will serve the purpose in hand.

Dr. Bean made a comparative study of the brains of forty-nine American whites and one hundred and three American Negroes. He found the variations according to race to be marked and important. The brain weight of the Negro was less than that of the whites; the frontal ends of the brains were found to be different in the two races, that of the Negro being smaller and more angular; the convolutions of the Negro brains were less elaborate, the fissures less deep, and the relative amount of white matter not so great; and the front end of the corpus callosum was relatively less in the white brains. He found the differences to be so marked as to separate the Negro and the white brains almost completely into racial groups. Dr. Bean's conclusions were widely quoted and very generally accepted as demonstrating Negro inferiority in brain weight and structure and, by implication, in mentality.

Dr. Mall submitted the conclusions of Dr. Bean to re-examination. He used in part the same brains but made use of more accurate projecting and measuring instruments. As a guard against any possible bias—in order to insure the greatest possible degree of scientific objectivity—all the labels were concealed and the tracings and measurements made without his knowing the race or sex of the individuals from whom the brains were taken. The results of this more careful study were markedly different from those of the earlier investigation. The dividing line between the Negro and the white brains disappeared and while some constant differences appeared the brains were overlapping and the racial difference appeared to be small if not negligible. The Negro and white brains were intermingled above the line that separated them in Dr. Bean's study.

These and such other careful observations as have been made indicate that, from the standpoint of size and weight, the great majority of Negro and European brains show approximately the same range of variation, but that there are normal Negro brains which are smaller in size and lighter in weight than any normal European brains as yet measured, and that the brains of certain Europeans have been found to exceed in size and weight any normal Negro brains so far reported. The result is that Negro brains average slightly less in size and weight than do those of Europeans. But the number of examinations has not been large and the degree of variability is high. Some recent data indicate that the mean brain weight of mixed-bloods seems to be lower than that of either the Negroes or the whites.

In making any inference in regard to relative Negro and white mentality from the measurements, several facts need to be borne in mind. The Negro brains measured are not known to be a representative sample of that racial group. Aside from the differences found at the extremes of the curve, Negro and European brains appear to be approximately alike in size and weight. But granting differences, the relation between mental capacity and brain weight does not appear to be a direct one. Some men of eminent ability have had brains of exceptional size and weight while the brain weight of other men of great ability has been relatively small. The range of brain size among men of exceptional ability seems to be the same as the range among groups unselected as to ability. The differences in size and weight between Negro and European brains may be significant but the present state of knowledge does not warrant any generalization in regard to relative mentality on that basis.

When attention is turned from the size and weight of the organ to its gross and microscopic structure, there again appears to be some racial peculiarities. But the significance, if any, of the differences is not clear. There does not appear to be any present scientific justification for interpreting them as evidences of superiority or inferiority.

The present state of scientific evidence on the subject of anatomical differences may be summarized by the statement that while such differences exist they are not uniform and do not seem to indicate any marked superiority or inferiority of one race as compared with the other.

CULTURAL RETARDATION OF THE NEGRO PEOPLES

A second patent difference between the races is their relative cultural status, and it is possible to approach the question of relative capacity for civilization from this angle. This historic approach to the problem has often been attempted, but the paucity of results that have followed its use is evidence of the unsuspected difficulties that the method involves. The cultural differences are the things that immediately leap to the eye of the observer, and they have been made the basis for much easy inference. The Negro is backward. The members of the race in America do not on the average and in most respects measure up to the cultural standards of the white population, they are poor, ignorant, and religious. In the native environment, while not so devoid of culture as is commonly assumed, the race has not produced an indigenous civilization comparable with the independent cultures of Egypt, China, the Valley of the Euphrates, Mexico, and Peru.

In the historic approach, the relative cultural sterility of the Negro people is commonly taken as an evidence of incapacity; the racial ability is judged on the basis of the racial history. This is, of course, a theoretically valid procedure. We may argue from achievement to capacity in races or in individuals, provided the number of observations is sufficiently large or the conditions of experimental observation adequately controlled. In the last analysis we have no way of judging the capacity either of individuals or of races except by what they can do.

In the controlled conditions of the laboratory, the relative ability of two individuals in a certain line may conceivably be measured by a single experiment. A single contest may determine the superiority, as a runner, of one athlete over another. But we would not pronounce one superior to the other because of their relative positions at any moment before the end of the race nor without taking into account their starting points, the difficulties of their routes, the accidents of their journeys, the goals of their courses, and their incentives to exertion. It is only after all the conditions have been taken into the reckoning that decision may be made.

Somewhat similar conditions obtain in the comparison of racial groups. The conditioning facts must needs be known and evaluated if valid conclusions are to be arrived at on the basis of their culture history record. It is not possible to use as a measure of any generation the civilization that that generation possesses. Human cultures grow with extreme slowness and in consequence the history of a people must be known through a very considerable period of time and must be very carefully analyzed before any cautious student would venture a generalization in regard to the capacity of the group. No fact is more firmly established than that the cultural positions of races change. The fact that a race has a low culture during one historic era is not evidence that its status will remain inferior. The historic record up to the last two thousand years gives no hint of Nordic cultural pre-eminence. The historic record gives no hint of what the Negro peoples will or will not achieve in the two thousand years immediately before us.

Civilization of a high order existed in Egypt for some thousands of years during which time the culture of the Greeks and Romans idled at the barbaric level. It is not probable that any Egyptian believed the race that was later to produce the Athenian civilization of the age of Pericles had a mental caliber and culture capacity equal to his own. The Egyptians disposed of the capacity of the Greeks and Romans to produce a civilization on the ground that they had never done so, just as these Greeks and Romans in the days of their glory disposed of our barbarian ancestors, and just as we, in the intolerance of our historic moment, are disposed to dismiss the Negroes and the Indians.

Another fact that makes general statement difficult is the superficial incomparability of cultures: there is no general objective standard. The claim to superiority of any culture so far produced rests upon a dominance in some one or a few respects. The superiority of the Greek was aesthetic. Rome was a legal and military triumph. The unquestioned superiority of the Anglo-Saxon of the twentieth century does not lie in the entire field of culture but in one narrow aspect of that field—scientific discovery, mechanical invention, and consequent industrial achievement. Aside from this he is probably outclassed in every type of human achievement; in literature, art, religion, ethics, social organization, he has no unquestioned superiority. To rank one culture superior to another, as the European to the Chinese, it is necessary to select the proper criterion of judgment. The uncritical person makes the judgment naïvely, by using the culture to which he is habituated as a standard by which others are judged. From this standard the cultures of other races and peoples of necessity diverge and the lack of conformity becomes at once a proof and measure of their inferiority.

Not only do racial claims to superiority rest upon achievement in a single or few lines, but also upon a brief and selected span in the history of a people. The age of Pericles was but a moment in the life of the Greek people, but their claim to superiority rests upon that flowering period. The present is the moment of the Anglo-Saxon and he measures himself by that, ignoring the age-long period of barbarism that preceded. To accept, on the evidence of culture achievement, the Nordic claim to innate superiority is, if we have due regard for logical procedure, to accept the similar claim of the ancient Egyptian who, in the moment of his triumph, might equally well have denied the potential equality of the ancestors of all the European peoples.

The only escape from this sort of absurdity is resort to the yet more untenable position that culture is a function of biological evolution. This is to infer racial capacity directly from the present status of the racial group. That certain races and peoples are culturally backward is obvious and indisputable. Just as the loose and incompetent thinker infers the biological and human worth and mental capacity of individuals from their achievement—economic prosperity, business or professional success, social prominence, and the like—without first correcting for a wide range of conditioning factors, so he tends to measure the capacity of a racial group by the present culture of its representatives. That the two sets of facts are of a different order and without any necessary connection is of course obvious on slight reflection. Racial capacity is a matter of hereditary biological equipment; present cultural status is, or may be, a matter of historic accident.

In general the weight of historical evidence lies against the tendency to infer racial worth from cultural status. The cultural status is essentially a matter of time and circumstance; it is not a fixed and permanent thing. Civilizations rise and fall; it is not possible to accept the momentary status of a racial group as evidence of its innate and inherited characters, else we would be forced to endorse the position that every change of status, the rise and fall of empires and states, is a biological instead of a political and social phenomenon. To accept this assumption is to accept the belief that the European peoples have in the past two thousand years undergone a biological evolution and change in innate mental capacity comparable with the change of culture that has taken place since Caesar described our barbarian ancestors. That such a change in mental capacity has taken place, or in fact that any change in capacity whatsoever has taken place, there is no convincing evidence. If we accept the position it would be necessary, for example, to endorse the absurd doctrine that the Japanese people underwent in less than a century a biological evolution that raised them from the ranks of the inferior and backward people, through the region of the *Dämmerungs-Menschen,* into the forefront of modern culture. The doctrine of a parallelism between racial ability and racial culture seems not to be a tenable one.

The cultural evidence advanced to prove the racial incapacity of the Negro people is certainly not inclusive; it is probably not even significant.

SCHOOL RECORDS OF NEGRO AND WHITE CHILDREN

Several more or less distinct types of proof have been advanced which tend in general to reinforce the popular assumption of Negro mental inferiority. The school records of Negro as compared with white children furnish one bit of evidence. More recently the development of the so-called mental tests and their application to children of different racial groups has given a body of experimental material. The application of such tests to a very large number of the adult male recruits of the army draft gave an additional body of comparative data. Whatever present scientific warrant there may be for the belief in the mental inferiority of the Negro people seems to fall within one or more of these groups. We will examine in order the evidence which comes from each of these sources.

A number of studies have been made to test the comparative educational ability and attainment of the Negro and white children in the schools. The facts brought out by these studies are, on the whole, in fair agreement. The colored children on the average enter school somewhat later than do white children. Their percentage of retardation is higher in all or nearly all the school grades. They make a poorer showing in school work, they remain in school a greater length of time, and they graduate at a somewhat later age.

It would be possible to criticize many of these studies from the standpoint of method. In some cases the children studied did not constitute an impartial sample. Where the efficiency of the pupils is arrived at on the basis of ratings given by teachers the standard is inexact, arbitrary, and subject to the possibility of indefinite distortion through personal bias. And when, as was the case in some of the best known of these studies, the problem was the practical one of determining the advisability of providing separate schools for the Negro children there is ground for the suspicion that an unconscious personal element may have biased the findings of the investigator.

If, for the purpose of the argument, the accuracy and complete objectivity of such studies be granted, there remain the problem of the interpretation of the findings and the question of the conclusions that may be legitimately drawn from the data presented.

It has been usual in these studies to explain the poor average showing made by the Negro pupils in terms of an inferior mental ability, or to infer a lower grade of mentality on the basis of the lower marks. A lower inherent mental capacity on the part of Negro children may be a fact but it is a thing that requires proof. To infer it as the cause of poor scholastic attainment, without first correcting for other facts of the same order, to draw conclusions in terms of ability, intelligence, or other similar concepts which imply hereditary equipment while the evidence runs not in terms of innate traits but in terms of school success, to derive biological conclusions from unrefined social data, is not a defensible scientific procedure. Before resorting to this easy explanation it is necessary to show that the facts cannot be explained in sociological and cultural terms.

The cause of school retardation among Negro children is complex but seems in general to lie in the same factors of the social heritage and environment that explain the retardation of white children. Chief among the causes of retardation of the Negro children is late entrance upon school life. This in turn is due to absence of school facilities, to over-crowded schools, to uneducated or indifferent parents, to poverty of the family, and to numerous other things that lie outside the personality of the child. The late entrance may or may not be related to low mental status. But granted a late entrance upon school life, whatever the cause, retardation through the grades and late graduation follow unless the late entrant be a child of more than average ability.

A second factor important in considerations of the cause of the retardation of the Negro children is the previous educational opportunity of the pupils. The investigations of the Chicago Race Commission disclosed the fact that the northern born Negro children had no higher retardation rate than had the white children. The great majority of the retarded Negro children were recent migrants from the South. The difference in this respect between children from different sections of the country is readily understood when the relative educational opportunities are compared. In many cases Negro children in the South have less opportunity to attend school; many Negroes live on plantations so far from school that regular attendance of young children is impossible. Again, the southern schools are in most cases inferior and the school terms short. In Mississippi, for example, the education law provides for a short school term in such districts as do not reject the law. The children may be up to grade in these schools, but are of necessity demoted on entrance in a northern school. In Chicago and other northern cities with the recent Negro migrations it became necessary to provide special rooms for the retarded children from the South.

Certain other facts and conditions operate in some cases to the disadvantage of the Negro children. The eagerness of many Negro parents for the education of their children causes many of them to keep over-age students in the schools. In most cases the Negro families are poor, the mothers are frequently employed away from home, and the home and family life broken and disordered to the disadvantage of the school life of the children. Whatever may be the cause it seems to be true that differences in economic status register in attendance and scholarship. The children of the low income classes of the whites register low and so do the children who come from the high income classes. The white children with high scholastic records seem to come from the classes in comfortable economic circumstances rather than from the wealthy or the poorer classes. In nearly all cases the Negro school children are from economically poor families.

Interesting and valuable as are the studies of the comparative success of Negro and white children in the schools, their failure adequately to evaluate the factors of the Negro child's environment, which condition if they do not determine the child's achievement in the school room, seems to render the conclusions of such studies unworthy of any high degree of scientific credence.

Psychological Tests and Racial Inferiority

A good deal of preliminary work has been done, designed to perfect a method for measuring more or less directly the higher mental capacities which we call intelligence. Various tests have been evolved and more or less standardized. To date the chief function of the tests has been the easy detection of backward and defective children.

A number of studies employing this technique have been made on Negro children and some comparative data are available. The results of the studies differ widely as to details but are in rather close agreement on the point here under consideration. The Negro children show a high degree of efficiency in the younger years and in the simpler mental processes. But the median Negro child is unable to perform the intellectual tasks performed by the normal white child of the same age; the performance is less accurate and more irregular. On the basis of comparative tests the average mental ability of the Negro child is lower, but not a great deal lower, than that of the white child. Also, the Negro children seem to show a less degree of variability than do the white children, but the differences in variability are not great.

Any adequate consideration of these findings would involve a critique of the whole psychological method of mental testing and the somewhat complicated philosophical presuppositions in which they, in the first hand, rest. Such a critique would obviously be out of place in the present discussion. Comment must be limited to a few of the more important objections that have been raised and lie with some force against the tests, in their present state of refinement, as a technique of race comparison.

These tests are designed to measure innate ability, natural intelligence, apart from information and training. That they, in their present state of development, do this with any high degree of accuracy is a thing not in general claimed by the careful students in the field—the critically competent men who use the tests rather freely and publicly admit their limitations. But the tests do show something. What they measure is apparently a native capacity along certain lines as it has been developed under environmental stimuli. How much of the thing measured is sheer intellectual ability and how much of it is sophistication, it is not at present possible to say. So far as the tests compare children differently trained, they of necessity fail just to the extent that they fail to separate native capacity from education and training and to measure the former as distinct from the latter. That there would be anything to test if the child had grown from birth without external stimulation, no psychologist, perhaps, would claim. That the thing to be tested would be the same had the earlier stimulations to which the child reacted been different is a gratuitous and apparently baseless assumption. It must also be noted that the tests measure only what they test. They test only the limited range of abilities to which they apply. But the concrete person is an integrated unity, too complex to be analyzed by his responses to a half a hundred verbal stimulations. Any random selection of persons registering the same score on the tests are found to have little or nothing in common other than their similar reaction to the tests. It has been one of the grievous errors of the experimenters to claim that the tests show more than they do.

In the application of the tests to the Negro children, the different environmental stimulations under which the children have developed have not been adequately appreciated. The casual and off-hand manner in which the "testers" have in general assumed a common environment in terms of some gross criterion, say of income of parents, is an adequate and conclusive demonstration of the failure to appreciate the almost indefinite complexity of social stimulation, and the large end results that may come from small and apparently trivial differences in initial stimulation. In much of the comparative work on Negro and white children, the incorporation of a methodological error detracts somewhat from the scientific conclusiveness of the findings. This is the too common practice of comparing averages and curves. To be valid it is necessary that there be some way by which the race may be judged by the test itself. But this appears nowhere to be the case. The norms have been standardized on children of a North European social heritage and accommodated to an urban environment. A classification is made on the basis of color, and a comparison is made of curves derived from tests that apply equally to the children of both races. The one group is thus used more or less directly as a measure of the other. In such a case the median lines of the groups may be quite separate, but there is no case where the curves are exclusive. There is always a large overlapping. So long as this is the case there is no validity for the classification other than that which would inhere in any arbitrary grouping.

In view of the highly tentative nature of the tests at the present time, no great confidence may be placed in the results derived from their application to children of differently circumstanced groups.

THE ARMY EXAMINATIONS

By far the largest body of psychological experimentation having a bearing on the problem of the comparative racial ability comes from the data collected incidentally to the hurried army mobilization. In 1917 the group of psychologists who were invited to assist in the allocation of the army personnel devised a series of tests and applied them to a little over one and three-quarter million draftees and officers. The result of these tests are popularly regarded as the most authoritative measurements so far made of the racial differences in mentality. They have been the occasion of much discussion.

The tests, so far as they relate to the Negro, seem to show the average of the race to be consistently and markedly below the average mental level of the white recruits. Eighty-five per cent of the Negroes were found to be inferior in intelligence, namely, in ability to pass the tests, to the average of the white population. The intelligence of the average American Negro was very greatly below that of the average white man. By making selection of 93,973 whites and 18,891 Negroes and throwing their rating upon a seven-point distribution curve the following comparative results were recorded.

Table 7-1: PERCENTAGES OF EACH GROUP MAKING GRADE INDICATED

Race	D−	D	C−	C	C+	B	A
Whites	7.0	17.1	23.8	25.0	15.0	8.0	4.1
Negroes	9.0	29.7	12.9	5.7	2.0	0.6	0.1

The test ratings also showed the distinct and marked inferiority of the southern to the northern Negroes. Taking the distribution of grades for a group of 8,165 northern Negroes and of 14,994 southern Negroes the following results were recorded.

Table 7-2: PERCENTAGES OF EACH GROUP MAKING GRADE INDICATED

Race	D−	D	C−	C	C+	B	A
Northern Negroes	19.6	27.6	22.1	21.4	6.7	2.3	0.6
Southern Negroes	55.7	26.4	9.8	6.2	1.4	0.4	0.1

The difference stands out in a similar striking way when the comparison is made of the northern and the southern Negroes by states. The data for the states of Illinois and Mississippi are shown in the following tabulation.

Table 7-3: PERCENTAGE FROM EACH STATE MAKING GRADE INDICATED

State	Cases	D−	D	C−	C	C+	B	A
Illinois	1,139	10.6	32.4	28.1	18.5	6.5	2.4	1.4
Mississippi	1,919	57.1	30.2	9.2	2.8	0.8	0.0	0.0

Accepting the results of these examinations as demonstrating the existence of mental differences between the whites and the Negroes, we turn to the question of the meaning of the findings. Are the differences disclosed to be accepted as a final and complete demonstration of the mental inferiority of the Negro which common sense has assumed or may the findings be better understood in other than racial terms? The former interpretation, being highly flattering to the racial pride of the white American, has been widely and uncritically accepted. Brigham, for example, on the basis of the findings asserted that "The average Negro child cannot advance through the educational curriculum adapted to the Anglo-Saxon child in step with that child." Terman asserted that over eighty-five per cent of the Negroes have less intelligence than a twelve-year-old white child. Trabue stated that "The average Southern Negro is about as capable in his intellectual capacities as the average nine-year-old white school boy." A host of similar statements on the basis of these examinations have gained a wide currency.

Are such generalizations to be accepted as final? There are two questions involved. First, do the conclusions come out of and follow inevitably from the data of the tests or may it be that they are opinions independently held and the army ratings used to illustrate and support them? The second point to be considered is whether or not the data on which the generalizations rest are of such a nature that valid scientific deductions may be drawn with these data as a basis?

A little critical examination of the tests and their results seems to show that the findings are somewhat less conclusive than is commonly believed and that the differences found are not inevitably to be accounted for in terms of the innate racial inferiority of the Negro people.

Before turning to the results themselves, it is necessary to raise the question as to whether or not there was anything in the nature of the tests or the manner of their application that was to the advantage or the disadvantage of any group. Were the army tests in any way unfair to the Negro? It would appear that their validity is open to question in a number of more or less important particulars.

The purpose of the tests was practical. They were "designed to facilitate the selection of personnel for the different branches of the service" and "the selection and study of scientific data were always incidental to this main purpose." The examinations undertook to decide which men were fit and which were unfit for positions in the higher branches of the service. They made no effort to ascertain the cause of the fitness or unfitness. Consequently, whatever light they may throw upon the question of comparative racial intelligence is incidental. The racial groups made different ratings but there is nothing in the results themselves as to the causal explanation of the differential scores.

The tests were so timed that "five per cent or less of any average group would be able to finish in the time allotted." That was the percentage of men needed by the army in the higher branches of the service. In the case of the Negro recruits a less percentage of men was needed in the higher branches of the service and the testing procedure was "determined by the practical needs of the Army." That is, the distribution of Negro grades was less important; Negroes were not needed in any considerable number in the higher branches of the service and the examiners were instructed to act accordingly. Now the Negroes making low scores, D minus and D, were in eighty per cent of the cases not recalled for re-examination. Yet all the evidence goes to show that a re-examination would have resulted in improved scores. Of the Negroes examined in Alpha, the test used for English-speaking literate persons, and making D minus and subsequently re-examined, 86.9 per cent made higher scores and the percentage receiving a rating above D increased from three to thirty per cent.

Another point that is apparently of some considerable significance is that a very high percentage of the Negroes were examined in Beta, a test used for illiterates and non-English-speaking persons. They were given in lieu of the Alpha tests to 65.5 per cent of the Negroes as against 24.7 per cent of the white recruits. The larger percentage of Negroes than of whites given the Beta was due in part to the higher percentage of illiteracy in the group—the illiteracy rate of the Negro recruits being more than twice that of the white recruits. But aside from the reason for giving the Negroes this test, the fact is that they were given the Beta in nearly three times as high a percentage of cases as were the whites.

In some cases the Negroes were all sent to the Beta without effort to separate the literate from the illiterate. Now it was at least in part the opinion of the examiners that the Beta was an unsatisfactory test for Negroes. In summarizing the reports from the various camps on this point, the previously quoted report of the psychological division of the Surgeon General concluded that "the general consensus seems to be that Beta is not as satisfactory a test for illiterate Negro recruits as it is for illiterate whites."

The fact that the Negroes were not needed in large numbers in the higher branches of the service, that the tests were administered to select the percentage needed, that the Negroes were in a larger percentage of cases examined in Beta where they were admittedly at a disadvantage, and that the Negro recruits making low scores were not as consistently re-examined as were the white recruits making low scores, certainly raise some questions as to the finality and scientific reputability of any conclusions derived directly from the relative racial ratings.

But suppose, for purposes of the argument, that the data of the tests be accepted as impartial and unbiased. The inferiority of the Negro is even then not demonstrated; it must first be shown that the results are not to be explained equally well on any other hypothesis. But this appears not to be the case. The differences found to exist are subject to a more immediate, complete, and adequate explanation on the ground of a difference in education and educational opportunity. The results are better explained without the assumption of any innate intellectual difference than they are on the hypothesis of racial differences in mentality.[1]

---

[1] It is necessary to avoid the confusion likely to result from the familiar quibble over terms. By intelligence we may understand the ability to perform problems that reflect an understanding of a familiar environment. But this is not the sort of thing the Army examiners undertook to measure. The Army Memoir defined intelligence as the thing measured by the tests. A person was intelligent to the extent that he was able to pass the tests. ". . . by 'intelligence' we mean the ability that manifests itself quantitatively in a set of consistent scores in all the types of examination upon which our data are based." Defined in this manner, the tests, or any other conceivable tests that anyone may wish to set up, are an irrefragable, indisputable, and perfect measure of intelligence. But quibbling of this sort is merely a form of obscurantism calculated to work utter confusion among the uninitiated: it shifts the question at the same time that it flatly contradicts the other assertion that ". . . We must assume that we are measuring *native and inborn intelligence.* . . ." Now native intelligence as such is not measurable. The thing which all the intelligence tests so far devised undertake to measure is developed intelligence and their validity depends upon the degree to which differences in native endowment may be inferred from differences in developed intelligence. This may validly be done provided a high degree of correlation consistently

The showing made in the Army tests by the northern Negroes was very much better than that made by the southern Negroes. The proportion of northern Negroes in the groups making a grade above the average was about ten times as high as that of the southern Negroes. In the groups making grades below the average, the southern Negroes had about twice as high a proportion as did the Negroes from the North.

In regard to the relative amounts of education, the report of the psychological examination of the recruits showed nineteen per cent of the southern and seven per cent of the northern Negro recruits to have reported no schooling whatever. Over fifty per cent of the southern Negroes had no schooling beyond the third grade and only seven per cent had finished the eighth grade. In the northern states fifty per cent of the Negroes do not go beyond the fifth grade while about twenty-five per cent finish the eighth grade. The correlation between years of schooling and rank in the tests is recognized in the memoir in the generalization that "Within each group such groups which were successively better schooled make successively better showing in the intelligence examinations." The median years of schooling of the white and colored draft is shown in the following tabulation.

Table 7-4: MEDIAN YEARS OF SCHOOLING, WHITE AND NEGRO DRAFT

Classification	Median Years of Schooling
Officers	14.7
White draft, native born	6.0
White draft, foreign born	4.7
Negro, northern	4.9
Negro, southern	2.6

The difference in schooling is strikingly parallel with the scores made by different types of recruits. But it is not possible adequately to appreciate the difference in educational opportunity when it is stated merely in terms of years in school. School years differ in length. The quality of the educational opportunity must also be taken into the reckoning. That there was a difference in quality is indicated by the fact that, in the decade of the examinations, Louisiana, for example, expended $1.31 for education per Negro child per year as against $45.32 expended by the state of New York; South Carolina expended yearly $1.44 for the education of each Negro child as against $36.20 expended by the state of Pennsylvania. The same difference between the educational opportunity of the Negro and

---

prevails between the phenomena measured and the phenomena whose measurement is inferred. This inference may with reasonable accuracy be made when, and only when, the individuals compared have a common experience.

the white is suggested by the relative amount of money expended for the instruction of each. Arkansas expended approximately three times as much per capita for teachers' salaries for white as for Negro children; Florida four times as much; Alabama, Georgia, and Mississippi five times as much; South Carolina seven times as much; and Louisiana nine times as much.

Certain other facts of interest and significance appear as the data of the examinations are studied. In all cases the literate members of every race made a better showing than the illiterates. Irrespective of the section of the country, the literate Negroes ranked higher than the illiterate whites. The northern Negroes very greatly surpassed the Italians in America. In the Alpha tests the New York Negroes made approximately the same ranking as the Alabama whites, while in the Beta tests the New York Negroes ranked approximately nine points superior to the Alabama whites. That is, the New York Negroes, on the basis of the tests, and in whatever the tests measure, were equal to or slightly superior to the whites of Alabama. Very clearly the accident of a southern birth was a determining element in intelligence, as measured by the Army tests.

It is not necessary to labor the point further. It is evident that the better scores of the northern compared with the southern Negroes are due to increased education, greater freedom and social contact, greater incentive, higher economic status, and to other elements of the social environment. One of two things is clear: either the Army tests were a measure of educational and social opportunity rather than a measure of innate and unalterable racial traits, or educational opportunity is so clearly a determining factor in the results that the tests mean little or nothing as an indication of relative racial mentality.

In summary, the customary proofs of racial inequality are scientifically worthless. The Negroes may be intellectually inferior to the white racial stock, but to date no one has marshalled in proof of the position any body of evidence that has scientific validity.

THE QUESTION OF RACIAL TEMPERAMENT

Some of the existing variations in cultures seem to indicate that certain types of temperament are more or less characteristic of large groups. In fundamental and essential respects all cultures are the same, but they also vary one from the other in more or less important ways. These variations may not be accounted for on the ground of difference in the intellectual capacity of groups, the existence of such differences in intellectual capacity not having been demonstrated. Moreover, the culture variations are those of difference rather than of degree: cultures do not stand in an hierarchal order. In some cases it apppears to be difficult to account for culture variations wholly in terms of historic accident. Such explanation is adequate to an understanding of the culture differences that obtain among the same people in different historic periods, as between that of the Germanic peoples of the tenth and the North European peoples of the twentieth century, or between that of the Japanese of the eighteenth and the Japanese of the twentieth century. But historic accident seems not always to furnish an adequate explanation of differences between nationalistic groups or to provide in all cases an adequate explanation of the differentiation of culture patterns within groups.

It is possible, and some students consider it probable, that as a result of variations, selection, and adaptation to a peculiar social environment and natural habitat, the Negro people may possess certain characteristic temperamental qualities. Popular observation has long characterized them by such descriptive terms as sunny, good-natured, lively, excitable, kindly, home-loving, convivial, improvident, and the like. So far as such terms are really descriptive of the people, and so far as the characteristics themselves are not a mere temporary expression of their recent historic status, they lend support to the belief in a racial individuality of temperament.

The period of Negro freedom in America has given some evidence in support of his hypothesis.

In the relatively simple social organization of a primary group, the individual life organization is largely, or completely, a replica of the inclusive social organization. The culture patterns are limited in number and rigidly defined, and the accommodation of the individual to them is complete and relatively perfect. There is no individual choice of work, no choice of metaphysical belief, no variation from the conventionalized sex patterns, and little opportunity in any direction for choice in accordance with individual inclination. The individual conforms to the relatively fixed group patterns. If the culture of the group is indigenous in origin, or completely modified through a long process of selective adaptation, these culture patterns may be assumed to reflect and to express with accuracy and with some degree of detail the wishes characteristic of the particular group as well as the more general needs of human beings.

But in any complex culture situation that permits of a degree of choice on the part of the group members, individual differences appear. The culture patterns are numerous and competing; frequently they are conflicting and contradictory. Within this system the individual life organization of each member of the group is based on the elements he selects or which are selected for him. He engages in a certain type of work to the exclusion of other types; he subscribes to some one of the various contradictory types of religious philosophy; he chooses one from among a variety of types of sex and family life; he selects certain forms of hedonistic activities and rejects or neglects others; and so for all the elements that go to make up his personal life organization. To the extent that he is a free person, the values which he selects and incorporates into a more or less consistent

individual life organization are those satisfying to his individual temperamental needs.

If the members of an alien race be introduced into such a complex culture situation and allowed freedom in their individual life organization,
and it is found that they more or less consistently select certain values and
neglect others, there is at least some reason to assume that these choices
are in harmony with their natural temperament or with the type of values
to which they have been habituated or both. The fact that the members
of one group go, in a larger percentage of cases than do the members of
another, into specific occupations or types of life is significant, so far as
we may assume a freedom of selection and so far as the tendency is consistent.

In American life the Negro people show a tendency to select certain
values and to reject others. During the long period of slavery their values
were of course selected for them. But in the brief period of relative freedom, since the Emancipation, there have been significant changes in the
behavior of the group. Certain occupations on which the race at one time
had a virtual monopoly have passed into the hands of other groups while
they have gone in increasing numbers into occupations from which they
were previously barred. While this period of freedom has been short and
their choice of values is still rather narrowly limited, they show a tendency to select from the complex American culture the artistic rather than
the utilitarian values. Dr. Park, observing this tendency, has with neatness
of expression and keenness of insight characterized the Negro as "the lady
among the races."

There is, of course, no complete segregation in this respect. But so far
as individuals are free to select the social values that make a fundamental
appeal, and so far as the Negro people select or neglect values in a proportion different from that characteristic of the white racial group, there is
a tendency toward cultural differentiation on the basis of differences in
racial temperament. Racial differences of this nature appear to have more
significance for an understanding of culture variations than do the possible
differences in average racial intelligence.

It must be re-emphasized, however, that the phenomenon of racial temperament has not been made the subject of any adequate scientific research.

CONCLUSIONS

The present status of the scientific study of racial phenomena is a considerable distance in advance of the points that have been discussed in the
present chapter. The idea of racial inferiority and superiority is not a present problem of research among students; it is a matter of debate among
laymen. For more than two decades there has been virtual agreement

among scholars; all accept as a provisional but fairly well-founded working hypothesis the position that the various races and peoples of the world are essentially equal in mental ability and capacity for civilization. The modern students of sociology and social anthropology, whose task it is to deal directly and scientifically with peoples and cultures, are interested in the individual and specific qualitative differences that may exist. There are qualitative excellencies in all races. In what lines do the Negro's peculiar capacities lie? This is a real problem of research: the search for the characteristic attitudes and interests as indicative of capacity and efficiency. To discover these and define the conditions necessary to their development is a thing of scientific and practical importance. The quantitative question, the question of which race or group has the largest number of excellencies concentrated, is a subsequent problem of addition that has no great scientific significance.

Barzun, Jacques, *Race: A Study in Modern Superstition.*

Boyle, E. M., "A Comparative Physical Study of the Negro," *Journal of the National Medical Association,* 4(1912), 124–130.

Brigham, C. C., *A Study of American Intelligence.*

Cooley, C. H., "Genius, Fame, and the Comparison of Races," *Annals of the American Academy of Political and Social Science,* 9(1897), 317–358.

Dewey, John, "Interpretation of the Savage Mind," *Psychological Review,* 9(1902), 217–230.

Faris, Ellsworth, *The Nature of Human Nature,* "The Mental Capacity of Preliterates," pp. 262–277. "Racial Superiority," pp. 328–337.

Garth, T. R., *Race Psychology.*

Hankins, F. H., *The Racial Basis of Civilization.*

Hertz, F. O., *Race and Civilization.*

Journal of Negro Education, 3(1934), 317–547. "Bibliography of Negro Abilities," pp. 548–564.

Klineberg, Otto, *Race Differences.*

Murphy, Gardiner, *Experimental Social Psychology,* 2nd ed., pp. 54–65.

Pearl, Raymond, "The Weight of the Negro Brain," *Science,* 80(1934), 431–434.

Radin, Paul, *The Racial Myth.*

Reuter, E. B., *Race Mixture,* "The Superiority of the Mulatto," pp. 129–163.

Thomas, W. I., *Primitive Behavior,* "The Relative Mental Endowment of Races," pp. 770–800.

Yerkes, R. M., ed., *Psychological Examining in the United States Army.*

Young, Donald, *American Minority Peoples,* "Race and Ability," pp. 419–430.

American Association for the Advancement of Science, Committee on Science in the Promotion of Human Welfare, "Science and the Race Problem," *Science,* 142(1963), 558–61.

Coleman, James S., et al., *Equality of Educational Opportunity.* Washington, D.C.: U.S. Government Printing Office, 1966.

Deutsch, Martin, "Happenings on the Way Back to the Forum," *Harvard Educational Review,* XXXIX(Summer 1969), 523–557.

Deutsch, Martin; Katz, Irwin; and Jensen, Arthur R., eds., *Social Class, Race, and Psychological Development.* New York: Holt, Rinehart and Winston, 1968.

Dreger, R. M., and Miller, K. S., "Comparative Psychological Studies of Negroes and Whites in the United States," *Psychological Bulletin* (September 1960), 361–402.

Garrett, Henry E., and George, Wesley C., "Science and the Race Problem," *Science,* 143(1964), 913–15.

George, Wesley C., *The Biology of the Race Problem.* Birmingham, Ala.: 1962.

Jensen, Arthur R., "How Much Can We Boost IQ and Scholastic Achievement?", *Harvard Educational Review,* XXXIX(Winter 1969), 1–123; and "Discussion" (Spring 1969), 273–356.

———, "Reducing the Heredity-Environment Uncertainty: A Reply," *Harvard Educational Review,* XXXIX (Summer 1969), 449–483.

Katz, Irwin, "Review of Evidence Relating to Effects of Desegregation on the Intellectual Performance of Negroes," *American Psychologist,* 19(1964), 381–99.

———, "Some Motivational Determinants of Racial Differences in Intellectual Achievement," *International Journal of Psychology,* 2(1967), 1–12.

Klineberg, Otto, ed., *Characteristics of the American Negro.* New York: Harper & Row, 1944.

Putnam, Carleton, "Science and the Race Problem," *Science,* 142(1963), 1419–20.

Rosen, Bernard C., "Race, Ethnicity, and the Achievement Syndrome," *American Sociological Review,* 24(1959), 47–60.

Shuey, Audrey M., *The Testing of Negro Intelligence.* Lynchburg, Virginia: J. P. Bell Company, 1958. 2nd ed., New York: Social Science Press, 1966.

Tumin, Melvin M., ed., *Race and Intelligence.* New York: Anti-Defamation League of B'nai B'rith, 1963.

V

THE BACKGROUND OF
RACE RELATIONS*

The American race problem in the present decades cannot be understood without some knowledge of the earlier relations and of the conditions out of which they developed. The existing racial status is not a rational body of human relations that can be understood as means consciously devised to achieve social ends, nor can the perpetuation of the existing order be understood as the rational behavior of men seeking personal and social welfare. The present arrangements are demonstrably uneconomic and morally stultifying; they retard the cultural advancement of the southern regions of the country, hence of the nation, and they make personally tolerable conditions of life impossible for large numbers of persons. They are an endless source of political corruption and governmental inefficiency; they perpetuate the educational backwardness of both the Negroes and the whites. In nearly every case, they operate to prevent the satisfaction of the real needs of the community life. Every consideration of economic, political, social, moral, and educational welfare calls for radical changes in the race relations.

The sentiments and beliefs that support and perpetuate a social order are themselves a product of the social order; they are not things apart or of independent origin, they are created by the going relations and they are nourished by participation in them. They are an integral part of the culture complex. The habit systems, the social attitudes, the emotional attachments, and other personal aspects of the culture support and are supported by the institutional structures and other external aspects of the regional life. In consequence, there is little real comprehension of a social order by the mass of persons who are in and a part of it; they are familiar with its workings and appreciate its values; they are bound to it by ties of

* This chapter is the same as in the second edition.

interest and sentiment; but they do not understand it. Appreciation comes from familiarity and participation; understanding comes from detachment and analysis and comparison.

This is in no sense a unique situation. The members of every group appreciate the group values, desire to perpetuate them, become emotionally disturbed when they show signs of decline. If the values become the object of criticism, the group members build up a philosophy in their defense and in justification of the practices offensive to the moral sense of the uninitiated. This body of rationalization becomes a part of the group culture and an important element in the resistance to social change; it gives a pseudo-intellectual basis for traditional practices and customary procedures. It defines the orbit within which the social thought of the group members revolves.

Cultural changes go on independently and for the most part in opposition to the prevailing system of rationalizations, through discoveries and inventions that undermine the social structure and make new modes of life necessary. In the American situation, the race relations in the past were determined by factors apart from the thought processes of the persons who established the system; the relations are undergoing change in the present but again in response to forces not understood by and not within the control of those within the system of existing relations. In the present stage of popular social intelligence, the social system—including the sentiments and attitudes toward the system, the ideas and beliefs and opinions in regard to its beneficence, and the types of human character and personality that appear under it—must be understood as a product of forces operating independently of the human will.

This is in no sense a denial of the fact that men may use the system for the exploitation of their fellow men, nor to deny that men struggle to perpetuate systems that enable them to prosper personally by the exploitation of other men. But this exploitation of others, as the disposition to exploit them, is itself a part of the system, not an explanation of it.

To understand race relations in America in the present and to understand the relations that will prevail in the future, it is necessary to understand the factors that determine their existence and control their change.

OPEN RESOURCES

At the time of the introduction of the Negroes into the American Colonies, the area was distinctly one of open resources. The country was very sparsely populated, much of it was not yet explored; even on the eastern seaboard the population was small and scattered. Only a fraction of the acreage was under cultivation; unoccupied and easily accessible land was plentiful and virtually free. In the circumstances, there was a desire for population increase; the country was operating under the economic law of increasing returns in the relation of men to land and other natural resources. There was an active demand for workers.

In a country where land is cheap or free one man will not enter or for long remain in the employ of another. In the American Colonies there was little need that he should do so. It was necessary only to move to an unoccupied or unpre-empted spot to become an independent farmer. The natural resources of the area were in general abundant. The type of agriculture was relatively primitive and the capital outlay necessary to set up an independent homestead on the frontier was negligible. The spirit of the times was such that the independent life of the frontiersman and the settler, though sometimes precarious and always rough and hard, was more attractive than wage labor.

The abundance of land and the shortage of labor were merely different aspects of the same fact. The former was a given condition and, in the existing situation, not subject to control; the latter was met in some part by a system of apprenticeship and indenture. Various persons, useless or troublesome in the European situation—paupers, vagabonds, criminals, political offenders, and the like—were shipped to America and sold into temporary servitude. This procedure provided laborers in the Colonies and freed the home population from burdensome members. As the demand became stable and the market active, many children and adults were kidnapped in the English port cities and sold as servants in the Colonies. Numerous prostitutes and other undesirable women were shipped to become indentured servants or wives of the colonists. Many poor and ambitious persons voluntarily accepted the status of indentured servants as a means of securing passage to America. This labor force was supplemented and made still more miscellaneous, in some of the Colonies, by the enforced labor of American Indian captives.

The Negroes were brought in to supply the demand for laborers. The attitude toward them was much the same as that toward other work animals. Their introduction was an experiment that at first met with little success; it was half a century after the first Negroes were sold in Jamestown before it became clear that they could be used profitably in large numbers.

In Pennsylvania and the northern colonies, the use of Negroes was not in general a success. The climate and the character of the resources favored the development of varied industries in the northern areas. In the circumstances, white servitude rather than Negro slavery tended to flourish. By the time of the Revolutionary War, the slavery of Negroes was nearly out in the regions north of Maryland, and there was a further period of decline after the Revolution.

In Virginia and the southern colonies generally the climate and the industries favored slavery. They were suited to a plantation rather than to an independent type of agriculture. The first real impetus toward slavery came from rice culture in Georgia and South Carolina. The crop was profitable but could not be extensively cultivated by free labor. Settlers and independent workers avoided the warm and humid climate, the malarial swamp lands, and the type of labor involved in the growing of rice. When the realization came that the swamp edges, rather than the ridges between the swamps, produced the best rice crops, and especially when the growers learned to flood the rice fields, there was a greatly increased demand for Negroes. Slave labor could be used profitably and if rice was to be produced—and its production held out great promise of profit—forced labor was necessary. Negro slaves could be driven to work that free men would not undertake.

The production of tobacco and sugar, like the cultivation of rice, demanded forced labor. Neither the climate nor the work conditions attracted free men. On the other hand, the work could be done by supervised gangs of low-grade and servile laborers.

The growth of cotton particularly favored a plantation slave régime. The crop requires a long and hot growing season, six or seven months without frost. Its cultivation is adapted to slave labor; the production of a crop provides nine or ten months of steady work, it is work that is suited to gang labor, and it is work that can be done by women and children as well as by men. The invention of the cotton gin in 1793, just as the English textile industry was at the factory stage of production, had prompt and far-reaching results. There was a steady market for the fiber, and so an active demand for slave labor.

Slavery was primarily an economic development. It grew and flourished where forced labor was profitable; it did not gain a permanent footing in other regions. It was profitable in the southern regions because the character of the agricultural crops was adapted to the use of low-grade servile labor. It was necessary in the situation because of the open resources—because there was more land than there was free labor to till; its development was favored by the climatic conditions in the South which repelled settlers, and by the fact that the type of labor involved in the production of the southern staples was avoided by free men. Slavery and the plantation system developed in the South in response to the climatic conditions and the condition of open resources.

THE PLANTATION SYSTEM

Negro slavery and the plantation economy were twin products of the natural and economic conditions—products of the climate and soil that determined the crops grown, and of the open resources that left men an alternative to working as laborers or tenants and made it impossible for landlords to secure abundant laborers except by coercion. The slavery of

the Negroes was an accompaniment—both a prerequisite and a consequence—of the plantation economy.

The plantation does not develop and flourish without an abundant supply of cheap and servile labor; in the absence of a dense native population
capable of exploitation, the system must rely upon the importation of
slaves, or upon contract or other laborers who, to all intent and purpose,
may be worked as slaves. As a going economic order, the plantation system produces an abundant population of servile workers economically
dependent upon the prosperity of the individual plantation and the plantation system. In the long run, the plantation economy, which is at first
dependent upon slave labor, makes a slave system unnecessary. In the beginning the southern plantation economy was dependent upon slave labor;
in the later periods, with all land appropriated and the growth of a large
property-less class, the landlord could secure abundant labor without coercion.

Once established in America, the plantation economy dominated all aspects of southern life. The use of gang labor and the one-crop system of
agriculture were virtually necessary to immediately profitable operation.
The system of social classes was in part essential to and in part an outgrowth of the type of agriculture; the planters and the slaves were the two
sharply separated castes essential to the economy; the small farmers—poor
whites—were a by-product of the plantation economy rather than an integral part of the system. The working plantation was essentially a self-
sufficing economic unit; it produced in major part the goods and services
necessary to its successful operation and to the needs of its personnel.
There was little place in the plantation system for an independent middle
class.

The plantation manner of life put its impress with equal effectiveness
on other aspects of life and social organization. It determined the traditions and customs of the regions, and came gradually to be defined in the
mores. Slavery and other practices necessary or incident to successful
plantation economy had the moral approval of the community, the legal
support of the state, and the religious sanction of the church. Philosophy
justified the system and literature romanticized and glorified it. Intellectually and morally as well as economically, the plantation tended to be
isolated and self-contained.

Similar aspects of the system appear on examination of the labor system
on which the plantation economy rested.

The Slave Order

In America slavery was first and foremost an economic system, an adjustment of differently circumstanced men to the impersonal competitive

processes. The struggle for life and place and power, in the unequal conditions of the struggle, reduced some to servitude, elevated others to an aristocratic and leisure class, and left still others physically free but economically impoverished.

Slavery, however, was a political order as well as an economic system. The political order, as seems always and everywhere to be the nature of political organization, was a secondary adjustment to the primary and basic economic factors. It was in general the organization developed to fight for the continuance of the established order, and it functioned to protect and advance the economic and personal welfare of those in possession and control. Slave owners were a united and homogeneous class, a solid political unit organized to defend their economic privileges. They were unified as to interests and many were alert and intelligent men. The political order, inevitably, was subsidiary to the control of the natural resources and control of the means of power. In contrast to the farm colonies where a degree of economic equality reflected itself in democratic political arrangements, the political aspect of the plantation and slave areas was aristocratic. The political machinery was directly in the hands or under the immediate control of the economic aristocracy.

Slavery must also be conceived as a system of social control. Ultimately, and from time to time in individual cases, slavery rested on force, on the ability physically to coerce weaker individuals to carry out the will of the master. But the exercise of physical force is everywhere an inefficient means of control, and in an established order the primary forms of coercion are little needed. Life must be lived within the existing social order. The institutional framework sets the channels in which life goes on, so determines the habits and the social attitudes that control personal behavior through adjusting the person to his social status in the social situation.

Slavery must also be understood as a system of ideas. It was a body of primary rationalizations, a philosophy attempting to explain and justify in impersonal terms the historically developed system of economic, political, and personal relations. Every slave and colonial system, as every system of exploitation, endeavors to justify itself in terms of wide or universal appeal—in terms of the "culture mission" of the advanced peoples, in terms of the "white man's burden," in terms of Christian education and native welfare, or in other terms of current popular appeal. Every such body of philosophical doctrine is at once an apology for the palpable injustices of the arrangements and an expression of a naïve belief in their unique and superior value as a system of human relations. It is necessary to conceive of slavery as a body of thought as well as to recognize it as an economic arrangement, as a political order, and as a system of social control.

Effects of the Slave Economy

The immediate effect of any system of economy is to exercise an institutional control over all those who live within the system. It defines immediately the range of activities possible in the situation; the individual's choice of vocation and means of livelihood is limited to the opportunities the social system provides. The wages of labor, the degrees of achievement, the rewards of success, the placement of recognition, and other incentives to human effort are fixed in the social system. The plantation economy and slave labor in the American South narrowly restricted the range of choice as to means of life and manner of living.

The dominant way of life in the economic area determines the run of attention and thereby defines the types of mind characteristic of the area. The daily work activities set the mode and manner of thought; the matters of interest, the body of information, and other evidences of mental activity are closely connected with the routine activities of daily life. The rural economy with its dependence on weather and other natural conditions for crop success, and the relations of masters and slaves in a system of forced labor were basic in the production of types of mind and modes of thought typical of the American South and agricultural plantation areas. In the South the influence of the plantation was toward cultural isolation; slavery retarded immigration from other areas, so shut off the introduction of new ideas, and it made for the growth of individualism and for the self-sufficiency of the individual plantation and the plantation area. The isolation resulted in sectional solidarity, cultural retardation, and a high degree of provincial self-consciousness.

The organization of the group life determines the types of personality developed. The institutional organization decides the status and rôle of individuals, hence their conceptions of themselves and their personalities.

And, finally, any social system defines the type of human relations—the moral order—that obtains in the situation.

From the human point of view, slavery was a set of reciprocal relations between and among the social classes and the personalities which were themselves products of the system. In the slave-holding South there developed a slave-owning, a master class; the system also developed a non-slave-holding, a poor-white class; a population of Negro slaves; and a population of free Negro peoples.

The White Aristocracy

The economic effect of the plantation economy was to concentrate wealth and power in a few hands. Of the four chief plantation crops, cotton, rice, and tobacco were most economically produced on large plantations; the fourth plantation crop, sugar, could be produced profitably only on a large scale. The result was a virtual monopoly of land in a few hands. In reality, in the period just preceding the Civil War, only one white man in five was an owner of slaves and of these the great majority owned a single or a few slaves. But the relatively few landed proprietors exercised a dominant influence on the social and moral as well as on the political and economic systems. The individual plantations were widely separated and virtually independent and self-contained units. Towns were few and uninfluential. Following the pattern set by the plantation owners, the middle-class group—lawyers, doctors, ministers, and the like—tended to be rural dwellers.

The nature of the life had a profound influence on the character and personality traits of the ruling whites. Like other Americans, they were of middle and low class origin; they were not "to the manor born"; the southern aristocrats were a development from a common class. The separation of the plantations forced a development of self-reliance. The large plantation was a sort of feudal domain and the owner was a sort of feudal lord. He had very great power and virtual independence. Within the situation, he was in reality an important person. He was responsible for the management of the estate with its wide range of work activities. In the circumstances he had to accept responsibility, assume leadership, and exercise control. The position developed the types of character and personality required to perform the functions—the types of character and personality characteristic of the plantation manager in all areas. Power leads to cruelty, to a contempt for the weak, to harsh and ruthless tyranny and to certain types of patriarchal and paternalistic and sentimental traits in certain relationships. The virtually unlimited power over helpless subordinates developed the domineering manner—one of the tricks of leadership. The various descriptive terms and epithets used alike by themselves and their critics—hard, proud, dignified, brutal, overbearing, imperious, intolerant, mentally narrow, politically unscrupulous, and the like—give the behavior characteristics of the petty tyrant in every situation. The slaveholder was a product of the system and an embodiment of the traits that the position and the system called for and made inevitable. The fundamentals of any system are embodied in the social types it produces. But the slave aristocrat was a person of much leisure, frequently a man of some education, and often an individual highly skilled in the social graces of the period. The romantic literature of the South has elaborated at length the benevolent and softer aspects of the plantation system and the slave master. These were of course very real and very important characteristics. But any real and realistic understanding requires a recognition of the fact that the slave-owning aristocracy was possessed of the traits of character and personality that made for success in the semi-feudal situation.

The plantation economy and the slave system of labor require the per-

formance of certain professional or service activities that are disagreeable
in character or held in social disrepute. On the smaller plantations, these
services were of necessity performed by the white master; on the larger
plantations, they could be delegated to subordinates or to semi-independent agents and operators. The work to be performed, if the plantation was
to operate efficiently and profitably, developed the types of men fitted to
do the work. These subordinate persons are not commonly, in the romantic literature, classed with the slave-holding aristocracy, though they
were very definitely a part of the slave régime and in the majority of
cases definitely of the slave-owning group.

The overseer was a by-product of the system. On the smaller plantations the owner was also the operator and the overseer. But the profession
of overseer and the type developed as slavery changed from the patriarchal to an industrial order. On the larger plantations and as absentee
ownership developed the overseer was the business manager. His obligation was to make the plantation pay dividends. The position was one of
great power and responsibility. But it carried no social status; the overseers were looked upon by the aristocracy as crude persons. Their success
depended upon driving the slaves and performing other functions of rough
and brutal character. They were despised by the aristocracy for doing the
very work that they were required to do, and the work that the masters
themselves did on most of the plantations.

The slave traders were an essential element of the system. If the plantation were to operate economically, an adequate labor force was necessary
and any over-supply of slaves had to be reduced promptly. This meant a
more or less active buying and selling of slaves. In many cases the buying and selling of slaves were local transactions between neighboring plantation owners. But this became increasingly inadequate as the system developed, and regular dealers took over the business. Slave markets were
established and the whole matter put on a strictly commercial basis. Negroes were purchased in the areas where they were plentiful and cheap
and shipped for sale in the areas where the demand was active and the
prices high. The commercial slave traders were the most despised persons
connected with the system. They brought boldly into the open the buying
and selling of Negroes, an aspect of the system that the apologists of the
system preferred not to stress. The commercial dealers made obvious the
crude monetary motives at the basis of slavery. There was no way to
camouflage or sentimentalize this aspect of the system; it made the ulti-
mate and basic character of slavery stand out in bold relief. The trader,
a necessary part of the system and an inevitable development in the situation, became a type of personal devil: attention was diverted from the
evils inherent in the system by heaping abuse on the agent of the system.
And the slave owner and master escaped the odium of the crude commer-

cial aspects of the system through allowing it to be handled by an agent who took the abuse. The social disrepute in which the occupation of slave-trading was held had its influence on the personnel; the occupation attracted crude and brutal and disreputable men and the business itself tended to increase their callous brutality. But it must be remembered that the plantation owners and managers were the buyers and the sellers of the slaves; the dealers were merely go-betweens.

While the overseers and the slave traders, who performed essential services in the slave economy, were not of the social aristocracy the same thing cannot be said of the slave breeders: they were very definitely of the aristocracy though their business was often held in ill-repute. The commercial breeding of slaves for the market was an incidental by-product of the system but one with wide and interesting ramifications. Of course all slave owners were slave breeders. There was no way of maintaining a slave population except by breeding them or buying them. Every slave owner was either a slave trader or a slave breeder or both. But it also had a definite business side. The generally unprofitable character of Negro slavery in the North caused many slave owners to dispose of their holdings in regions where the Negroes were in demand and brought a high price. The laws providing for the gradual abolition of slavery in New England and elsewhere in the North stimulated the tendency to sell the Negroes to the South. The importation of Negroes was stopped at the time that slavery was approaching its most profitable stage. The increased demand and the high prices that came with the boom in cotton culture led many plantations in the border areas to become virtually breeding stations for the southern market. The business was not one of the nicer aspects of the slave system, and the real nature of the business was generally not openly admitted. It was usual to assert that only the over-supply of Negroes was sold in the southern market, but every effort was made to assure the production of an annual over-supply. Mulatto and other Negroes of light skin generally brought a fancy price in the market; this may account in some part for the high percentage of part-white children produced on many of the slave-breeding plantations.

THE POOR WHITES

The "poor whites" were a product of the plantation system. In the romantic tradition, the doctrine prevails that the poor white class was descended from the indentured servants of the Colonial period, that they were of a racial strain unlike the aristocrats and the prosperous classes. This belief is a variant of the idea found in every caste area—the idea that the peasantry and the aristocracy are of separate biological origin. In America, at least, the doctrine has little evidence in its support; it is flattering to the prosperous classes—implies that their superior social and economic status is an expression of superior natural worth—but it does not describe the historic reality nor indicate a causal sequence.

The southern crops were most profitably produced on a relatively large scale. The organization of the plantations excluded an agricultural middle-class; the small farmer was at a disadvantage and was driven to the poorer lands and to the abandoned areas. In the slave régime, the small independent farmers were, wherever possible, driven out by the large planters. They were a bad influence on the slaves; the presence of poor and miserable whites living on a scale little if any superior to that of the Negroes tended to lower the prestige of the whites as a whole, and the presence of white men engaged in types of labor ordinarily done by Negro slaves further tended to blur the caste distinctions. In the code of slavery, the white man engaged in no menial labor.

The existence of slavery degrades all types of labor done by slaves. Labor was confused with slavery; to engage in any activity ordinarily done by slaves was to assume the slave level. One result was the destruction of independent industry by making most types of skilled and semi-skilled labor, as well as field work and unskilled labor, disreputable. The competitive processes operated in the same direction. On the larger plantations, slaves were trained for the various necessary vocational pursuits; each plantation had carpenters, tailors, harness makers, coopers, and other skilled workers among the slaves. Consequently, there was no place for the independent white mechanics and other skilled workers on the plantations. Moreover, the slave mechanics were frequently for hire, so came into direct competition with any free workers, hence narrowly limited their opportunities for profitable employment. By the time of the Civil War, practically all the skilled trades were in the hands of the Negroes; all avenues to profitable labor were closed to the poor whites.

This poor white class, approximately one-quarter of the southern white population, were, except for their physical freedom, in many cases scarcely better placed economically than the slaves.

Out of the situation developed the traditional attitudes of the Negroes and the poor whites. The early relations were generally friendly; the distinction between slavery and servitude was not sharply drawn and the working groups were not in obvious competition. As slavery became defined as the lot of the Negroes, the caste feeling arose. Even the most miserable of the whites assumed superiority to the Negroes because of the free status and the racial connections. As the developing slave economy progressively deprived them of means of livelihood, there developed a bitter hatred for the Negroes; the poor and ignorant whites attributed their miserable lot to the presence of the Negro rather than to the system of economy in which both the Negro and the landless whites were caught. On their part, the slaves developed a profound contempt for the poor whites; they did not conform in work or behavior to the servile man's conception of a superior man.

THE NEGRO SLAVES

The effect of slavery on the Negro will be considered in detail in the following chapters and is, in reality, the general theme of the entire volume. The purpose is to understand the Negroes—the social status, the cultural characteristics, the personality traits—and the existing race relations in terms of the present condition and the past experience. It is necessary here only to mention certain facts immediately related to the preceding sections.

The Negroes, as a servile class in the plantation economy, developed the characteristics that the status demanded. They were in the happy situation of having no responsibility. Food, clothing, shelter, and other necessities were provided by the masters who also made all decisions and assumed all responsibility. The slave's only duty was to perform the routine tasks assigned by the master. As a consequence the Negroes developed no resourcefulness, no self-reliance, and no sense of responsibility. The nature of their life provided no incentive to personal effort and it developed no habits of industry; there was no property and the concept of honesty in the property relation was in consequence undeveloped. In other ways the slave Negroes developed the traits of body and mind that life in the situation demanded.

Within the Negro group various class and caste divisions developed. The life conditions of the Negroes were not everywhere the same. Certain individual Negroes were outside the slave system. The free Negroes inevitably recognized the different status and held themselves superior to the slaves. The mixed bloods, in part because of relationship and a color like the masters and in part because of the prevailing idea of white superiority, believed themselves to be superior to the Negroes of unmixed blood. The house servants, because of the type of work and conditions of their work, enjoyed a prestige and tended to be a group apart from the field hands. The mechanics and skilled workers recognized the advantages they enjoyed in training, skill, and more pleasant work and considered themselves superior to the gang laborers. Various other lines of division were drawn and class distinctions made within the Negro population.

THE HERITAGE OF SLAVERY

The present relations of the races is a development out of these earlier conditions. The pattern of economic relations, the political organization, the class hierarchy, the social attitudes, and the body of social and racial doctrine are rooted in the arrangements of the earlier period. The existing racial situation is not a common-sense adjustment to the immediate economic and social needs; social and public welfare quite obviously demand somewhat radical alterations in the institutional structure and the manner of life. But the social order is not a logical construct; it is an historical growth, tinged with romantic memories and heavily freighted with emotional content. In consequence, derivative values of secondary and tertiary order quite commonly assume first rank; the basic and primary values, the imperative needs in the situation, are often sacrificed to perpetuate derivative values and historic relationships that are of positive disutility in the present situation. The irrational elements, the sentimental and emotional values, as well as the traditional economy and the historic political structure, are integral parts of the existing social order. They are extensions of the past into the present. Their importance lies in the fact that they cannot be evaluated or objectively understood by those within the culture; they are not recognized as traditional and irrational values; on the contrary, they are the values by which the people live, they determine behavior and it is in the light of them that behavior must be understood.

A basic element of this heritage is a plantation economy in agricultural areas where a one-crop system long ago exhausted the productivity of the lighter soils. The relative impoverishment of large regions, in comparison with other agricultural sections of lesser natural productivity, is to be understood in terms of the traditional agricultural system. The system of land holding with its semi-prosperous landed aristocracy, its impoverished and hopelessly defeated white tenant class, and its equally impoverished and servile Negro group is the plantation system operating under the coercion of poverty and in an area of closed resources.

This characteristic social stratification of the society is a second major heritage from the past social order; it is perpetuated in the present by the continuation of the old type of agricultural economy and its derivative caste ideology.

The racial sentiments and attitudes defined in the slave relation are operative in the present-day situation. The long-standing caste superiority of the white man is so completely a part of the white mind that there is not only an unwillingness to consider change but an inability to understand the possibility of other types of racial relationships. The general mental servility of the Negroes, like the mental set of the white men, is a heritage from the earlier status and is perpetuated by the conditions of life in the present.

The prevailing racial ideology is one of long standing. It was an inevitable development in a situation comprehending the contradictory facts of human slavery and the democratic doctrine of freedom and equality. It represented in its earlier stages a naïve effort to harmonize reality and doctrine; the only solution possible was to put the slave outside the human category and so outside the moral order. In later stages it hardened into a body of racial dogmas in defense and justification of an economic system that was under attack. It has continued into the present as a part of the social heritage; it persists because it offers an explanation, within the comprehension of the simple mind, of existing inequalities in racial status and because of its obvious utility in justifying and perpetuating the inequalities of status and opportunity.

The social and cultural complex—the economic order, the political arrangements, the class and caste system, the sentimental and emotional attitudes, the beliefs and idea systems, and the rest—is a heritage of slavery and it determines the racial problems in the present. The status of the Negro, his failures and achievements, his character and personality, his organizations and institutions, his beliefs and attitudes, and the other social and sociological characteristics of the Negro may be understood only in the light of the traditional and persisting culture of the American South.

RACIAL CHANGE

It is clear from the nature of the factors involved in the present-day system of race relations that no great change is to be anticipated in any short space of time. The basic economy is relatively stable, the political machinery is organized to perpetuate white control, and the body of sentiment favoring a caste and slave system is deeply intrenched in custom and tradition. Change in race relations may be anticipated only as a result of cultural growth and modification.

Such cultural change is going on, and a continued evolutionary development is to be anticipated; no culture is entirely static. Economic changes in the southern sections may go on with relative rapidity—through a modernization of agricultural methods, the invention and utilization of agricultural machinery, the growth of industry, or through other developments —and result in urbanization or migration or other shifts in population or in other adjustments that may, by disrupting the traditional system, initiate a new stage in the cycle of race relations. The modification of the moral order and the change in the relations of the races will not be in the nature of voluntary acts of conscious design. They will be blind and generally unrecognized acts of adjustment dictated by changes in the basic social structure.

READINGS

Bancroft, L., *Slave-Trading in the Old South.*

Dodd, W. E., *The Cotton Kingdom.*

Emerson, F. V., "Geographic Influence in American Slavery," *Bulletin, American Geographic Society,* 43(1911), 13–26; 106–118; 170–181.

Gaines, F. P., *The Southern Plantation.*

Haardt, Sara, "The Etiquette of Slavery," *American Mercury,* 17(1929), 34–42.

Johnson, C. S., *The Shadow of the Plantation.*

Kemble, Fannie A., *Journal of a Residence on a Georgian Plantation.*

Nieboer, H. J., *Slavery as an Industrial System.*

Phillips, U. B., *Life and Labor in the Old South.*

Reuter, E. B., ed., *Race and Culture Contacts.*

Sydnor, C. S., "Life Span of Mississippi Slaves," *American Historical Review,* 35(1930), 566–574.

Thompson, E. T., *The Plantation.*

Weatherford, W. D., and Johnson, C. S., *Race Relations,* "The Origin of Negro Slavery," pp. 99–111; "Economic Aspects of Slavery," pp. 146–162; "The Effect of Slavery on the Negro," pp. 274–288.

FURTHER READINGS

Aptheker, Herbert, *A Documentary History of the Negro People.* New York: Citadel, 1951.

Fishel, Leslie H., and Quarles, Benjamin, eds., *The Negro American: A Documentary History.* Glenview, Ill.: Scott, Foresman, 1967.

Franklin, John Hope, *From Slavery to Freedom: A History of American Negroes.* New York: Alfred A. Knopf, 1956.

Frazier, E. Franklin, *The Negro in the United States.* New York: Macmillan, 1949.

Klein, Herbert S., *Slavery in the Americas: A Comparative Study of Virginia and Cuba.* Chicago: University of Chicago Press, 1967.

Logan, Rayford W., *The Negro in the United States.* New York: Van Nostrand, 1957.

Meltzer, Milton, *In Their Own Words: A History of the American Negro 1619–1865.* New York: Thomas Y. Crowell Company, 1964.

Myrdal, Gunnar, *An American Dilemma.* New York: Harper, 1944.

Quarles, Benjamin, *The Negro in the American Revolution.* Chapel Hill, N.C.: University of North Carolina Press, 1961.

Willams, Eric, *Capitalism and Slavery.* Chapel Hill: University of North Carolina Press, 1944.

V I

THE ACCOMMODATION
OF THE RACES*

The accommodation of the races in America is a continuous process. It is not to be conceived merely as a condition once reached and thereafter remaining stable; it is rather a body of habitudinal adjustments that maintains an equilibrium in the working relations and at the same time changes in response to modifications in the culture. The mutually acceptable or tolerable relations of one period are unlike those prevailing at earlier and later dates, and the transition from one status to another may be made without overt conflict or notable friction. Accommodation is a relative condition; the group, or persons within the group, may be well adjusted or highly disorganized. Whether the tendency be toward increasing unrest or toward a more perfect accommodation depends upon whether or not the pace of cultural change—consequently the disturbance of personal habits and social routines—exceeds the rate at which habitudinal and sentimental readjustments may be made.

In the American situation, the process of racial accommodation has been a complex phenomenon involving the adjustment of both Negro and white persons to the rapidly changing culture complex, and the modification of each in the maintenance of working relations in the common political area. Moreover, as a condition, it has varied at different periods and in different economic areas.

The conditions of life in Colonial America were unlike those within the experience of the European settlers as well as unlike those to which the African Negroes were habituated. The individuals of each racial group had to adjust themselves to the climatic and other natural conditions of the geographic area as well as to the pioneer conditions of living, and to develop the types of mind and habits of action necessary to tolerable life

---

* Except for minor deletions, this chapter is the same as in the second edition.

in their situation. The adjustments and accommodations were somewhat different in the different colonies, and they were in continual process of change as the country gradually passed from a frontier to a settled area and from the rural and agricultural mode of life to the urban and industrial types of life and economy.

Within the natural conditions and the economic structure, the personal relations of the races had to be defined in custom and habit—each racial group had to become accommodated to its status in the social order, the whites to a position of mastery and leadership and the Negroes to a position of slavery. The master-slave relationship was highly variable; in some periods and areas it was mildly patriarchal, at other times and places it was ruthlessly industrial. In any case the slaves developed the social attitudes and types of mind that made for reasonable contentment in the situation. The masters developed reciprocal attitudes and personal characteristics that fitted them to the status.

The non-slave-owning whites and the free Negroes, while technically outside the slave relation, were quite definitely under its influence and the personal accommodations they made, while very different in individual cases, were those dictated by their subordinate position in the society. In neither case was the accommodation to a dependent status as complete as it was with the slaves. The freedom of the free Negroes was often sharply restricted by law and public sentiment and the freedom of the poor whites was sharply limited by the character of the economic system, but in each case there was a considerable area in which activities were more nominally free.

EARLY CONTACTS OF THE RACES IN AMERICA

Negro slavery was an old and well-established institution in Spain, Portugal, and elsewhere at the time of the discovery of America and, as a matter of course, was introduced into the New World with the first settlements. African slaves were used on many of the voyages of discovery and in various early exploratory expeditions. In the Spanish colonies the institution existed from the beginning; the first settlers brought Negro slaves as a labor force. Within a decade of the first Columbian expedition, the importation of slaves was approved by royal edict and in 1510 the direct importations of Negroes from Africa was begun. From the first, the number of Negroes imported was large; in 1517, Charles V of Spain granted a monopoly allowing an annual importation of 4,000 African slaves. In the following decades the trade was active and the number of annual importations increased.

Notwithstanding the very long period during which African Negroes had been subjected to slavery by European peoples and the century of Negro slavery in the Spanish and Portuguese settlements to the south, the introduction of twenty captive blacks into the Jamestown Colony in 1619 was the first experience of the English settlers with African slaves. Only a few years later Negro slavery was begun in the colony at Providence.

The early contacts of the races in the English colonies were more in the nature of physical than of social contacts. The Negroes were introduced as a labor force and were valued on that basis. The motives leading to their purchase and the attitudes toward them appear to have been essentially those that lead to the purchase, use, and care of domestic animals. The control exercised over their life and activity was of necessity physical rather than social: they were controlled from the outside as animals are controlled rather than through sharing a community of habit and sentiment. The attitude toward them was similar, often identical, to that manifested toward a valuable work animal. The Negroes were within the group rather than a part of it.

It could not well have been otherwise. The American communities into which the Negroes came were of a rude, pioneer type. The colonists were, for the most part, middle- and low-class persons. Agriculture was the chief, almost the only, occupation. There were few labor-saving devices. The cultivation of crops was almost exclusively by the hoe. Workers were needed and very low-class workers were equal to the tasks. The Negroes were very rude; in some cases they were brought directly from Africa and had no previous contact with Europeans or European culture; in other cases they came by way of the West Indies. In the latter and more usual case they had been to some extent subdued and partially habituated to the status of work animals. The newly arrived captives were "broken in" by being put to work in gangs with "seasoned" slaves. Later, as they became reconciled to slavery under the white masters and learned to follow simple directions, they were given individual tasks or sold to the planters and farmers on the mainland. But whether they were brought from the West Indies or direct from Africa they were primitive creatures with little or no knowledge of the language or other culture facts of the groups into which they were introduced. They were profoundly disorganized through the destruction of their social organization. They could communicate but imperfectly with the white masters and often, because of the separation of tribal members, they were unable to understand one another.

DEVELOPMENT OF THE SLAVE STATUS

In the Spanish colonies the slave institution existed from the first, developing by a simple extension of the European system and its adaptation to the needs of the colonial environment. But in the English colonies there was no precedent by which to determine the status of the Negroes. Slavery was not in the mores of the North European peoples and there was, in consequence, no traditional conception of slavery and of the place of the slave in the social order.

Moreover, the great majority of the English colonists had had no previous contact with the Negro people. In consequence of this historic fact, there was an absence of any traditional prejudice toward members of the race, there was no crystallized conception of the Negro and of his place in the social order. The relationships that came to prevail were the result in very large part of the biological and cultural differences between the races brought together in a geographic situation new to both. The status that developed was in minor degree only determined by traditional race conceptions. The Negroes were heathens and generally uncouth persons and the early personal prejudice against them ran in religious and hygienic rather than in racial terms.

It is probable that the first Negro slaves in what is now the United States were considered as servants rather than as slaves. The colonists were familiar with the system of indenture which prevailed in Europe during the period of American colonization. The system was transferred to America, and the socially heterogeneous indentured servant class was a numerically important part of the colonial population. The conception of the Negro's position in the society was determined or modified by the prevailing conception of social classes. The Negroes and the white indentured servants were closely associated during a considerable part of the early period and it appears that at first not much difference was made, formally, in the status of the two servile groups. In the census taken in the Virginia colony in 1624–1625, the twenty-three Africans were listed as "servants," the same as the white persons of the indentured class.

But the marked physical, mental, temperamental, cultural, and religious strangeness of the Negroes probably gave them from the first a status somewhat unlike that of any other group in the society. The general initial fear of the strange pagan people led often to their separation and to special precautions to prevent the possibility of uprisings. Other distinctions in treatment were inevitable in view of the language and other cultural differences between the African and the European servants. The special treatment became traditional and a distinctive status came gradually to be defined in practice and was well established and generally understood long before it anywhere received legal sanction. So far as Negroes were concerned, the status of servants came presently to mean servants for life and this came ultimately to mean servants in perpetuity. This transition was effected in custom long before it received formal legal sanction. The first legislation—Virginia 1662, Maryland 1663, and later in the other colonies—defining slavery was the result of cases brought to determine the status of mulatto children. The rule adopted—that the status of the child should follow that of the mother—implies that the slave status was already established and understood. As the system of white indenture fell into disuse the status of servitude came to be associated, more and more exclusively, with the alien, outcast, and degraded race and, conversely, the position of the slave became the presumptive status of all Negroes. By the beginning of the eighteenth century slavery of Negroes existed as an accepted practice in all the colonies and by the middle of the century it had everywhere in the colonies received legal sanction.

THE PLANTATION SYSTEM AND FORCED LABOR

The change in attitudes as slavery became profitable and well established is seen in the shift in the basis on which it rested. In the early decades it was justified on religious grounds; in theory at least the slave status was restricted to heathens and conversion to Christianity ended the period of servitude. This gave a justification for the system; it could be argued that slavery was an effective means of bringing the heathen under the influence of the Christian religion. But the effect of the doctrine was to destroy the system it rationalized; the Negroes readily embraced Christianity and became entitled to freedom. It became necessary, therefore, to shift the basis of slavery or to prevent the slaves from being Christianized. During the latter part of the seventeenth century, the test for slavery changed from religion to race.

The conception of slavery itself underwent a change as it came to be restricted to the members of a different race and as the social and economic life of the colonies developed and evolved. The idea of a slave as a person serving for life gave way to the conception of a slave as a thing rather than as a person.

After the Revolution, with the development of the country and its increase in area, wealth, and population, the status of the Negroes was yet more clearly defined. The climatic conditions and the rice, cotton, and tobacco industries of the South outlined the area in which the exploitation of slave labor was profitable. The invention of the cotton gin in 1793 with the resulting increased profit from the production of that staple further changed the nature of the institution. It increased the value of servile labor by increasing the productivity of the laborers and it definitely changed slavery from a semi-patriarchal to a business type of institution. This brought a corresponding change in the status of the servile class; from being quasi-personalities they became pieces of property.

As previously mentioned, the plantation economy of the South depended upon slave labor and provided the type of routine labor suited to slaves. The long growing season for cotton production gave a need for much unskilled labor throughout most of the year. All individuals, women and children as well as men, could be used in the fields and they could be worked in gangs under overseers.

In the situation, most of the human and personal relations between masters and servants disappeared. Before the development of the plantation system, the number of Negroes in the owner's family was generally small. The slaves quite usually worked with the master and the contacts were frequent, personal, and sympathetic. The slave was in many essential respects a member of the master's family. In the industrial types of plantation slavery the Negroes became an impersonal labor force driven by overseers. The contacts and association of the races were few and impersonal. On the large and efficiently operated plantations the Negroes had no human and personal relations with the whites; except for overseers and work bosses they saw little more of white men than before their importation. They were for the most part work animals rather than human beings.

ECONOMIC ADJUSTMENTS

In its developed form, the plantation system dominated all aspects of life throughout the entire South: it determined the form and development of the social institutions, set the culture patterns within which the individual activities and the social relations were carried on. The political institutions were molded into conformity with the economic system and functioned in the main to defend and perpetuate the system. The family, especially the slave family, was adjusted to the convenience of the plantation. Schools and public education were neglected or discouraged. The church too was auxiliary to the economic order; it provided moral support to the system through giving divine sanction to the slave system. Other institutions and community organizations took shape within the patterns set by the plantation and its system of labor.

As previously mentioned, the institutional arrangements in turn determined the types of character and personality possible and actual in the situation; the classes and sub-groups were in all cases subordinate to the major economic structure. The types of mind varied with the social groups within the economy—each class developed the specialized habits and activities necessary in the situation and the body of rationalization necessary to a tolerable life in the situation—and, within the social classes, with the individual's status. The basic accommodation was to the plantation system and manner of life which controlled not only the masters and the slaves but also the poor-whites and other individuals living within the economy.

THE ACCOMMODATION OF THE NEGRO

The Negroes on the whole yielded to the slave status with little show of resistance. To a very considerable extent, the master-slave relationship was within their tribal mores. Slavery was at the basis of most of the agricultural and industrial life of West Africa and subordination to alien races was also within the racial heritage, and within the experience of many individuals. It was the form that the institution took in America and the race that administered it rather than the status itself that was new to racial experience of the Negroes. The temperamental traits, or the socially acquired characteristics, of the race appear to be such as to make the initial stages of a slave order relatively easy to establish.

The external characteristics of the situation operated to the same end. The Negroes for a long period were few in number and were widely scattered. The plantation system of gang labor in the early stages of the slave institution did not in general prevail; the ownership of slaves rested with numerous individuals and the slaves were resident in many different households. As a result of this distribution the contacts with others of their race were comparatively few. The slaves brought to America represented many different tribal stocks and spoke many different dialects. In consequence, they were frequently unable to communicate until they had acquired some command of the English language. At all times the power of superior numbers rested with the whites and the infrequent revolts of individuals and small groups were promptly suppressed.

The imported Negroes soon became habituated to a servile position in the social order and resigned to a status from which there was no escape. Presently there were individuals born into the status, individuals who knew no other system of human relations and accepted their subordinate status as a part of the order of nature. The importation of raw Negroes from Africa and the West Indies continued, but more and more they were introduced into an ordered and established system which was supported and upheld by the sentiments and attitudes of the previous arrivals as well as by the power of the whites. The acceptance of the situation became easier for the new arrivals as the body of supporting slave sentiment increased.

The children born to slavery uncritically accepted it as their rightful status and equally uncritically accepted the superior status of the whites. They had no basis on which to question it. The caste order was all that they knew and the striking dissimilarity in the physical appearance of the races gave what seemed to be a natural basis for it. The difference in the cultural development of the races paralleled the caste lines and reinforced the tendency to accept the existing arrangements as being in harmony with the divine plan.

As slavery became an established and accepted institution, the slaves developed the complex of beliefs, sentiments, and attitudes which their position in the society demanded. Theirs was a typical psychology of inferiority. In terms of status they were inferior and they accepted their inferiority. The pattern of mind was in accord with the objective status. Like the disinherited and abused economic classes of modern and other societies, the slaves were much given to complaint over petty grievances but in their basic habits and attitudes supported the system that exploited them. While the ability to exercise physical force was always a reality behind the system, slavery did not rest upon force except in the early stages of the institution and in the case of unaccommodated individuals; the forces that controlled the slaves were within the slaves themselves. There was no general longing to escape and no general feeling of hatred and bitterness that comes from brooding over wrongs. They accepted the status and often took a certain pride in it. They looked up to the whites, desired them to be superior, and resented any behavior that seemed to put in question the superiority of the white master class. Conversely, they came to look upon their own race as inferior to the whites, as existing to serve the whites, and they resented any behavior of members of their race not in harmony with the master-man relationship. The mass of the slaves throughout most of the slave period were highly accommodated to their servile status.

The degree of their accommodation is indicated by the fact of their loyalty to the white families during the period of the Civil War. Unlike prisoners held in servitude by superior physical force, the slaves continued the habitual way of life and performed the routine tasks while the masters struggled with those who endeavored to liberate them. Their pathetic isolation and mental adjustment to the slave status kept them loyal to the system and the masters who exploited them.

The Accommodation of the Whites

The accommodation of the whites was not less complete than that of the Negroes. They became habituated to the rôle of domination and developed the complex of beliefs and attitudes appropriate to their position in the social order.

This white caste was of course the outcome of a long developmental process. It grew directly and inevitably out of the social situation. The slave cannot exist without the master. In the society the existence of a servile and inferior caste implies the existence of a master and superior caste. The relationship is a reciprocal one and the accommodation of the whites to their position in the society came in the course and as a part of the establishing of a slave order. The presence of a group of servile laborers made necessary the direction of their work and the control of their lives if they were to be economically valuable and were not to be a dangerous element in the society. The white owners were forced to assume responsibility, and with the exercise of power came the attitudes characteristic of a socially superior class. The tendency to look upon those who worked as inferior to those who directed the work and profited by it was inevitable. The racial difference between the slaves and the masters made it easy to assume that the difference in status was an expression of this fact. There developed a body of doctrine justifying the master-slave system and the white man's place in the system.

Once the slave economy was an established and going concern, the white children of the slave-owning families received, as an integral part of their social heritage, the sentiments and beliefs of their class in regard to their relation to and responsibility for the servile class. Slavery was a fact of their lives and was accepted as the child accepts other facts of his environment. The races were distinct in appearance; they differed in social position. One set of facts to the child was as natural as the other. He accepted the situation as he found it and learned to play the rôle appropriate to his station in life.

The accommodation of the whites was to the slave order as well as to the slaves as social inferiors. Certain types of work, including practically all involving physical exertion, fell to the lot of the Negroes, and whites could not engage in such work without loss of caste. The result of thus limiting the range of activity of the whites was to develop in them an habitual attitude of dependence upon their menials and a general helplessness in numerous simple situations.

A very large part of the white population, even in the slave-holding states, did not own Negroes and were technically outside of the system. They were, however, not independent of it; the system dominated the economic life and colored the entire social order. So far as the non-slave-holding individuals and families were dependent for livelihood upon their own exertions they were, more or less directly, in economic competition with the servile blacks, and the fact that they engaged in manual occupations put them, socially, in a class apart. They had little part in the political activities, were generally outside the influence of the schools, and had little part in the shaping of public policy. The slaves, reflecting and exaggerating the attitude of the master caste, looked upon the poor whites with contempt. In the situation the poor-white class developed the body of sentiments and attitudes necessary to a tolerable life. They hated the Negroes and stood in more or less fear and awe of the aristocracy. Though they were not a part of the slave economy, they were habituated to it. Their accommodation to the system, while in a different plane, was scarcely less complete than that of the Negroes and their masters.

The accommodation of the masters and slaves was reciprocal; each developed the traits of mind and manner for which the status called.

As a result of the relatively complete accommodation of the races, there was a virtual absence of racial strife. For the most part the relations of the races were friendly. Uprisings among the slaves were few in number and local in area. Such dissatisfaction as existed among the Negroes was in general the result of deviation from accepted standards, and was with individual men and masters rather than with the institution. Harsh discipline, overwork, poor food, and like forms of mistreatment gave rise to restless discontent on many plantations, and the presence of ill-adjusted individuals sometimes tended to disorganize an otherwise orderly group. As a whole the Negroes accepted their status and were in general contented and reasonably happy in their dependent position. The picture frequently drawn of the Negroes as unhappy and brooding persons held in servitude by the superior force of the whites and ready to rebel and throw off the yoke of oppression when opportunity came is of course completely out of focus. It misstates the historic situation and reflects a total lack of comprehension of the forces operating in social situations. Between the slaves and their masters there was in general a high degree of personal and social understanding and a good deal of intimacy in terms of the accepted status. There was a consciousness on both sides of the social distance that separated them. Each knew his place in the social order and the maintenance of the social distinctions enabled them to maintain friendly personal relations.

RACIAL FRICTION

But the accommodation of the races was by no means complete. The Negroes were not all and always willing and loyal slaves. The whites were not always confident and kindly masters. The slaves were frequently sullen and rebellious; they were guilty of numerous crimes; they plotted and attempted many insurrections; and they often took advantage of any circumstance that seemed to offer a chance to escape. The masters were often ruthless in the exploitation of the slaves and barbarous in their methods of control. The entire white population lived in continuous fear of slave uprisings. To insure public safety, elaborate and severe slave codes were enacted and enforced; any threatened uprising was an occasion for savage mob reprisals.

The fact that on occasions the slaves were ill-treated by the masters is abundantly evident in the various legislative acts designed to restrain the masters. The laws of Georgia, enacted in 1833, forbade, among other things, the unnecessary and excessive whipping of the slaves, starvation as a mode of punishment, and the failure to furnish sufficient clothing to protect the health of the slave. The laws of South Carolina, among other things, forbade the master to cut out the tongue, put out the eye, castrate, scald, or cut off a limb of the slave. They also restricted the amount of work of the slave to fifteen hours per day during the summer months and to fourteen hours per day during the winter season. The early laws of Virginia held masters blameless for whipping to death a resisting slave. But the presumption that the masters would not wantonly destroy their own property was not valid and each of the states enacted laws providing punishment by fine or imprisonment for masters who willfully or maliciously killed slaves. But exception was usually made in case a slave resisted the master or, in Tennessee, in case he died under "moderate corrections." The existence of regulations designed to curb the barbarities of certain masters is conclusive evidence that the barbarities were committed. But this is not the only evidence. The facts to show that slavery was a cruel and bloody business and that the masters were often guilty of monstrous conduct are excessively abundant.

The special laws relating to slave behavior were numerous and detailed, and often they provided excessively severe penalties. Slaves were generally forbidden to resist a white person in any way; they were commonly forbidden to assemble in the absence of a white person; they were forbidden to possess or carry weapons; and in innumerable other ways, which often had no reference to public security, their behavior was defined in law. In the Virginia law there were 68 slave offenses which carried the death penalty.

In spite of the minute regulations and the severe penalties, or perhaps because of them, slave crimes were numerous. For the most part slave offenses and their punishment did not get into the courts, hence are not a matter of public record. But the court decisions show hundreds of convictions for murder, burglary, arson, assault, rape, and other offenses. The punishment administered was often a barbarous form of torture. The record contains cases of cropping, castration and other forms of mutilation as well as hanging and burning at the stake.

The lack of accommodation and of friendly relations between the Negroes and whites also appears in the various insurrections that marked the period of slavery. In all there were over two score of slave insurrections or plots for uprisings of sufficient importance to excite widespread terror among the whites. The first major insurrection was that in New York in 1712. After its suppression 18 Negroes were put to death and many others committed suicide to escape the torture. An insurrection in South Carolina in 1739 resulted in the death of 21 white persons and in the execution of 44 Negroes. As a result of the Gabriel conspiracy in Richmond in 1800, at least 36 Negroes were executed and lesser punishments visited upon many others. The Vesey conspiracy in Charleston in 1822 resulted in 35 executions. The Nat Turner Rebellion in 1831 resulted in the massacre of some 55 white persons and the shooting and hanging of over 100 Negroes. As a result of the uprising in New York in 1841, 13 Negroes were burned, 18 hanged, and others transported. The frequency of plots and attempted uprisings as well as the ruthless and often hysterical severity with which they were suppressed show the discontent of the Negroes and the obsessive fear of the whites.

The dissatisfaction with the slave status is also indicated by the frequency with which the Negroes attempted to escape. In the early periods runaway slaves often escaped to surrounding Indian tribes and in many cases were protected and adopted into tribal membership. In later periods fugitive slaves, particularly from the border states, frequently reached Canada or free states where they were safe from pursuit. Some organization to assist fugitive slaves existed from an early date and by the time of the War of 1812 many escaped slaves were helped on their way to Canada. In the latter days of the slave régime the highly organized and widespread "underground railroad" facilitated the escape of the runaway slaves. From 1830 to 1860 probably 50,000 escaped from bondage chiefly through Ohio and Philadelphia. A few escaped into Mexico from Texas and the Southwest.

THE FREE NEGROES

The free Negroes occupied an uncertain and shifting status throughout the slave period. They were in general a poorly adjusted group. The anomalous social position of the free Negroes, their economic insecurity, restrictions on their freedom, and the frequent shifts in their legal status prevented any high degree of accommodation.

The free Negro group, which numbered nearly one-half million at the time of the slave emancipation, was of diverse origin and growth. Some of the early Negroes were freed after a period of servitude in accordance with the prevailing rule in regard to white indentured servants. A few Negroes were free from the time of their importation, owing to violation of non-importation laws or other circumstances. The number was recruited by the mixed-blood children of free white women. In a good many cases slaves were given their freedom, with or without the consent of the individual master, as a reward for distinguished or meritorious service to the state. More frequently slaves were freed by individual masters because of special or faithful service. Many masters freed their slaves by will because of a personal interest in their welfare and the fear that they would fall into the hands of unkind masters. Many individual slaves were freed because of affectional ties. This was particularly true of the part-white children of the master or other members of the master's family. The high percentage of mulattoes in the free Negro population is in some considerable measure accounted for by the owners freeing their own descendants and relatives. In some cases, slaves were purchased by the Quakers and others opposed to slavery in order to give them freedom. Other slaves, particularly skilled workmen, were able to purchase their own freedom with money earned by over-time work.

But the freeing of slaves was soon discouraged and presently vigorously opposed. This seems to have come about in the beginning because of the practice of individual masters, before the slave status was fully defined in law and custom, of freeing slaves when they became too old or crippled to be useful as laborers and leaving them to be supported at public expense. Virginia as early as 1691 denied the individual master the power to manumit slaves unless they were taken out of the colony. North Carolina in 1715 forbade the masters to liberate slaves except for meritorious conduct, and a few years later amended the act by requiring the meritorious conduct to be judged and certified by the court. Maryland allowed manumission only in case the slave was sound in mind and body, capable of work, and not over 50 years of age. Further restrictions were put upon the freeing of slaves as the fear of insurrection grew and as the anti-slavery agitation increased the pro-slavery sentiment in the South.

The first free Negroes enjoyed the same rights and privileges as other free persons in the society. But very soon they were made the object of special legislation and the restrictions on their movements and opportunities increased throughout the slave period. In 1691 Virginia forbade their intermarriage with whites and in due time similar legislation became the rule. In Maryland the free mulatto women were forbidden to marry Negroes or other slaves. The freedom of movement permitted the free Negroes in Colonial times was more and more restricted. In 1793, Virginia forbade the free Negroes to enter the state for permanent residence. In general in the South the free Negro was not allowed to go from place to place in search of work without a permit and proof of his freedom.

In the North, the free Negroes met severe economic competition. Jobs were scarce and the Negroes had little opportunity for skilled work. The bitter prejudice against them led to frequent race riots as in Cincinnati (1827, 1836, and 1841), Philadelphia (1834, 1838, and 1843), and elsewhere. The trades and professions were closed to them because they could not be apprenticed and could not be admitted to the professional schools. They were nominally free but they were not allowed to vote, they were excluded from the public schools, they were excused from military duty, they were excluded from jury service, they were barred from hotels and amusement places, they were segregated in the churches and on trains and other conveyances. For the most part they were restricted to domestic labor and menial jobs. They were taxed as other citizens.

In the South, the economic status of the free Negroes was in some respects at least better than in the North. They were allowed to engage in most occupations but the opportunities were greatly restricted in the later years. The stigma attaching to labor performed by slaves protected the slave and free Negro from the competition of white laborers in the so-called Negro jobs. But many of the free Negroes were without trades and, with the growth of repressive legislation, they were often denied the right to work at the trades. But the major restrictions were social. Every

Negro was presumed to be a slave unless he could prove his freedom. Unless he was in possession of a periodically renewable certificate with adequate description and attested by white persons he was subject to immediate arrest and sale at public auction. He was not allowed to vote and was exempt from jury service. If a white man was party to the suit, the Negro could not appear as a witness. He was restricted as to where he could sell goods. He could not sell liquor, maintain a house of entertainment, or be a type setter. For printing or circulating literature held to be liable to incite discontent, he was liable to a death penalty. He was commonly denied the right of jury trial except for capital offenses. In many of the states, especially after the Southampton insurrection in 1831, free Negroes were denied the right of public assembly.

On the whole the free Negroes were an unfortunate and unhappy class. They had no status with the whites. Their chief association was with the slaves who sometimes envied and sometimes openly despised them. They were always under suspicion by the whites who suspected them of fomenting unrest among the slaves. They were generally in poverty and were commonly accused of indolence and thievery. The degraded condition was generally taken as proof of racial inferiority. So miserable was the condition of the free Negroes that slaves in some cases refused proffered freedom: they chose slavery in the master's household to the uncertain life of the free Negroes.

There were, however, a few successful and outstanding free Negroes. Some of them accumulated a little property and a relatively secure position in the community life. In a few cases, free Negroes were themselves slave-holding planters. Perhaps as many as five or six thousand free Negroes held other Negroes in bondage, but in most cases these slave-owning Negroes held title to the ownership of their wives and children. The average number of slaves owned by free Negroes was about three. In a few cases the free Negroes succeeded in establishing exclusive mulatto societies whose members held themselves aloof from the slave and free Negroes of lowly status. There was a similar separation in sympathy between the free Negroes in the North and the fugitive slaves from the South.

In the circumstances, the free Negroes were perhaps less accommodated than any other major group in the population. They were, on the whole, a despised, abused, and poverty-stricken group excluded from most of the opportunities that freedom and citizenship seemed to imply or guarantee.

Bontemps, Arna, *Black Thunder*.
Bruce, P. A., *The Plantation Negro as Freeman*, "Master and Servant," pp. 29–43.
Dollard, John, *Caste and Class in a Southern Town*, "Accommodation Attitudes of Negroes," pp. 250–266.
Doyle, B. W., *The Etiquette of Race Relations in the South*.
Haardt, Sara, "The Etiquette of Slavery," *American Mercury*, 17(1929), 34–42.
Kirkland, W., "Slavery in the South Today," *Century*, 118(1929), 358–366.
Page, T. N., *Social Life in Old Virginia Before the War*.
Phillips, U. B., *American Negro Slavery*, "Plantation Life," pp. 309–330.
Warner, W. L., "American Caste and Class," *American Journal of Sociology*, 42(1936), 234–237.
Weatherford, W. D., and Johnson, C. S., *Race Relations*, "The Free Negro," pp. 238–258.
Wilson, C. D., "Black Masters: A Sidelight on Slavery," *North American Review*, 181(1905), 685–698.

FURTHER READINGS

Aptheker, Herbert, *American Negro Slave Revolts*. New York: Columbia University Press, 1943.
Buckmaster, Henrietta, *Let My People Go*. New York: Harper, 1941.
Fishel, Leslie H., and Quarles, Benjamin, eds., *The Negro American: A Documentary History*. Glenview, Ill.: Scott, Foresman, 1967.
Fitchett, E. Horace, "The Traditions of the Free Negro in Charleston, South Carolina," *Journal of Negro History*, XXV(April 1940), 139–152.
Franklin, John Hope, *From Slavery to Freedom: A History of American Negroes*. New York: Alfred A. Knopf, 1956.
———, "The Enslavement of Free Negroes in North Carolina," *Journal of Negro History*, XXIX (October 1914), 401–23.
———, *The Free Negro in North Carolina, 1790–1860*. Chapel Hill, N.C.: University of North Carolina Press, 1943.
Frazier, E. Franklin, *The Free Negro Family*. Nashville, Tenn.: Fisk University Press, 1932.
———, *The Negro in the United States*, rev. ed. New York: Macmillan, 1957.
Meltzer, Milton, ed., *In Their Own Words: A History of the Americn Negro, 1619–1865*. New York: Thomas Y. Crowell Company, 1964.
Myrdal, Gunnar, *An American Dilemma*. New York: Harper, 1944.
Tannenbaum, Frank, *Slave and Citizen: The Negro in the Americas*. New York: Alfred A. Knopf, 1947.

VII

THE ASSIMILATION
OF THE NEGROES*

In one usage, assimilation implies the process of incorporating culturally divergent individuals and groups into the political life and culture. Commonly in the contact of strange groups there is a mutual exchange of culture elements, first material and later more vital traits, and a consequent alteration of each pre-existing heritage. But in the Negro-white contacts in America, acculturation was a one-way process; there was practically no cultural borrowing from the Negroes. Nevertheless, the introduction of the Negroes had a profound influence on the American culture and way of life. Slave labor made possible the establishment of the plantation economy of the South and thereby determined the nature of the economic, political, and social order. But in any real and fundamental sense America has failed to assimilate the Negroes; they still constitute a group more or less apart and, by law and custom, they are denied many of the rights of citizenship and otherwise excluded from full participation in the culture. They are within the political order but they are not fully a part of it; they are culturally excluded and are in the way of becoming a permanent proletarian caste.

In another usage, assimiliation implies the gradual change in sentiments and attitudes that result from residence and participation in a foreign culture. The transplanted individuals gradually lose the body of memories, traditions, and personal attachments that defined their membership in the home group, and acquire the standards, beliefs, ideals, and appreciations that identify them with the new culture. The gradual and largely unconsious shift in traditions and loyalties is the essence of personal assimilation. It is a slow process of personal transformation that ultimately effects the incorporation of the individual into the group, assures his allegiance to the

* Except for minor deletions, this chapter is the same as in the second edition.

114

political order, and enables him to share the social experience by participating in the culture life.

The immediate interest is in the cultural and personality changes in the Negroes resulting from their forced introduction into the American economy. For purposes of discussion, the personal assimilation may be kept apart from the coincident and related changes effected in the biological character of the Negroes and from the habitudinal adjustments made to their social status. The latter was considered in the chapter immediately preceding; the former is discussed in the chapter immediately following.

THE AFRICAN BACKGROUND

Very little may be known concerning the African background of the American Negroes. For the most part they were shipped from the Guinea region of the West Coast but the slave trails extended far into the interior and, at the height of the trade, slaves seem to have been drawn from practically all parts of the continent. There was in consequence a great variety of physical types.

The African tribes differed as widely in culture and degree of civilization as in racial characters; some had developed civilizations of relatively high order and reasonably adapted to the climatic conditions, others were very primitive in their adjustments and manner of life. But in all cases they were backward when judged by European standards. Their control of the natural environment was at best partial and ineffective. Their industries and commerce were primitive. Their family institutions were in general not in accord with the European model. Their religious beliefs and practices were non-Christian, their political organizations poorly developed and militaristically impotent. In the situation all tribal differences were ignored; not only that, the whole culture heritage was destroyed. So far as the American Negroes are concerned, they have no African culture heritage, and scarcely a fragment of that heritage has found lodgment in the American culture.

THE EASE OF ASSIMILATION

The assimilation of the Negroes by the European culture went on with remarkable ease and unusual rapidity. The individual Negroes were highly plastic and the external conditions were highly favorable. The process was to be sure extended over a long period and there were at all times many unassimilated Negroes in the slave population. But this was due to historic circumstances rather than to any retardation of the sociological process: the traffic in slaves continued for a long period after the earlier importations and their descendants had lost all trace of the African heritage and become culturally indistinguishable from white Americans of similar status.

Even in their native environment, the Negroes were without a sense of nationality or of racial unity; they had no sentimental complex inhibiting their ready acceptance of alien culture facts. Moreover, the native African civilization in the regions over which the slave traders operated was thoroughly disorganized. The captives brought to America were separated from all the objective elements of their culture.

Incidentally or intentionally the slave trade separated tribal members and the Negroes came into the American situation as individuals. The slave régime completed the destruction of the tribal organization and social heritage of the captive people. As a consequence of the dispersion there was little opportunity to associate with fellow-tribesmen; their more frequent contacts were with slaves of a different tribal origin, so of different language and social heritage. All the material facts of their tribal culture disappeared at once and completely; there was no opportunity to practice or perpetuate a native culture. There was no opportunity to reproduce the values in the new world and no possibility of retaining or transmitting the non-material values. Their time was occupied in tasks set by their masters and the daily routine of their lives pretty effectively prevented attention being given to ancestral beliefs and practices. They were a broken people, realigned as individuals in a strange environment and subjected to a manner of living for which they had little inclination, without opportunity to practice their rites or transmit their culture tradition. They were completely stripped of their native social heritage and as completely as it is possible for any people to be at the mercy of a foreign culture.

Factors Favoring Rapid Assimilation

The sentimental and other facts that characteristically retard assimilation were absent, and there were present some positive facts of a general nature that stimulated the process.

The contact of strange peoples seems always to result in some degree in a modification of the culture complex of each. The groups may profit differently and perhaps never equally but the contacts are for each group culturally significant. The complex of values characteristic of each people is enriched or contaminated by the appropriation and incorporation of new values, or is changed by the addition of new elements or by the substitution of new values for the old. In any case the incorporation of new values may have far-reaching results and determine changes in the fundamental social organization through bringing changes in the basic conditions of life.

When the groups in contact are unequally advanced in culture the associated life influences their development in very unequal degrees. The advanced group has more to contribute; the backward group has more to learn. In each case the culture complex of one group may remain essentially unchanged and become the standard to which the other group tends to approximate. The sheer fact of number is an important element in the process of acculturation; the more numerous group, other facts equal, changes more slowly its traditional values and this is particularly so if it represents an old and relatively stable social order. There is also the factor of nativity and environmental adjustment. Every group of long residence in an environment has developed a set of values which adjusts its members with nicety to the prevailing conditions of life and offers greater resistance to social change than does a group recently migrant and still in a relatively early stage of folk adaptation.

In the American situation the Negroes were in the midst of an obviously superior type of culture. They were an unorganized minority in a strange environment. Even without the compulsion of their social situation and status, they would inevitably have taken over with great rapidity the material and technological facts of the white civilization.

The rapidity of personal assimilation turns in the main upon the number and intimacy of contacts between the individuals bearing the contrasted cultures. If the contacts be casual, formal, and intermittent the borrowing may be slight and usually is limited to such objective and superficial elements of the foreign culture as are obviously of superior utilitarian value. The weapons, work tools, hunting implements, personal ornaments, stimulants, and the like are readily appropriated and may pass into common use unless superstitious beliefs, magical practices, or other facts of the culture complex inhibit their spread. In the casual contacts of backward peoples with those of superior culture many material objects, conceived to have utility for ceremonial or magical purposes, may be taken over and converted to a new or grotesque use. But the cultural consequences of impersonal and superficial contacts are generally not far-reaching. Unless the secondary effect of the borrowed culture is the establishment of a new relationship between the people and the environment upon which they are dependent they bring no change in the fundamental social organization. The culture may be enriched or changed by the additions and substitutions but its basic character remains intact.

The slave status of the Negroes was thus an important, perhaps the most important, fact favoring their assimilation. The rapidity of the process is conditioned by the opportunity for association, and there is no form of social organization so well adapted to multiply the primary contacts of culturally divergent peoples as the patriarchal slave order. The Negroes, aside from those on the larger plantations and in the West Indies and in the Lower South, were in daily contact with the members of the master's family and with individuals of their own race who were already assimilated or partly assimilated to the white culture. So far as they were members of households owning a single slave or a few slave families—and such was the usual case—they worked side by side with their masters and mistresses. In the relationship of slave and master, the disorganized and helpless Negroes found a new security; the friendly and intimate relations which generally prevailed between the races, once they became mutually accommodated, opened the avenues along which the acquisition of the white culture facts came easily and inevitably.

There was at most times and places some active interest on the part of the whites in the assimilation of the Negroes, and some efforts, mostly of an informal sort, were made to bring them at least in part into the culture of the white group. Those whose lot fell with families of the more decent type received some instruction in the social and moral customs of civilized people and some control was exercised over their behavior. Some little effort was made at various times to instruct individual Negroes who showed ability or for other reasons attracted the attention and aroused the interest of sympathetic persons. The masters were interested in their learning English inasmuch as this increased their efficiency as workers, and the acquisition of the language was indispensable for any degree of participation in the community life. The clergy were interested in proselyting and the effect of the ministerial activities was to increase and vary the type of contacts.

THE DISAPPEARANCE OF THE AFRICAN HERITAGE

The native languages were essentially useless to the transported captives. They could not be used as a means of communication with the whites and, because of the separation of tribal groups and the distribution of the slaves, individuals rarely came into contact in America with others who spoke the same dialect. In the situation the native tongues were soon forgotten and the slaves learned to understand and speak the language of their conquerors. The language substitution was so complete and one-sided that practically no words of African origin found their way into English. The acquisition of the language was rapid in the case of the fortunate individuals who lived in small households and were in consequence in close and intimate association with white persons. The Negro children born in America to these fortunate slaves learned English as their native tongue and knew no more of the African dialect than did the American white children. On the plantations, and elsewhere that the slaves were used in numbers, the contacts with the whites were infrequent and impersonal and the Negroes acquired the English language more slowly and in a highly corrupted form.

The family institution was disorganized by the slave traffic and the family life of the Negroes completely destroyed by their capture and dispersion. With the destruction of the institutional control, the sex life was in large measure dictated by sexual needs as such; the sex demoralization was nearly complete. In the situation the only restraints were the ones imposed by the servile status; the only standards were those that the master class saw fit to enforce. Slowly the Negroes came to an understanding and acceptance of the monogamic family ideal. But the actual sex and family life of the slave population remained disordered. A marriage ceremonial was never necessary to the formation of a slave family. The unions formed could be discontinued at the will of the master. Slave parents had little control over or responsibility for their children and such as existed rested with the mother. No importance was attached to the promiscuous sex behavior of the slaves. Indeed, promiscuity was often encouraged as a means of increasing the slave population. Except in the personally favored class of slaves, the European sex and family mores were very slow of general adoption.

The religious and magical practices of the Africans were in large measure lost as a consequence of their dispersion. The sporadic appearances of tribal religious rites were generally suppressed. In the absence of observance the practices were forgotten and the beliefs lost. On the positive side they easily took on the white beliefs and practices. Fears aroused in the new form of life which they could in no way control made them ideal material for religious efforts. They readily accepted Christianity and found in it a philosophy admirably suited to their status.

In like manner the majority of their folk customs and practices were lost. In the absence of opportunity to associate with other persons of similar heritage the customs inevitably fell into disuse and were presently forgotten and lost. Little of either good or bad remained. Their moral ideas and tribal customs could not stand the shock of the slave traffic. Their systems of control and education were useless. Their political ideas, never more than a somewhat vague sense of loyalty to the chief, were soon gone. The whole culture complex collapsed and was not and could not be transmitted to their children. In place of the destroyed values they quickly came into possession of the objective culture values of their conquerors. They learned the agricultural and household activities of the whites through systematic training; they acquired through imitation the superficial vices and mannerisms of their white associates.

As time went on the contact of the members of the two races came to involve a high degree of intimacy and mutual dependence, and the cultural modification of many members of the servile group proceeded beyond the simple appropriation of objective values: they came to a more or less adequate appreciation of the values. The native-born Negroes shared in the common body of historic experience and had the same group of memories as did the native-born whites. The ethnic mixture of stocks, which is never absent when two culturally unequal groups occupy the same geographic region, increased the social contacts and promoted assimilation.

In the Negro children of American birth and ancestry little or nothing distinctly African remained; they had no knowledge of the country nor of African ways and culture. They spoke the same language as their masters and shared the same traditions. They had the same political conceptions, held the same social beliefs, and had institutional and cultural loyalties identical with those that prevailed in their familiar environment. They differed from the pattern type more in degree of conformity than in the kind of culture facts. The fusion of culture heritages and the formation of a community of interests, sentiments, and historic memories through participation in a common life proceeded rapidly.

The Incompleteness of Assimilation

In spite of individual exceptions, the Negroes had very incompletely assimilated the European culture heritages at the time of their emancipation. They were not fully in the white man's civilization. The complete destruction of their tribal heritage, as well as their servile status in the new world, was conducive to the adoption of foreign values, but their participation in the culture life was obstructed and partial. The foreign values they had adopted were often imperfectly understood: the externals of the new culture were acquired, often with ease and rapidity, but often with a very vague notion of the content and of the adopted forms. They took on the forms of Christian worship, for example, long before they came to any real appreciation or adequate conception of Christianity: the content, when the adopted forms had any real content, came from another source. The absence of any real comprehension on the part of even the more fortunately situated Negroes is seen in their educational and political activity following the Emancipation. They responded to classical and literary subjects but remained cold to technical and vocational training; they had the educational form without the content; they placed it strictly in the realm of magic. The same magical conception is manifest in the unlimited confidence they had in the franchise as the means to their social and economic salvation.

There were, of course, wide differences between individuals and groups, due to unequal periods of residence in America and to the unequal operation of the isolating factors. The first slaves were brought into the Colonies in the seventeenth century. At the time of the Emancipation there were Negroes in the population with five, six, or more generations of American-born ancestors. These persons were completely Americanized in the sense that they knew no more of Africa than did the white Americans; they differed from other native-born persons in their degree of civilization, perhaps, but such culture values as they had were American. But there were other slaves brought to America as late as the Civil War. At the Emancipation there were a good many African-born persons in the slave population and a much larger number whose parents, one or both, were of African birth. In most cases these late comers had had neither time nor opportunity to acquire the social heritage of their masters.

There were similar differences due to unequal opportunities for social contact. On the larger plantations the slaves came very little into contact with individuals of the white race; the gang laborers in the towns were sometimes almost equally isolated and retarded. In these circumstances the Negroes not infrequently underwent a cultural deterioration; there was nothing to replace the loss of their tribal heritage. An acquaintance with even the external facts of European life came to them slowly, indirectly, and imperfectly.

The complete assimilation of individuals and groups to a foreign culture comes only with their full participation in the common life. The participation of the Negroes in the group life was always limited and their assimilation of the culture values correspondingly retarded and imperfect. Even today there are many Negroes who are not in the European culture.

THE MODIFICATION OF EUROPEAN CULTURE VALUES

As previously indicated, the process of assimilating the Negroes to the white civilization was not without a profound influence on the culture.

It is possible to dismiss at once the position sometimes taken that the Negroes made an important cultural contribution: there are no elements of American culture that are African in origin. For better or worse, the slave traffic stripped the Negroes of their culture values and introduced them as work animals into the American environment. It does not follow from this, however, that they have made no contribution to the culture nor that the civilization would be the same today if they had not come: they have influenced the course of American life directly by their individual contributions and indirectly by their presence.

Their chief positive contribution to American life was the manual labor necessary for the exploitation of certain natural resources and the rapid development of an agricultural industry in the part of the country least suited climatically to white labor. But this unquestioned labor contribution was made at the expense of a modified economic order. The existence of slave labor made the growth of an efficient and self-respecting free labor group impossible. The presence of a servile group determined the form and development of political institutions—made impossible the free growth of a democratic political order. The presence of the Negroes perverted the democratic social institutions and led to the caste form of social organization.

Frazier, E. F., "Traditions and Patterns of Negro Family Life in the United States," in E. B. Reuter, ed., *Race and Culture Contacts*, pp. 191–207.

Guerard, A., "Southern Memories," *Scribner's Magazine*, 77(1925), 492–498.

Herskovits, M. J., "Acculturation and the American Negro," *The Southwestern Political and Social Science Quarterly*, 9(1927), 211–224.

Krapp, G. P., "The English of the Negro," *The American Mercury*, 2(1924), 190–195.

Mecklin, J. M., *Democracy and Race Friction*, "The Negro and His Social Heritage," pp. 77–122.

Page, T. N., "The Old Time Negro," *Scribner's Magazine*, 36(1904), 522–532.

Park, R. E., "Racial Assimilation in Secondary Groups," *American Journal of Sociology*, 19(1914), 606–623; also *Publications, American Sociological Society*, 8(1914), 66–83.

Pennington, P., *A Woman Rice Planter*.

Phillips, U. B., *American Negro Slavery*.

Settle, Ophelia, "Social Attitudes During the Slave Régime: Household Servants versus Field Hands," *Publications, American Sociological Society*, 28 (1934), 95–96.

Thomas, W. I., "Race Psychology," *American Journal of Sociology*, 17(1912), 725–775.

Woofter, T. J., *Races and Ethnic Groups in American Life*, "Assimilation," pp. 228–230.

FURTHER READINGS

Brink, William, and Harris, Louis, *The Negro Revolution in America*. New York: Simon & Schuster, 1964.

Broom, Leonard, and Glenn, Norval D., *Transformation of the Negro American*. New York: Harper & Row, 1965.

Fishel, Leslie H., Jr., and Quarles, Benjamin, eds., *The Negro American: A Documentary History*. Glenview, Ill.: Scott, Foresman, 1967.

Franklin, John Hope, *From Slavery to Freedom*. New York: Alfred A. Knopf, 1956.

Frazier, E. Franklin, *The Negro Church in America*. New York: Schocken Books, 1963.

———, *The Negro Family in the United States*. Chicago: University of Chicago Press, 1939.

Gordon, Milton M., *Assimilation in American Life*. New York: Oxford University Press, 1964.

Gomillion, Charles G., "The Influence of the Negro on the Culture of the South," *Social Forces*, XX(March 1942), 386–390.

Herskovits, M. J., *The Myth of the Negro Past*. Boston: Beacon Press, 1958.

Johnson, James Weldon, "Contributions of the Negro," *Southern Workman*, LXVII(February 1938), 57–60.

Mays, Benjamin E., and Nicholson, Joseph William, *The Negro's Church*. New York: Institute of Social and Religious Research, 1933.

Meltzer, Milton, ed., *In Their Own Words: A History of the American Negro*, 3 vols. New York: Thomas Y. Crowell Company, 1964.

Myrdal, Gunnar, *An American Dilemma*, Part I. New York: Harper, 1944.

Pettigrew, Thomas F., *A Profile of the Negro American*. Princeton, N.J.: Van Nostrand, 1964.

Prothro, E. Terry, "Ethnocentrism and Anti-Negro Attitudes in the Deep South," *Journal of Abnormal and Social Psychology*, 47(1952), 105–108.

Silberman, Charles E., *Crisis in Black and White*. New York: Random House, 1964.

Thompson, Daniel C., "The Rise of the Negro Protest," *The Annals of the American Academy of Political and Social Science*, 357(1965), 18–29.

VIII

THE MISCEGENATION
OF THE RACES*

The assimilation of the Negroes described in the preceding chapter—the gradual change in sentiments and attitudes, in memories and loyalties and social traditions, in manners and customs and habits of thought, the sloughing off of African and the acquisition of American social heritages—was accompanied by an amalgamation of racial groups, and an infusion of foreign blood that began a biological transformation of the race. The amalgamation assisted in the process of assimilation by the creation of an intermediate type that tended to bridge the cultural gap between the racial extremes, and the assimilation of the group, in turn, made more easy and natural the biological process of racial fusion.

But the contamination of the Negro groups by intermixture with other races began long before their introduction into the American social situation. The Negroes brought to America were in the main of West African descent. For the most part they were bought or captured along the West Coast, and the Guinea Negroes were by far the more numerous, constituting well over fifty per cent of the total importations. But the slaves secured along the Guinea Coast were by no means all of local origin. There were representatives of many different tribal stocks from many parts of the continent. The slave trails extended far into the interior of the continent and the slave coffles came by river and forest path sometimes for a thousand and more miles to the markets on the coast.

Moreover, the various Negro stocks were frequently very much mixed with each other. Many of the tribes were large slave holders and much contaminated by intermarriage with their captives. The domestic trade in slaves was generally active and resulted directly in a wide distribution of captive groups. There was also a very considerable scattering and inter-

* This chapter is the same as in the second edition.

mixture of stocks as a result of the tribal wars incident to the traffic in slaves.

Not only were the Negroes of different tribal stocks; they were also in many cases modified by previous contacts with other races. The Arabs came early into contact with various of the Negro peoples and intermixed rather readily with them. From the seventh and eighth centuries the Mohammedan trade in slaves and other African commodities led to the introduction of Berber blood into many tribal groups as well as to the introduction of some Negro blood into various populations about the Mediterranean. Of the Negroes brought as slaves to America, it has been estimated that possibly one-half showed some trace of previous contact and intermixture with the white race. The Senegalese, who were commonly considered the most intelligent of the slaves and were especially in demand, had a strong Arabic strain in their ancestry. Probably one per cent of the Negroes imported were able to speak some Arabic dialect.

THE NEGROES AND THE AMERICAN INDIANS

In America the Negroes have intermarried rather freely with the Indians wherever the races have come into contact. The two races have had some common basis for sympathetic association, the barriers to social equality between them have not been formidable, and there have been no legislative acts forbidding the intermixture.

Slavery of the native Indians existed in a number of the English colonies before the coming of the Negroes. The Indians captured in battle were in some cases sold into slavery in distant colonies. Others were kidnapped along the coast and sold as slaves in the more settled regions. The mention of Indian slaves and of slaves of Negro and Indian blood is frequent in the racial literature of the early slave period. With these enslaved Indians the Negro slaves came into close and intimate contact. The social status was the same and as slaves they met on terms of equality. Intermarriage followed and, as the body of Negro slaves increased and Indian slavery declined, the Indian slaves were gradually absorbed into the larger black population. The offspring of Indian slaves or of mixed Negro and Indian parentage came presently to be counted with the Negroes. Many of the broken tribes of coast Indians disappeared entirely into the Negro people. The amount of Indian admixture may of course not be known but was certainly very considerable. There is a similar trace of Indian blood in many white families of certain regions.

There is also a pronounced Negro strain in a number of the Indian tribes. Runaway slaves frequently made their way by accident or otherwise to the Indian camps. In some cases the Indians returned these escaped slaves to their masters; sometimes they were killed or otherwise mistreated. But in other cases they were protected and kept as slaves of the Indians among whom they sought refuge or were taken into the Indian tribes by adoption. The five civilized tribes owned many Negro slaves whom they were required to free and admit to equal Indian citizenship at the close of the Civil War. The Seminoles in Florida had in 1834 some two hundred Negro slaves who had gone to them as runaways from the whites and had been in turn enslaved by the Indians who intermarried freely with them. Also, other Negroes who were not classed as slaves made their way into Indian groups and many of the reservations became the joint home of Indians and free Negroes. In some cases the Negroes were more numerous than the Indians and the reservations became Negro and mulatto settlements with little more than a tradition of Indian ancestry. The so-called Croatan Indians in North Carolina, the "Redbones" of South Carolina, the "Moors" of Delaware, the "Melungeons" of West Virginia, and other similar groups of the present day are wasted Indian tribes that have been swamped by intermixture with escaped slaves, free Negroes and mulattoes, and white outlaws and rovers.

Much of the Negro-Indian intermixture has chosen to be Indian rather than Negro and so appears in the statistics. Some of the Indian tribes today are more Negro than Indian in their ancestry and many of them contain a large admixture of Negro blood.

THE EARLY NEGRO-WHITE INTERMIXTURE

The miscegenation of the Negro and white people in America dates from the first appearance of the Negroes. America was a pioneer society and in most of the colonies the excess of men was very great. The paucity of white women was an important factor in overcoming any racial repugnance and in stimulating the sexual use of Negro women. As time went on and the assimilation of the Negroes increased, the tendency to race crossing increased. The tendency was further increased as the physical features of the race became somewhat modified and softened by intermixture: there was less hesitancy to sex association with the mulatto girls than with the extreme African type. Consequently the miscegenation in the English colonies increased with the growth of the mixed-blood group.

The social composition of the colonial population favored a rapid racial intermixture.

In the English colonies there was a considerable use of indentured servants as well as of Negro slaves. These white servants formed a fairly distinct class before the coming of the Negroes. The group was of complex composition, a good number of them were free, poor people who contracted to pay the cost of passage to America by a period of servile labor. In the group there was a considerable number of children and others who had been kidnapped in European cities and sold into servitude in the American colonies. The group also contained many prisoners of war, political and other criminals, and dissolute persons who had been transported to rid the home country of their presence. In the group were many highly respectable and worthy persons who were poor or fallen into misfortune as well as paupers, convicts, prostitutes, and other no-account or vicious persons. In some of the colonies, notably Virginia and Maryland, this white servile class was a large and frequently a troublesome element in the population.

It was with this class of persons that the Negroes most frequently came into close contact and intimate association. At first the Negroes were in the minority. In Virginia in 1650 there were only thirty Negroes; twenty-one years later the white servants still outnumbered the Negroes three to one, and two years later they were four times as numerous as the Negro slaves. In Maryland, Pennsylvania, and some of the other colonies the same type of white servants was a numerically important element of the populations. The social condition of the two servile elements of the population was much the same; the chief difference in status was that the white servants were bound for a term of years while the Negroes were enslaved for life. During most of the seventeenth century there were many bonds of sympathy between the two classes. The Negroes were sought as agreeable and amusing companions. Illicit relations were inevitable and a half-breed population appeared and increased. Some of these mulatto children were the offspring of white serving women and Negro men. There were a few marriages between Negro men and low-class white women of both the servant and the free class. But the much larger percentage of the intermixture was between white men and Negro women and took place outside the marriage relation. The same sympathetic relations existed between the free Negroes and mulattoes and the low-class whites as between the Negro slaves and white servants.

The miscegenation of these servile elements early came to be a matter of concern throughout the colonies. Thoughtful men saw the dangers of this in a frontier society and denounced such unions, but the miscegenation was already advanced before the whites realized the need of efforts to control it and maintain racial integrity. Numerous laws were enacted designed to stop racial fusion and to determine the status of mixed-blood offspring. Other laws were designed to restrain white women from marrying or cohabiting with Negroes and to fix the status of the children of such unions as had already been formed. The laws also frequently contained severe penalties designed to reduce the number of bastard children of free Negroes and mulattoes. Where law failed to prohibit mixed marriages, they were frequently prevented by public sentiment expressing itself through extra-legal measures; mobs frequently punished the individuals who formed the odious unions.

But neither the severity of law nor the intolerance of public sentiment seemed to have much effect on the miscegenation of the races: they prevented intermarriage rather than race mixture. The clandestine intermingling tended to increase and the illegitimate progeny of the white servants and Negro slaves became in many places a serious public burden.

The white servant class was not alone responsible for the early miscegenation of the races. There was at all times some intermixture resulting from the association of the slave owners and their female slaves. As a free Negro and mulatto class appeared, numerous white men supported colored mistresses and reared families of mulatto children. In the slave-owning households, the association of the white boys with the Negro and mulatto housemaids was an important item in the racial intermixture; many slave owners were the fathers or grandfathers of some of their slaves.

THE PERIOD OF NATIONAL SLAVERY

The early sympathy between the white servants and the Negro slaves and the fraternizing of the two classes gradually declined as the number of Negroes increased and the distinction between the servant and the slave status became more strictly defined. The various laws designed to restrict the amalgamation emphasized racial and social differences and thus served to arouse a pride of race within the low-class white groups. The actual difference in social and economic status made by the upper classes was exaggerated by the white indentured group and the two dependent classes drifted apart. The white servants and poor whites in many cases still labored beside the slaves but they more and more held themselves socially aloof from the Negroes.

By the time that slavery became well established as an economic institution the early sympathy between the servant whites and the Negroes had been replaced by a caste and racial prejudice. Jealousies that had no place in the mutual attitudes of the slaves and the master class developed between the Negroes and the socially inferior whites. Partly as a compensation for their own inferior status, the poor whites developed a contempt and a hatred for the Negro that was one of the characteristic features of the later slave régime. When this antipathetic attitude developed it formed a most effective barrier to social intercourse and so operated to restrict the intermixture of the races. There continued to be a good deal of clandestine association between the slave women and the rougher classes of the whites but the freedom that marked the early association of the two dependent groups in the population had little place.

Another important factor also tended to retard the intermixture of these classes. Slavery as a developed economic institution regulated rather strictly the behavior of the servile class and thus in a measure limited the opportunity for irregular sex relations between this class and the general white population. This was notably the case on the larger plantations where the number of whites was small and where, in order to avoid the demoralization of the working population, the contacts of the slaves with the non-plantation population were kept at a minimum. There was also an effort in the better type of slave-holding families to instruct the Negro and mulatto house servants in the sex code of the whites and to enforce its observance by close supervision.

But there were no formidable barriers to intercourse between the slaves and the upper-class whites. The opportunities for association were practically unlimited, there was no attitude of racial jealousy to interfere, and the caste distinction was so clear that the relations of the sexes raised no question of social equality. The association of the slave-holding class and the slave women is not properly to be considered as a forced relationship. There were no doubt cases of the involuntary use of the female slaves. But it was more usual for the relationship to be courted by the slave women and girls as a mark of distinction and this was especially true as social distinctions arose between the house servants and other occupational groups of the slave population. It is of course easily possible and very usual to exaggerate the part played by the slave-holding class in the production of the mixed-blood population. But the only effective check on the relationship was the force of public sentiment in the community and there is no reason to assume that it was not at all times a factor of importance in the intermixture of the races.

In some sections there grew up a sub-surface type of polygamy that approached an institutional form. Free Negro and mulatto girls became the mistresses of white men by whom they were supported and by whom they reared families of mixed-blood children. In some cases these colored mistresses and children were deserted, with or without provision for their support, when the man married a white woman; in other cases the extra-legal relation was continued and the colored family supported in addition to the lawful household and the legitimate children. This type of dual family arrangement was particularly open and highly developed in New Orleans, Mobile, and certain other points of the Lower South. The free mulatto girls, whose families were frequently persons of some wealth and culture, aspired to such unions and, so long as there was hope of contracting one, scorned to marry with Negro or mulatto men. The keeping of Negro—more usually mulatto—mistresses was not uncommon in most parts of the country throughout the later slave period. Such establishments were of course limited to those members of the white society who were economically able to assume their support.

The rapidity of the intermixture as well as the nature of the relationship was strikingly different in different communities. The chief controlling force being the public sentiment, mixed-blood children tended to be numerous in communities where there was an apparent indifference to the relationship and few in the communities where the relationship was socially disapproved and the white men keeping Negro mistresses met public criticism and social ostracism. In the latter cases the relationship was largely confined to the low-class persons and differed only slightly from commercial prostitution; in the presence of the more tolerant social attitude the relationship frequently involved many reputable persons in the community, was more largely based upon some sentimental attachment, and was frequently of enough permanence to take on many of the attributes of regular family life.

As previously stated, the chief factor controlling the amount of intermixture was the opportunity for the contact of the races. Where the Negroes were numerous and the whites few, as on many of the plantations in the South, and in the more rural regions generally, the relative amount of race crossing was small. The rural Negroes were in large part segregated and their few contacts with the whites restricted to the plantation overseers. Where the proportion of Negroes in the population was less the intermixture was generally greater because the opportunities for interracial contacts were more numerous. There was always relatively more intermixture in the towns and cities, where opportunity for clandestine relations were numerous and where the proportion of mulatto girls was greater than in the rural districts. The percentage of mulattoes and their rate of increase was also much higher in the northern and border states than in the South. The difference in the rate of intermixture between town and country and between South and North was perhaps less than the mulatto statistics indicate. There were some selective tendencies at work. The mulattoes were always considered to be more capable than the black Negroes and were in greater demand as house and personal servants. The percentage of house servants was greater in the cities than on the plantations. There was in consequence a tendency toward an urbanization of mulattoes which accounts in part for their relative increase in the towns and cities as compared with the rural districts. There was also some northward migration of mulattoes produced elsewhere. Slave owners frequently freed their mulatto progeny and relatives and sent them into free territory. There were also in these northern regions a large number of free Negroes and mulattoes whose behavior was not supervised as was that of the slaves. The intermarriage of these mulattoes and their intermarriage with the black Negroes tended to increase the number of mulattoes. It is also true that the domestic slave trade took south a larger number of black than of mixed-blood Negroes. Each of these things tended to increase the mulatto ratio of the North. While the selective factors account in some part for the relatively high percentage of mulattoes in the northern regions and in the urban districts, there is also no question that the intermixture was decidedly more rapid in these environments. In the northern tier of slave states the percentage of mulattoes and their increase was greater than in states farther south; the slaves had greater freedom, they constituted a smaller percentage of the population, and their opportunities for clandestine association with the whites were more numerous.

Intermixture Following the Emancipation

Following the Civil War and the freeing of the Negroes there was a very great increase in the amount of racial intermixture. Slavery had shielded many members of the race from contacts with white men and probably operated on the whole somewhat to retard amalgamation. But slavery very generally failed to teach a sex code that would be effective when the institutional restraints were removed, hence the crisis of emancipation resulted in a prolonged period of sex irregularity and racial intermixture. Out of this period of social disorganization and personal demoralization there gradually appeared a sex code consistent with the new social and economic status.

The Present Status of Racial Amalgamation

In treating the nature and rate of the present day racial amalgamation it is necessary in the first place to remember that the amount of intermixture does not appear in the statistics. The enumeration figures show, within a rather wide range of error, the absolute and relative increase of the mulatto population. But the hybrid population may now increase without further intermixture and would in fact continue to increase were the race to receive no additional admixture of white blood. Mulattoes very generally marry other persons of mixed blood and to the extent that births exceed deaths there is a natural increase of the hybrid population. But mulattoes also intermarry with little hesitation Negroes of full blood, and the offspring, unless the amount of white admixture is very small, are counted as mulattoes rather than as Negroes. The hybrid population is also increased by the offspring from both Negro and mulatto crosses with white persons. The increase of the full-blood Negroes may come only by marriages or extra-matrimonial relations between individuals both of whom are of unmixed Negro ancestry. Neither the increase of mulattoes nor their relative increase is a measure of the extent to which racial fusion goes on.

On the other hand, the intermixture of the races may go on without the fact being reflected in the enumeration figures. So far as the crossing is between white persons and Negroes of full blood the mulatto offspring appear in the statistics as additions to the hybrid group. But this is the only type of crossing that registers in the statistics. If the crossing is between white persons and mulattoes or between mulattoes and Negroes of full blood, the fact of intermixture does not appear. It is in the one case a further infusion of white blood into an already mixed population and in the other a diffusion of white blood that already contaminates the Negro stock. A very great deal of the amalgamation in process is due to relations between white persons and mulattoes and between mulattoes and individuals of unmixed Negro blood, but since the statistics measure the fact and do not measure the degree of hybridization both these types of racial fusion are omitted.

At the present time as in the past, intermarriage of the Negroes and whites is responsible for a negligible part of the racial amalgamation. In the early colonial days mixed marriages were occasionally contracted between Negroes and members of the indentured servant class. But such unions usually aroused a public indignation that expressed itself in severe prohibitionary laws. Where this was not the case, they were prohibited by the popular sentiment of the white community. After the status of the Negroes became fixed and generally understood racial intermarriages almost never occurred; there were none in the slave states and very few in other parts of the country. There was some increase during the sentimental period centering about the Civil War but the number was not great. In the period since the Emancipation, intermarriages have been rare. It is not possible to know the exact number but such figures as are obtainable show the number to be negligible—an average of perhaps less than one hundred per year. Such marriages are prohibited in all of the southern states and in many states of the North and West. Where there is no legal prohibition, they nevertheless take place rarely; white sentiment is everywhere opposed to such unions and a similar attitude has recently appeared in the Negro population.

The mixed marriages that are from time to time solemnized are most frequently of white women with Negro or mulatto men. The cases of white men marrying Negro women are rare. In almost every case the white persons contracting mixed marriages are of the lower economic strata of the population. In many cases they are recent immigrants who have not acquired the American prejudice against social intercourse with the Negro people. A high percentage of the Negroes who contract mixed marriages are mulattoes and other light-colored individuals.

Nearly all the intermixture of the races goes on at the present time outside the marriage relation. The extent of the racial sex association may not be asserted. As pointed out above, the statistics of the hybrid population furnish no check and, since any sex relation outside the conventional marriage bond violates the middle-class code, the diverse dogmatic opinions of casual observers reflect the conventional sex attitudes rather than the objective situation. There has been no objective study on which an estimate may be based.

There is at present, as earlier, a certain amount of concubinage of colored women with white men. The mutual attraction of individuals of different racial extraction occasionally leads to sex association of a more or less permanent nature. The law prevents the marriage of the persons, keeps the relationship outside the realm of formal approval, but is of course powerless to control the association itself. As a result there are numerous Negro and mulatto women supported by white men and engaged in bearing and rearing their children. In some localities such relations are tolerated by the community, if not sanctioned by the local standards, and mixed families are fairly common. In other places the public attitude is less tolerant and such relations far less frequent. They have frequently been the occasion or excuse for action by mobs and other self-appointed discipline committees.

The sex contact of the races is for the most part aside from intermarriage or even from the custom of kept women. It is at the present time a relationship very closely bordering upon prostitution, and bears little resemblance to the unlawful but more or less decent and orderly concubinage of Negro and mulatto girls. In many communities there is little or no check upon such association of the races. The sex code of a very considerable percentage of the Negro population is not strict. Illicit relations within the race are common, and between the races such association is pretty much at the will of the white man. This of course must not be interpreted as a general indictment of the chastity of Negro women. The standards of a large and increasing percentage of the race are no doubt as conventional as those of any group in the population.

The racial sex behavior also varies with differences in community sentiment. The opportunities for the association of Negro and white persons are more frequent in the cities and towns than in the open country and the relationship may be concealed with relative ease. But there is also a marked difference between different communities. In many bi-racial communities in the South there is very little racial intermixture in process; in other communities the amount is very great. Any general statement is subject to many exceptions.

It is probable that the present contact of the races has less influence than formerly in the production of mulatto children; Negroes as well as whites are learning how to avoid the consequences of indulgence. It is also true that much of the present association of the races is between the sporting elements and has little effect upon the birth rate. On the part of the better elements there is a strong and growing sentiment opposed to all associations leading to farther amalgamation.

PHYSICAL AND CULTURAL DIFFERENTIATION

The transplantation of the Negroes resulted in a rapid modification of the physical type and in a remarkable differentiation of physical types. But the cultural differences that developed among the slaves were even more marked than the physical differences that appeared. In general the Negroes were in a barbarian stage of culture but there were great differences between tribal stocks. Some were still in savagery, others, particularly certain tribes that had been influenced by the Arab and other foreign contacts, had shown some sporadic examples of culture progress. In consequence the African captives differed considerably in the material facts of their culture as well as in custom, language, and tradition. In the American situation the social heritage of the transplanted groups was quickly sloughed off. As previously pointed out, the rapidity with which they acquired control of the American body of culture facts was directly proportional to their opportunity for social contact. This was determined by a combination of chance factors.

It was not, however, until the close of the slave régime that the individuality of the Negroes could appear fully. The Emancipation gave the first opportunity for the generality of the race to test their abilities and display their talents. In freedom, the cultural differentiation observable in slavery continued at an accelerated rate. The period of freedom is still too brief for the group to have outlived the effects of the earlier status, but in the time that they have been at liberty to move about and make individual selection of occupation and type of life there has been a realignment of men on the basis of interest and ability and an increase in personal differences. Amalgamation has continued and the physical types range from the near-white to the unmixed black with every degree of mixture and every variety of modified Negro features. The bulk of the race have remained agricultural laborers but individuals have established themselves in practically every type of economic activity. Educational differentiation has been very great, and the group embraces every type of person from those as illiterate and backward as the slaves to those possessed of the training afforded by modern universities.

As a result of the various differentiating factors that have been in operation—differences in race and tribal origin, unequal intermixture of blood, differences in legal and social status, varying degrees of restriction upon mobility and choice of occupation, differences in type and degree of isolation, and other forces making for differences in men—the social and racial heterogeneity of the group has greatly increased during the period of American residence. Ethnic differences, relatively small among the captive Negroes, have increased through the continued infusion of white blood until the group now includes every type of racial mixture from the near-white to the full black. The extremes of physical and racial type are greater among the American Negroes than among any other similar population. The negligible cultural differences that characterized the captive slaves have gradually widened; some have advanced but slightly beyond the African culture level, others have reached in all essential respects the highest standards of European civilization. The relative uniformity in the race and culture that characterized the captive Negroes has given place to a diversity as great as that which characterizes any modern people.

Baker, R. S., *Following the Color Line*, "The Mulatto: the Problem of Race Mixture," pp. 151–174.

Census Bureau, *Negro Population in the United States*, 1790–1915, "Color—Black and Mulatto Elements," pp. 207–231.

Day, Caroline B., *Study of Some Negro-White Families in the United States*.

Dodge, E., "The Mulatto Problem," *Journal of Heredity*, 16(1925), 281–286.

Frazier, E. F., "Children in Black and Mulatto Families," *American Journal of Sociology*, 29(1933), 12–29.

Gordon, E., "Negro Society," *Scribner's Magazine*, 88(1930), 134–142.

Hankins, F. H., *The Racial Basis of Civilization*, "The Problem of Race Mixture," pp. 328–351.

Herskovits, M. J., *The American Negro: A Study in Race Crossing*.

Linton, R., "An Anthropological View of Race Mixture," *Publications, American Sociological Society*, 19(1925), 69–77.

Park, R. E., "Mentality of Racial Hybrids," *American Journal of Sociology*, 36(1931), 534–551.

Reuter, E. B., *Race Mixture*.

——, *The Mulatto in the United States*.

——, "The Mulatto," *Encyclopaedia Sexualis*.

Stephenson, G. T., *Race Distinctions in American Law*, "Intermarriage and Miscegenation," pp. 78–101.

Weatherly, U. G., "Race and Marriage," *American Journal of Sociology*, 15(1910), 433–453.

Wittenberg, Philip, "Miscegenation," *Encyclopaedia of the Social Sciences*.

Woodson, C. G., "The Beginnings of the Miscegenation of the Whites and Blacks," *Journal of Negro History*, 3(1918), 335–353.

Woofter, T. J., *Races and Ethnic Groups in American Life*, "Intermarriage," pp. 208–209.

FURTHER READINGS

Barron, Milton L., *People Who Intermarry*. New York: Syracuse University Press, 1948.

Bernard, Jessie, "Note on Educational Homogamy in Negro-White and White-Negro Marriages, 1960," *Journal of Marriage and the Family*, 28-(August 1966), 274–276.

Burma, John H., "Interethnic Marriage in Los Angeles, 1948–1959," *Social Forces*, 42(1963), 1956–1965.

Chang, C. K., and Yamamura, Douglas S., "Interracial Marriage and Divorce in Hawaii," *Social Forces* (October 1957), 77–84.

Golden, Joseph, "Characteristics of the Negro-White Intermarried in Philadelphia," *American Sociological Review*, 18(April 1953), 177–183.

————, "Patterns of Negro-White Intermarriage," *American Sociological Review*, 19(1954), 144–147.

Heer, David M., "Negro-White Marriage in the United States," *Journal of Marriage and the Family*, 28(August 1966), 262–273.

Pavela, Todd H., "An Exploratory Study of Negro-White Intermarriage in Indiana," *Journal of Marriage and the Family*, 26(May 1964), 211.

Simpson, George Eaton, and Yinger, J. Milton, *Racial and Cultural Minorities*, 3rd ed., Ch. 17. New York: Harper & Row, 1965.

Stonequist, Everett V., "Race Mixture and the Mulatto," in Thompson, Edgar T., ed., *Race Relations and the Race Problem*. Durham, N.C.: Duke University Press, 1939.

Wirth, Louis, and Goldhamer, Herbert, "The Hybrid and the Problem of Miscegenation," in Klineberg, Otto, ed., *Characteristics of the American Negro*. New York: Harper, 1944.

I X

RACIAL PREJUDICE AND
SOCIAL ISOLATION*

The universal fear of things new and strange to individual experience may have its roots in the original nature of man. There is a negative organic reaction to stimuli offensive to the senses. Vile-smelling and foul-tasting objects excite disgust; there is an involuntary shrinking in the presence of ugly and repulsive objects and of diseased and deformed persons; slimy substances are offensive; there is a general human shrinking from blood and bloody things. Similar antipathies may be observed elsewhere in the animal world: the dog is violently excited at the first odor of a camel; cattle and horses run amuck at the odor of blood.

These antipathies—organic attitudes—presumably have been of some biological utility in the evolutionary process; their universality cannot well be understood except in terms of survival value. The fundamental and intimate way in which many offensive things are related to the senses of taste and smell indicates their utility in food choices; the involuntary withdrawal in the presence of strange phenomena suggests a selective adaptation to an environment in which danger was inherent in the unfamiliar.

Whatever the origin or biological utility of these original attitudes, they may be conditioned and controlled, if not eliminated, with relative ease, and modified or opposing reactions may be determined in the individual's social experience. It is, for example, the force of convention rather than the native reactions that determines many food habits; oysters, fish, eggs, milk, and many other things are not originally attractive items of diet. Also, the needs of the organism may override, temporarily at least, the native antipathies and give rise to behavior contrary to them: extreme hunger may lead to the use, as food, of substances that at other times are

* Except for minor deletions this chapter is the same as in the second edition.

highly offensive; excited sex passion may overcome the normal aversion to contact with strange or dirty persons.

On the other hand, these organic attitudes may be modified, culturally conditioned, and extended into the social field. Disgusts arise fundamentally from the sense of taste and smell in connection with food, but the range of objects becomes extended by association, resemblance, and analogy until disgusts are aroused by purely conventional stimuli that are in a remote way only connected with the senses. A natural aversion to certain things, in the presence of an habitual code of personal cleanliness acquired in the primary group relations, may be conditioned into an aversion to dirt unknown to the child, the savage, the peasant, and other unspoiled persons. By further extension it may be made to include things displeasing to the mental and moral sentiments of the fit and proper. This cultural extension of organic attitudes is basic to an understanding of the characteristically negative reactions toward individuals and groups with food habits, moral customs, social beliefs, or other behavior patterns of unfamiliar type.

In these extensions we are in the realm of prejudice rather than in that of native reaction. Contrasted to the native antipathies, prejudices are always attitudes acquired in or as a result of social experience. They may exist wholly apart from and independent of any organic repulsive reaction, or the two, as just pointed out, may be connected in more or less intimate and subtle ways. The antipathies may determine or help to determine the social attitudes, in which case the prejudices are in part an extension into the realm of socially modified antipathies.

The antipathies may be and possibly are an essential element in the explanation of racial prejudice. Fears, vague or well-defined, appear always to arise in the presence of uncontrolled phenomena and they are always present in racial contacts until time has allowed the opposing groups to become mutually accommodated to a mutually worked out social order and the individuals of each race habituated to the racial status. The disgusts also play an important rôle. The human animal has the vestiges of a sense of smell that at one time in racial evolution functioned strongly and it is even now stimulated by and reacts to odors, and so determines personal prejudices, without the conscious awareness of the person. At the same time the bodies of all men secrete aromatic substances which rather quickly become rancid. The body odor differs from individual to individual and from race to race. That characteristic of the individuals of one race is commonly offensive to individuals of other races: the Japanese and other Orientals profess an extreme dislike for the body odor of white persons; to many white persons the characteristic body odor of the Negro is nauseating; and certain African Negroes have commented upon the disagreeably rancid odor of the white man. The extensive use of aromatic substances for toilet purposes reflects a folk realization that body odors are personally offensive.

Strong racial prejudices whether independent of or supplementary to organic attitudes were unquestionably of utilitarian value in the conditions prevailing throughout most of the life of man. In most times and places, the unknown was the dangerous, the familiar was the safe. The fear of the strange was a character of survival value. And it is a fact not without significance in the present connection that the fear of the strange and the prejudice of race are prominent and active in the provincial groups.

The Social Character of Race Prejudice

When full allowance has been made for the antipathies, that is, for whatever biologically determined reactions may underlie and condition the relations of the races, the specific attitudes that prevail at any time or place are still not explained.

If racial prejudices were biological phenomena, they would be relatively uniform in intensity and in form of expression; they would exist at all times and in all situations where diverse races meet and associate. But this is not the case: in an historical sense the prejudice of race seems to be of recent origin; it varies in strength and form of expression from one situation to another and in the same area from time to time. Like other social attitudes, the prejudices of race are culturally determined; they must be understood in terms of the culture of which they are a part.

Race prejudice is a function of conflict. It arises in those situations and areas where one group feels its security or existence menaced by the presence or behavior of another. The fears, vague or clearly defined, well-grounded or hallucinatory, get dual expression: on the one hand they generate an in-group solidarity and sense of loyalty, on the other hand they lead to a stereotyped conception of the competitors and to the invention or exaggeration of offensive or menacing characteristics. In this respect, race prejudice differs from class or other types of group prejudice chiefly in the object toward which it is directed.

The fact that race prejudice exists in regions of incomplete control is shown by the fact that it declines in times of racial accommodation and becomes active in times of change and readjustment. In the equilibrium of a slave or caste régime where the exploited group accepts its inferior status, the personal relations are often patronizing, sentimental, or even friendly. The slave masters, the employers of labor, and the landed proprietors are generally contemptuous of rather than prejudiced against the slaves, the workers, and the peasants. Prejudice reappears in active and violent form as the established order disintegrates and as proletarian movements and threatened or actual uprisings of the slaves or peasants menace the security of the masters.

The perpetuation of racial as of other group prejudices is a matter of the transmission of the social heritage. They are essentially emotional and non-rational in character. But men desire to feel and appear reasonable and rational. Consequently, the racial prejudices are presently explained and justified; a whole body of opinion in regard to the race appears and is accepted as accounting for the feelings and the treatment out of which it arose. This body of opinion, the racial attitudes that it rationalizes, and the customary treatment accorded the out-group, are learned by the children and continued through the generations as an integral part of the group culture.

EARLY ATTITUDES TOWARD THE NEGROES

The early attitude of the American colonists and settlers toward the Negroes was determined by physical rather than by conventional facts. The slaves were of a strange race and the physical type was, from the point of view of the white people, ugly and personally repulsive. They were coarse and degraded persons of strange habits and uncouth behavior. In the presence of these facts, the common attitude was one of avoidance; the ill-defined native fear of the strange and unknown was reinforced by the more definite reaction to the personal traits resulting from servile status.

But when personal characteristics become familiar they may cease to be offensive; the repulsive reactions may disappear without change in the marks that at first excited them. As the Negro slaves became a familiar part of the environment and habitual relations were established, conventional attitudes replaced the original reactions. The divergent appearance and other physical marks of the race ceased to be offensive or even noticed once they were no longer strange. But the fact that for the most part they ceased to be conscious phenomena enhanced rather than lessened their rôle in the social situation. They helped to determine personal relationships and to define status in subtle and little understood ways once they ceased to excite a pronounced negative reaction.

The fact that the Negroes were not Christians was a factor of importance in fixing their status and in determining the early attitudes of the whites. The strange beliefs and practices of the slaves, in a time when much importance was attached to such matters, helped to fix a gulf between the races. Their stage of culture development set them apart from the other race and gave a further basis for assigning them an inferior position in the society. The language isolation tended to put them more or less into the category of dumb brutes. The nature of the work in which they were engaged helped to fix the popular attitude toward them. And various other more or less incidental facts of life and culture set them apart and helped to define their status.

Many of the things originally significant in determining the relations of the races disappeared after a little contact with the white civilization. The slaves soon acquired something of the technology, language, manners, customs, religion, and general culture of the white man. But the antipathetic reactions to the strange race, though often lost sight of in the customary situation, remained to reinforce the social attitudes fixed in the early contacts. These attitudes persisted and constantly were reinforced owing to the continued importation of raw Negroes. A category was defined in terms descriptive of the work, habits, and general behavior of the common slaves. The position of individuals was then fixed in categorical terms: as Negroes, individuals were assumed to have the characteristics of the type. Without knowledge of the origin or consciousness of the basis, a common attitude toward Negroes as such passed into and became an integral part of the culture tradition.

SLAVERY AND RACIAL ATTITUDES

As the slave status of the Negroes became an accepted fact and an understood relation there was little place for racial prejudice. Like every other well-established slave régime, that in America was characterized by a more or less complete and perfect accommodation of both the subject and the master race. On the part of the slave was the tendency to submit to the will of another, to expect and accept direction; on the part of the master, the disposition to command and assume leadership was a necessity. In the situation the slaves acquired the character that the masters demanded; their characters conformed to what the whites wanted but did not themselves want to be. It was a caste order of society in which the slaves had a definite place which they understood and accepted. They were not only in a position of inferiority but they accepted the inferior status as a part of the natural order. The whites were in a position of superiority and they accepted the position with little if any more fundamental criticism.

As previously pointed out, there was, throughout the slave period, some fear of Negro uprisings and at times these fears became acute and led to exceptionally harsh treatment of the servile group. Among the laboring and non-slave-holding whites there was sometimes a bitter hatred of the Negroes. But race prejudice as such was not an important factor during the slave period. The Negro had a clearly defined place in the social economy and he was in his place. There was a uniform enforcement of the inferior status. So far as there was prejudice it was that of caste rather than that of race and it expressed itself toward the free Negro rather than toward the slave. Within the slave system itself there was a reciprocal accommodation of the races, so there was no place for racial prejudice.

In the situation there presently came into existence a body of opinion in justification and support of the existing social order and of the relative place of each race in that order. Like every social order the slave-holding society had a philosophy to explain its practices and justify its existence. The philosophy was very simple and direct. The Negroes were in a servile position and possessed the social and psychological marks inevitably resulting from it. These characteristics were a matter of common observation, so could be taken and were taken as fundamental data. The ignorance, indolence, vice, shiftlessness, untruthfulness, dishonesty, and other traits were, in the thought of the time, evidence and proof of the inferiority of the race, and the inferiority was accepted as the reason for the inferior status and justified its continuance. The poor showing of the free Negroes was further evidence, when any was needed, that the race was not capable of self-direction and needed the tutelage of the white. The facts were as patent to the Negroes as to the whites and were given the same interpretation in their body of thought.

The total effect of the slavery experience was to build up an elaborate race and class hierarchy with characteristic sentiments and attitudes and with a body of rationalization designed to explain the peculiarities of status and to make life tolerable within the limits defined.

PREJUDICE AND CULTURAL ISOLATION

Racial prejudice against the Negro in America is an heritage of slavery but it is very largely a development and characteristic of freedom. It is a phenomenon that exists in the region of incomplete control. There was little place for it when the Negro was in and accepted a legally defined servile status. It is most pronounced today in the stratum of the white population least secure in its economic and social superiority to the Negroes. It is most active in the sections of the country where the Negroes have made the greatest advancement and where they are most disposed to insist upon fair and equal treatment.

The sudden emancipation of the slaves destroyed the economic and social organization of the South. The caste order that had prevailed throughout the history of the section was left without legal support. The Negroes were legally changed from dependents and slaves into free and independent persons. The former master and the former slave were made legally equal and each was made the peer of the man of the poor-white class.

But the reciprocal attitudes could not and did not undergo a correspondingly sudden and racial change. These personal attitudes, which had been for two centuries and a half in process of growth and definition had become an integral part of the psychology of both white and Negro. They remained after as they had been before the granting of freedom. The Negro continued to look up to the white man as superior and the white man continued to look upon the Negro as an inferior and a child. The social and class distinctions between the races and within each race and the supporting sentimental complexes were not immediately disturbed by the legal change in status. There was no immediate change in fundamental relations; between the old masters and their former slaves there continued to exist a high degree of mutual sympathy and understanding.

But gradually and by degrees the basis of the old order disappeared and a new order made its appearance. With the death of the older masters and their former slaves the sentimental bonds weakened and presently, with the maturing of individuals who had not known slavery, the break between the races was relatively complete. The long period of disorganized social life and of personal demoralization contributed to the growing loss of sympathy. On the positive side the change in legal status brought an increased number of Negroes into direct and individual competition with the white laboring classes and increased the traditional hatred for these groups. And there were added sources of friction as Negroes advanced in wealth, education, and self-respect. The Negro menial of humble attitude was known and accepted; often he had the affection and sometimes the respect of white men. The independent and self-respecting Negro was intolerable. Racial antagonisms increased as the efforts of individuals to advance resulted in business and other relations implying equality.

As the races drifted apart in sympathy and understanding prejudice increased. This was in part a prejudice of race and in part a caste prejudice. The fear of the Negro—partly an emotion of native origin, partly a vague uneasiness respecting the behavior of the depressed and exploited —came to be a universal and persisting element of the white psychology. The aversion to individual and personal association and the inability to accept the individual Negro as a concrete reality increased as the races drew apart. But in the South the important prejudice was against the Negro out of his traditional status. There was a fixed conception of the place of the Negro in the social order and a dislike for him in any other relation. There continued to be a liking for individual Negroes, a toleration of their faults, an understanding of their problems, and a recognition of them as personalities. The caste prejudice is not a dislike of the Negro as a person but a dislike for him in a certain relation. The prejudice expresses itself as an intolerant insistence upon the customary caste relationship; it is exemplified in the southerner's insistence that he likes the Negro "in his place."

As the races drew apart and prejudice and misunderstanding developed, the cultural isolation of the Negroes increased. Presently there were ef-

forts to institutionalize and make permanent the isolation in order to reinstate and perpetuate the caste order. The Negro was to be kept in his
place by preventing his participation in the community life. The disfranchisement of the race and the segregation movement exemplify the concrete development.

DISFRANCHISEMENT OF THE NEGROES

In the early Colonial days there were no laws limiting the franchise to
white men. Political discriminations grew slowly in practice but it was
only after a hundred years that they found legal definition.

In 1715 North Carolina passed an act disfranchising the Negroes, mulattoes, and the Indians but a royal edict in 1734 commanding its repeal guaranteed all freemen the right to vote. The law as re-enacted about the middle of the century limited the suffrage to freeholders; the free Negroes,
at least in law, met no discrimination. South Carolina inserted the word
"white" in the franchise law of 1716 and retained it in later enactments
and in the state constitution. Virginia passed an act in 1705 forbidding
Negroes to hold office and in 1723 they were disfranchised. The latter act
was repealed by proclamation after being in force for over a decade. The
final and complete disfranchisement of the Negro in Virginia came in
1762. The Georgia law was passed a year earlier and the limitation was
written into the constitution of 1777.

During the period from the Revolution to the Civil War the Negroes
in general did not vote. In some states—Virginia, South Carolina, Florida,
Alabama, and a number of others—the ballot was specifically limited to
white men. North Carolina did not have a definite color qualification in
her franchise laws and it is uncertain whether or not it was the intention of
the constitution of 1776 to exclude the free Negroes. They appear to have
voted without opposition until the activities of the colonization and emancipation societies aroused a popular hostility. The revised constitution of
1835 excluded them from the suffrage. This act marked the end of Negro
suffrage in the South until after the Civil War.

The attitude of the northern and western states was less uniform than
in the South but it was not always more liberal. Certain of the New England States with a negligible number of Negroes made no mention of color
as a voting qualification. Vermont in 1838 and New Hampshire in 1857
passed laws stating that Negroes should not be excluded from the ballot.
But Maine was the only New England state in which the Negroes were
actually allowed to participate equally with the whites. In certain states
Negroes were at first allowed to vote and at a later date denied the privilege. Most of the middle group of states either withdrew or restricted
suffrage. A color qualification was introduced in Delaware in 1792, in
Kentucky in 1799, in Maryland in 1809, in Connecticut in 1818, in New

Jersey in 1820, and in Pennsylvania in 1838. All of the new western states refused the Negro the privilege of voting. Certain of the states—California, Colorado, Illinois, Indiana, Iowa, Kansas, Michigan, Mississippi, Nebraska, Nevada, Ohio, Oregon, Utah, and Wisconsin—limited the suffrage to white men from the beginning. Of all the states that fought for the preservation of the union only four granted suffrage to the Negroes on the same terms as to the whites. In 1861 the Negroes were allowed to vote in but five of the thirty-four states: Maine, New Hampshire, Massachusetts, Rhode Island, and New York.

Immediately following the Civil War the right of suffrage was extended to Negroes on the same basis as to the whites. Federal pressure amounting to compulsion led the state conventions to adopt constitutions enfranchising the freedmen. The fifteenth amendment to the federal constitution, ratified in 1870, safeguarded the newly acquired political rights by forestalling any attempt to withdraw the franchise by later changes in the state constitutions. It removed all suffrage restrictions on the basis of race in the northern as well as in the southern states.

Almost immediately thereafter a movement arose in the southern states to prevent the participation of the Negroes in political affairs. The size of the Negro vote was materially reduced by intimidation, violence, and fraud as the whites regained political control. After 1876 the Negro vote ceased to be an item of importance in the state governments.

It presently became evident that the illegal prohibition of Negro suffrage could not continue indefinitely and about 1890 a movement began to disfranchise them by legal means. The fifteenth amendment was an effective bar to direct legislative actions; the problem was to devise measures that would apply to the Negroes but not to the whites without at the same time violating the prohibition on special race legislation. The state of Mississippi in the amended constitution of 1890 limited the franchise to those who paid poll taxes and were able to read any section of the constitution or were able to "understand the same when read to them and give a reasonable interpretation thereof." Fairly executed, this would have debarred alike the illiterates of both races, but it was easily possible for registration officials to rule anyone unqualified after examination. In practice it was applied to Negroes only.

Among other constitutional amendments adopted to circumvent the "race, color, or previous condition of servitude" clause of the fifteenth amendment to the Federal Constitution was the notorious "grandfather clause." This provided that all persons who had served in the army or navy of the United States in any of its wars, all who served in the Confederate army or navy, or of the armed forces of the state in which they resided, and all lawful descendants of such persons might register to vote provided they possessed the other necessary qualifications. In Louisiana and North

Carolina the form of this clause provided for the registration of all persons who had a right to vote prior to 1867 and of their lawful descendants. This type of legislation was ruled unconstitutional by the Supreme Court of the United States in 1915. Various other restrictions on the suffrage appear in constitutional provisions of general nature but capable of special application. Educational and property qualifications are most common. These include such things as the demonstrated ability to read and write, the ability to interpret the constitution of the United States, and the ownership of a stipulated amount of property. There is in general no objection to such laws. The states are clearly within their rights in limiting the suffrage to intelligent and property-holding citizens and it is possibly a wise governmental policy to do so. But that there is racial discrimination in the administration of the laws is seldom denied. Prior to 1964 several states required the prepayment of a poll tax, sometimes for a considerable term of years, as a voting qualification and in two of the states proof of the payment had to be shown at the polls. The tax provision probably prevented more Negroes from voting than did any other restriction; the masses of the race were not sufficiently interested in the suffrage to pay a poll tax if it could be escaped.

It was generally assumed that the application of the various constitutional provisions was such as practically to disfranchise the race in the South. It would be of interest to know the extent to which legally qualified Negroes were discriminated against and prevented from registering and voting. In some states and parts of states where there are two parties a considerable number do vote at all elections; in other states the Negro vote is small. It is not known to what extent the laws are made to apply to one race and not to the other.

The one-party system in the South is perhaps more effective in eliminating the Negro from participation in the political life than are the constitutional and legal provisions. The historic fear of Negro domination prevents the political division of the whites even on local issues. The result is that in most states of the South the nomination of a Democratic candidate is equivalent to his election. The Republican party exists but is without competitive power. In the Democratic primaries voting was restricted to the whites until very recent years.

The Negroes were out of politics but they dominated the whole political situation. Their agitation for re-enfranchisement roused deep-seated fears and prejudices and intensified the determination of the masses to prevent it.

SEGREGATION AND CULTURAL EXCLUSION

The segregation movement was another expression of the growth and hardening of racial and caste prejudices and the consequent increasing social isolation of the Negroes. It may be viewed as a process by which individuals in the free society redistributed themselves in accordance with natural ability and personal interest; noting how this natural tendency was in part directed and controlled and everywhere limited by the existing racial and caste attitudes. From the point of view of social condition, the movement shows the gradually increasing exclusion of the group and the isolation of its members from social contacts and from participation in the general cultural life.

In many relations of life a fairly complete separation of the races existed throughout the slave period. The slaves were a group apart and had no participating part in the public life. The arrangement of their life experiences was subject to arbitrary control; it differed with family and master but there was general uniformity. They were generally provided with living quarters apart from the whites. Their church and religious activities were frequently separate and in all mixed congregate groups they had a segregated place. They had their own amusements and provisions for recreation and took no part in those of the whites. Their dead were buried apart. The civil rights of the free Negroes were restricted in numerous ways both in law and custom and their cultural isolation in some cases was equal to that of the slaves.

With freedom the separation of the races increased. On the side of the Negro group there was a voluntary segregation in many of the relations of life and the beginnings of a semi-independent racial life. With the readjustment of the social and economic order the whites placed various legal restrictions upon the activities of the Negroes, in part as police measures looking toward harmony in race relations and in part as repressive measures designed to maintain the customary status of inferiority. Efforts at residential segregation by law and ordinance grew up to restrain individuals who for one reason or another wished to live outside the Negro sections. The recognition that the exclusion policy, by keeping the race together and forcing them to develop their own institutions, operated to their economic welfare and to the development of self-confidence and self-respect led to its being advocated and extended not only as a device for avoiding racial disorder but as an effective legal method of inducing the Negroes to take advantage of the wonderful economic advantages open before them.

The movement was somewhat retarded by certain acts of the federal government. The Emancipation Proclamation, read into the fundamental law in the form of a thirteenth amendment, specifically guaranteed the Negroes the same rights as enjoyed by other citizens. A little later the Civil Rights Bill stated that "all people within the jurisdiction of the United States should be entitled to full and equal enjoyment of accommodations, advantages, facilities, privileges of inns, public conveyances on land and water, theaters, and other places of public amusement, subject only to conditions established by law applicable to citizens of every race and color." Social status is an intangible thing little subject to control by legislative edict. It resides ultimately in the attitudes of the people and the status enforced in the practices of the society may depart indefinitely from the status as defined by law. The Negroes did not anywhere enjoy the equality defined by the legislative bodies, but these acts stood in the way of a systematic legal isolation. When the Supreme Court of the United States in 1883 declared the federal Bill of Rights unconstitutional and returned the explicit civil rights of the Negroes to the control of the states the chief barrier was removed and the states with a large Negro population took advantage of the judicial decision to enforce distinctions through all the various relations of social and civil life.

The church life of the races was separated by the voluntary withdrawal of the Negroes. The schools were separated by legislative acts of the whites. The fear of disorder resulting from the mingling of the races in public conveyances was the excuse for separate accommodations on trains, electric lines, and street cars as well as in depots and other public places. The separation of the races came to be enforced in theaters and practically all other places of amusement. They were excluded from hotels and restaurants. They were denied the use of libraries and often excluded from lectures and public concerts. The tendency after the eighties was toward an extensive application of a policy of segregation.

THE ORGANIZATION OF NEGRO LIFE

The growing prejudice and separation of the races was an incidental, probably inevitable, result of working out a new basis of relations. It was necessary to make some adjustment in accordance with the changed legal status. There was no precedent to furnish guidance; no two races had ever evolved mutually satisfactory working relations except on the basis of superiority and subordination, the enslavement of the one by the other. The transition to a new order that held any promise of being either mutually satisfactory or relatively permanent was not easy. There was no intellectual leadership either North or South able to visualize a free, democratic, social order. The South was so thoroughly habituated to a slave régime that only the rare individual could picture any other tolerable order; the North was equally profoundly habituated to the master-man relationship functioning through a wage system. A reorganization of the society on the basis of human values did not come within the orbit of thought of either section. The actual direction of affairs was at all times in the hands of politicians and on the level of popular thought: there was no statesman-like policy. The period of doctrinaire experimentation following the War was too brief and weak to work any thorough-going change in the institutional life or to form new habits of thought and action, and the leadership was too unintelligent and uninformed to initiate any vital social movement. The withdrawal of foreign influence from the South and the restoration of local control did not improve the quality of the statesmanship. The long, stupid period of trial and error that followed was characterized by an absence of political and social vision and dominated by a fixed determination to restore and maintain as much as possible of the former order.

On the side of the Negroes the changed legal status necessitated a profound social reorganization, and the period of psychological and social transition from a slave to a free order was one of bewildered disorder, of individual demoralization, of personal failure. The natural difficulty of reaccommodation was intensified by the anticipation of a governmental redistribution of real property. The problem of the Negroes was to adjust behavior to the social policy of the whites which they were powerless to control. The separation of the races, whether as a voluntary act or in compliance with the exclusion laws and ordinances of the whites, isolated the Negroes, shut them out more or less effectively from culture contact, stimulation, and example. The race was forced back upon itself, forced to depend upon its own leaders for guidance, forced to reorganize the social life upon a semi-independent basis. But there was no real racial leadership, no trained men. The greatest economic opportunity ever presented to the peasantry of any country was before the freedmen, but they were not prepared to accept it and there were no leaders to direct them along the obvious lines of racial advance. The natural reaction of the newly freed individuals was away from the type of life on which their advance depended. Labor was associated with servitude; it was the badge and symbol of inferior status. The numerous individuals who entered the South at the close of the war with aspirations to racial leadership were in the great majority of cases unfitted for the task; they were indoctrinated with the sentimental prepossessions of abolitionism and uninformed as to the social and economic situation of the region and as to Negro character. Bewildered, ignorant, and without intelligent leadership, the Negroes were a helpless and economically exploited group in the population.

Out of the confusion a reorganized Negro life gradually came into being. Its form was determined by the immediate demands of the local situation, not by any design or statesmanlike policy or forethought. The new interracial relations that grew up came as blind trial and error adjustments.

Economically the races were and remained mutually dependent—the whites upon the Negroes for labor, the Negroes upon the whites for the opportunity to work for the means to existence—and work relations, suited to the local economy and the type of labor, were developed. But in almost every other relation of life the races were separated, either by voluntary withdrawal or by compulsory exclusion, and independent and race-limited institutions grew up to serve the needs of the segregated people. The church organizations, in some cases separate before the Emancipation, were the first to develop and for a time the whole social and intellectual life centered about them. But other institutions followed and the number and variety increased as the life of the races became more separate.

The growth of an independent Negro life reacted in the situation to increase the cleavage between the races: as they gained in experience, so in individual and racial self-confidence, the tendency to a voluntary and complete separation increased. It marked the beginning of a sense of racial unity, a race consciousness, which, however, did not reach an articulate stage before the present century.

The advance of the Negroes during the first half century of their liberation was slow. Their success in many places and in many lines was retarded by the prejudice and discrimination of the whites, the separation of the races deprived them of much needed advice and encouragement and isolated them from valuable culture contacts. A spurious leadership often directed attention away from the obvious business of life in the circumstances, stimulated racial antagonisms, and encouraged futile and unprofitable types of activity. But measured by any of the conventional standards there was progress. The amount of privately owned property, chiefly in the form of homes and farms, increased; there was a steady growth in the value of churches, school houses, and the like owned by racial organizations. The number of business enterprises increased. There was an increase in education and a rapid decline in the percentage of illiteracy. The stability of family life increased. In many respects the moral standards improved.

SOCIAL STATUS AND DIFFERENTIAL TREATMENT

The denial of political rights and the residential and other types of segregation are typical rather than inclusive of racial discrimination. In practically all aspects of their life the Negroes' cultural opportunities are restricted and their rights curtailed. The degree and character of racial discrimination varies with the section of the country: in some areas it is undisguised and in accord with public expectation, in other places it is less frank and open, but the progress of the race in various lines and certain consequences of racial prejudice and cultural isolation will be considered in following chapters.

Baily, T. P., *Race Orthodoxy in the South,* "The Race Problem and Race Prejudice," pp. 7–115.

Chicago Commission on Race Relations, *The Negro in Chicago,* "Racial Contacts," pp. 231–326.

Detweiler, F. G., "The Rise of Modern Race Antagonisms," *American Journal of Sociology,* 37(1932), 738–747.

Dollard, John, *Caste and Class in a Southern Town,* pp. 363–388, 433–444, 445–585.

Faris, Ellsworth, *The Nature of Human Nature,* "The Natural History of Race Prejudice," pp. 354–366.

Frazier, E. F., "The Pathology of Race Prejudice," *Forum,* 77(1927), 856–862.

Gosnell, H. F., *Negro Politicians.*

Hart, A. B., "Negro Suffrage in the United States," *American Government Encyclopaedia.*

Park, R. E., "The Basis of Race Prejudice," *Annals of the American Academy of Political and Social Science,* 140(1928), 11–20.

Reuter, E. B., ed., *Race and Culture Contacts.*

Schuyler, G. S., "Traveling Jim Crow," *American Mercury,* 20(1930), 423–432.

Smith, W. R., *Negro Suffrage in the South.*

Stephenson, G. T., *Race Distinctions in American Law,* "Civil Rights of Negroes," pp. 102–153; "Suffrage," 281–347.

Thomas, W. I., "The Psychology of Race Prejudice," *American Journal of Sociology,* 9(1903–1904), 593–611.

Wallis, W. D., "Some Phases of the Psychology of Prejudice," *Journal of Abnormal and Social Psychology,* 24(1930), 418–429.

Washington, B. T., *Up From Slavery.*

Weatherford, W. D., and Johnson, C. S., *Race Relations,* "Political and Civil Rights," pp. 403–422.

Wood, C. C., "Alabama: A Study in Ultra-Violet," *Nation,* 116(1923), 33–35.

Woofter, T. J., *Races and Ethnic Groups in American Life.*

Young, Donald, *American Minority Peoples,* "Racial Prejudices," pp. 1–21.

FURTHER READINGS

Adorno, T. W., et al., *The Authoritarian Personality.* New York: Harper & Row, 1950.

Allport, G. W., *The Nature of Prejudice.* Cambridge, Mass.: Addison-Wesley, 1954.

Berkowitz, Leonard, *Aggression: A Social-Psychological Analysis.* New York: McGraw-Hill, 1962.

Bettelheim, Bruno, and Janowitz, Morris, *Social Change and Prejudice*. New York: Free Press, 1964.

Blumer, Herbert, "Race Prejudice as a Sense of Group Position," in Masuoka, Jitsuichi, and Valien, Preston, eds., *Race Relations Problems and Theory*. Chapel Hill: University of North Carolina Press, 1961.

Christie, Richard, and Jahoda, Marie, eds., *Studies in the Scope and Method of the Authoritarian Personality*. New York: Free Press, 1954.

Cox, Oliver Cromwell, *Caste, Class, and Race*. New York: Doubleday, 1948.

Dollard, John, et al., *Frustration and Aggression*. New Haven: Yale University Press, 1939.

Hartley, Eugene L., *Problems in Prejudice*. New York: King's Crown Press, 1946.

Kardiner, Abram, and Ovesey, Lionel, *The Mark of Oppression*. Cleveland: World Publishing, 1962.

Kelly, J. G.; Ferson, J. E.; and Holtzman, W. H., "The Measurement of Attitudes toward the Negro in the South," *Journal of Social Psychology* (November 1958), 305–317.

Pettigrew, Thomas, "Personality and Socio-Cultural Factors in Intergroup Attitudes," *Journal of Conflict Resolution* (March 1958), 29–42.

———, "Regional Differences in Anti-Negro Prejudice," *Journal of Abnormal Psychology* (July 1959), 28–36.

Price, H. D., *The Negro and Southern Politics: A Chapter of Florida History*. New York: New York University Press, 1957.

Rhyne, Edwin H., "Racial Prejudice and Personality Scales: An Alternative Approach," *Social Forces* (October 1962), 44–53.

Silberstein, Fred B., and Seeman, Melvin, "Social Mobility and Prejudice," *American Journal of Sociology*, LXV(1959), 258–264.

Simpson, George E., and Yinger, J. Milton, *Racial and Cultural Minorities*, 3rd ed. New York: Harper & Row, 1965.

Vander Zanden, James W., *American Minority Relations*, 2nd ed. New York: Ronald Press, 1966.

Woodward, C. Vann, *The Strange Career of Jim Crow*. New York: Oxford University Press, 1957.

X

THE HEALTH OF THE NEGRO

One of the more serious problems of the present-day* American South is the condition of the public health. The sickness and death rates from tuberculosis, pellagra, the hookworm disease, typhoid and malarial fevers, and from other less well advertised diseases are excessively high. The recency of accurate registration statistics makes a comparative quantitative statement difficult, but that the South is far behind other sections of the country and other parts of the white world in the matter of freedom from infectious disease is not open to question.

This backward condition of the South has been due in some part to poverty and general educational backwardness. But it has also been due in other part to the attitude of indifference that the white people have assumed toward the welfare of the Negro people. The health problems of the Negroes have not been a matter of serious social interest. The housing and sanitary conditions of the Negroes have been neglected and, in consequence, Negro health compares very unfavorably with that of other classes in the population. Since they are an important numerical element of the population, their high sickness and death rates materially lower the average health and efficiency standards of the total population.

But Negro health influences the health of the nation, particularly of the South, in a far more significant way. The white people of the South cannot establish and maintain high health and efficiency standards while neglecting the vital welfare of the Negro people. The contact of the races is such that the health of the one is conditioned by that of the other. The Negroes serve and care for the whites, prepare their food, wash their clothing, nurse their children, and otherwise come into frequent contact with them, and in such circumstances the ill health of the Negroes inevita-

* In 1938.

bly contaminates the whites. Many communities have followed the short-sighted policy of providing more or less adequately for the medical inspection of white school children, while neglecting to provide similar inspection for the Negro school children. So far as infectious diseases are concerned such a policy defeats itself: infection arising in the Negro quarters spreads rapidly to the white schools and there undoes the work of the medical inspection. Where a population is bi-racial, a diseased colored community means a diseased white community; the mutual interdependence of the racial groups is such that most public health measures must fail unless they include both racial elements.

THE ECONOMIC IMPORTANCE OF NEGRO HEALTH

Poor health on the part of the Negro operates to the social disadvantage in other ways. The economic loss resulting from sickness is enormous. The worker's chief asset is his ability to work continuously and effectively. Sickness detracts from his industrial efficiency and this is a matter of concern to the individual employer unless the existence of a redundant labor supply makes it possible for him to secure other workers without additional expense. But to the worker, ill health means the loss of wages, so a more intense poverty with its consequences of greater economic exploitation and lower living standards. To the family it means an increase of woman and child labor with its results in the way of ignorance, illiteracy, social inefficiency, and general cultural retardation. It puts an additional burden upon the efficient members of the group in that the results of their labor must support the diseased and inefficient persons. It handicaps the economic and social advance of the group. When a person is injured or sick the society suffers a serious loss, a loss in both goods and services. It has been estimated that the cost in loss of earnings alone due to preventable, hence unnecessary, sickness and death in the South amounted in the 1930's to over $300,000,000 annually. Whatever may be true of the individual employer of labor, the society cannot afford to scrap workers.

But to take a narrow economic attitude toward Negro health is to remain blind to things of more importance. The human powers and energies of persons composing the population are the most important part of the nation's resources. Disease and unnecessary deaths are an economic and social loss but the human costs of bearing and rearing children and the human waste of disease and premature death are matters of greater concern. If human life is a value in and of itself, man is not to be regarded as a means for the production of wealth but as an end for which wealth is produced.

From any point of view the condition of physical welfare of the Negro people is a matter of grave concern. It is fundamental to the well-being of the group itself; it is probably the most outstanding problem that con-

fronts the Negro people today.* It is important from the point of view of
economic and industrial efficiency; it bears upon the problem of education; it is a controlling factor in poverty and dependence; it is a significant
factor in vice and delinquency. The health and vitality of the Negro people, as of any other class in the population, is of concern not alone to the
group itself but to the community as a whole. Negro health is a national
as well as a racial problem.

NEGRO HEALTH PRIOR TO THE CIVIL WAR

Until recent decades little may be known concerning the health of the
Negro people. In Africa, as the result of climatic conditions and the pre-
literate state of culture, the death rate was high and the life span short.
But prior to the entrance of the white man in numbers, they appear to
have been free from a number of diseases to which they are particularly
susceptible in America. On the other hand they are relatively free in
America from the effects of various diseases from which they suffered in
Africa. In the case of still other diseases, they appear to suffer excessively
in either environment; even in the Tropics they are especially subject to
affections of the lungs.

Very little may be known in regard to Negro health prior to the Civil
War and, in many areas, for some decades thereafter. There are two conflicting opinions, but the body of pertinent objective data in support of
either is almost nil.

One position holds that the poor sanitary conditions of the Negro quarters resulted in early deaths and a high death rate. The other emphasizes
that, in the American slave régime, the economic advantage of the master
as well as considerations of human kindness led to relatively adequate
measures for the preservation of the health of the slaves. They were
largely rural and led an active outdoor life, there was an enforced regu-
larity of habits, the diet was simple and generally wholesome. On the
large plantations as well as in the better city environments, the sanitary
condition of the slave quarters was assured by more or less regular and
systematic inspection. As a result of the vigorous and orderly life imposed
on the slaves, the mortality and morbidity rates were probably low.

There are almost no statistical data and neither position can be demonstrated by that technique. The few scattered figures are from urban areas
and the slaves were for the most part rural. Some early reports from
Charleston, Savannah, and New Orleans give Negro and white death rates
as about equal. It was high for both races. The races suffered unequally
from certain diseases. In 1838, a yellow fever year, the white mortality of
Charleston was given as 54.5 per 1,000 as against 30.3 per 1,000 for the

* In 1938.

Negro population. In 1836, a cholera year, the situation was reversed; the Negro mortality was reported as 51.0 per 1,000, the white was reported as 24.6. In Mobile, Alabama, in the period 1843–1846, the Negro death rate was reported as only one-half that of the whites—23.1 per 1,000 for the Negro and 45.8 per 1,000 for the whites. In the period 1822–1830, the annual average Negro death rate in Charleston, South Carolina, was reported as 28.2 per 1,000 Negroes as contrasted to 32.7 per 1,000 whites. In Baltimore, the mortality record dates from 1812. With the exception of four years—1821, 1853, 1854, and 1858—the Negro rate has been above that of the white. Other scattered reports are frequently quoted in comparing Negro health in the past and present. While these early reports are probably without value—the frequent remarkable showing of the Negroes being due to incomplete reporting of Negro deaths—it is possible that at the time of the Emancipation the Negroes enjoyed the best health in the history of the race up to that time.

In the North, where in general the statistics were more nearly adequate, the mortality rate of the Negroes was always higher than that of the whites. In the decade ending in 1840, the Negro death rate in Philadelphia was approximately 31.0 per 1,000 as contrasted to 22.0 per 1,000 for the whites. Similar differences in the Negro and white deaths prevailed in Boston, New York, and other northern cities.

Vital Statistics of the Negro People

The first definite figures bearing upon the question date from 1850. At that time the Census Bureau undertook to secure certain information in regard to each person who had died within one year preceding the date of enumeration and similar data have been secured at each subsequent enumeration. That the mortality data secured in this way are incomplete and highly inaccurate is generally obvious on the face of the returns, and the fact has been pointed out in the various reports. According to the returns of 1850, the mortality rate appeared to be 16.4 per 1,000 for the slave population and 13.5 per 1,000 for the free population. That is, the returns indicated a mortality rate lower than had anywhere been reached up to that time. Obviously there were wholesale omissions; probably over one-third of the deaths for the year were not reported. In later decades the mortality statistics of the registration areas furnish a partial check upon the degree of inaccuracy of the enumeration figures. In 1900, for example, the number of deaths in the death registration areas was 30.2 per 1,000 of the Negro population and 17.3 per 1,000 of the white population. But according to the enumeration returns the rate was 13.7 for the Negro population and 10.6 for the white populations. Since there is little reason to believe that the death rate was higher within than without the registration areas, the difference between the two sets of figures may be taken as representing with some approximation to accuracy the omissions made by the enumerators. These enumeration data are not without value for other purposes but they furnish no satisfactory basis for determining rates of mortality.

The only index of mortality that comprehends the entire Negro population is that derived from the age classifications of the several census enumerations. The Negro population is almost exclusively native; consequently it is little disturbed by immigration or emigration. This being true, it is possible to assume that those enumerated in 1920, for example, as from ten to nineteen years of age include all the survivors of the Negro population returned at the previous census as being under ten years of age. Since the net immigration is negligible, whatever decrease appears is presumably due to mortality.

As just indicated, the United States has not always had a comprehensive system of registration of vital statistics. But certain states and cities have provided by state laws or municipal ordinances for the registration of such data. In 1880, Congress authorized the compilation and publication of birth and death statistics by the census bureau, the information to be obtained from the states and municipalities providing the machinery for its collection. The first census report on mortality, issued for the year 1900, gave statistics for ten states and the District of Columbia, which comprised approximately forty per cent of the American population. Since that beginning, the area has gradually expanded until in 1930 it contained 96.2 per cent of the estimated population. At present all states are included in the death registration area.

But for much of the period since 1900 these registration areas did not include the territory where the bulk of the Negroes resided. The extension of the area was for the most part confined to the northern sections of the country; only a limited number of the more important cities of the South were included until recently; the large rural population of the South has until recently been almost wholly excluded. Since the Negroes are largely a southern and a rural population, the mortality statistics for this racial element are particularly incomplete. It should also be borne in mind that the reporting of deaths has probably been, at most times and in most places, less complete and accurate for the Negroes than for the whites.

NEGRO DEATH RATES IN THE UNITED STATES

In 1930, the death registration area contained 96.2 per cent of the estimated population and 94.4 per cent of the total Negro population of the United States. In 1920, the death registration area included 34 states and the District of Columbia, and 16 cities outside of the registration states. But beginning with 1933 all the states and the District of Columbia were

Table 8-1A: DEATH RATE BY SEX AND COLOR, 1900–1965* †

	1900	1910	1920	1930	1935	1940	1945	1950	1955	1960	1965
White											
Both Sexes	17.0	14.5	12.6	10.8	10.6	10.4	10.4	9.5	9.2	9.5	9.4
Male	17.7	15.5	13.0	11.7	11.6	11.6	12.5	10.9	10.7	11.0	10.8
Female	16.3	13.6	12.1	9.8	9.5	9.2	8.6	8.0	7.8	8.0	8.0
Nonwhite											
Both Sexes	25.0	21.7	17.7	16.3	14.3	13.4	11.9	11.2	10.0	10.1	9.6
Male	25.7	22.3	17.8	17.4	15.6	15.1	13.5	12.5	11.3	11.5	11.1
Female	24.4	21.7	17.5	15.3	13.0	12.6	10.5	9.9	8.8	8.7	8.2

* Source: Data taken from *Historical Statistics of the United States*, p. 27, and from Dept. of Health, Education, and Welfare, Public Health Service, Annual Report, *Vital Statistics of the United States*

† Rates per 1,000 population (excluding fetal deaths)

included in the death and birth registration area. It is therefore possible at the present time to state certain health facts and tendencies with a higher degree of accuracy than was possible prior to 1933.

The general Negro death rate is comparatively and absolutely high. This is true of both sexes and of all age groups in both rural and urban areas and in all sections of the country.

In the death registration area, in 1920, there were 130,147 Negro deaths (exclusive of still births) from all causes, giving a crude death rate of 18.7 per 1,000 of the Negro population. In 1930 the number of deaths was 185,503, a rate of 16.5. In 1932 the rate had fallen to 14.1. There is no reason to assume that prior to 1933 the rates were lower—and they may have been higher—in the territory lying outside of the registration areas. In 1960 there were 206,647 deaths from all causes, giving a crude death rate of 10.1. In 1964 the number of deaths was 219,377—a rate of 9.7.

The comparative death rates of the Negro and white populations in the years 1900 to 1965 and 1933 to 1964 are given in Tables 8-1A and 8-1B.

Table 8-1B: CRUDE DEATH RATES, BY COLOR, IN DEATH-REGISTRATION
STATES, 1903–1932, AND UNITED STATES, 1933–1964* †

	Total	White	Nonwhite
1903–07		15.7	24.9
1908–12		14.0	21.6
1913–17		12.9	20.0
1918–22		13.0	18.4
1923–27		11.2	17.0
1928–32		10.9	16.0
1933–37		10.7	14.7
1938–42		10.3	13.5
1943–47		10.2	11.9
1948–52		9.5	11.2
1953–57		9.3	10.3
1958–62		9.4	9.9
1963		9.5	10.1
1964		9.4	9.7

* Source: Data are from *Historical Statistics of the United States*; also *Vital Statistics of the United States, 1965*, Vol. II, Table 1-1
† Data refer to deaths occurring within the specified area. Rates per 1,000 population (excluding fetal deaths)

The racial mortality rates show greater variation when taken by smaller areas. The smaller units give an opportunity for the variation in health conditions, occupations, climatic influences, and other facts influencing death rates to stand out—the facts are often concealed in the general figures. The death rates of Negroes and whites for 1930 and 1960 are given in Table 8-2 for selected states typical of the areas.

It is obvious from the comparative rates set out in the table that the Negro rates are higher than the white rates. In general the rates of Negro mortality are higher in the northern and western states than in the southern sections of the country. These figures may not, of course, be accepted without interpretation. They are crude rates that do not take into account differences in age and sex distribution. Some part of the regional variation may be due to differences in the degree of accuracy in registration procedure. Then, too, some of the states in the West are not representative of the Negro population, for in these states other nonwhites outnumber Negroes.

The variations in the figures from state to state are probably more a matter of rural and urban residence than of geographic location. In the North and West the Negroes are in major part a city population, while in the South they are more largely rural. The Negroes have fared poorly

Table 8-2: WHITE AND NEGRO DEATH RATES FROM ALL CAUSES, IN SELECTED STATES, 1930 AND 1960* †

	Whites		Negroes	
State	1930	1960	1930	1960
Alabama	9.4	8.3	15.2	11.5
Arkansas	9.1	9.6	13.5	11.4
Connecticut	10.6	9.5	17.5	8.7
District of Columbia	13.0	7.2	21.0	9.6
Georgia	9.8	8.0	16.0	11.4
Idaho	9.2	8.1	19.5	10.0
Illinois	10.7	10.2	17.7	10.3
Iowa	10.6	10.4	17.1	13.7
Massachusetts	11.5	11.1	15.9	10.6
Minnesota	9.9	9.3	20.8	14.6
Mississippi	9.2	8.9	14.8	11.5
Nevada	12.3	9.0	27.1	8.2††
New York	11.5	10.7	16.6	9.8
North Carolina	....	7.8	....	10.5
Oregon	10.9	9.5	24.6	9.0††
South Carolina	....	7.6	....	10.6
Virginia	10.5	8.0	18.0	11.2

* Source: 1960 data computed from Dept. of Health, Education, and Welfare, *Vital Statistics of the United States, 1964,* Vol. II, *Mortality,* Part A, Table 1-1
† Rate per 1,000 population
†† Refers to nonwhite population

when settled in cities. Taking the figures of 1910 as illustrative, the general death rate among the Negroes was 21.7, while that of the whites was 14.5, a difference of 7.2 points. In the part of the population living in rural and semi-rural conditions—the open country and villages and towns of less than 10,000 population—the general death rate was lower than for the urban population.

Similar though less marked differences existed twenty-two years later. In 1932 the death rate per 1,000 population was 10.9 for the registration states, 10.5 for the white population, and 14.1 for the colored, chiefly Negroes. In the cities of over 10,000 population the rate per 1,000 population was 11.6, for the whites it was 11.2, and for the colored 16.9. In the smaller cities and rural areas the general rate was 10.2, that of the whites 9.8, and that of the colored 12.3. Urbanization seems to affect the death rates of both races adversely, the rates of the colored more markedly than those of the whites.

The comparative death rates of the colored and white populations in cities of 10,000 or more inhabitants, and the rates in the remainder of the area, are given in Table 8-3.

Table 8-3: COLORED AND WHITE DEATH RATES BY CHARACTER OF RESIDENCE AREA, 1929-1933*

Area	1929	1930	1931	1932	1933
Cities of 10,000					
or more	13.0	12.3	11.9	11.6	11.5
White	12.4	11.7	11.4	11.2	11.0
Colored	20.6	18.5	18.1	16.9	16.2
Remainder of Area	10.9	10.5	10.2	10.2	9.9
White	10.4	10.0	9.8	9.8	9.6
Colored	14.9	13.8	13.3	12.3	11.8

* Rate per 1,000 population (excluding still births)

It should be noted that these figures are for the entire colored population, not exclusively Negro. Table 8-4 gives rates for several selected central cities of standard metropolitan statistical areas in 1960, showing a range from a high of 14.1 in Chattanooga, Tennessee, and 14.0 in Louisville, Kentucky, to a low of 6.7 in Los Angeles-Long Beach, California, and 6.3 in San Francisco-Oakland, California.

The Negro death rate in the 1930's was higher than that of any other large group in the population. The relatively high rates of Negro mortality were not a peculiarity of a single region, or of a single or few groups in the population; these rates appeared to prevail in all sections of the country and in about the same degree in each sex. Through most of the age scale, the proportion of deaths was greater for the Negro than for the white population.

Up to 1930 the status of Negro mortality in the United States stood out when it was compared with the rates of different European countries. It was not only higher than that of the general population of the United States but also higher than that of most European populations. The status

Table 8-4: DEATH RATE BY COLOR AND REGION FOR SELECTED STANDARD
METROPOLITAN STATISTICAL AREAS, UNITED STATES, 1960

City	North Nonwhite	White	City	Nonwhite	White
St. Louis, Mo.	11.2	9.8	Wilmington, Del.	12.2	8.7
Indianapolis, Ind.	11.2	9.4	Jacksonville, Fla.	12.0	7.6
Kansas City,			Shreveport, La.	11.7	7.5
Mo./Kan.	11.9	9.4	Birmingham, Ala.	11.7	8.2
Pittsburgh, Pa.	11.5	10.2	New Orleans, La.	11.4	9.8
Columbus, Ohio	10.0	8.6	Richmond, Va.	11.2	9.2
Philadelphia, Pa.	9.9	10.4	Norfolk-		
New York City	9.5	10.6	Portsmouth, Va.	11.2	6.9
Chicago, Ill.	9.8	10.0	Charleston, S.C.	11.0	6.7
Dayton, Ohio	9.7	8.3	Charlotte, N.C.	11.0	6.9
Newark, N.J.	9.6	10.3	Atlanta, Ga.	10.9	7.4
Detroit, Mich.	9.3	11.2	Fort Worth, Tex.	10.5	7.6
Cleveland, Ohio	8.8	9.8	Baltimore, Md.	10.4	9.6
Buffalo, N.Y.	7.9	10.1	Baton Rouge, La.	9.9	5.7
South			Washington, D.C.	9.6	7.2
Chattanooga, Tenn.	14.1	8.4	Jackson, Miss.	9.4	6.9
Louisville, Ky.	14.0	9.0	Houston, Tex.	8.8	6.8
Nashville, Tenn.	13.5	8.2	West		
Savannah, Ga.	13.4	8.1	Los Angeles-Long		
Winston-Salem, N.C.	12.6	6.6	Beach, Calif.	6.7	8.9
Macon, Ga.	12.3	7.0	San Francisco-		
Little Rock-North			Oakland, Calif.	6.3	9.7
Little Rock, Ark.	12.3	8.2			

was one of long standing, as may be seen in the comparative figures in Table 8-5.

In spite of the high death rates, the present state of Negro health shows marked improvement from earlier decades and the present rate compares more favorably than at any previous time with that of other populations. The mortality rates of both races are decreasing; in recent years the downward trend of the Negro rate has been abrupt. From 1910 to 1920 the decline in the registration areas was 22.7 per cent for the whites and 33.8 per cent for the Negroes.

In 1900 the general death rate of the Negro population of the registration areas was 29.4 per 1,000 population. In 1910 this had dropped to 25.5, a decrease of 3.9 per 1,000 population in the ten-year period. In 1930 the death rate dropped to 16.5, a decrease of 12.9 per 1,000 population in the thirty-year period. However, these figures may not be taken as an entirely accurate index of health improvement, since the registration areas at the three dates are not identical—the figures for 1910 and 1930 representing a much larger proportion of the Negro population. The improvement during the decades may have been greater or less than the improvement indicated by the decline in the registration areas. Also, the rate each year rep-

Table 8-5: DEATH RATES OF SELECTED COUNTRIES, 1910, 1920, 1930, AND 1966*

Country	1910	1920	1930	1966
Australia	10.4	10.5	8.6	9.0
The Netherlands	13.6	12.0	9.6	8.1
United States (white)	14.6	12.6	10.8	9.5
England and Wales	13.5	12.4	11.4	11.8[a]
Sweden	14.0	13.3	11.7	10.0
Switzerland	15.1	14.4	12.1	9.3
Scotland	15.3	14.0	13.3	....
France	17.8	17.2	15.6	10.7
United States (Negro)	25.5	17.7	16.5	9.7[b]
Spain	23.3	23.2	17.3	8.6
Japan	20.9	22.8[c]	18.2	6.8
Ceylon	27.3	29.6	22.1[d]	9.1 (1959)
Chile	31.1	30.8	24.7	10.7 (1965)

* Source: 1966 data taken from *Statistical Abstract of the United States*, 1969, Tables 69 and 1248
[a] Rate for United Kingdom
[b] Rate for nonwhite population
[c] (1919)
[d] (1931)

resents a population that was largely urban, so it probably exceeds the true rate for the Negro population as a whole.

The 1966 death rate (9.7) of the nonwhite people appears to be about that of the whites in 1950 (9.5). However, in 1930 the nonwhite rate of 16.5 was higher than the white death rate (14.6) in 1910. It is interesting to note that the 1932 nonwhite rate of 14.1 compared favorably with that of France (15.8), Italy (14.7), Spain (16.4), and various other relatively advanced countries. But the 1966 nonwhite death rate (9.7) compares favorably with that of such nations as Italy (9.3), the United Kingdom (11.8), Spain (8.6), and France (10.7).

A number of factors were operating favorably on the life and health conditions of the Negro race in the 1930's. There had been a considerable development of public health activities in southern sections of the country, and in this development the Negroes had shared both directly and indirectly. The economic status of many Negro groups had improved, with a consequent improvement in living conditions. Migration had operated to the same end—directly, by giving large numbers the advantage of the higher wages and the more advanced social, health, and educational conditions in the North; indirectly, by temporarily influencing the wage and labor conditions in the South and by stimulating efforts to improve the educational, sanitary, and general living conditions of the Negroes.

It is, however, easy to overemphasize the significance of certain figures. The very rapid decline in the Negro death rate prior to 1930 in Chicago,

Philadelphia, New York City, and other northern cities in the registration area has frequently been cited as disproving the general idea that the Negro people cannot survive in industrial competition in the colder regions. The decline was no doubt due in some part, perhaps in major part, to improvement in the economic status of the Negroes and to intensive health activities. But it is also well to remember that the very remarkable migration of Negroes in the past decades had brought into these northern cities a large number of young, active, and relatively healthy Negroes, and that the effect of this selective migration was reflected in the downward trend of the Negro rate in these cities. The gains in health, while they were marked and important, were perhaps less spectacular than a noncritical reading of the figures led many persons to believe.

THE AGE FACTOR IN NEGRO DEATHS

The death rate of infants and young children is an important item in the explanation of the excessively high death rate of the Negro people. Whether measured by absolute or relative standards, the rate has been high. In 1910, the number of deaths of male Negro children under one year of age for each 1,000 male Negro infants in the population was 280.3; the corresponding figure for the female infants was 243.2. That is to say that more than one-fourth of the Negro children born died within the first year of life.

At the present time, the rate for deaths under one year is much higher in the Negro than in the white group. In 1930, of each 1,000 deaths in the white population, 103 were of babies under one year; in the Negro population 130 of each 1,000 deaths were of babies under one year. The rate varies somewhat with different sections of the country being, in general, higher in the South than in the North. The rate also appears to be lower for the urban than for the rural parts of the population though very little dependable information is available for the most of the rural Negro population. Infant mortality seems to decline as the Negroes migrate to cities of the North and West where prenatal care and obstetrical work is better organized and open to Negroes. Everywhere the Negroes suffer excessively as compared with the whites. In 1910 the infant mortality rate for the registration area was over twice that of the white—261.6 for the Negroes and 129.7 for the whites. In 1931 the rates were 92.7 for the Negroes and 56.7 for the whites; in 1933 the corresponding rates were 85.4 and 52.8.

In spite of the very high rate prevailing in most places at the present time, it is a marked improvement over those of earlier years. In 1900 the infant Negro death rate was reported as 344.5 for each 1,000 of the Negro population under one year of age: the rate for male infants being 380, that for female infants 309.7. During the following decade there was remark-

Table 9-1: INFANT MORTALITY RATES, BY COLOR, BIRTH-REGISTRATION
STATES OR UNITED STATES, 1915–1966* †

Year	Total	White	Nonwhite
1915–19	95.7	92.8	149.7
1920–24	76.7	73.3	115.3
1925–29	69.0	65.0	105.4
1930–34	60.4	55.2	98.6
1935–39	53.2	49.2	81.3
1940–44	42.6	39.2	67.2
1945–49	33.5	31.3	49.8
1950–54	28.1	25.4	44.8
1955–59	26.4	23.4	43.7
1960	26.0	22.9	43.2
1961	25.3	22.4	40.7
1962	25.3	22.3	41.4
1963	25.2	22.2	41.5
1964	24.8	21.6	41.1
1965	24.7	21.5	40.3
1966	23.7	20.6	38.8

* Source: Dept. of Health, Education, and Welfare, *Vital Statistics of the United
States, 1964*, Vol. II, *Mortality*, Part A, Table 2-1; and U.S. Bureau of the Census,
Pocket Data Book U.S.A. 1969, Table 30
† Rate per 1,000 live births

able improvement. The decline was greater for the Negro than for the
white infants though at the end of the decade it was still greatly in excess
of the white rate. In 1910 the deaths per 1,000 population under one year
of age were 129.7 for the whites and 261.9 for the Negroes. In the earlier
decades the rates were even higher. In 1890 the figures show an infant mortality of 430.2 for New Orleans, 461.7 for Charleston, and 529.8 for Richmond. The corresponding rates for the white babies were 269.4 for New
Orleans, 200.4 for Charleston, and 186.9 for Richmond. The white infant
mortality in 1890 was thus far above the present Negro rate in many
places. The sharp downward trend is seen in the fact that the situation of
the Negroes in 1930 was better than that of the whites a decade earlier. In
1920, of each 1,000 deaths in the white population, 150 were of babies
under one year; in the Negro population, 173 of each 1,000 deaths were of
babies under one year.

The causes of the high infant rate for Negroes are in general the same
as those which account for a high infant rate in any group. The respiratory diseases such as pulmonary tuberculosis and pneumonia play a large
rôle and whooping cough appears to be particularly dangerous to Negro
infants. But the infant mortality is high in every group that lives under
social and economic conditions similar to those of the Negro population.
Poverty is the greatest enemy of babies: most infant deaths occur in fam-

ilies where the father's wage is low, where the mother goes out to work, where poverty compels the group to live in alley houses or rear tenements. The causes are, of course, the ignorance of child care and the inability to provide adequate care which go with poverty rather than the poverty itself; mortality and morbidity rates may be greatly reduced without great change in wages or housing conditions.

Rickets, which is so nearly universal among Negro city infants, illustrates how poverty, combined with ignorance, affects the health conditions. It is generally estimated that seventy-five per cent of all children suffer from this disease during the first two years of life. The Negro rate is higher than the white; it is estimated that fully ninety per cent of Negro children in New York City suffer from the disease in infancy. In 1931, there were 138 Negro deaths from rickets, and 143 in 1930. It is probable that the Negro child in the northern cities is peculiarly susceptible to rickets. But the chief cause lies in the poor environment of the child—the improper diet and the absence of sunlight. The disease, even when not extreme, permanently affects the bone structure causing flat feet, chest deformities, and other defects. As a result the person goes through life less able to resist disease and particularly prone to such respiratory troubles as pneumonia and pulmonary tuberculosis. It is possible that there is some direct causal relation between this childhood disease and the respiratory diseases from which the young Negroes suffer so excessively. The marked decline in recent decades of the Negro general death rate discussed above has been due in large part to the wider economic opportunities of the Negro with a consequent improvement in housing and living conditions, and to more drastic public health measures bringing tuberculosis and other diseases somewhat under control. The decline has been due chiefly to the reduction in the mortality of children under fifteen years, the period at which the proportion of Negro deaths is highest in comparison with the white.

The experience of New York City indicates what may be done by community effort to lessen the destruction of Negro child life. In 1915 an investigation was made of Negro infant mortality. In one section of the city where incomes were smallest and where the percentage of lodgers was largest and overcrowding in consequence greatest, and where the largest percentage of mothers was employed, the infant mortality was 314 per 1,000. The Negro rate for the entire city was 202 per 1,000 and that for the whites was 96 per 1,000. As a result of the investigation a health improvement campaign was organized and participated in by the Health Department, the schools, and various social welfare and other agencies. In two years the Negro infant mortality of the city fell from 202 per 1,000 to 173 per 1,000 a decline of 29 points. In 1919 the rate had fallen to 151 per 1,000. In the following year the Negro infant mortality in the district which in 1915 had a rate of 314 per 1,000 was lower than the white rate in the same district.

The declines in infant mortality in New York City from 1929 to 1933 are shown in Table 9-2.

Table 9-2: DEATHS UNDER ONE YEAR OF AGE PER 1,000 LIVE BIRTHS IN NEW YORK CITY, 1929–1933

Years	Total	White	Colored
1929	58.9	55.7	111.0
1930	57.8	54.9	104.8
1931	55.7	52.4	105.6
1932	50.8	48.0	92.6
1933	53.0	50.0	94.8

The death rate of Negro babies is also excessively high in the early childhood years. In 1930, of each 1,000 deaths in the white group 35 were of babies from one to four years; the corresponding figure in the Negro population was 45. Thirty-four years later the corresponding figures for white and Negro population were only 7 for white and 18 for Negro babies one to four years old.

In the following five-year period, the chances of death are the same in the Negro and white populations: 17 of each 1,000 deaths are in the age-group five to nine years. In the following age-groups the Negroes again show relatively high numbers of deaths, the greatest divergence appearing in the 15- to 19-year period when the number of Negro deaths is over twice that of the white.

The comparative Negro and white deaths at different ages are shown in Table 9-3.

NEGRO MORTALITY BY CAUSE OF DEATH

The death rate of the Negro people when examined from the viewpoint of the cause of death seems to show some peculiar health problems. Some diseases appear to be common to both racial elements in about the same degree. In the case of typhoid fever and malaria the Negroes appear to be less susceptible than the whites and a similar thing is true in regard to measles, smallpox, and certain other diseases. The cancer rate relatively is very low. But in the case of other diseases they have a decidedly higher mortality rate. They suffer excessively from diseases of the lungs and pleura and of the digestive tract. Heart disease, Brights' disease, and other chronic diseases cause relatively many more deaths among colored than among white persons of the same economic classes.

Table 9-3: NEGRO AND WHITE DEATHS IN THE REGISTRATION AREA OF THE
UNITED STATES, BY AGE GROUPS, 1920, 1930, AND 1964*

Age Groups	1920 White	1920 Negro	1930 White	1930 Negro	1964 White	1964 Negro
All Ages	1,000	1,000	1,000	1,000	1,000	1,000
Under 1 year	150	173	103	130	46	123
1 to 4 years	64	70	35	45	7	18
5 to 9 years	24	24	17	17	5	8
10 to 14 years	16	23	12	17	4	6
15 to 19 years	25	49	20	42	8	11
20 to 24 years	34	71	26	59	8	14
25 to 29 years	41	65	26	59	7	17
30 to 34 years	42	57	28	58	9	23
35 to 39 years	43	67	36	67	14	34
40 to 44 years	40	55	42	68	23	46
45 to 49 years	44	58	50	75	34	55
50 to 54 years	50	55	60	80	50	75
55 to 59 years	56	40	69	62	67	83
60 to 64 years	67	41	84	57	86	106
65 to 69 years	71	38	93	46	110	107
70 to 89 years	222	96	284	101	478	252
90 and over	11	15	13	14	43	21
Unknown	1	5	1	4	1	1

* Source: Dept. of Health, Education, and Welfare, *Vital Statistics of the United States, 1964*, Vol. II, *Mortality*, Part A. 1964 data computed from Table 1-25

The death rate by classes of diseases at the present time shows characteristic differences between the racial groups. The figures for a few important causes of death, in which the rates are sharply different among the races, are given in the following table. The rates shown in Tables 10-1A and 10-1B are for the white and nonwhite, not exclusively Negro.

It is evident from these figures that there are important differences between the races in susceptibility to disease, or in the liability to fatal results.

Table 10-1A: DEATH RATES PER 100,000 POPULATION BY
SPECIFIED CAUSES, 1932

Causes of Death	White	Nonwhite
All causes	1,070.8	1,431.0
Infectious and parasitic diseases	105.5	318.6
Cancer and other tumors	117.5	71.7
Diseases of the circulatory system	265.3	235.3
Diseases of the respiratory system	83.8	143.0
Diseases of the digestive system	69.8	89.6
Violent and accidental	96.6	119.0
Ill-defined	6.6	64.4

Table 10-1B: DEATH RATES AND AGE-ADJUSTED DEATH RATES PER 100,000
POPULATION FOR SELECTED CAUSES, BY COLOR, 1964*

| | White | | Nonwhite | |
Causes of Death	Death Rate	Age-Adjusted Death Rate	Death Rate	Age-Adjusted Death Rate
All Causes	935.5	706.8	971.6	1,031.1
Major cardiovascular-renal diseases	523.7	370.3	444.8	504.1
Malignant neoplasms, including neoplasms of lymphatic and hemato-poietic tissues	154.9	124.5	124.8	145.6
Accidents	52.8	49.9	65.2	68.4
Influenza and pneumonia, except pneumonia of newborn	29.1	20.3	45.8	40.8
Diabetes mellitus	16.4	12.5	20.1	23.6
Cirrhosis of liver	12.1	10.9	12.5	15.2
Tuberculosis, all forms	3.6	3.0	9.8	11.5

* Source: Dept. of Health, Education, and Welfare, *Vital Statistics of the United States, 1964*, Vol. II, *Mortality*, Part A, Tables 1-7 and 1-9

The relative importances of various specific diseases in the Negro death rate is indicated in Table 10-2, which gives the total Negro deaths in 1931 and 1964 and the number of deaths from a few of the more important causes.

It is evident from these data that tuberculosis is a major cause of death

Table 10-2: NEGRO DEATHS BY IMPORTANT CAUSES,
REGISTRATION AREA, 1931 AND 1964*

| | Number of Deaths | |
Causes of Death	1931	1964
Total deaths	174,023	209,065
Tuberculosis, all forms	20,683	14,358
Pneumonia	15,040	9,495
Chronic nephritis	11,246	2,404†
Cerebral hemorrhage	10,263	15,164
Cancer and other malignant tumors	6,528	26,839
Influenza	5,558	264
Syphilis	4,657	707
Pellagra	2,832	8
Diabetes mellitus	1,465	4,312
Malaria	1,195	.....

* Source: 1964 data Dept. of Health, Education, and Welfare, *Vital Statistics of the United States, 1964*, Vol. II, *Mortality*, Part A, Table 1-25
† Includes unspecified nephritis and other renal sclerosis

in the Negro population. The various types of tuberculosis and the various forms of pneumonia accounted for nearly one-fifth of all Negro deaths in 1931. The tubercular death rate has fallen sharply in the recent decades; in 1910, about one-fifth of the Negro deaths were from this cause. It is still a scourge, especially in the younger age groups.

Table 10-3: DEATH RATES FROM TUBERCULOSIS OF THE RESPIRATORY SYSTEM BY SELECTED STATES, 1920, 1930, AND 1960*

State	1920 White	1920 Nonwhite	1930 White	1930 Nonwhite	1960 White	1960 Nonwhite
Florida	56.9	158.4	38.2	123.0	3.3	10.3
Kentucky	111.5	309.9	73.7	198.7	10.0	20.2
Louisiana	72.6	211.9	48.3	128.2	7.0	11.8
Maryland	96.5	271.4	62.1	220.9	6.6	18.6
Mississippi	43.8	189.0	35.1	128.5	4.5	9.6
North Carolina	73.0	171.4	45.5	129.3	3.0	8.4
South Carolina	57.7	155.8	33.5	119.9	4.0	9.0
Tennessee	110.2	260.4	78.7	228.9	6.0	13.4
Virginia	82.0	225.6	53.9	164.2	4.3	13.9

* Source: 1960 data, Dept. of Health, Education, and Welfare, *Vital Statistics of the United States, 1960*, Vol. II, *Mortality*, Part B, Table 9-6; and *Statistical Abstract of the United States*, 1969, Table 28

The tubercular death rates vary sharply in different sections of the country and at different dates. In 1921, for example, the rate in Pennsylvania was 83.3 for the white and 330.0 for the nonwhite population, chiefly Negro. The rates for Negroes and whites in 1920 and 1930 in selected states are given in Table 10-3.

It is evident from these figures, taken at their face value, that the tubercular death rate varies enormously from state to state.

In certain states the general rate is over twice that of others: in 1931, the rate was in Nebraska 22, in Iowa 26, and in Kansas 32; the rate was in Tennessee 98, in Virginia 83, and in Delaware 80. In all cases the rates for both the white and nonwhite populations were lower—in most cases very much lower—in 1930 than in 1920. In every case the rate for the nonwhite population was very much higher than the rate for the white population—in general about three times the white rate. Approximately the same differential prevailed in 1930 as in 1920.

The comparative death rates from tuberculosis are shown in Table 10-4 for a few selected cities for 1920 and 1930.

These data show the tubercular death rates of the nonwhite populations of urban centers, as in the state populations, to be far in excess of the white rates. A comparison of the two tables is enlightening. In some cases,

Table 10-4: DEATH RATES FROM TUBERCULOSIS OF THE RESPIRATORY SYSTEM BY
SELECTED LARGE CITIES, 1920 AND 1930

City	1920 White	1920 Nonwhite	1930 White	1930 Nonwhite
Atlanta, Ga.	67.4	125.0	36.5	153.3
Baltimore, Md.	97.9	285.4	58.4	218.1
Birmingham, Ala.	46.8	259.6	26.6	172.3
Chattanooga, Tenn.	96.2	300.3	68.0	225.2
Cincinnati, Ohio	112.7	380.3	55.5	317.5
Columbus, Ohio	73.1	258.7	46.1	144.6
Dallas, Tex.	55.6	287.3	32.6	130.8
Houston, Tex.	66.0	176.4	44.3	150.5
Indianapolis, Ind.	81.1	295.2	51.7	173.8
Jacksonville, Fla.	58.8	240.9	51.3	236.5
Kansas City, Kan.	75.9	143.0	44.4	170.3
Kansas City, Mo.	68.7	361.1	49.0	310.4
Knoxville, Tenn.	119.8	146.7	46.0	115.6
Louisville, Ky.	90.1	219.3	38.0	170.5
Memphis, Tenn.	87.1	259.9	54.1	236.3
Miami, Fla.	53.2	239.3	42.0	166.7
Nashville, Tenn.	105.7	308.5	53.0	223.8
New Orleans, La.	144.4	316.4	91.8	230.8
Norfolk, Va.	80.7	261.9	23.4	151.6
Philadelphia, Pa.	100.3	291.1	53.0	232.3
Richmond, Va.	94.8	203.5	47.6	158.5
Saint Louis, Mo.	68.8	249.1	35.3	251.8
Tampa, Fla.	84.9	227.2	62.2	111.6
Washington, D.C.	74.3	215.6	54.6	227.8
Wilmington, Del.	74.6	212.0	33.9	107.1

the urban rates are higher and in other cases lower than the state rates. In 1930, for example, the white rate for Florida was given as 38.2, that for Miami was given as 42.0, the nonwhite rate for the state was given as 123.0, that of Miami was given as 166.7. The rate for Kentucky was reported as 73.7 for the white and 198.7 for the nonwhite; the rate for Louisville was reported as 38 for the white and 170.5 for the nonwhite. In Louisiana, the rates for both white and nonwhite are much higher in New Orleans than in the state as a whole. The white rate for the state is 48.3, the nonwhite rate is 128.2; the white rate for New Orleans is 91.8, the nonwhite rate is 230.8. In Virginia the white rate for the state is 53.9, the rate for Richmond is 47.6; the nonwhite rate for the state is 164.2; the rate for Richmond is 158.5.

The variations from state to state, from city to city, and from urban centers to general populations make it abundantly clear that high tubercular death rates are an unnecessary if not a willful destruction of human life. The nonwhite rates, often two, three, or four times the white rates in the same state or city, measure for the most part the popular indifference to Negro life and health. In most of the states and cities listed in the two tables, a minimum of attention to Negro health would reduce the tubercular death rates to one-half or one-third of the present rates.

Death rates from tuberculosis for both whites and nonwhites have continued to decline sharply through the 1960's, though the nonwhite rate is approximately three times higher than the white rate. The prospect for the continued decline of tubercular deaths is bright in view of the fact that a greater emphasis is now given to public health programs for early detection and treatment.

It is possible of course, that the Negroes may be racially more prone to tuberculosis and to diseases of the respiratory system than are the whites and that their death rates may in consequence remain relatively high, but the prevailing rates are an index of living conditions rather than a measure of racial vitality.

Certain other specific diseases were more widespread and destructive among the Negroes than among the whites in the 1930's. The venereal diseases were very widespread and important in the sickness and death rates. Until recently in their racial history the Negroes seemed to have been relatively free from syphilis, and the disease was in consequence very severe. It appeared to spread rapidly, and the death rate increased. Of the total of 174,023 Negro deaths in 1931, some 4,657—2.7 per cent—were reported as due to syphilis. The disease was very imperfectly reported but the data indicated that infection among Negroes was perhaps five times the rate among the whites. Following public health and medical advances, relatively few deaths were attributed to syphilis in 1964: 1,889 for whites—a rate of 1.6 per 100,000 population for males and 0.6 for females—and 730 for nonwhites—a rate of 4.4 for males and 2.1 for females.

The maternal mortality rate is high among the Negroes, and particularly high among the young Negro mothers. In 1931 there were 2,634 deaths of Negro women from diseases of pregnancy, childbirth, and the puerperal state, and in 1964 there were 570 such deaths among Negro mothers. The death rate from these causes was more than double the rate among the whites in 1930 and almost three and a half times greater in 1964. The deaths from these causes would be reduced to a fraction of the present number by providing adequate medical and nursing care.

In the case of other important diseases the Negro death rates are below the white rates. Cancer and other malignant tumors, for example, appeared to be only about half as frequent in the Negro as in the white populations in 1930, but the rates have increased so that in 1964 the white rate was 154.9 per 100,000 population and the nonwhite rate was 145.6.

Table 10-5: MATERNAL MORTALITY RATES IN SELECTED YEARS BY COLOR,
BIRTH-REGISTRATION STATES OR UNITED STATES, 1915–1966* a

Year	Total	White	Nonwhite
1915–19	727.9	700.3	1,253.5
1930–34b	636.0	575.0	1,080.7
1945	207.2	172.1	454.8
1950	83.3	61.1	221.6
1955	47.0	32.8	130.3
1960	37.1	26.0	97.9
1961	36.9	24.9	101.3
1962c	35.2	23.8	95.9
1963c	35.8	24.0	96.9
1965	33.3	22.3	89.9
1966	29.1	20.2	72.4

* Source: Dept. of Health, Education, and Welfare, *Vital Statistics of the United States, 1964*, Vol. II, *Mortality*, Part A, Table 1-16
a Rate per 100,000 live births
b For 1932–34 Mexicans are included in Nonwhite category
c Figures by color exclude data for residents of New Jersey

IMMUNITY AND SUSCEPTIBILITY TO DISEASE

When attention is turned from the fact of the high Negro mortality to its causes, the question at once arises, To what extent are the observed conditions explainable in racial terms, and to what extent in environmental terms? Is the high death rate indicative of a lesser degree of vitality and disease resistance in this element of the population or is it simply an expression of the lower economic status and the poorer living conditions?

In the 1930's general opinion was doubtless to the effect that the Negro people were constitutionally weak and that the race was peculiarly prone to disease. If this be the case, the high death rate cannot be brought under complete control and probably cannot be materially reduced—the weakness bearing no essential relation to the environment over which human agencies can exercise control. This position appears to be, for the most part, a naive inference drawn directly from the fact of the high death rate itself. Even when more labored it is perhaps not more valuable; the nature of the data upon which any statistical argument, in the last analysis, rests has been indicated. Many other persons of opposite opinion assert or assume that racial differences are negligible and that the difference in mortality rates is virtually a measure of environmental difference.

There is even some evidence for the position that the Negroes under equally favorable environmental conditions would show a lower rate of mortality than the whites.

A general dogmatic position is scarcely justified, considering the present state of knowledge on the subject. The biological and environmental factors do not operate separately and may not be segregated by statistical methods. The problem has not been at all adequately approached on the qualitative side. But there is no doubt that the Negro mortality and morbidity rates could be easily and greatly reduced.

Factors Involved in Negro Mortality

The Negro people appear to be characterized by a high resistance to particular local diseases and by a high susceptibility to others. The relatively great differences in mortality that prevail between the races in the American environment are in part the result of particular diseases. This difference is to be expected.

A high immunity to a certain disease is the result of racial experience, natural forces having operated through a selective mortality to eliminate the more susceptible. In the case of certain diseases the Negroes have been free for generations, perhaps for their entire racial history, and as a consequence they have never acquired or have not maintained an immunity. A similar statement would hold for any racial group. All peoples appear to experience difficulty in becoming acclimated to environments radically different from those to which their race is adjusted. The white race appears not to have learned to live in the tropics. The American Indians had only slight immunity to measles and died in great numbers from the disease in the early decades of their contact with the European settlers. It is to be expected that the Negro would have some difficulty in meeting the health requirements of a temperate zone.

The high resistance that the Negroes show to certain other diseases is subject to a similar explanation. As a result of a biological adaptation to a peculiar environment, they have, like other acclimated races, developed an innate character fitting them to cope with the rigors of that environment. The high resistance to certain diseases may very well be the selective result of an age-long struggle with the microorganisms of the tropics, just as the skin color may be an environmental adaptation, a racial uniform, protecting the organism against the injurious actinic rays of the tropic sun, and as the high degree of fertility which seems to characterize the race may represent a character acquired by selection operating in the interest of racial survival in a difficult environmental situation.

But the fact of a difference between races in the degree of immunity to specific diseases may be the present expression of unlike historic experience and racial in the popular sense only. It need not be an expression of a peculiar germinal constitution due to mutational change; it may be merely a difference in the percentages of individuals in the two groups that enjoy an immunity. A high death rate of the North Europeans in the tropics is not, of itself, proof of the biological weakness of the white race. The susceptibility to tropical diseases may be due to the historic fact that the white groups have had little racial experience with the diseases peculiar to these regions and have not acquired an immunity to them. This lack of experience is an historical and not a racial or biological fact but, as a result of it, their death rate in the tropics may be far in excess of that of the native peoples living in similar circumstances. But there is apparently no reason to believe that it would be impossible for Europeans to become acclimated to a tropical environment and develop an immunity to tropical diseases. Acclimatization through historic experience does not mean that hereditary traits are modified; it means that the percentage of individuals having certain traits is increased. The same type of statement holds true for the Negroes in a temperate climate and exposed to diseases foreign to their racial experience. In either case, if the race be given a little time—a few generations—an immunity will be established, or re-established, and susceptibility to attacks of the disease will fall to the level characteristic of acclimated groups.

To make a case for the position that different degrees of immunity or susceptibility to disease are racial, that is, biological, it would be necessary to show, not only that under equally favorable external conditions the individuals of one race contract the disease more readily or suffer more severely from the effects of infection than do individuals of another, or die in a larger percentage of cases from its attack, but also to show that the members of the group always contract the disease on exposure, or always suffer excessively from its attacks, or always succumb from the effects of its attacks, and that the germinal constitution of the race is such that it lacks the capacity to build up an immunity through the selective effects of long exposure to the disease. If there were no possibility of the race acquiring an immunity through the selective effects of long exposure, because of racially peculiar innate characteristics, the fact would be properly racial and the only hope for the race would lie in its complete and permanent isolation from infection or in the disappearance of the disease through evolutionary changes in the infecting microorganism which would destroy or materially modify the virulence of the disease. But if there are individual differences in the susceptibility to infection or in the seriousness of the attacks, or in the liability to death from its attacks, there exists in the racial constitution the power to acquire a more and more complete immunity through a more extended process of selection, and the difference between this group and groups that have acquired relative immunity is that the one group has already passed through a selective process that the other is now undergoing. The difference is thus not one of unalterable racial nature; it is a statistical difference due to historic experience. One group has had more experience with the disease than has the other and consequently, at the present racial moment, there is less destruction in the one group than there is in the other. It is thus clear that race as such has nothing to do with the theoretical situation. Any two groups of exactly the same biological characteristics and racial ancestry would show similar relative differences in immunity to specific diseases if one had through a series of generations been exposed to its selective effects and the other isolated from the ravages of its attacks.

This, of course, is not to deny that there may be differences in disease susceptibility or immunity that are more accurately designated as racial. The Negroes may lack as a mark of their racial separateness, characteristics that other racial stocks possess and may not be able to acquire them by similar racial experience but may acquire them only through the biological process of racial fusion. The Negro is possessed of a thick, tough, active, and highly pigmented skin. This valuable body covering seems to account for his relative immunity to certain diseases communicated through the bites or stings of insects, either because of the mechanical protection it affords or because of the chemical effects of its profuse secretions on the microorganisms responsible for the diseases. If this racial uniform is the result of biological mutation, not the product of environmental adaptation, and hence not to be acquired by other racial groups except through the biological process of racial fusion, the disease immunity consequent upon its possession is truly racial. But if the same covering may be acquired by any racial stock exposed to the selective effects of a tropical habitat, the immunity it gives must be classed as an environmental adaptation rather than as a mutation. The bodily frame-work of the Negroes is characterized by a peculiarly narrow chest which may or may not account in part for their high tubercular mortality rate. If this or other character peculiar to the Negroes is the explanation of the high mortality resulting from tubercular infection, and if this lung capacity may be increased only by the Negroes ceasing to be Negroes through biological mutation or fusion with other racial types and selective processes operating to the establishment of a new type not characterized by the bodily structure in question, the susceptibility to diseases of the lungs and pleura may be rightly classed as racial. But if this or other peculiarity is the result of previous conditions of racial life and may undergo change in a changed environment, or if the Negroes may develop, through a period of exposure to the disease, an immunity to infection as other races appear to have done, their present high mortality rate from this cause is an accident of their historic experience, so far as it is not the expression of the immediate sanitary and nutritional situation.

The various factors involved in the question of relative racial health appear most clearly perhaps in the case of cancer. This disease appears not to be contagious, so the question of an acquired immunity does not arise. The disease is not curable, hence a differential treatment is not an item of importance in the death rate. So any racial differences should appear with clearness and certainty. It is frequently alleged that the white race is peculiarly prone to the disease. In the United States the death rate for the whites in 1932 was 112.6, that for the colored, chiefly Negroes, was 64.5. It would thus appear that the white race is more susceptible than the Negro race. But when the cancer rate is studied from the point of view of the distribution of the disease it is found to fall rapidly from the North to the South. This would indicate that there is a relation between the disease and latitude. If a comparison be made by occupations it is found that cancer is of greater relative frequency in some than in others. Poverty is another factor of very great importance as may be illustrated by the comparative rates of Austria and Hungary. There is no difference in race and no essential difference in climatic conditions, yet the Austrian rate is approximately twice the rate for Hungary. But there is a great difference in cultural development; Austria is superior to Hungary in wealth, education, and the degree of medical development. This has a two-fold effect on the cancer death rate. In the more backward country a larger percentage of persons die without adequate medical attention and without having the cause of their death properly diagnosed. Also, the poorer country has a higher general death rate and a higher rate of infant mortality and consequently there are fewer persons to die of cancer and other diseases of old age. It would appear then that the higher cancer death rate of Austria is a function of the older population; civilization tends to raise the cancer rate by increasing the age of the population. A similar thing appears in the case of the Negroes: the rate in South Africa is given as 14, that for the Negroes in the United States as 64.5. In the United States the rate increases for Negroes and the whites remain parallel, each rising as we go from the South toward the North. The Negro rate remains lower in all cases. The explanation appears to be not that the Negroes are immune to the disease in any greater degree than the white, but they are economically depressed and so have poorer health, less medical care, inferior diagnosis, live in lower latitudes, and in rural regions. It is such facts as these that appear to account for the racial differences in the cancer mortality rates. If they do not account for the differences in their entirety, they do show that the cause is overwhelmingly environmental. It appears to be highly doubtful if racial heredity enters at all as a causal factor.

In the case of other diseases which are more directly and obviously influenced by environmental conditions it is still more hazardous to assert that racial heredity plays any considerable part in the comparative death rates.

IMPROVEMENT OF NEGRO HEALTH CONDITIONS

While some part of the excessive mortality among the Negro population may be the result of inherent constitutional weakness of the race and so not subject to control, this does not provide a complete and adequate explanation of the health situation. Nor does the recognition of certain constitutional weaknesses of the Negro people give reason for assuming that the differences in the mortality rates are natural differences in the sense that they would persist should the social and economic conditions of the racial group improve. The probability is always that any differential mortality is explainable in environmental terms unless the determining influence of the natural and racial factor is demonstrated. In the present case the only reasonable and practical point of view is that the environment is the dominating factor and, in the absence of proof to the contrary, it is necessary to assume that the racial differences in mortality would largely disappear with improvement in social, economic, and hygenic conditions.

The poverty of the Negroes with all of its attendant circumstances appears to be the major factor in the health situation. The Negroes are typically unskilled laborers. This type of work frequently involves exposure and over-exertion which increase the sickness, disability, and death rates. Poverty makes it very generally necessary that the mothers work away from home with results disastrous to the proper care and feeding of children. In sickness, adequate medical attention is the exception rather than the rule. Hospitals are few, overcrowded, and beyond the financial means of any save the exceptional family.

The Negroes normally live under the most miserable health conditions that the community tolerates. In nearly every case the Negro sections are the meaner and less desirable parts of the city. In part they are driven to these sections by restrictions upon their place of residence, and in part they are attracted to them by the relative cheapness of rent and real estate. But whether the cause be poverty or prejudice, the neighborhoods in which they chiefly live are the least sanitary which the cities afford. In the rural regions the conditions are often not superior to those of the towns. Among the uneducated and poor there is an improper disposal of waste material and the soil and water supply are frequently polluted.

Some part of the high death rate must certainly be laid to the general ignorance of the Negroes. They are commonly uninformed concerning even the simpler rules of health, and heedless of sanitation and personal hygiene. In the rural regions there is no school inspection and epidemic and contagious diseases spread, and the spread is facilitated by the highly social disposition of the Negroes. There is little knowledge of child care and children perhaps generally receive improperly prepared and unwholesome food. The general absence of well-cooked food throughout the South particularly affects the Negroes; they live in innumerable cases on scraps.

The social and sanitary conditions resulting from the poverty and ignorance of the mass of the Negro people is an element in explanation of the high death rate. The unvarying relation which obtains between the diseases that kill the most Negroes and the conditions under which they must live has led many students of Negro health to the conclusion that the social and environmental conditions are chiefly responsible for their bad health record.

Organized efforts to improve the living conditions, and so the health standards of the population, have been slow to reach the mass of Negroes. As in most other things, they have been among the last groups to receive the benefits of the public health movement. Until recently few organizations have been interested in the health of the race; the first conscious definite efforts extend back little more than the 1920's. But the success that has attended the initial efforts has been most encouraging and enough has been accomplished to justify the conviction of workers that further improvement is possible.

In 1914, Booker T. Washington initiated a health education movement through the Negro Business League. In this movement the National Urban League presently joined and in later years various other health and social organizations have co-operated. At present a very large number of organizations are carrying on an active health propaganda among the Negroes in the effort to spread elementary information in regard to personal cleanliness and sanitary surroundings in their relation to the control of disease. There is also an increasing amount of medical and sanitary work being done and this results directly in health improvement.

The recent migratory movement of the Negroes has reacted and will perhaps continue to react favorably on the health conditions. The higher wage and the better opportunities to advance have been reflected in a lower infant and general mortality rate. It has also brought many individuals and families into a more sanitary environment and within the reach of medical and hospital care. The movement also promises to improve the wage scale as well as the living conditions and educational facilities of the South and so to lower the sickness and death rates.

There is a rather rapid extension of general education throughout the southern sections of the country. Poor community health is in large part the direct result of community ignorance. As education spreads there is a growing recognition on the part of both races of the value of public health. The Negroes are coming to realize the need and are making efforts to increase their health standards. And the white leaders are realizing the interdependence of the races, that there is no way to protect the educated and the white and at the same time to neglect the ignorant and the black. The health question is national, not racial. Any effort to divide the problem and make Negro health a separate issue is more and more recognized as an unworkable program. Good community health is purchasable but the daily touch of the races is such that any effective white program cannot ignore the Negro.

There are, however, certain obstacles to be overcome before health conditions can greatly improve. The masses of the Negroes, particularly the rural Negroes, are densely ignorant and with ignorance go various superstitions. The poverty of the group stands in the way of health; unable to afford medical and hospital service, they depend upon druggists and patent medicines. It is reported that four out of each five Negro deaths in Savannah, Georgia, in 1908 were not attended by a physician. The health facilities are wholly inadequate. In 1930 there was one physician or surgeon for 3,125 Negro inhabitants and one trained nurse for 2,076 Negro inhabitants. But the physicians and nurses are very poorly distributed in relation to the Negro population. The distribution is indicated in Table 11-1, which gives the number of Negroes for each Negro physician or surgeon and for each trained nurse in the sections of the country and in selected states.

Table 11-1: AVERAGE NUMBER OF NEGROES PER NEGRO PHYSICIAN AND PROFESSIONAL NURSE, 1930 AND 1960*

| | Average Number of Negroes Per | | | |
| | Physician | | Professional Nurse | |
Section and State	1930	1960	1930	1960
United States	3,125	4,005	2,076	588
The North	1,582	2,519	1,231	374
The South	4,286	6,614	2,567	999
The West	1,228	2,504	971	312
Colorado	910		2,366	
Illinois	994		1,241	
New Mexico	950		1,425	
New York	1,966		536	
Maryland	2,764		1,738	
District of Columbia	691		763	
Virginia	3,964		1,826	
Georgia	5,550		1,800	
Alabama	8,145		2,304	
Mississippi	14,221		8,078	
Louisiana	7,255		4,913	

* Source: 1960 figures were computed from *U.S. Census of Population, 1960, Nonwhite Population by Race*, Tables 1 and 50; and *U.S. Census of Population, 1960, United States Summary*, Table 257

Of the 119 hospitals and sanitariums for Negroes in 1920, perhaps half a dozen were adequately manned and equipped. The poverty-stricken nature of community life in the South makes the spread of health information difficult. Tenant houses are widely scattered, villages are few, communication is poor, the population shifting, and the scattered and poorly equipped schools and churches are the only rural institutions. There is a lack of organization for spreading health information. The churches and schools are the only starting points. But the preachers are typically ignorant and generally indifferent, except to the extent that co-operation brings personal glory, and the teachers are generally untrained.

There is a very general indifference to Negro health. In some part this is an outcome of the general belief that the poor health of the Negro is the result of constitutional weakness of the race.

There is, however, consciously or unconsciously a sinister aspect of much of the white indifference to improving Negro health or lowering the Negro death rate. The fecundity of the Negro people is very great. In spite of the high death rate their increase has been approximately as rapid as the natural increase of the whites. There is a possibility that the natural increase of the race would very greatly exceed that of the whites should the forces that have operated to retard it be brought under control. An effective health program that would jeopardize white control of large sections of the country by allowing a disproportionate increase of the Negroes will meet indifference or opposition from many whites to the extent that its racial significance is understood. The whites will not enthusiastically nor for long support a program that will in the end mean their own elimination. Southern white support of an effective Negro health program is contingent upon assurance that Negro fecundity will also be brought under control; to expect it without such assurance is fanciful. No one thing would do more perhaps to assure active and effective support to a health program than would a drop in the Negro birth rate—through a spread of birth control information—to a point where the southern white fear of Negro domination would be allayed. However, there appears some reason to anticipate continued improvement in the health conditions of the Negroes. Their death rate has declined and their health improved in spite of the partial and inadequate community facilities. It may be further reduced as the community desires its reduction.

Census Bureau, *Negro Population in the United States, 1790–1915*, "Mortality in the Registration Area," pp. 298–312.

Census Bureau, *Negroes in the United States, 1920–1932*, "Vital Statistics—Mortality," pp. 443–493.

Chicago Commission on Race Relations, *The Negro in Chicago*, "The Negro Housing Problem," pp. 152–320.

Clark, C., *The Control of Syphilis in Southern Rural Areas.*

Dublin, L. I., "Effect of Health Education on Negro Mortality as Shown by the Metropolitan Life Insurance Company's Figures," *Proceedings, National Conference of Social Work*, 1924: 274–279. Also, *Opportunity*, 2(1924), 232–234.

Gover, Mary, and Sydenstricker, Edgar, *Mortality Among Negroes in the United States.*

Hoffman, F. L., *Race Traits and Tendencies of the American Negro.*

Johnson, C. S., *The Negro in American Civilization*, pp. 132–198.

Jones, S. B., "Fifty Years of Negro Public Health," *Annals of the American Academy of Political and Social Science*, 49(1913), 138–146.

Love, A. C., and Davenport, C. B., "A Comparison of White and Negro Troops in Respect to Incidence of Disease," *Proceedings, National Academy of Science*, 1919.

Pearl, Raymond, "Biological Factors in Negro Mortality," *Human Biology*, 1(1929), 229–249.

Stoughton, Amanda L., and Gover, Mary, *A Study of Negro Infant Mortality.*

Transactions, National Tuberculosis Association, 1920, "Tuberculosis Among Negroes," pp. 226–233.

Weatherford, W. D., and Johnson, C. S., *Race Relations*, "Health of the Negro," pp. 368–382.

Woodbury, R. M., *Infant Mortality and Its Causes.*

Woofter, T. J., *The Basis of Racial Adjustment*, "Health," pp. 57–74.

FURTHER READINGS

Baumgartner, Leona, "Health and Race in the Sixties," *American Journal of Public Health*, April 1965.

Bogue, Donald J.; Misra, Bhaskar D.; and Dandekar, D. P., "A New Estimate of Negro Population and Negro Vital Rates in the United States, 1930–60," *Demography*, 1.1(1965), 339–358.

Frazier, E. Franklin, *The Negro in the United States*, rev. ed., Ch. XXII. New York: Macmillan, 1949.

Goldstein, Marcus S., "Longevity and Health Status of the Negro American," *Journal of Negro Education*, 32(Fall 1963), 337–348.

Holmes, S. J., *The Negro's Struggle for Survival*. Berkeley, Calif.: University of California Press, 1937.

Hunt, Eleanor P., and Huyck, Earl E., "Mortality of White and Nonwhite Infants in Major U.S. Cities," *Health, Education, and Welfare Indicators* (January 1966), 23–41.

Huyck, Earl E., "White-Nonwhite Differentials: Overview and Implications," *Demography*, 3:2(1966), 548–565.

Malzberg, Benjamin, "Mental Disease Among American Negroes: A Statistical Analysis," in Klineberg, Otto, ed., *Characteristics of the American Negro*. New York: Harper, 1944.

Myrdal, Gunnar, *An American Dilemma*, Ch. 7. New York: Harper, 1944.

National Office of Vital Statistics, *Death Rates for Selected Causes by Age, Color, and Sex: United States and Each State, 1949–1951*. Washington, D.C.: U.S. Government Printing Office, 1959.

Parker, Seymour, and Kleiner, Robert J., *Mental Illness in the Urban Negro Community*. New York: Free Press, 1966.

Pettigrew, Ann Hallman, and Pettigrew, Thomas F., "Race, Diseases, and Desegregation: A New Look," *Phylon*, 24(Fall 1963), 315–333.

U.S. Department of Health, Education, and Welfare, "White-Nonwhite Differentials in Health, Education, and Welfare," *Health, Education and Welfare Indicators*. Washington, D.C.: U.S. Government Printing Office, 1966.

U.S. National Center for Health Statistics. *Vital and Health Statistics. Infant Mortality Trends, United States and Each State, 1930–1964*. Washington: U.S. Government Printing Office, November 1965.

Wilder, Charles S., *Family Health Expenses: United States July-December 1962*. Public Health Service Publication No. 1000, Series 10, No. 41. Washington, D.C.: U.S. Department of Health, Education, and Welfare, 1967.

X I

NEGRO SEX AND FAMILY LIFE

The African Negroes, representing as they do many separate tribal groups, have a variety of sex mores and marriage and family customs differing widely from one another. The reliable data are still fragmentary; dependence must be had in some part upon the reports of missionaries and officials and upon the impressionistic accounts of travelers. These accounts are of course prone to a considerable degree of biased error. The scientific and dependable studies are mainly local and of somewhat limited tribal application. A further difficulty to the understanding of the African Negro family organization results from the fact that the present native family structure is in many cases highly disorganized through tribal intermixture and as a result of foreign contacts and missionary activities. General statements are in consequence difficult and subject to numerous individual and tribal exceptions.

But so far as the American Negro family is concerned, the African organization is of academic interest only. The African types of family and the sex mores and practices were the folk adjustments of a relatively primitive people to the conditions of life; the present forms of sex life and the family institution are consequences of the American experience. The African organization is of interest in its own right but has nothing to contribute to an understanding of the present American adjustment.

The Negro Slave Family

The American Negro family has no unbroken social history connecting it with the family in Africa. The tribal customs and the sex and family mores of the African Negroes were thoroughly disorganized in the transfer of the captives from the tribal home. The slave trade ruthlessly destroyed the family connections and upset the balance of the sexes. Individuals of different regions, of different tribal stocks, and of different language areas were systematically intermixed in order to simplify the problem of control. This practice made impossible the perpetuation of native sex and family heritages in the new environment. In consequence of this early disorganization as well as the suppression during the slave period of any outcropping of tribal practices, it is impossible to connect in any historic sense the present condition of the Negro sex and family life with an African past. The present situation must be understood in terms of the original nature of the Negro as developed under the American historic situation.

The ruthless and complete destruction of the tribal mores was of necessity accompanied and followed by a period of profound personal demoralization. In the circumstances any restrained or high type of sex life was not to be expected and did not exist. The marriage tie was loose but in some cases there was a degree of stability. Promiscuous sex life was common if not usual. The slave régime in North America pretty effectually crushed out the African type of marriage and sex life but it did not in all cases familiarize the Negroes with the monogamic family ideal nor permit their adherence to it.

Out of the inevitable demoralization following upon the systematic destruction of the native sex and family heritage there gradually appeared a Negro sex and family life modeled upon that of the whites but modified by the limitations imposed by the slave status. Many masters exercised some control over the sex life of their slaves, prohibited polygamy, and discouraged sex promiscuity. European family morals were taught to certain slaves, especially the house servants, by many white families and, among these groups, there gradually appeared a Negro sex and family life of the European type. Almost from the first, owing to fortunate chance which brought them into contact with the more settled type of American family, certain individuals conformed in all respects to the conventional white standards and the number of such families increased as the Negroes came more and more into the culture.

The process of developing an effective monogamic family ideal in the Negro group as a whole was extremely slow. The Negroes in general were immersed in a vicious social environment. Their most intimate and frequently their only personal contacts were with other Negro and Indian slaves or with indentured servants of a nondescript sort. The number of slaves was continually increased by fresh importations from Africa or the West Indies and each consignment of new slaves was a shock to the slowly developing standards of the partly assimilated groups. The natural balance of the sexes was usually disturbed and this resulted in widespread sexual irregularity.

The slave status of the Negroes was frequently an additional force in the sex and family life. The recognition of the slave family was optional with the master and was subject to disturbance or destruction at the will of the master. In some places there were legislative enactments forbidding the separation of mothers and young children but in general slave families could be, and frequently were, broken up by the sale and transfers of slaves. The slave régime familiarized the Negroes with the monogamic ideal at the same time that it frequently made impossible any close adherence on their part to the ideal. Slavery did not develop the type of character conducive to a high order of family life nor did it provide the conditions necessary to the institution. The dependence of the slave on the master for food, clothing, shelter, and the other things necessary to life and physical comfort destroyed any tendency toward the development of responsibility. The Negroes received their keep in return for their services and the master likewise provided the necessities of life for the wife and offspring. There was little in the conditions to stimulate a desire for home and family life or to make it possible to develop ideals of sex restraint.

The marriage ceremony was not usually such as to impress the Negro with the sanctity of the relation. It was in general nothing more than a sex association with the consent of the master. The slave marriage was not recorded and could be dissolved at any time that either person desired or at the will of the master. In a sense there was no legal marriage or legal family. The relationship carried no civil rights; the parents had no control over their children. The husband and father was in general an occasional visitor rather than a responsible member of a family group. Incontinence, fornication, adultery, bigamy carried no punishment and were the rule.

Illicit sex relations between the races were numerous and made more difficult the establishment of a Negro family life. The debauchery of Negro girls was easy and the extent of this type of association is suggested by the rapid growth of a mixed-blood group. The colored servant and slave girls were generally powerless to resist the approaches of white men and without doubt cases of rape occurred, were perhaps numerous. But the sex association of the Negro girls and white men was not in general a matter of compulsion. Conventional sex behavior is a result of training; the individual attitudes spring pretty directly from the prevailing sex code; they are in no sense innate. The slaves were without a body of inhibiting sex standards and they occupied an inferior social status. In the situation, sex association with individuals of the superior caste was a thing to be courted, an honor to be merited, and a distinction to be treasured. In some cases the relation was sought by the slave women in the interests of themselves and their children; an easier type of life and greater chances of freedom frequently resulted from a sentimental or blood relationship with the master's family.

At most times and places, increase in the number of the slave group was to the financial profit of the master, and a high birth rate was very generally encouraged: the larger the number of the babies the greater the profit of the owner. Where this was the case, the sex irregularity of the slave women was not discouraged, unless it became so promiscuous as to interfere with fecundity, and was very frequently encouraged especially in case of female slaves who had produced few children. More control was exercised over the sex behavior of the slave women in those places and at those times where the rearing of slave children was a loss and looked upon by the masters as one of the burdens incident to the system. But aside from these cases little if any restriction was placed upon the birth rate and the slave women very generally produced children at a rate pretty close to physiological capacity. Slave families of from fifteen to twenty-five children were not unknown. In some places the annual crop of babies was an item of importance in the plantation economy and planters frequently purchased slave women because they were known to be good breeders.

SLAVE HOMES

Under the slave régime the typical Negro homes were small, roughly-constructed, one-room shacks or log cabins. They were generally without windows, the single door serving for light and ventilation as well as for entrance and exit. The floors were usually of earth. In some places frame cabins with board floors were in use, and these were in some cases provided with windows. There were no sanitary provisions and the cabins gave no privacy; all ages and both sexes occupied the single room. A rude stone fireplace sometimes with and sometimes without a chimney served a double purpose: it kept the cabin warm and over it were cooked the simple meals of the slaves. The furnishings were few and rude and simple.

After the Emancipation the typical Negro home remained a cabin of one room. To this was added in some cases a "lean-to" and presently a porch. Gradually there was added a little furniture as it could be provided. But progress was slow; half a century after the Emancipation forty per cent of the Negro families were still living in one-room cabins, another forty per cent were living in cabins of two rooms, and less than ten per cent of the families were living in houses of four or more rooms. In these Negro homes the light was generally poor, the windows being characteristically without glass and closed by a shutter except in fair weather; the air was bad, the room being used as a kitchen and sleeping room as well as a living room; there were no sanitary appliances and the houses almost invariably were dirty and infested with vermin. The homes afforded little privacy—the crowding was often greater than in the city slum—and frequently they did not even furnish an adequate protection against the elements.

The village Negro homes were not essentially different from the plantation cabins. They were rude shelters and without sanitary provisions.

The windows were typically without glass and generally provided with wooden shutters. The crowding was equally as great as in the rural cabins and standards of living were equally low. There was more vice in the village than in the open country and the conditions surrounding children were of the most demoralizing nature.

FAMILY LIFE OF THE FREEDMAN

The period following the emancipation of the slaves was one of general family disorder and readjustment. Whatever external control had been exercised over the sex and family life of the slaves disappeared. Freedom gave an opportunity to develop a stable sex and family life but it also gave an opportunity for unlimited sex indulgence and family disorder. There was an opportunity to form new sex unions and to discontinue those not in accord with personal inclination and the early part of the period was one of great sex and family disorganization. The personal contacts of the Negroes were greatly increased: previously their contacts had been pretty largely limited to the personnel of the slave plantation, now they came into contact with larger numbers of other Negroes and also into a very considerable contact with the low class whites. Sex promiscuity became general and the little stability of the slave family seemed for a time about to disappear.

There is, of course, no way to measure accurately the amount of sex irregularity that prevails in any group and descriptions of the sex life of the freedmen may understate or exaggerate the actual state of affairs. The amount of illegitimacy is almost the only index of sex standards. But there are no general figures for illegitimacy in the Negro population in the post-Emancipation period on which an estimate might be based. The very general idea that practically all Negro women were unchaste is of course grossly unjust, though it is hardly possible to overstate the degree of sex looseness in the emancipated group. Such fragmentary figures of illegitimacy as are available indicate an amount of sex irregularity greatly in excess of that found among other groups in the population. In 1879 the figures for Washington, D.C., where the Negro sex morals were not below and probably considerably above an average for the country, showed the percentage of Negro births reported as illegitimate to have been 18.8 per cent of the total. These figures are, of course, of doubtful value but they are an evidence that the standards of sex life among the freedmen were far from strictly monogamic. The rapid spread of venereal diseases in the Negro population dates from the war and post-war period, and this is a further bit of evidence indicating how completely the Negroes threw off the restraints of slavery.

Out of the virtual sex promiscuity of the post-war days there gradually appeared an increasing number of stable families and an increasing number of individuals with high personal sex standards. The development was of course slow; the home life was generally poor and the chances of a decent life small. It must be understood, of course, that male continence and female chastity are artificial cultural values that are acquired by each individual only as the result of precept and example, and that it requires time for any group to develop a system of taboos effective in the control of the sex appetite. The mass of the Negroes remained more or less promiscuous but more and more individuals acquired a sense of conventional sex morality and the number increased as education and better home conditions made possible the more careful rearing of children.

THE MARITAL STATUS OF THE NEGRO PEOPLE

The sex composition of the Negro population has received attention in another connection. It will be recalled that in the total Negro population there is a considerable excess of females and that this sex composition has characterized the race since before the Civil War. It will also be recalled that, owing to a heavy short-distance migration of Negro girls who are in demand as unskilled servants in the cities, there is a considerable degree of masculinity in the Negro rural population and a correspondingly greater excess of females in the urban centers; that the excess of women is greatest in the ages of early maturity; and that it is enormously in excess in the mulatto division of the population, especially in the urban centers and in the years of early maturity.

These facts must be borne in mind as factors influencing the sex and family life. An excess of one sex over the other, especially in the years of early maturity, influences adversely the age and rate of marriage, so the legitimate birth rate. It has a marked effect also upon the illegitimate birth rate and upon the sex standards maintained by the group.

The marital status of the Negro peoples, being a matter of inquiry at the periodic census enumerations, may be known within the limits of accuracy of these returns. There are, of course, various sources of error attaching to the returns of marital condition. Men who are widowed, divorced, or for any reason living apart from their families are apt to be returned as single. Unmarried mothers frequently return themselves as married or as widowed or divorced and the married women, who have been deserted by their husbands, as well as divorced women, frequently return themselves as widowed. The general trend of such errors is to an overstatement of the number of single men and an understatement of the number of men in other marital groups. In case of women, the opposite error tends to exist. The number of the two sexes married is necessarily equal and any inequality in the figures is an evidence of the incorrectness of the returns.

In 1930 approximately one-third of the Negro men and one-fourth of the Negro women above the age of fifteen years were returned as unmarried. Of each sex approximately sixty per cent were returned as married. Approximately six per cent of the men and nearly sixteen per cent of the women were returned as widowed. In 1960 roughly thirty per cent (29.6) of the Negro men and slightly above one-fifth (21.7 per cent) of the Negro women above the age of fourteen years were returned as single. The percentage of the Negro men returned as married increased from 59.8 in 1930 to 62.6 in 1960, and for the Negro women the corresponding percentages were 58.5 and 60.6. Approximately five per cent of the men and fourteen per cent of the women were returned as widowed. The percentages of men and women in each marital group, for each of the eight census enumerations, are given in Table 12-1.

Table 12-1: MARITAL CONDITION OF THE NEGRO POPULATION 15 YEARS OF AGE AND OVER, 1890–1930, AND MARITAL STATUS OF THE NONWHITE POPULATION 14 YEARS OF AGE AND OVER, 1940–1960*

Year	Males Single	Married	Widowed	Females Single	Married	Widowed
1890	39.8	55.5	4.3	30.0	54.6	14.7
1900	39.2	54.0	5.7	29.9	53.7	15.4
1910	35.4	57.2	6.2	26.6	57.2	14.8
1920	32.6	60.4	5.9	24.1	59.6	14.8
1930	32.2	59.8	6.3	23.3	58.5	15.9
1940	35.5	58.2	5.3	26.1	56.9	15.4
1950	28.5	64.4	5.2	20.7	62.0	14.6
1960	30.4	62.6	4.5	22.0	60.6	13.8

* Source: 1940–50 data, U.S. Bureau of the Census, *Census of Population: 1950, United States Summary*, Part I, *Characteristics of the Population*, Vol. II, Table 102; 1960 data, U.S. Bureau of the Census, *Census of Population: 1960, United States Summary*, *Detailed Characteristics*, Table 176

These percentages reveal: (1) a decreasing number of Negroes reported as single—the percentage-point decrease over a seventy-year period was for men 9.4 and for women 8.0; (2) an increasing number of Negro men and women returned as married—a 7.1 percentage-point increase for men and 6.0 for women; and (3) a relatively unchanged number, over the same period, of persons returned as widowed—roughly five per cent for men and fourteen per cent for women.

Until very recent decades the percentages for single Negro males were markedly lower than those for single white males during each of five census years. After around 1940 the differences in the percentages of single whites and Negroes became much smaller. The percentages of males of each race returned as married were approximately the same in 1930, but showed a considerable difference by 1960. The percentage of widowed males was much greater in the Negro than in the white group. In the female groups, the percentage of both single and married was consistently higher in the white than in the Negro groups in 1930, but the reverse was the case in 1960 for women returned as single—21.7 for Negroes and 18.6 for whites. The percentage widowed was greater for both sexes in the Negro than in the white groups, in 1930 and also in 1960. The percentage of each marital class in 1930 and 1960 is given by race and sex in Table 12-2.

Table 12-2: MARITAL CONDITION OF THE NEGRO AND WHITE POPULATION OF THE UNITED STATES, 15 YEARS OF AGE AND OVER, 1930, AND 14 YEARS OF AGE AND OVER, 1960*

| | *Males* | | | | *Females* | | | |
| | *Negro* | | *White* | | *Negro* | | *White* | |
	1930	1960	1930	1960	1930	1960	1930	1960
Single	32.2	29.6	34.1	24.4	23.3	21.7	26.8	18.6
Married	59.8	63.3	60.2	70.3	58.5	60.3	61.3	66.7
Widowed	6.3	4.6	4.5	3.3	15.9	14.3	10.5	11.9

* Source: 1960 data, U.S. Bureau of the Census, *Census of Population: Nonwhite Population by Race*, PC(2)-1C, Table 9, p. 9

In the period covered by the statistics, there has been a fairly marked increase in the percentage of Negroes married and a corresponding decline in the percentage reported as single. The two sexes show the same trend and in about the same degree. The percentage of persons returned as widowed has remained practically the same at each enumeration. The same changes in marital status appear in the figures for the white population: there has been a decline in the percentage of single persons of marriageable age, an increase in the percentage married, and no significant change in the percentage returned as widowed. The changes in marital status appear to be due to causes operating equally on the two races.

The age of marriage is somewhat lower among the Negro than among other groups in the population. In 1930 3.7 per cent of Negro males in the under-twenty age group were married. This was not only higher than the average of the population but higher than that of any other single element of the population. In all classes of the population 1.7 per cent of the males in the age group from 15 to 19 years, and 1.5 per cent of white males in this age group, were reported married. In all ages under thirty years in 1930 the Negroes maintained the lead in percentage of males married. After the age of thirty there was no great difference in the different population groups. Among the females there was a similar excess of married women in the younger age groups. In the age group from 15 to 19 years, 20.5 per cent of the Negro girls were married in 1930 as against 12.6 per cent for the general population and 11.5 per cent for the white group. In the other age groups under twenty-five years, a larger percentage of the

Negro girls were married than in any other group of the population. However, thirty years later the percentage of men and women returned as married increased for whites and Negroes of both sexes. The increase was far greater for the white than the Negro groups. As a result, color difference in respect to the per cent married became considerably more marked. In 1960, in all ages except females aged 15 to 19, the whites maintained the lead in the percentage married. (See Table 12-3.)

In 1930 the greatest differences in the marital status of the races appeared in the younger age groups. In the age groups of 20 to 24 years, for both sexes, the percentage married was much higher for the Negro than for the white in both urban and rural-farm sections. But in 1960 the color differences in the percentage married for urban Negro and white persons of the younger age group, 20 to 24 years, became much smaller for both sexes. A considerable difference between the colors appeared in married females classified as rural-farm (76.7 for the whites and 54.6 for the Negroes) and rural-nonfarm (72.9 for the whites and 61.0 for the Negroes). Rural-nonfarm males also show an important difference by race, 46.0 for the whites and 36.4 for the Negroes. Economic prosperity has affected both whites and Negroes; for the whites, more than the Negroes, it has meant a tendency toward earlier marriage. The corresponding percentages appear in Table 12-4.

Table 12-3: PERCENTAGE OF THE NEGRO POPULATION AND OF THE WHITE POPULATION MARRIED, BY SEX AND BY AGE GROUPS, 1930 AND 1960*

	Male				Female			
	Negro		White		Negro		White	
Age Groups	1930	1960	1930	1960	1930	1960	1930	1960
15 years and over	59.8	62.6	60.2	70.3	58.5	60.6	61.3	66.7
15 to 19 years	3.7	3.7	1.5	3.8	20.5	15.8	11.5	15.7
20 to 24 years	42.8	42.0	26.5	46.3	60.4	62.2	50.3	70.5
25 to 29 years	67.9	70.2	60.8	78.1	73.5	78.9	74.3	87.2
30 to 34 years	75.1	79.1	76.3	86.4	76.0	82.3	82.0	89.6
35 to 39 years	78.7	82.4	81.4	89.0	75.2	81.7	83.0	89.0
40 to 44 years	78.9	84.2	82.5	89.6	71.2	79.0	81.6	86.7
45 to 49 years	80.2	83.9	82.4	88.9	67.9	75.1	78.6	83.3
50 to 54 years	79.6	81.5	81.3	87.5	60.3	68.9	73.5	77.9
55 to 59 years	78.6	77.8	79.7	85.5	55.1	60.7	67.0	70.9
60 to 64 years	74.8	76.5	76.3	83.5	43.7	52.0	57.8	62.3
65 to 69 years	69.9	72.9	71.6	80.0	35.9	42.5	47.2	52.4
70 to 74 years	63.4	68.0	64.8	73.5	25.7	32.4	35.5	39.6
75 to 79 years	51.5	61.2	50.4	65.0	14.9	22.9	18.5	27.8
80 to 84 years		53.6		53.7		14.8		16.3
85 years and over		42.9		38.3		9.3		8.1

* Source: 1960 data, U.S. Bureau of the Census, *Census of Population: 1960, United States Summary, Detailed Characteristics*, Table 176

Table 12-4: PERCENTAGE OF THE NEGRO AND OF THE NATIVE WHITE POPULATION 20–24 YEARS, MARRIED IN 1960*

Race and Age Group	Males						Females					
	Urban		Rural-nonfarm		Rural-farm		Urban		Rural-nonfarm		Rural-farm	
	1930	1960	1930	1960	1930	1960	1930	1960	1930	1960	1930	1960
20–24 years												
White	30.0	45.0	36.0	46.0	28.5	34.1	49.7	61.3	62.5	72.9	57.3	76.7
Negro	40.1	46.9	41.9	36.4	46.5	34.1	58.2	63.6	63.9	61.0	61.8	54.6

* Source: 1960 data for Negroes, U.S. Bureau of the Census, *Census of Population: 1960, Nonwhite Population by Race*, PC(2)-1C, Table 19, pp. 30–31 (based on 25 per cent sample); 1960 data for whites, U.S. Bureau of the Census, *Census of Population: 1960*, Summary

The marital condition of the Negro population shows some slight variation with different sections of the country. As a consequence of the selective nature of the migratory process, the percentage of single men in 1930 was slightly lower in the South than in the West and North. But with the slackening in the number of single men moving out of the South, the percentage of single men was higher in the South than the other two regions in 1960. The percentage of single women was higher in the South in both 1930 and 1960 than in the North and West. In the West, where the excess of males makes marriage contacts easier for women, the percentage of single females is relatively low. In the past, the hesitancy of unmarried women to undertake long-distance migration also accounted in part for the small percentage of unmarried women in the West. In all sections of the country the percentage of single men and single women has declined at successive enumerations. The only exception was in the case of males in the South in the decade 1920–30. These facts, however, are not distinctive of the Negro population. The same general differences between the sections of the country are true of the white population.

The percentage of single people of both sexes is somewhat lower in the urban than in the rural Negro population. In 1930, in the urban Negro population fifteen years old and over, 31.3 per cent of the males and 22.2 per cent of the females were returned as single. In 1960 both sexes showed a significant decrease in percentage returned as single—27.1 per cent for the Negro males and 20.3 per cent for the Negro females. In 1930, 33.0 per cent of the males and 25.6 per cent of the females residing in rural-farm areas were returned as single; thirty years later the single percentage in these areas increased by 4.5 for the males and 4.4 for the females. The percentage distribution by marital status for the two sexes is given in Table 12-5 by urban, rural-farm, and rural-nonfarm distribution.

The maximum percentage of marriage at one time was reached at a somewhat earlier age in the rural than in the urban population.

The proportion married in 1930, for both sexes and in all age groups, was higher in the rural-farm population than in the rural-nonfarm population, and higher in the rural-nonfarm group than in the urban. However, in 1960 the percentage married was higher for urban dwellers than rural-nonfarm and rural-farm.

There were important differences in the marital status of both men and women from city to city in the heyday of Negro migration. Such differences as have existed between cities of different size appear to be the result of the geographic location of the city—with the consequent influence of migration on the sex composition—and of the migratory character of the population, rather than the result of its size as such. In the case of cities of 10,000 or more Negro inhabitants, the percentages married in 1930 vary from the rates of Wilmington, Delaware (53.3), and Boston,

Table 12-5: MARITAL CONDITION OF THE NEGRO POPULATION 15 YEARS OLD AND OVER IN 1930, AND 14 YEARS OLD AND OVER IN 1960, BY SEX AND PLACE OF RESIDENCE*†

	Males						Females					
	Single		Married		Widowed		Single		Married		Widowed	
	1930	1960	1930	1960	1930	1960	1930	1960	1930	1960	1930	1960
Urban	31.3	27.1	60.4	65.4	6.4	4.6	22.2	20.3	56.6	60.9	18.4	14.4
Rural-nonfarm	33.4	35.7	57.4	57.9	7.1	4.8	21.8	24.7	58.7	58.2	17.1	15.6
Rural-farm	33.0	37.5	60.3	57.6	5.7	5.9	25.6	30.0	61.3	59.3	11.7	10.7

* Source: 1960 data refer to the Negro Population. U.S. Bureau of the Census, Census of Population: 1960, Nonwhite Population by Race, PC(2)-1C, Table 9, p. 9 (based on 25 per cent sample)
† Percentage distribution

Massachusetts (53.7), to Kansas City, Kansas (66.2), and Queens Borough, New York (69.0). The percentages married among Negro women varied from Raleigh, North Carolina (47.3), and Baton Rouge, Louisiana (47.7), to Gary, Indiana (69.9), and Youngstown, Ohio (70.5). Similar differences appear, of course, when the populations are examined from the point of view of the percentages of unmarried persons. Progressively these cities today are less dependent for their population growth on a large volume of immigrants, predominantly young and single men. There is some evidence that many of those coming to the cities are coming as families. As a consequence of these changes in the character of migration, marked differences in marital conditions that once existed between cities of varied size have now been greatly reduced. For example, Wilmington, Delaware, in 1930 had 53.3 per cent of the Negro men and 55.9 per cent of the Negro women married; in 1960 the per cent married for men increased to 61.1 and for women to 61.6. Kansas City, Kansas, which had in 1930 the highest per cent of Negro men returned as married (66.2), remained virtually unchanged in the per cent married. Montgomery, Alabama, in 1930 reported the lowest per cent of Negro women married (47.8), but in 1960, 52.4 per cent of the women were married. The following tabulation gives the percentages married in a few selected cities with large Negro populations, in 1920, 1930, and 1960.

Table 12-6: MARITAL STATUS OF THE NEGRO POPULATION 15 YEARS OLD AND OVER, BY SEX, PERCENTAGE DISTRIBUTION FOR SELECTED CITIES OF 10,000 OR MORE NEGRO INHABITANTS, 1920–1930 AND 1960*

City	Males			Females		
	1920	1930	1960	1920	1930	1960
Wilmington, Del.	52.2	53.3	61.1	55.5	55.9	61.6
Boston, Mass.	53.5	53.7	61.3	53.7	54.0	59.4
Newport News, Va.	52.2	56.4	64.9	64.4	55.1	65.4
Louisville, Ky.	56.8	58.3	64.9	52.5	54.2	59.7
Montgomery, Ala.	64.4	60.8	63.0	49.4	47.8	52.4
Akron, Ohio	47.5	60.9	65.3	74.2	68.9	63.9
Youngstown, Ohio	53.2	62.1	65.4	73.3	70.5	65.2
Macon, Ga.	66.3	62.9	65.4	59.5	50.1	56.6
Fort Worth, Tex.	58.8	64.4	66.7	60.7	60.4	61.1
Kansas City, Kan.	64.2	66.2	66.5	64.2	62.9	60.7

* Source: 1960 data, U.S. *Census of Population: 1960, General Population Characteristics*, Final Report PC (1), *Alabama, Delaware, Georgia, Kansas, Kentucky, Massachusetts, Ohio, Texas, Virginia*, Table 21

The proportion of widowed persons is higher for the Negro than for the white population. This is true, with a single exception, of both sexes at all age levels and in both the rural and urban populations. In all age groups the percentage of females widowed is higher than the rate for men.

In the total male population 4.5 per cent of the whites and 6.3 per cent of the Negroes were widowed in 1930. The corresponding percentages were 3.3 and 4.6 in 1960. In the total female population 10.5 per cent of the whites and 15.9 per cent of the Negroes were widowed in 1930; thirty years later 11.9 per cent of the white women and 14.3 per cent of the Negro women were returned as widowed. The excess of widowed females is everywhere marked in the older age groups, owing to the greater longevity of women, and this excess is much greater in most age groups in the urban districts.

The percentage of widowed varies sharply from one city to another, reflecting in part the migratory character of the city population and in part the general age distribution of the Negro population. For the males in 1930 the percentages varied from 3.4 for Bronx Borough, New York, to 9.8 for Tulsa, Oklahoma; female percentages varied from 10.8 for Port Arthur, Texas, to 27.3 for Columbus, Georgia. But in 1960 the variation in percentages widowed became less marked—for Negro men, from 4.0 for Akron, Ohio, to 7.0 for Louisville, Kentucky; for the women, from 10.7 for Gary, Indiana, to 21.2 for Augusta, Georgia. Table 12-7 gives the percentages for selected cities of 10,000 or more Negro inhabitants.

Table 12-7: PERCENTAGE OF WIDOWED PERSONS IN THE NEGRO POPULATION OF THE UNITED STATES, FOR SELECTED CITIES OF 10,000 OR MORE NEGRO INHABITANTS, 1920–1930 AND 1960*

City	Males 1920	1930	1960	Females 1920	1930	1960
New York City	...	...	4.5	....	....	13.2
Bronx	6.5	3.4	...	15.0	11.6	....
Brooklyn	4.4	3.5	...	15.8	14.1	....
Richmond	4.6	6.3	...	9.9	10.9	....
Detroit, Mich.	3.6	4.8	4.4	10.0	13.3	11.3
Akron, Ohio	3.5	5.0	4.0	8.7	11.5	11.1
Gary, Ind.	3.8	5.4	4.2	10.2	13.9	10.7
Youngstown, Ohio	4.4	6.1	4.8	9.8	12.7	11.8
Montgomery, Ala.	7.1	6.5	5.5	24.1	23.8	20.1
Atlanta, Ga.	7.4	6.9	5.3	24.1	23.1	17.6
Houston, Tex.	7.2	7.3	4.6	17.1	18.0	12.5
Newport News, Va.	3.2	7.7	4.5	11.1	18.7	11.5
Nashville, Tenn.	8.9	7.9	6.1	23.3	22.0	17.9
Columbus, Ga.	6.4	8.0	4.6	23.1	27.3	19.2
Dallas, Tex.	9.2	8.6	5.3	20.3	19.8	14.2
Augusta, Ga.	7.8	9.0	5.9	21.8	25.9	21.2
Louisville, Ky.	7.5	9.5	7.0	22.3	22.3	17.3
Tulsa, Okla.	6.4	9.8	6.7	13.7	19.8	16.4

* Source: 1960 data, *U.S. Census of Population: 1960, General Population Characteristics,* Final Report PC (1), *Alabama, Georgia, Indiana, Kentucky, Michigan, New York, Ohio, Oklahoma, Texas, Tennessee, Virginia,* Table 21

The dissolution of marriage through divorce varies widely from city to city. For males the percentage divorced was lowest in 1930 in Greenville, South Carolina (0.2), Bronx Borough, New York (0.3), Wilmington, North Carolina (0.3), and Columbus, Georgia (0.3). It was highest in Beaumont, Texas (4.3), and Galveston, Texas (7.3). In the case of women the percentage divorced was lowest in Greenville (0.2) and in Winston-Salem, North Carolina (0.5), and highest in Beaumont (7.0) and Galveston (9.4). The percentage divorced, with a few exceptions, has increased rapidly in most of the cities of large Negro population during the past four decades. Table 12-8 gives the percentages of Negroes divorced in selected cities of 10,000 or more Negro inhabitants.

Table 12-8: PERCENTAGES OF DIVORCED PERSONS IN THE NEGRO POPULATION OF THE UNITED STATES FOR SELECTED CITIES HAVING 10,000 OR MORE NEGRO INHABITANTS, 1920–1960*

City	Males			Females		
	1920	1930	1960	1920	1930	1960
Greenville, S.C.	...	0.2	0.8	...	0.2	1.1
New York, N.Y.	0.2	0.3	1.6	0.3	0.6	2.9
Wilmington, N.C.	0.3	0.3	1.3	0.9	0.8	2.1
Columbus, Ga.	0.6	0.3	1.8	1.0	0.6	3.1
Wilmington, Del.	0.4	0.6	2.7	0.6	0.8	3.9
Atlanta, Ga.	0.2	1.2	1.9	0.5	3.1	3.4
Boston, Mass.	0.9	1.7	3.7	0.8	2.2	6.1
Memphis, Tenn.	1.2	2.0	1.7	2.5	3.3	2.8
Louisville, Ky.	2.3	2.7	3.7	3.0	3.1	5.3
Kansas City, Kan.	2.6	3.3	4.0	2.5	4.1	5.8
Houston, Tex.	3.4	3.9	4.0	5.4	6.4	6.6
Beaumont, Tex.	2.1	4.3	3.8	4.6	7.0	6.2
Galveston, Tex.	3.8	7.3	6.2	6.0	9.4	9.0

* Source: 1960 data, *U.S. Census of Population: 1960, General Population Characteristics*, Final Report PC (1), *Delaware, Georgia, Kansas, Kentucky, Massachusetts, New York, North Carolina, South Carolina, Texas, Tennessee*, Table 21

THE FERTILITY OF THE AMERICAN NEGROES

The Negro birth rate for most of the American period may not be stated with accuracy. Until recently very few of the states maintained reliable birth registration systems. In 1922, for example, the birth registration area included slightly over eighty-five per cent of the total population. But several states with large Negro populations—Alabama, Arkansas, Florida, Georgia, Louisiana, Missouri, and Oklahoma—were outside the registration area. It was not until 1933 that all states were admitted to the registration area for births. The figures in Table 13-1 up to 1933 are for the registration area; since then the figures are for the entire population.

Table 13-1: BIRTH RATES BY COLOR IN THE UNITED STATES, 1915–1966* [a]

Year	Total	White	Nonwhite
1915–19[b]	28.3	27.6	32.8[d]
1920–24	26.8	24.6	34.4
1925–29	23.2	22.4	30.9
1930–34	19.7	18.9	26.6
1935–39	18.8	18.0	25.9
1940–44[b]	21.2	20.4	27.5
1945–49[b]	24.1	23.4	30.3
1950–54	24.9	23.8	33.9
1955–59	24.9	23.6	34.8
1960	23.7	22.7	32.1
1961	23.3	22.2	31.6
1962[c]	22.4	21.4	30.5
1963[c]	21.7	20.7	29.7
1964[c]	21.0	20.0	29.2
1965[c]	19.4	18.3	27.6
1966[c]	18.4	17.4	26.1

* Source: Data based on Anders S. Lunde, "White-Nonwhite Fertility Differentials in the United States," *Health, Education, and Welfare Indicators*, Sept. 1965. Washington, D.C.: U.S. Department of Health, Education, and Welfare
[a] Births per 1,000 population; births adjusted for underregistration 1915–59 and registered births 1959–66
[b] For 1917–19 and 1941–46, data for nonwhites based on population including Armed Forces abroad
[c] Based on a 50 per cent sample of births
[d] Prior to 1917 data are not available

Moreover, prior to 1933 the figures for the birth registration area may not be taken as typical of the Negro as a whole. The Negroes lived chiefly in the South and for a long period were outside of the registration area; they were largely rural; they were in general of low economic, social, and educational status. There is, therefore, every reason to believe that the Negro birth rate was for most of the period higher than the rate in the registration area would indicate, and such partial information as is available indicates that it was appreciably higher.

The race, sex, and age data of the general censuses afford some information in regard to racial fertility differentials in the United States. In the total population there has been a long and continuous decline in the proportion of children. In 1820, forty-three per cent of the Negro population were children under fourteen years of age; the percentage of children in the white population was approximately the same, 43.7. The number of children per each 1,000 women of childbearing age was somewhat less for the Negroes than for the whites. In the following hundred years there was a marked decline in the proportion of children in each race. The decline represents in part a decrease in the mortality rates as well as a decline in the birth rates; both phenomena, if operative over a period of years, tend to increase the age of the population. Racial comparison is also distorted by the higher infant mortality among Negroes.

Table 13-2: PERCENTAGE OF POPULATION UNDER 10 YEARS OF AGE, BY RACE, 1830–1960*

Year	Negro	White
1830	34.2	32.5
1840	33.2	31.6
1850	31.3	28.6
1860	30.5	28.4
1870	29.7	26.4
1880	32.5	25.9
1890	28.7	23.7
1900	27.4	23.3
1910	25.5	21.8
1920	23.0	21.5
1930	21.8	19.2
1940	19.8	17.3
1950	22.8	20.7
1960	27.2	21.1

* Sources: *Historical Statistics of the United States, Colonial Times to 1957*, Series A 71–85, pp. 10–11; and *U.S. Census of Population: 1960*, Vol. I and PC(2)-1C

The partial information seems to indicate that the Negro race in America has been slightly more prolific than the white. The average number of children born to Negro women who bore children in 1931 was 3.6, as compared with three for white women. At each enumeration the number of children per 1,000 women in the childbearing ages was above that of the white. The proportion, however, has been lower for the Negroes than for certain other elements of the population. In 1930, for example, the number of children under five years of age per 1,000 women within the age group 15 to 44 was, for all classes, 391; for the Negro 393; for the white, 386. The corresponding figures for 1920 were 467, 429, and 471. The figures for 1940 were 468 for the Negro and 375 for the white; the corresponding figures for 1950 were 513 and 469; and for 1960 the figures were 694 for the Negro and 549 for the white.

The ratio of children to women has declined from census to census for both races up to approximately 1940. The decline has in general been more rapid for the Negro than for the white elements in the population. Commencing with 1950, the ratio of children to 1,000 women of childbearing ages began once more to increase. The figures for each census from 1850 to 1960 are shown in Table 13-3.

Table 13-3: CHILDREN UNDER 5 YEARS OF AGE PER 1,000 WOMEN
15 TO 44 YEARS OF AGE, 1850–1960*

Year	Negro	White
1850	741	659
1860	724	675
1870	692	610
1880	760	586
1890	621	517
1900	582	508
1910	519	484
1920	429	471
1930	393	386
1940	468	375
1950	513	469
1960	694	549

* Sources: 1940, 1950, and 1960 figures were computed from *U.S. Census of Population*, 1940, 1950, 1960, Vol. I

The decline in the percentage of Negro children in the younger age groups has been irregular but continuous. The number of children under five years of age in each 100 of the Negro and white populations at the past seven enumerations appears in Table 13-4.

Table 13-4: PERCENTAGE OF POPULATION UNDER 5 YEARS OF AGE,
BY RACE, 1900–1960*

Year	Negro	White
1900	13.8	11.9
1910	12.9	11.4
1920	10.9	10.9
1930	10.3	9.1
1940	10.2	7.8
1950	12.5	10.5
1960	14.4	10.9

* Sources: *Historical Statistics of the United States, Colonial Times to 1957*, Series A 71–85, pp. 10–11; and *U.S. Census of Population: 1960*, Vol. I and also *Nonwhite Population by Race*

The abruptness of the decline in the Negro population appears in the fact that in spite of the considerable increase in the Negro population and the increase in the marriage rate, the actual number of Negro children under five years of age has not greatly changed in the first half of the present century. The total numbers are shown in Table 13-5.

The decline is shown by the number of children under five years per 1,000 women 15 to 44 years of age. In 1900 the number was 508 for the

Table 13-5: NUMBER OF NEGRO CHILDREN UNDER 5 YEARS OF AGE, 1900–1960*

Enumerations	Number†
1900	1,216
1910	1,263
1920	1,144
1930	1,230
1940	1,312
1950	1,884
1960	2,722

* Sources: *Historical Statistics of the United States, Colonial Times to 1957*, Series A 71–85, pp. 10–11; and *U.S. Census of Population: 1960, Nonwhite Population by Race*
† In thousands

whites and 582 for the Negroes; in 1930 the number was 386 for the whites and 393 for the Negroes; and in 1960 the number was 549 for the whites and 694 for the Negroes.

For both races in the population, the proportion of children is higher in the southern than in the northern and western states. In 1930, for example, the number of children under five years per 1,000 Negro women of childbearing age was 393 for the country as a whole, 423 for the South, 295 for the North, and 239 for the West. The corresponding figures for the white population were 386, 468, 364, and 326.

In each race there has been an abrupt decline in the percentage of children, the decline being greater for the Negro than for the white. Table 13-6 allows a comparison of the two races at four different enumerations for the total population and for the population of the three sections of the country.

These figures show the significant facts in regard to the number of children per married woman at the separate enumerations and allow a comparison of the two races in the different sections and years. At each enumeration the number of children per married woman was greater for the Negroes than for the whites, but the apparent trend is toward a lessening of the differences. A comparison of the separate sections shows the number of children per married mother to be greater for the Negroes in the South but less in the North and West. In the North and West, however, there is apparently a trend toward racial equality; in the South the trend is apparently toward greater racial differences.

The division of the Negro population into urban or rural categories roughly parallels the division according to sections of the country; the southern Negroes are predominantly a rural population, those in the North and West chiefly urban. The difference that obtains between the rural and urban populations—the higher proportion of children to women in the

Table 13-6: CHILDREN UNDER 5 YEARS PER 1,000 MARRIED WOMEN 15 YEARS
OF AGE OR OVER, BY SECTIONS, 1910–1930 AND 1960*

Section and Year	Negro	White
United States		
1910	711	588
1920	561	540
1930	513	423
1960	709	448
The South		
1910	757	749
1920	608	642
1930	559	523
1960	749	442
The North		
1910	396	539
1920	335	513
1930	373	399
1960	647	446
The West		
1910	315	518
1920	283	465
1930	286	339
1960	705	468

* Source: 1960 data, *U.S. Census of Population: 1960 Subject Reports, Nonwhite Population by Race* and *U.S. Summary (Detailed Characteristics)*

rural than in the urban areas—is characteristic of each racial group. The range of difference is very great.

The comparative figures for the Negro and white population in 1930 and 1960 are given in Table 13-7. The distribution is made for the total populations of the different sections.

The racial patterns are strikingly parallel. The urban numbers are in all cases far below those for the rural populations, and within the rural populations the number of children per 1,000 women is less in the village than on the farm. In the urban populations in 1930 the number of children per 1,000 women was much greater in the white than in the Negro groups, and the excess was much the same in all sections of the country; the greatest differential was in the South, where each 1,000 white women had 65 more children under five years than the corresponding number of Negro women. In the rural-farm population as a whole, the proportion of children was greater for Negro than for white women, and the same was true of the North and the West. In the South the rural-farm white women, like the southern white women in all groups, had proportionately more children under five years than did the Negro women.

Table 13-7: CHILDREN UNDER 5 YEARS PER 1,000 WOMEN 15 TO 44
YEARS OF AGE, BY RACE AND AREA OF RESIDENCE, 1930–1960*

	Negro		White	
Section and Area	*1930*	*1960*	*1930*	*1960*
United States				
Urban	268	652	316	525
Rural	521	838	504	596
The South				
Urban	261	677	326	516
Rural	525	847	560	553
The North				
Urban	282	625	321	524
Rural	436	663	469	622
The West				
Urban	216	672	259	544
Rural	387	879	448	635

* Source: *U.S. Census of Population: 1960, U.S. Summary (Detailed Characteristics)*

SEX STANDARDS

As previously mentioned, there is no satisfactory index of conformity
to the sex mores. The number of illegitimate births is one index, but one
of doubtful validity; the amount of sex irregularity may be very great
without registering in the statistics of illegitimacy.

In the groups of the population in which a knowledge of contraceptive
methods is general, and in the classes economically able to afford abortion
operations, the number of illegitimate births may be very small as compared with the number in the economically unfortunate and unenlight-
ened groups. Inasmuch as the mass of the Negroes belong to the poor and
ignorant segment of the population, it is to be expected that their rates of
illegitimacy would be comparatively high.

The statistics of illegitimacy given for the years 1930 and 1931 are for
the registration area of the United States. The statistics for the years after
1940 are estimated from numbers reported in thirty-four states and the
District of Columbia.

In 1964 the estimated number of illegitimate births in the United States
was nearly 275,700, or 68.5 illegitimate births per 1,000 live births. For
whites the ratio was 33.7, and for nonwhites 245.0, illegitimate births per
1,000 live births. The 1964 ratios, when compared with those of 1930,
clearly show a quite similar pattern of increase in the occurrence of illegitimate births for both races. Both increased during World War II; following the war, white ratios declined slightly and nonwhite ratios held
steady up to about 1950; subsequently the ratios increased steadily for
both races. The ratios of Negro illegitimate births show a wide range from

Table 14-1: NUMBER OF ILLEGITIMATE BIRTHS AND THE RATIO OF
ILLEGITIMATE TO TOTAL LIVE BIRTHS, BY RACE OF MOTHER,
1930–31 AND 1940–1963*

Race of Mother	1930	1931	1941	1945	1950	1955	1960	1963	1964
	Number (in thousands)								
Total	67.0	69.4	89.5	117.4	141.6	183.3	224.3	259.4	275.7
White	30.0	31.0	40.3	56.4	53.5	64.2	82.5	102.2	114.3
Nonwhite	34.0	35.7	49.2	60.9	88.1	119.2	141.8	150.7	161.3
	Ratio: per 1,000 total live births								
Total	32.7	35.4	37.9	42.9	39.8	45.3	52.7	63.3	68.5
White	19.1	20.3	19.5	23.6	17.5	18.6	22.9	30.7	33.7
Nonwhite	143.4	153.9	168.3	179.3	179.6	202.4	215.8	235.9	245.0

* Source: U.S. Dept. of Health, Education, and Welfare, *Vital Statistics of the United States: 1964*, Vol. I, *Natality*, Table 1-26

state to state. In general the states with the larger number of illegitimate births are also the ones with the higher ratios. They are also in general the states with large Negro groups of low economic and educational status. For example, in 1964 Delaware had the ratio of 372.0, Tennessee 343.7, Kentucky 308.1, Illinois 301.9, Florida 295.5, Alabama 295.4, South Carolina 273.5, Mississippi 267.1, North Carolina 266.8, and Louisiana 246.1.

For the most part the states with relatively few Negroes in the total population show lower illegitimacy ratios. In 1930 Arizona, for example, reported only 7 Negro illegitimate births, a ratio of 53.0; Michigan, with only 240 Negro illegitimate births, had a ratio of 74.3; Iowa, with only 20 such births had a ratio of 82.6. But there is no close correspondence between numbers and ratios. Colorado, with only 14 Negro illegitimate births, had a ratio of 116.7, as compared with New Jersey, which had 457 illegitimate births and a ratio of 91.7.

Too much reliance should not be placed on such data. The accuracy of the statistical reporting is not always beyond question, and the significance of the data for sex standards is not entirely clear. The rate of illegitimacy is influenced by a number of factors including economic status, family traditions, educational level, and home and living standards. It is probable that the sex standards of the Negroes are approximately the same as those of the whites of the same social classes.

MATERNAL FAMILIES

In the slave régime the Negro family tended to follow a maternal pattern; the mother was the important person, the husband was incidental; the father had no control. The great influence of the women in the Negro family has continued in the later generations.

After the emancipation of the slaves, many types of family life appeared. In some cases the freedmen assumed the responsibility for wife and children and developed stable families according to the conventional social pattern. In other cases the affectional bonds were weak; the freedman had no interest in his wife and family, and the women and children were neglected or deserted. The family of a mother and her children without permanent male support or headship was a common type.

This maternal type of family has continued to be a prominent feature of Negro social organization. It is in no sense African in origin or tradition. It was developed in the slave plantation system and has persisted into the present, partly as a survival of the earlier period, partly as an adjustment to persisting conditions of Negro life. In this type of family organization the father is a casual visitor who does not figure in the group. The woman is the economic support and the responsible head; the man contributes little or nothing to the support of the family and has no authority over the woman or children. Often there are several men, and the children may be of different paternity. The persistence of these families is favored by the fact that it is often not possible for a man to marry and support a family, and also by the fact that extramarital sex relations and the birth of illegitimate children do not result in a loss of social status. Moreover, the relation leaves the woman economically as well as sexually independent; marriage involves certain dangers and obligations; a husband may very well prove a liability.

The frequency of this type of Negro family is indicated in part by the census returns covering Negro families with female heads. The percentage of maternal families is much higher among the Negroes than in the native white population in both the urban and rural areas. Table 15-1 shows the relative frequency of maternal families in the racial groups by place of residence.

The presence of families with female heads is accounted for in part by desertion and divorce. But the excess number in the Negro population indicates the measure of independence of Negro women in their economic and sex life. In certain areas and classes in the South one-third or more of the Negro families are without a male head.

It must not be assumed that these maternal families are of necessity disorganized. On the contrary, they are often very stable families representing several generations of the same type of organization. The lack of conformity to conventional standards does not mean disorganization. It represents, rather, the ineffectiveness of institutional control of sex behavior in cases when tradition opposes the conventional norm.

The frequency of such families in the urban areas is accounted for in part by the disorganizing effect of urbanization, which destroys the rural folkways of the peasant Negro, and by the conditions of urban employ-

Table 15-1: FAMILIES CLASSIFIED BY SEX OF HEAD FOR THE UNITED STATES,
1930 AND 1950–1965*

| | WHITE | | | | NONWHITE | | | |
Year	All Fami-lies	Husband-Wife Families	Other Families with Male Head	Fami-lies with Female Head	All Fami-lies	Husband-Wife Families	Other Families with Male Head	Fami-lies with Female Head
1930	100	88.1	...	11.9	100	80.7	...	19.3
1950	100	88.4	3.1	8.4	100	76.8	4.3	19.1
1955	100	87.9	3.0	9.0	100	75.3	4.0	20.7
1960	100	88.7	2.6	8.7	100	73.6	4.0	22.4
1965	100	88.6	2.4	9.0	100	73.1	3.2	23.7

* Source: *U.S. Census of Population: 1960, U.S. Summary (Detailed Characteristics)*, Table 186; and *Current Population Reports*, Series P-20

ment, which enables the woman, because of her earnings, to be in a measure economically independent. Specific studies show that the percentage of maternal families decreases sharply with improvement of economic status and increase in the employment of Negro men.

HOME AND FAMILY STANDARDS

The range of Negro home and family standards is as wide as that of any group in the population. The standards are in general those of other Americans of similar economic and educational status; the Negroes conform to the prevailing patterns except as conformity is made impossible by economic, legal, or other insuperable handicaps.

While Negroes have in large measure conformed their sex life and family ideals to the dominant patterns of society, the actual conditions of home and family life are often unfortunate and the efforts to conform commonly encounter peculiar difficulties.

The great majority of the race lives in the rural sections of the South. Here the typical Negro home, whether owned or rented, is a rude one- or two-room cabin, always ugly, usually insanitary, and generally lacking the minimum of furniture and equipment essential to physical comfort. The poverty of the group makes improvement in the living conditions slow and often impossible. The characteristic shiftlessness of a discouraged group as well as their habituation to hardship, discomfort, and low living standards are forces operating to retard improvement in the physical conditions incident to home and family life. As a result of the profound and general ignorance characteristic of this black peasantry and because of the general absence in the situation of inexpensive but attractive, comfortable, and sanitary cottages that might serve as models for imitation, they seldom make good use of the advantages which the natural situation provides. The almost equal backwardness of the rural whites limits the possibility of learning from that source. The situation is made more difficult by the Negro's lack of confidence in the white man's honesty—an attitude frequently exploited to the limit by the local Negro leadership—by their frequent unwillingness to accept leadership from outside, and by the paucity of honest and competent local leaders within the racial group.

In certain respects the housing conditions of the urban Negro laboring classes in the South are inferior to those of the rural districts. From choice or necessity the Negroes live in segregated colonies in the poorest and most undesirable residence districts. In most of the towns and villages and in some of the larger cities such as New Orleans the houses are duplicates of the plantation shacks, typically dilapidated and usually devoid of sanitary conveniences. In Baltimore, Washington, and many towns of the South, many of the working-class Negroes live in alley tenements—one- or two-room shacks, cheaply constructed of rough boards, without ceiling or windows or sanitary arrangements.

In the northern cities the housing conditions of the laboring-class Negroes are not greatly if at all superior to those in the South. The Negro population is generally concentrated in one or a few neglected and undesirable districts to which they have been attracted because of the relatively cheap rents or into which they have been forced by the difficulty of securing living quarters in the better residential areas. The buildings are generally old and frequently dilapidated, the surroundings usually neglected, the sanitation poor, and the health regulations not enforced. Even in the better class of houses occupied by laboring classes the ordinary conveniences are often lacking; the heating is usually from wood or coal stoves, the lighting is commonly by gas or by oil lamps, and bathrooms are unusual.

The Negro of means often meets extreme difficulty in finding a desirable neighborhood in which he may live, and the reputable elements frequently cannot afford the cost of decent homes. It is a frequent complaint of worthy Negroes that they can neither buy nor rent a house in a decent locality; city zoning, administrative or real estate devices, or property owners' agreements shut them out of the best districts. If by subterfuge they buy property in a desirable neighborhood it presently results, in many cases, in neighborhood deterioration; the migration of Negro families, seeking a decent neighborhood in which to live, frequently results in the course of a few years in the conversion of a relatively desirable residence district into an undesirable neighborhood. When Negro families move in, the whites move out, property values fall, deterioration takes place, and more Negro families move in. The first Negro families are frequently followed by a sporting element, from which they seek to escape, and the neighborhood presently becomes a Negro slum. In many of the northern cities the educated and more economically prosperous Negroes live in settlements away from the congested business district, in residence areas that do not differ in character from those of the whites of similar economic status.

The absence of privacy incident to the miserable housing conditions of the bulk of the race is conducive to extreme laxity in sex and family relationships. The amount of family disorganization is perhaps greater than in white families; the incomes are less and home conditions poorer. The general ignorance of parents and the general inefficiency of Negro family life among the poorer classes makes impossible a proper care of children. In the lower class homes there is little direct training of children and little direct control exercised over their behavior. Because of poverty both parents frequently work away from home; proportionally many times as many Negro as white women work away from home. The children are in consequence neglected, left unsupervised to play in the streets and alleys where, because of the neighborhood environment in which the great majority of Negro families live, they almost inevitably come into contact with vicious persons and have every opportunity to observe and become familiar with debased standards of life and conduct.

There are also some special conditions conducive to family disorder among the Negroes. Racial discrimination, public abuse, exclusion from playgrounds, and other forms of segregation make the education and family training of Negro children particularly difficult.

The homes and home life and the sex standards of the middle- and upper-class Negroes are essentially the same as those of white Americans of similar economic, educational, and social strata. So far as differences exist they are differences of degree which are to be explained and understood in historic and social terms—in terms of tradition, ignorance, poverty, isolation, and the modifying, retarding, and disturbing factors of a difficult environment.

The same tendency to avoid marriage or, married, sharply to limit the size of the family is observable in the upper-class Negro groups as in the cultured and upper economic strata of the white population. The explanations lie, doubtless, in the divergence of standards and incomes, and in the discouraging conditions of life faced by the Negroes of culture. Children are a source of worry and expense and lessen the personal opportunities of the parents. Moreover, many cultured persons hesitate to bring children into the world to face the difficult life they would meet. They differ in this respect from the more ignorant classes chiefly in the fact that they have come into possession of knowledge of means of controlling impregnation.

Trends in Negro Family Life

The review of Negro sex standards, family life, and home conditions shows a remarkable assimilation all along the line. For the mass of the Negro population, an independent and self-responsible family life is a matter of only two generations. In view of the relatively short period of freedom and the general economic and social conditions of Negro life, the degree of conformity to the white standards is surprisingly complete.

In every respect the trends in Negro family life parallel those going on in the white families.

Bruce, P. A., *The Plantation Negro as a Freeman*, "Parent and Child," pp. 1–14; "Husband and Wife," pp. 15–28.

Census Bureau, *Negro Population in the United States, 1790–1915*, "Home Ownership and Size of Family," pp. 459–501; "Fertility—Proportion of Children to Women of Childbearing Age," pp. 283–297; "Marital Condition," pp. 235–282.

Census of the United States, *Negroes in the United States, 1920–1932*, "Marital Conditions," pp. 146–200; "Fertility," pp. 201–207; "Families," pp. 253–286.

Chicago Commission on Race Relations, *Negroes in Chicago*, "The Housing Problem," pp. 152–230.

Comstock, A. P., "Chicago Housing Conditions: The Problem of the Negro," *American Journal of Sociology*, 18(1912), pp. 241–257.

Day, Caroline B., *A Study of Some Negro-White Families in the United States*.

Frazier, E. F., *The Negro Family in Chicago*.

——, *The Free Negro Family*.

——, "Traditions and Patterns of Negro Family Life in the United States," in E. B. Reuter, ed., *Race and Culture Contacts*, pp. 191–207.

——, "An Analysis of Statistics on Negro Illegitimacy in the United States," *Social Forces*, 11(1932), 249–257.

Johnson, C. S., *The Negro in American Civilization*, "The Problem of Homes," pp. 199–223.

Mallard, R. Q., *Plantation Life Before Emancipation*, "Marriage and Family Relations," pp. 47–53.

Park, R. E., "Negro Home Life and Standards of Living," *Annals of the American Academy of Political and Social Science*, 49(1913), 147–163.

Reed, R., "Illegitimacy Among Negroes," *Journal of Social Hygiene*, 11(1925), 73–91.

Weatherford, W. D., and Johnson, C. S., *Race Relations*, "Home Life of the Negro," pp. 384–401.

FURTHER READINGS

Bernard, Jessie, *Marriage and Family Among Negroes*. Englewood Cliffs, N.J.: Prentice-Hall, 1966.

Billingsley, Andrew, *Black Families in White America*. Englewood Cliffs, N.J.: Prentice-Hall, 1968.

Davis, Allison W., and Havighurst, Robert J., *The Father of the Man: How Your Child Gets His Personality*. Boston: Houghton Mifflin, 1947.

Drake, St. Clair, and Cayton, Horace R., *Black Metropolis*, rev. ed. New York: Harper & Row, 1962.

Frazier, E. Franklin, *Black Bourgeoisie*. New York: Collier Books, 1962.

Frazier, E. Franklin, *The Negro Family in the United States*. Chicago: University of Chicago Press, 1939.

Glick, Paul C., *American Families*. New York: John Wiley & Sons, 1957.

Gordon, Joan, *The Poor of Harlem: Social Functioning in the Underclass*. New York: Office of the Mayor, Interdepartmental Neighborhood Service Center, 1965.

Lewis, Hylan, "The Changing Negro Family," in Eli Ginzberg, ed., *The Nation's Children*, Vol. 1. New York: Columbia University Press, 1960.

Office of Policy Planning and Research, U.S. Department of Labor, *The Negro Family: The Case for National Action*. Washington, D.C.: U.S. Government Printing Office, 1965.

Rainwater, Lee, "Crucible of Identity: The Negro Lower-Class Family," *Daedalus*, 95 (Winter 1966), 172–216.

———, and Yancey, William L., eds., *The Moynihan Report and the Politics of Controversy*. Cambridge, Mass.: M.I.T. Press, 1967.

Schulz, David A., *Coming Up Black*. Englewood Cliffs, N.J.: Prentice-Hall, 1969.

XII

THE ECONOMIC STATUS
OF THE NEGRO

At all periods the Negroes have been an important factor in the economic life and development of the American South. As slaves they were employed chiefly in plantation agriculture, especially in the production of cotton, rice, tobacco, and sugar, but they were also the chief element in the supply of common labor in the towns. A small percentage of the slaves was employed in the skilled and semi-skilled trades; every considerable plantation had workmen trained in various handicrafts. Judged by present-day standards, on the basis of such samples of their handicraft as remain, this slave work was very crude and indicates nothing in regard to native ability along these lines. But regardless of the quality of Negro craftsmanship and of the general inefficiency of the unskilled labor, the slaves performed practically all the work.

No group in the population, in proportion to its contribution, has profited so little from the economic development of the country and the region. For most of the American period, they shared not at all in the wealth that their labor produced. Their status was that of work animals; they owned no property and had no economic status in the society.

Whatever status the Negroes have reached must be evaluated in the light of the recency of their opportunity; the independent economic life dates no farther back than the Civil War period. It is true that in the period of bondage the slaves acquired some knowledge of American life and some control of simple work processes; at their emancipation they were wholly without capital.

The only exception to be made is in the case of the free Negroes. This element of the Negro population, numbering nearly one-half million in 1860, nominally at least had the same legal rights as white men in respect to the acquisition and ownership of property. There were some restrictions, varying with time and place, but they could engage in most of the occupations open to white men. The regulations in regard to residence and travel as well as restrictions on their occupational mobility interfered seriously with economic advance of the free Negroes.

THE FREE NEGROES

A considerable number of the free Negroes accumulated a little property and a few became fairly prosperous and highly respected members of their communities. A few members of the free group were slave holders. In general, restrictions were placed upon their ownership of this form of property but the ownership of Negro slaves by Negroes began quite early and the number of slaves so owned increased with the years. In 1790 there were 195 free "colored," presumably Negro, families reported as slave holding and the number may have been larger since data on this point are not available for several of the states. In 1860 there were 132 slave-owning Negroes in the city of Charleston and it has been estimated that approximately 6,000 Negroes owned a total of 18,000 slaves during the life of the institution. One effort to determine the extent of slave holding by free Negroes is requoted in Table 16-1, taken from W. D. Weatherford and Charles S. Johnson, *Race Relations.*

Table 16-1: NEGRO SLAVE OWNERS AND NEGRO-OWNED SLAVES

State	Negro Slave Holders	Negro-Owned Slaves
Alabama	48	197
Arkansas	1	3
Connecticut	1	1
Delaware	9	21
District of Columbia	133	242
Florida	15	92
Georgia	61	205
Illinois	7	11
Kentucky	120	265
Louisiana	956	4,277
Maryland	655	1,575
Mississippi	17	74
Missouri	4	6
New Hampshire	3	3
New Jersey	16	32
New York	21	41
North Carolina	192	624
Ohio	1	6
Pennsylvania	23	50
Rhode Island	3	3
South Carolina	467	2,788
Tennessee	69	153
Virginia	983	2,236
Totals	3,805	12,905

The considerable number of Negro slave owners and Negro-owned slaves is better understood when it is recalled that in many cases free Negro men bought their wives and owned them as slaves and that in such cases the children by the slave wife were slaves of their father. The great majority of Negro slave owners were in the areas where the free mulatto cast was organized and divorced in sympathy from the slave Negroes of darker hue.

The great majority of the free Negroes were unskilled laborers who owned little or no property. They had in many places a traditional monopoly on certain occupations. But in the decades before the Civil War they suffered a severe economic setback due to the coming of large numbers of European immigrants. In the new competition the Negroes were quickly displaced from many of their traditional occupations. As cooks, house-servants, waiters, barbers, coachmen, and in various forms of rough labor their monopoly disappeared as soon as an alternative labor supply appeared. The opposition to their entrance into skilled industry increased: the white workmen opposed them and master mechanics usually refused to take them as apprentices. The abolitionists carried on an agitation for the establishment of manual labor schools in which Negro children would be given the industrial training which they could not get as apprentices. A convention called in 1830 to consider the problem of the free Negro recommended the reconstruction of their schools on the manual labor basis. The abolitionists approved the recommendation but popular sentiment remained opposed to the industrial training of Negroes. The few industrial schools established were not successful, partly for the reason that they were not honestly industrial but undertook to subordinate industrial training to literary education or endeavored to combine the two. The riots in Washington, New York, Cincinnati, and elsewhere in the thirties and forties were due in some part to the bitter antagonism of white skilled laborers against Negro competition.

THE ECONOMIC REORGANIZATION OF NEGRO LIFE

At the time of the Emancipation a few Negro individuals had some savings. There were a few planters and small tradesmen. It is estimated that there were perhaps 12,000 Negro-owned homes and 20,000 Negro-operated farms at the time of the Civil War. About 2,000 Negroes were operating small business concerns. A number of free Negroes were skilled or semi-skilled tradesmen. But the overwhelming majority, both North and South, were unskilled workmen without savings. The total amount of property owned by Negroes in 1866 is liberally estimated to have been valued at under $20 million.

The granting of freedom left the former slaves without guidance or protection. Many of them, disinclined to continue regular work, drifted to the towns and army posts awaiting federal aid and anticipating a redistribution of southern lands and other property. The irregular life and extreme poverty resulted in a great increase in disease, vice, and crime.

As the white South came again into control various restrictions were placed upon the Negroes in the effort to restore order and to reinstate, in so far as possible, the status of slavery which could no longer exist in name. To control the idleness and wandering, various states enacted vagrancy laws of special application to Negroes, the term often being so defined as to include not only all idle and disorderly Negroes but also those engaged in any activity not approved by the white group. Many apprenticeship laws applicable to Negroes only were enacted and these effected in some cases a virtual reinstatement of slavery. The restrictions placed upon the occupations that Negroes might follow differed from state to state. It was commonly made unlawful for them to sell liquor or run taverns and in most cases they were forbidden to own or carry firearms and weapons. In some cases the provisions were such as seriously to interfere with their economic progress: South Carolina virtually restricted their activity to farming, domestic service, and common labor, and in some other states the legal obstacles to economic advance were equally great.

In the long period of experimentation and reorganization the race gradually advanced its economic position. The advance was irregular, at times halting and uncertain. In certain respects there was deterioration; there was a pretty general decline in craftsmanship, and certain occupations in which the race at one time had a virtual monopoly were lost. But gradually the Negroes acquired an interest in land ownership and gained an entrance into a more varied group of occupations. A small property-owning, middle-class group emerged. The advance was retarded in many respects by prejudice and discrimination but gains were made. Around the 1930's the value of the property owned by Negroes was estimated to be approximately $2,500,000,000.

OCCUPATIONAL DISTRIBUTION

At the present time the proportion of Negroes fourteen years of age and over engaged in gainful occupation is slightly less (50.4 per cent) than the proportion of the white population (51.3 per cent). Prior to 1960 the proportion of Negroes employed was always greater than in any other group in the population. In 1950 gainfully employed Negroes fourteen years of age and over numbered roughly 5,370,000 or 56.3 per cent; in 1930 there were 5,503,535 Negroes gainfully employed, which was 59.2 per cent of the Negro population of ten years or over. Ten years earlier the number was 4,824,151 or 59.9 per cent of the total of these age groups.

The foreign-born whites, who are closest to the Negroes in this respect, had 60.3 per cent employed in 1910, and 57.4 per cent in 1920, and 56.1 per cent in 1930.

Table 17-1 gives the facts in regard to employment for the different divisions of the population, 1910–30 and 1950–60.

Table 17-1: PERCENTAGE OF THE POPULATION 10 YEARS OF AGE AND OVER IN GAINFUL OCCUPATIONS, 1910–1960* †

Class of Population	1910	1920	1930	1950	1960
All Classes	53.3	50.3	49.5	53.4	51.2
Native White	49.0	47.4	47.0		
				49.9**	51.3**
Foreign-born White	60.3	57.4	56.1		
Negro	71.0	59.9	59.2	56.3	50.4
Other Colored	61.1	53.4	51.2	....	....

* Source: U.S. Department of Commerce, Bureau of the Census, *Census of Population: 1950*, Vol. II, Part I *United States Summary, and Census of Population: 1960*, Vol. II, Part I *United States Summary*
† Data for 1950–60 refers to population 14 years of age and over
** Refers to total whites

The high percentage of Negroes employed was due in large part to the number of women workers, and the sharp decrease in the decade ending in 1920 was due to the change in the percentage of women workers. There were more men gainfully employed in 1920 than in 1910, though the percentage employed fell from 87.4 to 81.1; there was a further percentage decline to 80.2 in 1930, to 69.0 in 1950, and to 63.8 in 1960, though the total number employed increased from roughly 3,500,000 men in 1950 to 3,600,000 in 1960. The percentage of Negro men gainfully employed was less at each enumeration than was that of certain other population groups. The percentage of men gainfully employed by different population classes is shown in Table 17-2, p. 219.

In the decade ending in 1920 the percentage of women employed declined from 54.7 per cent to 38.9 per cent, and there was an actual as well as a percental decline. In 1930 the per cent employed was the same as in 1920, though there was a gross increase in the number of females over ten years old from 1,571,289 in 1920 to 1,840,642 in 1930. There were 1,870,-000 employed women (33.8 per cent) in 1950, and ten years later the number increased to 2,455,000 or 38.5 per cent of the total. At each enumeration the percentage of Negro women employed was greater than for any other population group.

Table 17-3, p. 219, shows the comparative facts in regard to the employment of women 1910–60.

Table 17-2: PERCENTAGE OF MALES 10 YEARS OLD AND OVER
GAINFULLY OCCUPIED 1910–1960* †

Class of Population	1910	1920	1930	1940	1950	1960
Total	81.3	78.2	76.2	66.8	73.3	72.9
Native White	77.9	75.1	73.4			
				66.9**	73.6**	73.1**
Foreign-born White	90.0	89.3	88.4			
Negro	87.4	81.1	80.2	65.3	69.0	63.8
Other Races	80.8	75.4	78.0	....	....	....

* Source: Data for 1940, 1950, and 1960, U.S. Department of Commerce, Bureau of the Census, *Census of Population: 1940*, Vol. II, Part I *United States Summary*; *1950*, Vol. II, Part I *United States Summary*; and *1960*, Vol. II, Part I *United States Summary*
† Data for 1940–60 refers to population 14 years of age and over
** Refers to total whites

During the 1920–30 decade there was a somewhat marked improvement in the economic position of the Negroes. This is reflected in the decline in the number of women employed and in the shift in numbers in different occupations. The following tables give the number of Negro women in the chief occupations in which they were gainfully employed in 1930 and in 1950–60.

The bulk of Negro workers have been employed in a comparatively few lines. In 1910 the percentages of the gainfully employed in the five main occupations were as follows: agricultural pursuits 54.6; domestic and personal service 21.6; manufacturing and mechanical pursuits 12.6; trade and transportation 7.2; professional service 1.3. In 1920 the distribution was as follows: agricultural pursuits 44.2; domestic and personal service

Table 17-3: PERCENTAGE OF WOMEN 10 YEARS OLD AND OVER
GAINFULLY OCCUPIED, 1910–1960* [a]

Class of Population	1910	1920	1930	1940[b]	1950	1960
Total	23.4	21.1	22.0	22.0	27.6	34.5
Native White	19.2	19.3	20.5			
				21.0[c]	26.3[c]	33.6[c]
Foreign-born White	21.7	18.4	18.8			
Negro	54.7	38.9	38.9	32.2	33.8	38.5
Other Races	17.6	13.7	15.2	....	....	....

* Source: Data for 1940, 1950, and 1960, U.S. Department of Commerce, Bureau of the Census, *Census of Population: 1940*, Vol. II, Part I *United States Summary*; *1950*, Vol. II, Part I *United States Summary*; and *1960*, Vol. II, Part I *United States Summary*
[a] Data for 1940–60 refers to population 14 years of age and over
[b] Employed (except public emergency work)
[c] Refers to total whites

Table 17-4A: NUMBER OF NEGRO WOMEN, 10 YEARS OLD AND OVER,
IN THE CHIEF OCCUPATIONS OF NEGRO WOMEN, 1930

Occupations	Total	Number Employed Per 1,000 Employed Women
All occupations	1,840,642	
Servants	727,342	395
Farm laborers (wage workers)	120,114	65
Farmers (owners and tenants)	76,422	41
Laundry operatives	47,546	26
Teachers	45,672	25
Waiters	17,628	9
Tobacco factory operatives	14,976	8
Hairdressers and manicurists	12,816	7
Janitors and sextons	6,033	3
Clerks	4,930	3
General labor	4,620	2
Elevator operators	4,443	2
Saleswomen	4,378	2
Retail dealers	3,849	2
Labor in tobacco factories	3,391	2
Cleaning and pressing-shop workers	3,200	2
Musicians and teachers of music	2,836	1
Laborers (cotton mills)	2,050	1

22.0; manufacturing and mechanical pursuits 18.7; trade and transportation 9.4; professional service 1.7.

The distributions for 1930 and 1950–60 are given in Tables 17-5A and 17-5B, (pp. 222, 223), which allow a comparison of Negro workers with the gainfully employed of other population groups.

It is clear from the figures that the Negroes are rather rapidly shifting from agriculture to other pursuits. In most lines there has been a gradual advance in the amount of Negro employment. But the occupational distribution of the Negroes is still excessive in the agricultural pursuits and in domestic service. In these occupations, they comprise a considerable percentage of all persons so employed.

THE NEGRO FARMERS

Prior to 1940 Negroes were engaged in largest numbers in the agricultural pursuits. Of the Negroes ten years old and over gainfully employed in 1930, 36.1 per cent were in some form of agriculture. With the exception of the relatively small group classed as "other races" (Mexicans, Indians, Chinese, Japanese, Filipinos, Hindus, Koreans, Hawaiians, etc.) this was greatly in excess of the per cent of agricultural workers in any other class of the population; the percentage of the total population, and of the native whites, engaged in agricultural pursuits was in each case 21.4. Of

Table 17-4B: NUMBER OF NEGRO WOMEN EMPLOYED, 14 YEARS OLD AND OVER, IN THE CHIEF OCCUPATIONS OF NEGRO WOMEN, 1950–1960*

	1950		1960	
	Number (1,000)	*Per 1,000*	*Number (1,000)*	*Per 1,000*
Chief Occupations of Negro Women	1,839	1,000	2,260	1,000
Private household workers	744	421	888	393
Operatives and kindred workers, durable and nondurable manufacturing	136	74	103	46
Laundry-dry cleaning operatives	99	54	99	44
Farm laborers (wage-workers)	67	36	58	26
Teachers	68	37	100	44
Waiters, bartenders, counter workers	42	23	54	24
Charwomen, janitors, and porters	35	19	51	22
Laborers, except farm and mines	28	15	24	10
Hairdressers, cosmetologists	27	15	32	14
Secretaries, stenographers, typists	22	12	52	23
Managers, officials and proprietors, salaried and self-employed	22	12	21	9
Saleswomen and sales clerks, retail trade	20	11	29	13
Attendants, hospital and other institutions	19	10	67	30
Practical nurses, midwives	16	9	32	14
Nurses, professional and student	15	8	34	15
Bookkeepers and cashiers	7	4	17	7
Insurance and real estate agents and brokers (including other specified sales workers)	4	2	4	2
Social, welfare, and recreation workers	4	2	9	4
Telephone operators	2	1	8	3
Musicians and music teachers	..	..	4	2
Librarians	1	..	3	1
All other occupations	..	..	571	254

* Source: *Census of Population: 1950*, Vol. II, Part I *United States Summary*; and *1960*, Vol. II, Part I *United States Summary*, Table 257

the foreign-born whites, only 9.1 per cent were engaged in agricultural pursuits. In the case of males the percentages were as follows: total 25.1; Negro 40.7; native white 26.0; foreign-born white 10.3; other races 41.8.

The percentages engaged in agricultural pursuits were less for each racial group than in the earlier decades. In 1910, 54.6 per cent of the Negroes, 33.8 per cent of the native whites, and 40.1 per cent of the other race groups were so engaged. In 1920, 25.6 per cent of the gainfully employed population was engaged in agricultural pursuits; the percentage of Negroes so engaged was 44.2, the percentage of native whites was 26.3,

Table 17-5A: PERCENTAGE DISTRIBUTION BY GENERAL OCCUPATIONAL DIVISIONS
OF GAINFUL WORKERS 10 YEARS OLD AND OVER, BY RACIAL CLASSES, 1930

General Division of Occupations	Total	Negro	Native-born White	Foreign-born White	Other Races
All occupations	100.0	100.0	100.0	100.0	100.0
Agriculture	21.4	36.1	21.4	9.1	39.4
Forestry and fishing	0.5	0.6	0.5	0.6	0.9
Extraction of minerals	2.0	1.4	1.9	3.1	2.6
Manufacturing and mechanical industries	28.9	18.6	27.5	44.1	21.1
Transportation and communication	7.9	7.2	8.2	6.6	10.9
Trade	12.5	3.3	13.7	13.7	6.7
Public service (not elsewhere classified)	1.8	0.9	1.9	1.6	0.9
Professional service	6.7	2.5	7.9	4.4	1.9
Domestic and personal service	10.1	28.6	6.6	12.7	14.5
Clerical occupations	8.2	0.7	10.4	4.1	1.3

Table 17-5B: DISTRIBUTION OF GAINFULLY EMPLOYED NEGRO WORKERS
14 YEARS OLD AND OVER, BY INDUSTRY, 1950–1960*

	Negro		White	
	1950	1960	1950	1960
Total	100.0	100.0	100.0	100.0
Agricultural	19.0	8.9	11.4	6.2
Forestry and fisheries	0.3	0.1	0.2	0.1
Mining	0.8	0.3	1.7	1.0
Construction	5.5	5.4	6.2	6.0
Durable goods manufacturing	10.8	10.8	14.2	15.7
Nondurable goods manufacturing	7.8	8.1	12.6	12.3
Transportation, communications, other public utilities	6.1	5.3	8.0	7.1
Wholesale and retail trade	11.5	12.3	19.5	18.9
Finance, insurance, and real estate	1.6	1.6	3.6	4.5
Business and repair services	1.4	1.7	2.6	2.6
Personal services	22.8	21.6	4.4	4.3
Entertainment and recreational services	0.8	0.8	1.0	0.8
Professional and related services	6.6	11.0	8.5	11.8
Public administration	3.4	4.8	4.5	5.0
Industry not reported	1.6	7.3	1.6	3.7

* Source: *Census of Population, 1950*, Vol. II, Part I *United States Summary*; and
1960, Vol. II, Part I *United States Summary*, Table 257

Table 17-6A: DISTRIBUTION OF GAINFULLY EMPLOYED WORKERS 10 YEARS OLD
AND OVER, BY GENERAL DIVISIONS OF OCCUPATIONS, 1930

| | Distribution per 1,000 Gainfully Occupied | | |
| | Negro | Native White | Foreign-born White |
Occupations	1,000	1,000	1,000
Agriculture	361	214	91
Domestic and personal service	286	66	127
Manufacturing and mechanical industries	186	275	441
Transportation and communication	72	82	66
Trade	33	137	127
Professional service	25	79	44
Extraction of metals	14	19	31
Public service (not elsewhere classified)	9	19	16
Clerical occupations	7	104	41
Forestry and fishing	6	5	6

Table 17-6B: DISTRIBUTION OF GAINFULLY EMPLOYED WORKERS 14 YEARS OLD
AND OVER, BY GENERAL DIVISIONS OF OCCUPATIONS, 1960*

| | Distribution per 1,000 Gainfully Occupied | |
| | Negro | White |
Occupations	1,000	1,000
Personal services	216	43
Wholesale and retail trade	123	189
Professional and related services	110	118
Durable goods manufacturing	108	157
Agricultural	89	62
Nondurable goods manufacturing	81	123
Construction	54	60
Transportation, communication, and other public utilities	53	71
Public administration	48	50
Business and repair services	17	26
Finance, insurance, and real estate	16	45
Entertainment and recreational services	8	8
Mining	3	10
Forestry and fisheries	1	1
Industry not reported	73	37

* Source: *Census of Population, 1960*, Vol. II, Part I *United States Summary*, Table 257

the percentage of foreign-born whites was 11.2, and the percentage of the other race groups was 41.3.

In spite of the fact that the Negroes had made advances in a number of occupations, agriculture was still the most important pursuit in 1930, and Negroes were an important part of the agricultural workers of the country. This is a condition of long standing. In 1910, Negroes composed 22.9 per cent of the agricultural workers of the country; in 1920, they composed 19.0 per cent; this percentage remained the same up to 1950. Since then, those engaged in agricultural pursuits declined sharply to 8.9 in 1960. For the white population the decline was equally dramatic: from 21.4 per cent in 1930 to 11.4 per cent in 1950, to only 6.2 per cent in 1960.

Table 18-1: NUMBER OF NEGRO FARM OPERATORS, BY SOUTHERN REGIONS AND STATES, 1910–1964*†

	1910	1920	1930	1940	1950	1954	1959	1964
United States	(NA)	926	883	682	560	(NA)	273	184
The South	881	916	871	672	551	460	267	180
South Atlantic								
Maryland	6	6	5	4	4	3	2	2
Virginia	48	48	40	35	28	24	16	12
North Carolina	64	75	75	57	69	63	41	27
South Carolina	97	109	77	61	61	54	31	20
Georgia	122	130	87	59	50	39	20	11
Florida	15	13	11	10	7	6	4	3
East South Central								
Kentucky	12	13	9	6	5	4	3	2
Tennessee	38	38	35	28	24	21	15	11
Alabama	110	95	94	73	27	26	29	21
Mississippi	164	161	183	150	123	101	55	37
West South Central								
Arkansas	64	72	80	57	41	31	15	9
Louisiana	55	62	74	60	41	33	18	12
Oklahoma	13	13	15	9	6	4	3	2
Texas	70	79	86	53	34	27	15	11

* Source: *U.S. Census of Agriculture,* 1959, Vol. II, and 1964, Vol. II
† Numbers in thousands

The number of Negro farm operators has increased irregularly during the present century. In 1900, the number of Negro farm operators was 746,715; in 1910 the number was 893,370; in 1920, the number was 925,708; and in 1930, the number was 882,850. The increase is not in proportion to the growth of Negro population; the Negro numbers increased over 3,000,000—nearly 35 per cent; the Negro farms increased about 18 per cent. In the decade 1920–1930, there was a decrease of 4.6 per cent in the number of Negro farm operators. This was parallel with the movement of white farm operators which represented a decrease of 2.3 per cent during the decade. Of the total number of Negro farm operators, 98.7 per cent were in the South in 1930. In the South the number of Negro farmers decreased 44,659; in the North and West the number increased—1,724 in the North and 77 in the West.

A much smaller percentage of Negro than of white farmers own the land they cultivate. About one-fifth of the Negroes and over three-fifths of the white farmers own the property they are operating. In 1930 there were 181,016 Negro-owned farms and 700,911 Negro tenant farms. The owners were 20.5 per cent and the tenants 79.4 per cent of the total. Of the white farm operators, 3,365,674 or 62.6 per cent were owners and 1,954,137 or 36.4 per cent were tenants.

The number of farm owners of each race decreased during the 1930's and the amount of farm tenancy correspondingly increased. There was, in the Negro group, a decrease of over 37,000 farm owners. The percentage of Negro-owned farms is greater in the North and West than in the South: in the West over one-half (57.0 per cent) of the Negro farmers are farm owners; in the North over one-third (39.8 per cent) own the land they till; in the South about one-fifth (20.2 per cent) of the Negro farm operating groups are owners. The Negro farm groups are mostly in the South; some 98.7 per cent of the Negroes engaged in agricultural pursuits are in the southern states.

The average size of Negro-owned farms is considerably below that of farms owned by white farmers, and there is a tendency for the average to decrease. In 1910 the average acreage per farm of all land owned by white farmers was 156.3 acres; in 1920, this average acreage had increased to 168.0; in 1930 the average acreage per white farmer was 179.6 acres. The colored-owned farms, chiefly Negro, in 1910 averaged 79.1 acres; in 1920 the average acreage had decreased to 71.6; in 1930 the average acreage was 68.0 acres. The average acreage of Negro-owned farms in 1930 was 61.9 acres. The smaller average size of the Negro-owned farms is in part due to location: nearly all Negro-owned farms are in the South and, generally speaking, the size of all farms is smaller in the South than in other sections of the country.

The size of Negro and white operated farms in the different sections of the country in 1920 and 1930 is given in the following table.

Table 18-2: AVERAGE ACREAGE PER FARM OF NEGRO AND WHITE OPERATORS, BY SECTIONS, 1920 AND 1930

Section	Negroes		Whites	
	1920	*1930*	*1920*	*1930*
United States	44.8	42.6	165.7	176.0
The South	44.3	42.2	135.2	130.3
The North	81.9	64.9	156.5	166.5
The West	163.7	145.4	369.8	446.6

The value of Negro-owned land fluctuated violently in the decades following 1910. In 1910 the valuation of all colored-owned farm property (land and buildings) was $440,922,439; in 1920 the valuation was $648,-760,084. This remarkable increase was due to the general rise in the valuation of all farm property in the decade, and to the fact that the valuation of farm property in the South increased more, proportionally, than did similar values in the North and West. In 1930, the valuation of all colored-owned farm land and buildings was set at $410,534,526; that of the Negroes was set at $334,451,396.

The average value of lands and buildings is much less for Negroes than for whites. In the United States in 1910, the average value of Negro farms was reported as $22.23 per acre; the average value of white farms was reported as $40.57 per acre. In 1920, the average value per acre of Negro land and buildings was $54.49; in 1930 it was $37.32. The average value per acre of land and buildings on farms operated by whites was $70.02 in 1920 and $48.94 in 1930.

The present status of Negro farm operators may be stated briefly as follows: (1) percentage-wise about the same number of Negro operators, (97.8 per cent) are in the South as they were in 1930. They are most numerous in the tobacco-growing areas and the older cotton-growing areas, as they have been in the past; (2) the number of Negro operators reveals a steady, sharp decline, from 871,000 in 1930 to 180,000 in 1964. During the same period full owners decreased by nearly 51,000 or 36.1 per cent, part owners by 4,000 or 9.8 per cent, and the tenants by as large a number as 560,000 or 80.1 per cent; (3) the movement of people from farms was especially heavy in the South between 1950 and 1959; in this short period the number of farms decreased by 38.0 per cent; (4) Farms of nonwhite operators in the South continued to be small, with an average size of 56 acres of cropland harvested as compared with an average size of 382 acres and 93 acres of cropland harvested for white operators. In 1959 the average value of land and buildings was $7,328 for nonwhite operators as compared with $37,816 for white operators; (5) the future outlook for Negro farm operators is far from optimistic.

Negro Tenant Farming

The typical Negro farmer is a tenant rather than an independent farm owner. Only about one-fifth of the Negro farmers are owners or part owners of the land they cultivate; approximately four-fifths are tenants. In 1930, some 15.8 per cent were classed as owners and 4.7 per cent as part owners, 11.1 per cent were cash tenants, 44.7 per cent were croppers, and 23.5 per cent were classed as other tenants. The percentage distribution at the last three enumerations is given in the following table for the different sections of the country.

Table 19-1: PERCENTAGE DISTRIBUTION OF NEGRO FARM TENANTS,
1910–1930

Section	1910	1920	1930
United States	75.3	76.2	79.4
The South	75.9	76.6	79.7
The North	35.9	36.1	59.3
The West	15.6	28.6	39.8

The large southern plantations are commonly subdivided into an acreage that a single family can operate. These small plots are rented by the season and worked by the renter and his family. The degree of independence of the renter depends upon his ability and financial responsibility. If he pays a cash rent he is free from supervision and interference.

But the typical Negro renter is without means, and gives a share of the crop in lieu of a money rent. This system developed through trial and error in the period of readjustment of the labor to the land at the close of the Civil War. The overthrow of the slave labor system left the Negroes with the problem of making a living. Their chief asset was physical strength but they were wholly irresponsible and not disposed to work beyond the necessary minimum. In order to hold the necessary labor until the crop was harvested the planters would employ the Negro for a period of six months or a year, the wage not to be paid until the end of the period of employment, the planter furnishing rations for the Negro and his family during the period of employment. Another common arrangement was to pay a monthly wage and to furnish in addition a plot of ground that the laborer might cultivate for his own profit, the landlord furnishing teams, machinery, and seed and allowing the man certain days of each week to cultivate and harvest his crop. The four-day plan was an arrangement by which the Negro worked four days for the employer and was allowed the other days to cultivate a plot furnished him by the landlord who also provided the seed, stock, and farm implements. The laborer under this arrangement received a weekly ration. Out of the various experiments tried the share-crop system gradually developed and at the present time a very large percentage, approximately two-fifths, of the southern Negro farm tenants are croppers.

In this arrangement the tenant is supplied with tools, machinery, seed, and other necessaries as well as with land and farm equipment in return for which the landlord receives a stipulated share of the crop, usually fifty per cent. In another system of tenancy rather widely practiced in certain parts of the South, the tenant furnishes the stock, implements, seed, and fertilizer, paying the landlord one-quarter to one-third of the crop produced. A common division is one-fourth of the cotton and one-third of the corn and other crops. In either arrangement the tenant furnishes the labor. The landlord frequently advances the tenant money or provisions which stand as a charge against his share of the crop. If the tenant neglects the crop, and the typical share cropper, whether Negro or white, is not inclined to do more work than is absolutely necessary, the landlord may hire the necessary labor and deduct the cost from the tenant's share of the crop.

The system, which grew up and persists because of the poverty and weakness of the southern white and Negro peasantry, often operates to keep the cropper dependent. The landlord has considerable financial investment and assumes the risk of crop failure. Consequently, he takes a very active interest in, and assumes supervision of, the tenant's activity. The value of the arrangement varies with the character of the landlord. The average cropper is uneducated and dull, often stupid and irresponsible. The landlord's supervision may determine the success rather than the failure of the joint enterprise and be as much to the advantage of the tenant as to the land owner. The tenant receives the supervision needed to be successful. It is the system that has enabled the Negroes in the South to make such agricultural advance as they have; it has led to the independence of many ambitious and industrious Negroes.

Toward the Negro croppers the landlords, by choice or necessity, often assume a patriarchal attitude. They care for them in sickness, settle family and community quarrels, protect them from exploitation by others, and see that they are fed, clothed, and cared for in time of disaster.

The system contains latent possibilities of fraud and exploitation; the dishonest landlord may take advantage of the system. The average Negro cropper will spend as much money during the season as the man who is financing him will permit. He is sometimes charged exorbitant rates for money and supplies advanced and may end the year so deeply in debt to the landlord that his share of the crop may be insufficient to cover the obligation. The supplies are often furnished from a plantation store and the tenant not allowed to buy elsewhere. This is a method of protecting both the landlord and the tenant but one that can be used by the unscrupulous landlord for purposes of robbing the tenants. The "classing" of cotton requires a degree of skill and ability that the Negro commonly does not possess and the dishonest planter profits by taking advantage of this ignorance.

The common desire of the Negroes is to escape the supervision of the landlords. This they can do by becoming renters, paying cash for the use of the land, and assuming the responsibility for crop failure. The landlords, too, are glad to free themselves of responsibility and rent without risk. But success still very largely depends upon the continuous and minute supervision from which both landlord and tenant wish to be free.

Negro Peonage

A type of debt slavery, often loosely referred to as peonage, has frequently developed in the South from the system of farming and the laws governing labor contracts on the one hand and the operation of the criminal law and penal system on the other.

The paternalistic system of agriculture may be a great aid to the penniless Negro who is ambitious to establish himself as an independent farm operator. It tides him through periods of scarcity, provides him the means necessary to the successful harvesting of his crop, and affords him the advice and direction of a landlord who has assumed the financial responsibility for the enterprise.

But the tenant in the situation loses some of his independence; he is in the debt of another person and subject to that person's supervision. Because of poor judgment, crop failure, or other reason he may be unable to discharge his obligation and virtually cease to be a free person. As a protection to the landlord he may be required to remain on the plantation until he has by another crop worked out the debt contracted. It may be necessary that he borrow in order to live, thereby going deeper into debt, and his obligations may become such that he virtually becomes a serf. An unscrupulous planter, by indulging the shiftless tendency of the Negro tenant and his disposition to borrow against the crop, may get a tenant so deeply in debt that the tenant's share of the crop will not cover the amount of the indebtedness. In such case the tenant is legally bound to the plantation until the obligation is discharged.

The criminal law and practice of many of the southern states has fostered another and slightly different type of slavery. In the case of Negro petty offenders it has been customary to impose a fine-work sentence, that is, the offender has the choice of paying a cash fine or working a specified number of days in the chain gang. The offenders are commonly unable to pay the fine. In such cases the fine may be paid by a white friend and the Negro freed. In some cases it is paid by the employer or planter on agreement that the offender work out the amount for him at a small wage, perhaps fifty cents a day. On such agreement the contract labor law allows the planter to hold the convict until the debt is paid. The offender is then charged for food, clothing, and money advanced him by his employer. If the offender runs away, refuses to work, or disobeys the commands of the master he may be returned to jail and this results in the imposition of a new sentence.

Obviously, the system is open to abuse and often is grossly abused. Plantation owners and employers may conspire with the authorities to recruit cheap labor in this manner. Negroes may be arrested for slight of-

fenses and farmed out to employers. The shiftlessness and extravagance
of the offenders are then taken advantage of and instead of discharging
the obligations they may go deeper and deeper into debt; the white man
is the bookkeeper and his statement of the account is accepted by the
court. With or without the consent of the debtor, the employer may sell
or transfer his claim against the Negro to some other farmer who is in
need of labor. This is, of course, equivalent to selling the Negro.

Other laws also foster peonage. For example, the probation law of Georgia, passed in 1913, allowed the defendant, in counties having no regular
salaried probation officer, to serve a sentence outside the jail or chain gang
under the supervision of the court. The purpose was doubtless an effort to
mitigate the evils of the penal system so far as young children were concerned. The court was allowed to appoint a volunteer probation officer to
aid the probationer in carrying out the terms of the probation. Since only
a few of the counties had regularly appointed probation officers, the delinquents were farmed out. Like the practice above, this plan was open to
grave abuse and was often grossly abused. The parole law of 1908 was
also grossly abused in this way through the provision that made it possible
for a prisoner, after serving a minimum time, to be paroled to an individual for an indefinite period which might be for years.

Legalized peonage through the leasing out of convicts has stopped:
its legislative basis was declared unconstitutional by the United States
Supreme Court in 1911. That the practice has not ceased is evident from
time to time in exposures that come to public attention. There is no
strong public opinion opposed to it and the employer is often a law unto
himself. It has attracted wide comment because of its spectacular features
but is of trifling importance in comparison with the type of peonage inherent in the tenant system operated by powerful landlords and weak and
ignorant Negroes.

THE NEGRO IN INDUSTRY

Negro workers have been and still are a comparatively unimportant factor in the industrial life of the nation. In various non-manufacturing pursuits their labor has always been in demand but within the industrial field
they have been for the most part restricted to unskilled work. Even in the
unskilled occupations they have been in many cases unable to succeed in
competition with the recent immigrants. They have had little opportunity
and have made little advance in the skilled trades. In the decade prior to
World War I there was a steady migration of northern Negroes to the
South for the reason that they could not earn a living in the North in
competition with immigrant labor.

The outbreak of the war gave the Negroes an industrial opportunity
they had not previously enjoyed. The stoppage of immigration, the army

mobilization, and the sudden stimulation of industrial activity created a scarcity of common labor. Men and women were needed in large numbers to do work supplying food, clothing, and war supplies and to take the place of more efficient men sent elsewhere. To secure workers the industrial plants stimulated a flow from the great reservoir of black labor in the South. There was a general exodus of Negroes from the South: approximately 330,000 migrated during the decade ending in 1920. After the emergency, in the period of readjustment, there was a disposition to replace Negro workers or use them in less skilled capacities and at lower pay. In the fall of 1922 there was a renewal of this migratory movement. The imposition of new restrictions on immigration and the expanding business created a demand for unskilled labor and the industrial plants again turned to the southern Negro supply. Probably 500,000 Negroes migrated northward within the following year. A considerable percentage of these migrants found work, chiefly as common laborers, in the steel industry, in the packing plants, in coal mining, and in various other industries.

It was during World War II and the years immediately following that Negro workers made a significant breakthrough in some lines of industrial work heretofore closed to them. An acute labor shortage, particularly the dearth of qualified young white males as they were drawn into the armed forces, led the northern industrialists to look to white women and Negroes of both sexes to fill the labor vacuum. Negro workers were able to wedge themselves into new types of work, without at the same time arousing fear of racial competition for jobs. There was that famous Executive Order 8802 of President Roosevelt: it forbade discrimination on the basis of race, creed, or national origin by employers who held government war contracts. The FEPC was set up in 1941 to implement the order, and in several cases the committee was able to prevent outright racial discrimination and to open new jobs to Negroes. The decade 1940–50 was a period of considerable geographical shifting of Negro workers, accompanied by changes, albeit small, in the occupational structure of the race.

In comparison with the white race and other nonwhite races, except for American Indians, occupational gains by Negro workers in the period of national crisis and economic prosperity that followed the war were tragically small and unimpressive. Even as recently as 1960 Negroes classified as white-collar workers constituted only 11.0 per cent of the total of employed Negro men (the corresponding figure for white men was 37.0 per cent). For the same year Negro men classified as blue-collar workers comprised 54.6 per cent of the total (white men, 45.6 per cent); the percentage for male Negro service workers continued to be high, 14.7 (for whites, 5.3 per cent); and farm workers decreased to 11.3 per cent (white farmers, 7.9 per cent). In short, Negro male workers are still highly concentrated in the semiskilled, unskilled, service, and farm operator occupations. Out of every 100 employed Negro men nearly 24 are operatives, 20 are laborers, 15 are service workers, 10 are craftsmen or foremen, and 11 are farm operators or farm workers.

Negro women are even more highly concentrated in a few lower-level occupations than Negro men. The lower rung of operatives, unskilled laborers in durable and nondurable manufacturing, comprised 13.6 per cent (16.2 for white women) of the total of employed Negro women; service workers, 57.3 per cent (whites 16.5), and farm operators or workers, 3.4 per cent (whites 1.4). The whys of this occupational gap require some explanation.

The initial employment of Negroes in industry was due in nearly all cases to the fact that white laborers were not available. Their adaptability to skilled labor has not everywhere been accepted, and in processes demanding highly skilled work they have not been widely employed. For work that assumes the mastery of a trade—painting, carpentry, brick-laying, and the like—they are seldom considered if other labor is available. A general belief still persists that Negroes are not fitted to perform technical tasks of other than a routine nature. The steretotype of the shiftless and undependable Negro man has militated against the employment of individuals in positions of responsibility. When individuals have been given a trial at skilled labor the results have sometimes been surprising to employers and superintendents. On the other hand, many employers who have used Negro labor in manufacturing industries believe them to be less satisfactory than white laborers. On the whole, reports from nonmanufacturing industries have been much more favorable to the Negroes. The difference lies probably in the fact of greater experience in nonmanufacturing types of pursuits. If the Negroes are to gain and hold a place in industry they must do so by measuring up to prevailing labor standards—or above them. Sentiment and inertia may help or hinder the rapidity of their advance but in the end their success will depend upon their ability to meet competition.

A number of facts for which the Negroes themselves are in no way responsible have operated severely to limit their occupational field and to virtually exclude them from many occupations. As industrial workers they are seldom employed for positions that entail authority over a large number of white workers, and the popular prejudice against Negroes in certain relations often prevents the advancement of competent men. It is widely believed that promotion would sometimes raise unpleasant social questions. It is sometimes feared that to advance a competent Negro worker and allow him to occupy a position in which he would be the superior of white workers would antagonize the latter and thus tend to reduce the efficiency of the plant. A similar story can be told in regard

Table 20-1: OCCUPATIONS OF EMPLOYED NEGROES AND WHITES, BY SEX, 1960*

Occupation Group	Negro Total Number (1,000)	Negro Total Per Cent	Negro Male Number (1,000)	Negro Male Per Cent	Negro Female Number (1,000)	Negro Female Per Cent	White Total Number (1,000)	White Total Per Cent	White Male Number (1,000)	White Male Per Cent	White Female Number (1,000)	White Female Per Cent
	6,099	100.0	3,644	100.0	2,455	100.0	58,010	100.0	39,462	100.0	18,548	100.0
White-collar workers	819	13.5	401	11.0	418	17.0	25,585	44.1	14,595	37.0	10,990	59.2
Professional, technical	288	4.7	112	3.1	175	7.1	6,880	11.9	4,324	11.0	2,556	13.8
Managers, officials, proprietors	88	1.5	63	1.7	25	1.0	5,288	9.1	4,539	11.5	749	4.0
Clerical workers	360	5.9	179	4.9	182	7.4	8,883	15.3	2,814	7.1	6,069	32.7
Sales workers	83	1.4	47	1.3	36	1.5	4,533	7.8	2,918	7.4	1,615	8.7
Blue-collar workers	2,339	38.3	1,989	54.6	350	14.2	21,244	36.6	18,005	45.6	3,239	17.5
Craftsmen, foremen	372	6.1	357	9.8	16	0.6	8,317	14.3	8,082	20.5	235	1.3
Operatives	1,198	19.6	887	24.4	310	12.6	10,621	18.3	7,702	19.5	2,919	15.7
Nonfarm laborers	769	12.6	745	20.4	24	1.0	2,306	4.0	2,221	5.6	85	0.5
Service workers	1,943	31.9	535	14.7	1,408	57.3	5,148	8.9	2,082	5.3	3,067	16.5
Private household workers	915	15.0	27	0.8	888	36.1	795	1.4	32	0.1	764	4.1
Other	1,028	16.9	508	13.9	520	21.2	4,353	7.5	2,050	5.2	2,303	12.4
Farm workers	495	8.1	411	11.3	84	3.4	3,396	5.9	3,128	7.9	268	1.4
Farmers and farm managers	169	2.8	154	4.3	15	0.6	2,313	4.0	2,212	5.6	101	0.5
Farm laborers	326	5.3	257	7.0	69	2.8	1,083	1.9	916	2.3	167	0.9
Not reported	503	8.2	307	8.4	195	8.0	2,637	4.5	1,652	4.2	985	5.4

* Source: *Census of Population: 1960*, Vol. II, Part I *United States Summary*, Table 257

to work that implies association on an equal footing with white employees; a small percentage of Negroes are employed or are advanced to such positions. If the nature of the work is such that the employees must meet customers in any capacity other than that of menials, the Negro has a small chance of employment. As yet, white persons are employed as sales people, conductors, solicitors, and the like when white people are the customers. The employer in such cases is making a business adjustment to the racial attitudes of the public his business serves.

THE NEGRO AND THE LABOR UNIONS

The entrance of the Negroes into skilled industry has been consistently and at times bitterly opposed by the labor unions. Up until very recent years, the efforts of these organizations have been to restrict and monopolize skilled labor so as to force the payment of a living wage. The idea has been current among white workmen that the Negroes should be kept down and eliminated whenever their labor seems to compete with that of the whites.

The American Federation of Labor consistently expressed itself as opposed to racial discrimination. But the Federation could not control the attitude of the local unions, and these separate organizations often discriminated against or refused to admit Negroes. The friendly attitude of the Federation resulted in the organization of locals affiliated directly with the national organization. Of the affiliated unions, some expressly barred Negroes from membership especially prior to the 1960's; in certain cases the local chapters excluded them even though they may have been eligible for membership in the national or international unions. Other unions had no Negro members, though they did not expressly exclude them. In some cases this was explained on the ground that there were no Negroes following the trade or that if there were such they had not applied for membership.

The types of union relations in the present may be briefly summarized under several categories arranged in order of increasing degrees of friendliness toward Negro membership.

A large number of national and international organizations specifically excluded Negroes in the past by constitutional provisions. A list of national unions that had long-standing formal race bars as late as 1963 reads as follows: the Brotherhood of Boilermakers, Iron Shipbuilders, and Helpers of America; the Brotherhood of Railway Carmen of America; the Brotherhood of Railway and Steamship Clerks, Freight Handlers, Express and Station Employees; the Brotherhood of Dining Car Conductors; the Order of Sleeping Car Conductors; the Order of Railway Conductors of America; the Grand International Brotherhood of Locomotive Engineers;

the Brotherhood of Locomotive Firemen and Engineers; the International Association of Machinists; the Railway Mail Association; the National Organization of Masters, Mates, and Pilots; the Neptune Association; the American Federation of Railroad Workers; the Switchmen's Union of North America; the Order of Railroad Telegraphers; the Commercial Telegraphers' Union of America; the American Train Dispatchers' Association; the Brotherhood of Railroad Trainmen; the American Wire Weavers' Protective Association; the Railroad Yardmasters of America; the Railroad Yardmasters of North America. These various organizations, which pretty well covered in the 1930's the various branches of commercial transportation, included some 400,000 members and excluded perhaps 40,000 Negroes who, except for the race discrimination, would have been eligible for membership. The Blacksmiths and Helpers' Union permitted auxiliary locals of Negro helpers but did not allow Negroes to be promoted to blacksmiths. The Brotherhood of Maintenance of Way Employees and the National Rural Letter Carriers' Association admitted Negro members but barred them from office holding and representation in conventions.

In the 1930's certain unions which did not specifically bar Negroes from membership either excluded them unofficially or kept the numbers very small. The International Brotherhood of Electrical Workers, with some 140,000 members, had practically no Negro members though there were perhaps 1,200 Negroes eligible for membership. The Sheet Metal Workers had no Negro members. The plasterers' union had very few Negro members though there were perhaps 6,000 Negroes eligible. The Plumbers and Pipe Fitters Union had no Negro members. The Flint glass workers' organization had no provision against Negroes but admitted no Negro members. The Journeymen Tailors' Association had a very limited number of Negro members.

Another group of unions admitted Negroes but did not encourage their membership. The largest of these was the carpenters' union, with about one-third of a million members; they have only a few hundred Negro members though there are perhaps 30,000 Negro carpenters. The painters admitted only two or three hundred of some 10,000 Negro painters. In part the small number of Negroes in these unions was due to the fact that union membership often operated to their personal disadvantage; outside of union jurisdiction they could bargain individually, but within the union white workers were generally given preference over them by employers.

One group of unions admitted Negroes freely but only to separate unions. The American Federation of Musicians, with a membership of close to 125,000, had some 3,000 Negro members in the thirties. The organization of Hotel and Restaurant Employees had about 1,000 Negroes in a total membership of about 40,000. Other large groups with separate Negro unions were the journeymen barbers, the laundry workers, the tobacco workers, and the union of cooks and waiters.

The unions which admitted Negroes freely to separate and mixed unions include the International Longshoremen's Association, the Hod Carriers and Common Laborers Union, and the Tunnel Workers. These were the unions with the largest Negro memberships.

Certain unions admitted Negroes to mixed unions only. Chief of these were the United Mine Workers, which endeavored to prevent racial discrimination, and the Garment Workers' Union. These two groups had in the neighborhood of 10,000 Negro members.

Finally, in the thirties, there were a number of independent Negro unions with a few thousand members. Chief of these were the Railroad Men's Independent and Benevolent Association, the Dining Car Men's Association, and the Pullman Porters' Organization.

A number of unions have few or no Negro members for the reason that there are few or no Negroes in the trades. The pattern makers, operative potters, leather workers, metal engravers, and others have no Negro members because the trades are largely or exclusively restricted to whites who will not work with Negroes nor instruct them in the crafts.

There is, of course, no doubt that the action of the unions as a whole has greatly curtailed the opportunities of the Negroes in industry. The Negroes' first and often their only entrance into some industries has been secured by "scabbing" in time of strikes; the only reason for the first employment being the employer's inability to secure other labor. The attitude of the unions has in many cases antagonized the Negroes. They remember the discrimination practiced by their white fellow workers and look upon the employers as their friends. Overlooking the fact that the employer's only interest is in securing an efficient labor supply at the lowest possible wage, they side with them rather than with other workers in times of industrial dispute. The Negro workers are often advised by their leaders to remain outside the labor organizations when they are given a chance to join. It is also true that the Negro workers have in some cases profited by the exclusion policy of white unions, their exclusion from the union being the thing that enabled them to retain a place in the industry. Since the policy of the unions is to insist upon a uniform wage the Negroes, by joining the unions often lost all chance of employment; if compelled to pay the same wage to Negro as to white workers, few employers hired the Negroes in those days.

At present the Negro workers are making gains in organization. The present-day attitude of labor leaders is in general favorable to their organization and inclusion in the unions. There is a growing recognition of the interdependence of all workers and a consequent growing tolerance of the black men in labor organizations. It is coming to be accepted doctrine in labor circles that this must be the case for the protection of all workers as well as for the good of the Negro laborers.

THE NEGRO IN BUSINESS

Negro business is almost entirely a development of the period of freedom and in major part a development of very recent years. In 1866 the establishments operated by members of the race were few in number and small in size. *The Negro Year Book* estimated that possibly 4,000 members of the race were engaged in some sort of business enterprise at the time of the Emancipation. In this total it included such activities as dressmaking, barbering, draying, huckstering, and the like, as well as others of a slightly more ambitious nature, but all were small and represented a very trifling capital investment.

The same authority gives a presumably complete list of all business enterprises in which, in 1920, as many as 200 Negroes were engaged. (See Table 21-1, to which approximately comparable data have been added for 1930.)

It is obvious from this list that the bulk of the business concerns were small undertakings and represented a very small outlay of capital. The total annual amount of business of all the concerns was estimated liberally in 1930 at $1,500,000,000. The enumeration returns of 1920 gave 41,473 as the number of Negroes engaged in various sorts of business.

The first nationwide census of retail business was in 1930, for the business operations of the preceding year. The returns for stores operated by Negro proprietors were classified separately and, in states with numerous Negroes, by the kind of business. The census reported 25,701 stores operated by Negroes with sales of over $100,000,000. The more important classifications were grocery stores, filling stations, restaurants and lunch rooms, cigar stores and cigar stands, and drug stores.

A comparison of the stores operated by Negro proprietors with all stores shows food to be the item of first importance in each case. But it is an item of much greater importance in Negro-operated stores than in all stores: in the former the percentage was 36.25 in 1930; in all stores of the United States the percentage was 22.07. Beyond the sale of food, there is little parallel between the all-stores group and stores under Negro proprietorship. In the all-stores group automotive products were 19.58 per cent of the total; in the Negro group they were 9.68 per cent of the total. The third most important item in the all-stores group was general merchandise, with 13.12 per cent of the total; in the Negro group general merchandise was less than one per cent of the total. In the stores under

Table 21-1: BUSINESS ENTERPRISES IN WHICH 200 OR MORE
NEGROES WERE ENGAGED, 1920 AND 1930

	1920	*1930*
Restaurant and lunch-room keepers	7,511	10,543
Grocers	6,339	7,547
Truck gardeners	6,242	. . . . .
Hucksters and peddlers	3,194	4,356
Butchers and meat dealers	3,009	. . . . .
Undesignated retail dealers	2,123	935
Coal and wood dealers	1,754	1,853
Pool-room attendants	1,582	4,120
Undertakers	1,558	2,946
Contractors and builders	1,454	2,570
Real estate dealers	1,369	4,050
Junk and rag dealers	1,132	2,445
Hotel keepers and managers	1,020	1,064
Proprietors of transfer companies	990	1,878
Drug stores	910	1,482
General stores	884	807
Produce and provisions dealers	689	. . . . .
Candy and confectionery	573	1,333
Dairying	526	. . . . .
Fruit growers	345	. . . . .
Manufacturers and proprietors of clothing factories	340	460
Garage keepers and managers	309	646
Stock raising	296	. . . . .
Drygoods, fancy goods, and notions	262	564
Furniture	256	250
Ice dealers	253	775
Jewelry	224	88
Saw and planing mill proprietors	219	265
Fruit dealers	216	. . . . .
Buyers and shippers of grain and live stock	214	149
Employment office keepers	213	287

Negro proprietorship, restaurants and eating places occupied second place with 21.09 per cent of the sales; in the all-stores group, restaurants and eating places made only 4.33 per cent of the sales.

The general comparison shows that the preponderance of stores under Negro proprietorship are those that may be operated on a very small investment in goods and wages. Food stores, restaurants and eating places, and all other retail stores constitute nearly four-fifths of Negro retail business; of all stores they constitute less than one-third.

The following summary tabulations give a view of the principal kinds of business reporting net sales of $100,000,000 and over, and of the absolute and relative importance of stores operated by Negro proprietors.

Of business endeavors of more individual consequence, the Negroes have been most successful in insurance. From the point of view of capital involved it is the largest field of business they have entered. According to

Table 21-2: SELF-EMPLOYED NEGRO BUSINESSMEN,
BY INDUSTRY, 1950 AND 1960*

	1950	1960
Retail trade	38,730	26,303
Eating and drinking places	15,030	11,344
Food and dairy products	14,520	8,740
Gasoline service stations	1,290	2,153
General merchandise and limited-price variety	750	640
Apparel and accessories	600	321
Furniture and home furnishings	360	182
Motor vehicles and accessories	180	163
Hardware, building materials	120	80
Other retail trade	5,880	2,680
Personal services	5,970	4,349
Construction	3,390	3,978
Wholesale trade	2,640	2,610
Transportation	2,430	1,241
Manufacturing	1,050	1,376
Automotive repair and garages	870	1,083
Insurance and real estate	600	794
Business services	570	890
Miscellaneous repair services	450	414
Communication, utilities, and sanitary services	270	82
Banking and finance	90	41
Other industries	2,760	3,239
Total	59,820	46,400

* Source: adapted from John P. Davis, ed., *The American Negro Reference Book*, Table XX, p. 292. Englewood Cliffs, N.J.: Prentice-Hall, 1966

Table 21-3: KINDS OF RETAIL BUSINESS OPERATED BY NEGRO
PROPRIETORS IN THE UNITED STATES, 1929

Kind of Business	Number of Stores	Proprietors and Firm Members	Number of Employees	Net Sales in Millions
Total	25,701	28,243	12,561	101.1
Principal kinds, total	22,969	24,979	10,398	83.4
Grocery stores	8,450	9,118	1,475	28.4
Restaurants, etc.	5,729	6,209	4,742	17.3
Drug stores	712	852	955	7.3
General stores	761	892	229	4.8
Lunch counters, etc.	2,189	2,321	683	4.0
Filling stations	799	869	302	3.4
Motor vehicle dealers	39	46	166	3.1
All other food stores	631	707	182	2.9
Meat markets	537	576	252	2.8
Candy stores, etc.	1,137	1,193	230	2.6
Garages and repair shops	732	838	525	2.5
Coal, wood, ice	549	594	337	2.1
Cigar stores, etc.	704	764	320	2.1

the 1930 reports of the National Negro Insurance Association, twenty-one companies in the Association had some $260,000,000 insurance in force. The total assets of these companies were reported as somewhat over $18,000,000. As of Dec. 31, 1962, the twenty leading Negro insurance companies for whom accurate statistics were available had nearly $1,644,-000,000 insurance in force. The total assets of these companies were reported as approximately $311,000,000.

In 1924 there were seventy-three Negro banks doing business. Like the insurance companies, they were all small concerns and catered chiefly to Negro depositors and businessmen. The total capital of the seventy-three institutions was $6,250,000; the annual volume of business was about $100,000,000.

At present the number of banks and the business transacted are considerably reduced. The number of Negro banks in 1932 was reported as fifty-one, with a total capitalization of $3,000,000 and resources of about $20,000,000. The annual volume of business was reported as about $75,-000,000. In 1963 thirteen Negro banks listed total assets of $76,864,368.

An additional indication of the progress of the Negroes in business and industry comes from the numbers who are in proprietary, official, managerial, and supervisory pursuits. The following tabulation gives industries and occupations with 200 or more Negroes in some official or other responsible capacity.

Table 21-4: CERTAIN INDUSTRIES AND OCCUPATIONS IN WHICH 200 OR MORE NEGROES ARE IN PROPRIETARY OR OTHER RESPONSIBLE CAPACITY, 1930

Industry and Occupations	Total Number
Builders and building contractors	2,410
Suit, coat, and overall factories	370
Saw and planing mills	265
Printing, publishing, and engraving	235
Garages, greasing stations, and automobile laundries	891
Truck, transfer, and cab companies	1,916
Banking and brokerage	270
Insurance	511
Automobile agencies, stores, and filling stations	470
Wholesale and retail trade (except automobiles)	31,479
Hotels, restaurants, boarding houses, etc.	26,354
Laundries	500
Cleaning, dyeing, and pressing shops	1,754

The Negroes in America lack business experience and are limited in their opportunities to obtain it. In the 1930's there were almost no openings in white establishments for Negro youths who would learn; the type of position commonly open afforded little or no opportunity to learn the business technique. The going business concerns of the race were too few and small to afford apprenticeship to many ambitious individuals. Consequently the Negroes who aspired to a business career often made the venture without adequate training and often without sufficient capital to give reasonable assurance of success. The percentage of failure in business ventures was very high.

PROFESSIONAL STATUS

Relative to population the number of persons engaged in professional pursuits is very much less in the Negro than in the white population. In the white population of native parentage 7.9 per cent of gainfully employed persons were giving some form of professional service in 1930; in the Negro population the professional group included 2.5 per cent of the gainfully employed. The percentage for both racial groups has increased but the same disproportion appears at the different enumerations. In 1920, 6.4 per cent of the gainfully employed native whites were in some form of professional service as compared with 1.7 per cent for the Negroes. In 1910 the comparable rates were 5.7 for the native whites and 1.3 for the Negroes.

The number of persons reporting themselves as members of the different professional service groups is given in Table 22-1 for the last four enumerations.

The teachers, the largest professional group, composed over forty per cent of the total of Negroes in professions in 1930 (over forty-five per cent in 1960). In general in the thirties, they were inadequately trained, poorly paid, and under the direction of white supervisors and administrators. They did not form a learned or self-directing body; they gave a professional type of service but did not form a professional group. Almost without exception they served in segregated schools where the possibility of advancement was small. Outside of these schools there was apparently no immediate future for the Negro teachers, in part because of an opposition on the part of white parents to placing their children under Negro teachers and in part because their qualifications were rarely such as would enable them to secure such positions, in the absence of discrimination, in competition with white teachers. The development of the educational institutions is discussed in detail in a later chapter.

In 1930 the Negro preachers composed nearly twenty per cent of the Negro professional service groups (12.4 in 1960). This is the only type of professional service in which the proportion is higher in the Negro than in the white population (4.2 per cent in 1960). The ministers as a whole are of limited education and there are very few professional standards. Their service is largely confined to the racial group. The church and religious development of the Negroes is considered in more detail in a later chapter.

Table 22-1: NEGROES IN PROFESSIONAL SERVICE GROUPS,
1920–1930 AND 1950–1960*

	1920	1930	1950	1960
Total, professional service	80,183	135,925	180,166	287,969
Accountants	.....	.....	1,272	3,662
Actors, showmen, etc.	1,973	4,130	733[a]	556[a]
Architects	50	63	135[b]	233[b]
Artists and art teachers	259	430	976	1,858
Authors, editors, and reporters	315	425	790	1,161
Chemists, assayers, and metallurgists	207	361	967	1,539[b]
Clergymen	19,571	25,034	18,817	13,955[b]
College presidents, professors, instructors	1,063	2,146	4,039	5,415
Dentists	1,109	1,773	1,525	1,998[b]
Designers, draftsmen, and inventors	145	217	952	3,209
Dietitians and nutritionists	.....	.....	1,733	3,507[a]
Lawyers, judges, and justices	950	1,247	1,450	2,180
Librarians	.....	.....	1,469	3,144[a]
Musicians and music teachers	5,902	10,583	8,505	9,305
Natural scientists	.....	.....	488	1,418
Osteopaths	215	19	.....	.....
Pharmacists	.....	.....	1,147	1,462[b]
Photographers	608	545	.....	.....
Physicians and surgeons	3,495	3,805	4,026	4,706
Social scientists	.....	.....	602	1,059
Social, welfare, and recreation workers	.....	.....	2,052	14,276
Teachers (n.e.c.)	35,563	54,683	86,620	130,659
Technical, engineers	184	351	1,662	4,378
Technicians, electrical and electronic	.....	.....	.....	1,613[b]
Technicians, medical and dental	.....	.....	2,558	9,767
Trained nurses, professional and student	3,341	5,728	14,871	33,752
Veterinary surgeons	145	134	N.A.	N.A.
Other professional and semiprofessional pursuits	5,088	24,251	22,777	33,157

* Source: 1960 data taken from *U.S. Census of Population: 1960, United States Summary*, Table 257
[a] Women only
[b] Men only

The little body of physicians and surgeons is the only Negro group maintaining professional standards at all comparable with those of white professional groups. The training, broadly speaking, is the same, and individuals regardless of color must meet certain examination standards before being licensed. The profession has attracted many of the most capable men. The Negro dentists have a virtual monopoly of the business of the race, and the profession includes many highly capable practitioners.

The number of men in other vocations implying professional training is small. The lawyers are perhaps better trained than any group other than the physicians but they are in a peculiarly difficult position because of the small amount of business they can successfully handle, and the number of men in the profession is relatively small. There are a few editors and newspaper men but they are for the most part untrained and with few exceptions have shown no particular ability. The number of men in other professions is increasing but the possibilities in most cases are rather narrowly limited—except in the few cases where the Negroes show real superiority or arouse the sentimental interest of the whites. In the 1930's they had to depend for patronage upon their own race, and the race was not then in need of or in a position to support a greatly increased number of professionals.

THE ECONOMIC FUTURE OF THE NEGROES

The economic future of the race is at present uncertain and in certain respects the outlook is not bright. There has been, of course, a great advance but when measured by any external standards the rate has been slow and the progress uneven. The retardation is subject to explanation but the fact should be recognized as should the very real obstacles in the way of future advance. The degree of improvement in certain lines is rather definitely limited. In the South the Negroes apparently have an assured position in agriculture, but not a promising one; the trend is toward a subsistence type of peasantry. At the same time they are barred from almost every avenue of social advancement. In the fields of domestic and personal service they have rather consistently lost ground. Opportunities in public service, except as laborers, are not numerous.

The present industrial position is a most disturbing feature of the Negroes' situation. Their status is not fixed nor assured; whether they can gain and hold a position in the industrial world is still in doubt. Historically they have been displaced wherever they have come into competition with other groups. The immigrants have displaced them in the menial employments as well as in the trades and industries except in the South where they have made a showing because of numbers, the absence of competition, and the local prejudice against foreigners. Their recent inclusion in numbers in northern industry was the result of a scarcity of white labor. Their success in retaining the position gained, and in improving their position will turn apparently upon factors over which they have no control, partly upon the federal immigration policy. If the supply of immigrant labor remains restricted during such time as is required for the Negroes to gain skill, experience, and discipline and for their use in certain capacities to harden into an industrial folkway, their position as an industrial proletariat is assured. But the renewal of a heavy immigration from a disciplined labor group would mean their prompt elimination from many of their present positions.

Negro business in the predictable future will continue to be restricted to such establishments as can exist on the patronage of the race. The same limitation, if it be a limitation, exists in the professional field: they cannot anticipate much patronage from the whites.

Various efforts toward the development of a self-sufficient racial group are pointed out in the discussion of the growing nationalistic psychosis. The economic aspect of this movement involves the idea of developing business, industrial, and professional classes which will cater to the Negroes and have a monopoly of their buying power at the same time that they will furnish employment to the members of the race; the group will be economically and culturally independent of the whites and produce everything from food and service to art and literature that it consumes. It is inevitable that this emotionally conditioned movement should continue and it may go far in spite of the fairly obvious economic fallacy that underlies the movement. The advantage that comes to certain specialized individuals from a segregated economy is obvious, and is obviously at the expense of the group that supports the economy. The general racial welfare requires that the individuals become an integral part of the national economy. If the service they are able to render is of superior quality, there is no occasion to fear open competition, and in any case competition cannot be avoided merely by a refusal to recognize its existence. To put competition on a group rather than on an individual basis does not erase the brute fact that in the end individuals and groups must find the occupations in which they can survive. There is no means by which they can escape being measured by the same standards as are applied to other citizens and the same conditions control their success as control that of other men. They will get out of their historic status, that of menials, by success in competition, not by segregation.

Census Bureau, *Farm Tenancy in the United States*, "Race and Nativity," pp. 71–79.

Census Bureau, *Negro Population in the United States, 1790–1915*, "Occupation," pp. 502–551; "Negro Agriculture," pp. 552–764.

Chicago Commission on Race Relations, *The Negro in Chicago*, "Migration of Negroes from the South," pp. 79–105; "The Negro in Industry," pp. 357–435.

Feldman, H., *Racial Factors in American Industry*.

Frazier, E. F., "Occupational Classes Among Negroes in Cities," *American Journal of Sociology*, 35(1930), 718–738.

Frey, P., "Attempts to Organize Negro Workers," *American Federationist*, 36(1929), 296–305.

Hill, T. A., "Negroes in Southern Industry," *Annals, American Academy of Political and Social Science*, 153(1931), 170–181.

Johnson, C. S., *The Negro in American Civilization*, pp. 38–131.

"Occupational Distribution of the Negroes," *Monthly Labor Review*, 42(1936), 975–976.

Peters, P., "Dockwollopers," *American Mercury*, 20(1930), 319–326.

"Relative Efficiency of Negro and White Workers," *Monthly Labor Review*, 40(1935), 335–338.

Raper, A. F., *Preface to Peasantry*.

———, *Report on the Economic Status of the Negro*, Julius Rosenwald Fund, 1934.

Spero, S. D., and Harris, A. L., *The Black Worker*.

Weatherford, W. D., and Johnson, C. S., *Race Relations*, "Economic Aspects of Slavery," pp. 146–162; "Present Economic Relations," pp. 309–329.

Wolfe, T. E., *Admission to American Trade Unions*, pp. 566–588.

Woofter, T. J., et al., *Landlord and Tenant on the Cotton Plantation*, Research Monograph V., Division of Social Research, Works Progress Administration.

Woofter, T. J., "Economic Status of the Negro," *Monthly Labor Review*, 32(1931), 847–851.

Beale, Calvin L., "The Negro in American Agriculture," in Davis, John P., ed., *The American Negro Reference Book*, Ch. 3. Englewood Cliffs, N.J.: Prentice-Hall, 1966.

Becker, Gary S., *The Economics of Discrimination*. Chicago: University of Chicago Press, 1957.

Bond, Horace Mann, "The Negro Scholar and Professional in America," in Davis, John P., ed., *The American Negro Reference Book*, Ch. 14. Englewood Cliffs, N.J.: Prentice-Hall, 1966.

Brimmer, Andrew F., "The Negro in the National Economy," in Davis, John

P., ed., *The American Negro Reference Book*, Ch. 5. Englewood Cliffs, N.J.: Prentice-Hall, 1966.

Cruse, Harold, *The Crisis of the Negro Intellectual*, Part IV. New York: William Morrow, 1967.

Drake, St. Clair, "The Social and Economic Status of the Negro in the United States," *Daedalus*, 94(Fall 1965), 771–814.

Edwards, Franklin, *The Negro Professional Class*. Glencoe, Ill.: Free Press, 1959.

Ferman, Louis; Kornbluh, Joyce L.; and Miller, J. A., eds., *Negroes and Jobs: A Book of Readings*. Ann Arbor, Mich.: University of Michigan Press, 1968.

Foley, Eugene P., "The Negro Businessman: In Search of a Tradition," *Daedalus*, 95(Winter 1966), 107–144.

Gibbs, Jack P., "Occupational Differentiation of Negroes and Whites in the United States," *Social Forces*, 44:2(December 1965), 159–165.

Ginzberg, Eli, ed., *The Negro Challenge to the Business Community*. New York: McGraw Hill, 1964.

Hare, Nathan, "Recent Trends in the Occupational Mobility of Negroes, 1930–1960: An Intracohort Analysis," *Social Forces*, 44.2(December 1965), 166–173.

Haynes, Marion, "A Century of Change: Negroes in the U.S. Economy, 1860–1960," *Monthly Labor Review*, 85(December 1962), 1359–1362.

Henderson, Vivian, *The Economic Status of Negroes: In the South*. Atlanta, Ga.: Southern Regional Council, 1963.

Kessler, Matthew A., "Economic Status of Nonwhite Workers, 1955–1962," *Monthly Labor Review*, 86(July 1963), 780–788.

Lipset, Seymour M., and Bendix, Reinhard, *Social Mobility in Industrial Society*. Berkeley: University of California Press, 1959.

Marshall, Ray, *The Negro and Organized Labor*. New York: John Wiley and Sons, 1965.

Marshall, Ray. *The Negro Worker*. New York: Random House, 1967.

Masuoka, Jitsuichi, and Valien, Preston, eds., *Race Relations: Problems and Theory*, pp. 252–266. Chapel Hill. University of North Carolina Press, 1961.

Miller, Herman Phillip, *Rich Man, Poor Man*. New York: Thomas Y. Crowell Company, 1964.

National Urban League, *Economic and Social Status of the Negro in the U.S.* Washington, D.C., 1961.

Northrup, Herbert, *Organized Labor and the Negro*. New York: Harper, 1944.

Pierce, J. A., *Negro Business and Business Education*. New York: Harper, 1947.

Ross, Arthur, and Hill, Herbert, eds., *Employment, Race, and Poverty*. New York: Harcourt, Brace & World, 1967.

Schmid, Calvin F., and Nobbe, Charles E., "Socioeconomic Differentials Among Non-White Races," *American Sociological Review*, 30:6(December 1965), 909–922.

Schuchter, Arnold, *White Power/Black Freedom: Planning the Future of Urban America*, Part III. Boston: Beacon Press, 1968.

Sovern, Michael I., *Legal Restraints on Racial Discrimination in Employment*. New York: The Twentieth Century Fund, 1966.

Sterner, Richard, *The Negro's Share*. New York: Harper, 1943.

U.S. Department of Labor, *The Economic Situation of Negroes in the United States*, Bulletin S-3. Washington D.C.: Government Printing Office, 1960, rev. 1962.

U.S. Department of Labor, Bureau of Labor Statistics, *The Negroes in the United States: Their Economic and Social Situation*. Bulletin No. 1511, June 1966.

Weaver, Robert C., *Negro Labor: A National Problem*. New York: Harcourt, Brace & World, 1946.

XIII

THE EDUCATION OF THE NEGRO*

The previous discussion has from various angles emphasized the fact that the simple conditions of life during the early decades of the Colonial period brought the slaves into frequent contact and close association with the white population. For the most part they proved to be tractable servants and docile laborers. They worked side by side with the white indentured servants whose status was not very different from their own and the two groups frequently associated on terms of essential equality. The work of the servants and the conditions under which they lived were not very unlike those of their masters. In the social situation the Negroes manifested a surprising ability to adapt themselves to the American environment and conditions of life. They speedily acquired some command of the language of their masters, took on the habits of the white people, and developed proficiency in the routine and mechanical tasks of their daily life.

In the Colonial era the social and economic life of the masters and slaves often assumed a feudal aspect. The Negroes were few in number and their relations with their owners were close; they often worked with the white farmer in the fields and with the family as servants in the house. The personal relations of the plantation owners and their dependents were at first largely patriarchal in nature. For the most part the slave owners were farmers and middle-class folk without education or special refinement. In some cases the Colonial plantation owners were men of some general education with at least a superficial knowledge of history, literature, law, and politics who maintained a somewhat tenuous cultural contact with European life. The Negro servants fortunate enough to be associated with these farm and plantation families assimilated many of the better elements of the white social heritage.

* This chapter remains the same as in the second edition.

Many of the slave masters, in order to increase the economic efficiency of their servants or for other reason, had the slaves instructed in various farm and household tasks. Sometimes they received a bit of literary education and often they received some religious training. On the larger plantations, certain slaves were instructed in the various trades essential to efficient plantation economy. In some cases the Negroes showed considerable mechanical ability and acquired a respectable degree of skill. In the slave population of the larger establishments were tailors, carpenters, wheelrights, shoemakers, tanners, smiths, weavers, and workmen skilled in various other lines. Even the routine work on the plantation taught a degree of punctuality, application, thoroughness, and other virtues essential to life in a civilized community. The household and personal servants were in a particularly happy position to acquire the social customs and personal habits of civilized life.

The greater part of Negro education throughout the slave régime was just this habituation to civilized, albeit rude and simple, standards. As a result of the slave status they incidentally but inevitably acquired the language, the religion, the family ideals, and other values of European culture.

EDUCATION DURING THE COLONIAL PERIOD

Throughout the Colonial era there was little formal schooling of either white or Negro children. The idea of general education was not in the social heritage of the group, and school training was not necessary to success in the ordinary affairs of life. The little secular education provided was dominated by the idea of moral discipline. The interests of the time were religious rather than intellectual and the burden of instruction was in piety and the tenets of Christianity. Education was almost everywhere regarded as an affair of the church; the clergy were almost the only teachers. The subjects common to the present-day elementary school curriculum were not taught. Such institutions of higher learning as existed in the colonies were for the purpose of training men for the ministry and for governmental service.

Since their contacts were in major part with the lower elements of the white population, the slaves tended to take on the vices more rapidly than the virtues of the master race. The need of some instruction to counteract the moral tendencies was generally recognized. For the most part, the ministers of the time assumed a common-sense attitude toward the moral failings of the Negroes, recognizing that their vices were due chiefly to the influence of contact with and the example of the vicious whites. They urged the masters to instruct the slaves in piety, to furnish them with Bibles, teach them to read, and to require their presence at the religious exercise of the family. Schoolmasters were urged to assist in the Sunday instruction of Negroes. It was considered a duty of the church to instruct the slave children. The early opposition to the conversion of Negroes to Christianity lapsed after the church and legislature decided that conversion did not imply manumission.

The attitude toward Negro education and the practices in regard to it varied with the religious beliefs of the people and with the occupational use of the servile population. In Puritan New England the town was a kind of religious republic in which the governing authorities performed both civic and religious duties. They believed in religious education and maintained schools at public expense. The form of slavery was mild—most of the Negroes were farm hands and house servants—and the slaves had some opportunity for mental and moral instruction. Since the religious and political organizations were so closely related and the whites were unwilling to admit the Negroes to the political organization though anxious to convert them, there grew up separate churches and schools for the two races. The Quakers offered the same educational and religious opportunity to the Negroes as they provided for themselves. The Catholics admitted Negroes to their churches and Negro children to their parochial schools. In the southern colonies there was no interest in general secular education. The plantation type of settlement, with its use of indentured servants and Negro slaves and consequent caste order of society, was against it. Private schools of an elementary sort existed for the children of those able to pay and at certain times and places there were church and charity schools for the poor. The instruction in reading and writing given to the white and black apprentices was incidental to the teaching of religion and profitable forms of labor.

By the Revolutionary period a good deal of the early religious fervor and intolerance had abated. The religious and sectarian monopoly of education was about over and new secular interests were appearing. Opinion in regard to slavery was defined and definite attitudes concerning the education of the slaves had become established.

One body of opinion, held for the most part by southern planters and those reflecting their interests, was to the effect that the Negro was an inferior order of man destined to serve the interests of the superior whites. The race was looked upon as a source of cheap unskilled labor and was to be kept from so changing its social status as to endanger the supremacy of the white race. The only education the Negroes needed was such as would enable them to do the work that the white man could not or would not do. They should be trained to do heavy manual labor and work in the less congenial trades without coming into competition with white men. A directly opposite opinion was taking form among ministers, philanthropists, and other idealistically minded men who came little into personal contact with the Negroes. It opposed the apparent determination of the repressionists to keep the Negro inferior and argued for equality of race on religious and humanitarian grounds. There were various shades of intermediate opinion which recognized the cultural inferiority of the Negroes but believed that they should, under tutelage of the white man, be given the opportunity to develop their native capacities.

The Revolutionary period was marked by the prevalence of humanitarian sentiments and the diffusion of liberal ideas and democratic sentiments. But during the War and the years following there was a general decline in the educational opportunities. In the South the tendency was to discard education as superfluous except for the few. The church and charity schools decreased in number and effectiveness.

THE PERIOD OF NATIONAL SLAVERY

There was little interest in the education of the people in the early decades of national history. Life was simple and very little formal education was required for the transaction of routine affairs; in the ordinary walks of life illiteracy was not a handicap. As the church interest in secular education declined there was a decrease in the school facilities and an increase in illiteracy. The idea of schools for all children supported by general taxation came slowly to acceptance.

In the North the Negro children had essentially the same educational opportunity as the white children. The development of schools for the Negroes parallels the development of those for white children, and was determined primarily by the attitude of the whites toward education in general and toward the Negroes in particular. In some cases the Negro children attended the white schools; in other cases separate schools were established and received some part of the public funds provided for education. Connecticut adopted the plan of separate schools as early as 1830 and only a little later separate schools were authorized in Illinois, Indiana, and Ohio. In general as the public school system developed, the Negro children attended the white schools in rural districts and elsewhere when the numbers were small; they were generally excluded from the schools for white children when they came to form any considerable percentage of the school population.

The Negroes took reasonable advantage of whatever educational provisions were made for them. The school attendance of the Negroes increased rapidly in the North especially in the decades before the Civil War and the percentage of illiteracy declined. When separate schools were provided they were generally inferior to the schools for white children in both instruction and equipment but they were in both respects superior to the church and private schools.

The trend of events was very different in the South. In the latter part of the eighteenth and early part of the nineteenth centuries the agricultural conditions in the South underwent a rapid transformation. The inventions of Hargreaves, Arkwright, Crompton, Cartwright, and Whitney revolutionized the cotton industry and, by creating a great demand for that staple, led to the extension of the plantation system and prevented the development of mixed farming. Slavery became economically profitable and the plantation type of the institution, previously limited in the main to Georgia and Carolina, was extended throughout the cotton areas of the Lower South.

In the plantation system the education of the slave was unnecessary and had some positive disadvantages. There was a growing fear of slave insurrections. Some news of the San Domingo revolt reached the Negroes and created restlessness in certain areas. The agitation carried on by the abolitionists roused discontent among the literate slaves. The southern whites suspected the free Negroes and literate slaves of spreading discontent in the slave population. The fears of the whites were further stirred by several attempted Negro insurrections. It became increasingly clear that if the institution was to be preserved and the dangers of insurrection avoided the general slave population would have to be kept in ignorance and isolation. The slave-owning interests came more and more to an active opposition to Negro education and in response to this sentiment the southern legislatures enacted laws prohibiting the literary education of slaves and restricting the mobility of free Negroes. In some cases even the religious instruction of Negroes was prohibited. The clergy, responsive to the dominant interests of their wealthy parishioners, discontinued their efforts to teach the Negroes to read and write.

But opposition to the instruction of Negroes was never unanimous. In spite of legislative prohibition, many masters continued to give favorite slaves the rudiments of an education as well as to instruct the Negroes when education was needed for the tasks to be performed. In the District of Columbia some small schools, partly supported by the free Negroes, were kept open. In Maryland the Catholic Church conducted parochial schools from which the Negroes were not excluded. In Baltimore there were some educational facilities provided for the free Negro children and the same was true in New Orleans where there was a considerable population of free mulattoes. The teaching of free Negroes was never prohibited in some of the southern states, notably Texas, Tennessee, Kentucky, Florida, and Maryland. But in spite of exceptions, the amount of education available to the Negro in the South was always small and in the antebellum period it was almost zero.

NEGRO EDUCATION DURING THE WAR PERIOD

The first real educational opportunities open to the mass of the Negro population had their beginnings at the time of the Civil War and developed out of conditions that had to be faced during and following the period of civil strife.

Almost as soon as the Union forces advanced into southern territory fugitive slaves, for the most part plantation hands and rough laborers, began to arrive within the Union lines. As the war progressed there were large numbers of destitute Negroes concentrated near the principal fortifications. Many of them were employed in various sorts of rough camp work and ultimately the physically fit were mustered into the Army. But there was a very large number of destitute men, women, and children who could not be employed and had to be supplied with the necessities of life and for many of these some permanent provision had to be made.

The various army officers, under whose protection these fugitives had placed themselves, made repeated appeals to northern charity. The response was always generous and in many communities Aid Societies were formed. These organizations undertook to relieve the temporary physical wants of the refugees and to provide secular and religious instruction. The principal aim of the Societies presently came to be the education of the former slaves. They established primary schools, provided teachers, and systematized instruction. Many plantations were abandoned by the owners or seized by the invading forces and the slave population was disorganized and bewildered. Supervisors were placed in charge of many of these plantations and efforts were made to restore order; in many cases schools were established as an incidental part of the program. Schools, frequently under the direction of army officers and chaplains, sprang up about the fortified places where large numbers of fugitive slaves were found. The Aid Societies, particularly the New England Society and the American Missionary Association, were the main educational and relief agencies in the first years of the war. Their work was marred by endless petty jealousies and struggles for personal glory. Even their federation in 1863 did not result in harmonious relations.

THE PERIOD OF RECONSTRUCTION

The relief work and incidentally the education of the freedmen was systematized by the creation of the Freedman's Bureau in the War Department. The Bureau, established by Congressional act in 1865, exercised almost unlimited power and assumed the general guardianship of the Negroes.

This Bureau was instrumental in founding the Negro public school system of the South. When it entered upon the work there were a few tax-supported schools, a few schools maintained by the free Negroes, and a somewhat larger number supported and directed by Aid Societies. The Bureau immediately assumed the supervision of all schools and opened numerous others in unused government buildings. The Bureau supplemented its appropriation from the United States by the sale or lease of property formerly held by the states of the South and by the use of funds from the philanthropic societies.

No race distinctions were recognized in the schools established; they were free to all who cared to attend them. If the whites desired instruction they had to take it with the blacks. The result was that, with few exceptions, the pupils were all Negro children: of the 111,000 school children under the Bureau in 1867, the whites numbered 1,348 and the Negroes 109,652.

On the part of the white South there was a general and bitter opposition to the education of the Negroes and this was increased by the highhanded methods of the Bureau. White teachers who undertook the work were ostracized and sometimes manhandled. The Negroes were largely indifferent to the efforts being made for their education. Only a small percentage of the Negro children of school age were under instruction and the number increased slowly. Only one-tenth of the children of the freedmen were attending school in 1869. The progress of Negro education during this period is shown in the following table.

Table 23-1: PROGRESS OF NEGRO EDUCATION
IN THE SOUTH, 1860–1870

Date	Schools	Teachers	Scholars
1866 (Jan. 1)	740	1,314	90,589
1866 (July 1)	975	1,045	90,778
1867	1,839	2,087	111,442
1868	1,831	2,295	104,327
1869	2,118	2,455	114,522
1870	2,677	3,300	149,581

In the early years the teachers were nearly all white persons from the North. But it very soon came to be the practice to use Negro students to teach the more elementary students. In 1869 about one-half of the teachers employed by the Bureau were Negroes. When the Bureau went out of existence the work of Negro education passed into the control of the philanthropic and denominational societies which had co-operated with it.

The whole history of this Bureau was characterized by harshness and gross military stupidity. But it was instrumental in organizing a school system where none had been before. Perhaps the most important single act of the Bureau was the establishment in 1867 of Howard University at Washington, D.C.

THE RISE OF DENOMINATIONAL SCHOOLS

During the war period the various organizations engaged in relief and educational work among the freedmen were liberally supported. Humanitarian sentiment and emotional enthusiasm ran high. Various denominational groups co-operated in the work. The American Missionary Association was supported by various denominations and confined its work to education along undenominational lines. In 1867 it had 528 missionaries and teachers in the South and its income in cash and clothing for the year was close to $500,000. After the war many of the co-operating societies withdrew their support. The enthusiasm for the work of relief and education rapidly subsided, money donations declined, and many societies discontinued their work for lack of funds. By 1870, most of the workers had been withdrawn from the field. The New England Society continued its work until 1874 though it had only two teachers and a total income of $21,700 for the last two years. The period of co-operation for the uplift of the freedmen was over; denominational competition was beginning.

The various churches of the North were interested in building up and extending their denominations among the Negroes. Pious persons who had become indifferent to Negro education and deaf to appeals to support undenominational work for Negro education and welfare, responded willingly and liberally when appeal was made for funds to proselyte the freedmen and propagate sectarian doctrines among them. These religious organizations carried on some relief work but this was always subordinated to the educational and sectarian propaganda. They devoted their energies chiefly to religious instruction and to training their promising converts for the ministry. The denominations, particularly the Baptists, Methodists, and Presbyterians, that had previously established churches among the Negroes, took measures to extend their influence by establishing special schools to train Negro teachers and preachers. In 1865 the Methodist Episcopal Church established Walden at Nashville; two years later it established Morgan at Baltimore; in 1870 it established Clark at Atlanta; and in later years several other institutions. The Baptists founded Shaw University at Raleigh in 1865; Roger Williams at Nashville in 1867; Leland at New Orleans in 1869; and several other institutions in later years. The Presbyterians had founded Lincoln University before the war. St. Augustine at Raleigh was founded by the Episcopal church in 1867. Church schools were also founded by the Unitarians, Reformed Presbyterians, Southern Methodist Episcopalians, and other religious and sectarian groups. The Negro denominations were also active. The African Methodist Church founded Western College at Kansas City in 1864, having previously established Wilberforce in Ohio. In later years this organization established Allen University at Columbia, South Carolina, and similar schools at Atlanta, Georgia; Waco, Texas; Jackson, Mississippi; Selma, Alabama; and elsewhere. The Zion Methodist Church, the Colored Baptists, and other Negro denominations also established church schools.

The social and economic disorganization resulting from the War and the Emancipation was conducive to a state of mind peculiarly receptive to religious doctrines, and religious sects multiplied with great rapidity. But in spite of the religious and sectarian activity, the period was not wholly barren of educational beginnings. Some organizations devoted their energies to building schools for training Negro teachers on whom ultimately would rest the responsibility for instructing the race in the rudimentary branches of knowledge. The American Missionary Association was responsible for building more teacher training schools than any other organization of the period.

The high-sounding names given the schools expressed the hopes and aspirations of enthusiastic founders. But they also had a practical value: many people would contribute to the maintenance of a college or university who would not contribute to the support of an elementary school. In reality the schools were neither colleges nor universities; they were primary schools with some teacher training when conditions were favorable. They depended on charity for support and led an uncertain and precarious existence.

The work of even the best schools conducted along sectarian and classical lines was barren of results: the schools contributed practically nothing to the real education of the Negroes nor to the improvement of the social and economic conditions of the race. The whole movement, particularly the bringing of northern Negro churches into the South, widened the breach between the races, intensified race hatred, and increased the social and cultural isolation of the Negroes.

The Rise of Industrial Education

The early Negro schools embraced the traditions of the classical studies. This pseudo-education, except in the more culturally backward regions, was on the decline when the Negroes came within the educational orbit. But it was the only education in the South. It was a sign of leisure and a mark of the gentleman. The régime of slavery had engendered in the Negroes a sentiment against education of a practical nature; superiority they associated with a classical and literary training. The idea of industrial education made no appeal; they wanted the education of the gentleman. In the situation they eagerly embraced a discredited type of semi-intellectual activity which has continued to handicap the educational progress to the present time.

A fairly obvious need of the freedmen was an education that would stress practical knowledge and lead to the formation of habits of persistent application to productive work. It appeared evident to many people, thoughtful Negroes as well as white friends of the race, that there should be a close relation between the occupation and the education given in the schools. Many thoughtful persons came to regard industrial education as possibly the only means of uplifting the race. The agitation for an industrial education grew stronger as the workers among the Negroes were confronted with the problem of making them self-supporting and capable and intelligent in participation in the civic affairs of their community.

The majority of the southern whites were apathetic and generally opposed or indifferent to any kind of education for the Negroes. The intiative came primarily from northern sources. A successful beginning was made in 1868 when the American Missionary Association founded the Hampton Normal and Agricultural Institute. Two years later the Institute received a charter from the Virginia Legislature and became an independent institution. Its purpose was to furnish practical training in agriculture and in the industrial occupations, and to train teachers for Negro schools. In 1875 the Institute was allowed one-third of the federal land grant, the sale of which gave a small but permanent supporting fund. The institution has continued to flourish. At the present time the Institute has an endowment of about $10,000,000 and an income of about $600,000.

The vocational movement grew slowly and several other institutions were founded for the industrial education of the Negroes, the most noteworthy of which was the Tuskegee Normal and Industrial Institute. It was this school, under the leadership of Booker T. Washington, the ablest politician the race has so far produced, that won a large percentage of the Negroes as well as of the whites to the support of schools for the vocational and industrial training of the Negroes. The school opened in 1881 on a legislative appropriation of $2,000 annually for instructional salaries. But Washington made the idea popular and got the support of private philanthropists, and gifts from various sources raised the endowment to about $7,000,000 at the present time. It has grown to over 100 buildings and owns a large body of land. In 1937 it had a faculty and staff of 238 and a total student enrollment of about 2,000. Industrial training is one of the principal features of the school. Training is offered in all lines from the simplest trades to electrical engineering. Industrial training of women along the lines of their customary life activities is given. The Institute carries on considerable extension work in the field of agriculture.

These industrial schools have had a marked effect through the students that they have trained and turned back into the communities to become leaders in various occupations. They have done a great deal for the Negro in the South by teaching the common duties of life and inculcating habits of persistent application. They have given the Negro a hope and an outlook for a brighter future. In spite of the fact that a considerable part of the support of these schools has come from the North, they have kept in close and friendly touch with the South and its public school system and have exercised a marked influence on it.

The industrial education of the Negro received little public support prior to 1890. The Merrill Land-Grant Act of 1862 provided means for the establishment of Agricultural and Mechanical colleges for the white population in the several states and territories but made no provision for the industrial education of the Negro. Some of the states, however, diverted a part of the funds to Negro education: in Virginia a third of the grant was given to Hampton Institute; in South Carolina a part of the grant went to Claflin; in Mississippi, Alcorn was opened and presently became a Negro school. In 1890 the amended Merrill Act increased the federal appropriation and provided that a certain proportion should be used for the benefit of the colored people. The act specified that none of the fund should be used for building purposes; the realization of the plan obligated the states to make additional appropriations for buildings, equipment, and administration. The funds were to be used for salaries in teaching agriculture and mechanic arts; the state had to provide funds for buildings, administration, and general education.

The result of the amended act was the establishment of separate agricultural and mechanical schools for colored people in the southern states. By 1893 there were fourteen such schools in the South receiving federal aid. By 1914 there were seventeen land-grant schools. This is the present number.

Something of the character of these schools is shown in Table 24-1, p. 259.

It is perhaps obvious that the support of these schools is most inadequate. The administration of most of the institutions has been in the hands of colored presidents and boards of white trustees with uncertain interest in the education of the Negroes. The industrial work is also hampered by the fact that it is necessary to maintain an elementary grade school. The schools are generally poor. Most of them are equipped to teach carpentry, blacksmithing, brick masonry, and to train girls in the household arts, but few of them teach trades effectively. The time allowed for industrial courses is very limited and the projects undertaken are often in the nature of manual training.

THE NEGRO PUBLIC SCHOOLS

The public school system of the South is of comparatively recent development. Except in a few cities there were practically no schools for either white or colored children maintained at public expense prior to 1868. The traditional attitude was one of opposition to education at public

Table 24-1: LAND-GRANT COLLEGES FOR NEGROES

School	Number of Teachers	College Enrollment	Total Enrollment	Total Income
A. and M. Institute, Normal, Ala.	30	78	382	69,012
A. and T. College, Greensboro, N.C.	45	249	1,009	97,617
Alcorn A. and M. College, Alcorn, Miss.	31	159	745	117,284
Arkansas State College for Negroes, Pine Bluff, Ark.	34	60	502	86,648
Colored A. and M. University, Langston, Okla.	35	388	631	214,567
Florida A. and M. College for Negroes Tallahassee, Fla.	72	259	622	153,709
Georgia State Industrial College, Savannah, Ga.	26	131	504	106,311
Kentucky State Industrial College, Frankfort, Ky.	30	110	353	262,000
Lincoln University, Jefferson City, Mo.	30	190	395	153,925
Prairie View State College, Prairie View, Tex.	92	790	1,153	420,500
Princess Anne Academy, Princess Anne, Md.	28	0	120	73,120
Southern University, Baton Rouge, La.	59	472	886	647,533
State A. and M. College, Orangeburg, S.C.	77	288	1,345	192,217
State College for Colored Students, Dover, Del.	15	17	191	40,133
Tennessee A. and I. Teachers College, Nashville, Tenn.	53	1,162	1,760	149,850
Virginia State College for Negroes, Petersburg, Va.	82	384	2,425	365,006
West Virginia State College, Institute, W.Va.	59	513	1,052	268,527
Total	798	5,250	14,077	3,417,959

expense, and the education of the Negroes was generally thought to be useless if indeed not positively dangerous to society.

The opposition to Negro education was intensified by the course of political events following the freeing of the slaves. The desire was general in the white South to restrict the personal liberties of the Negroes so as to place them in a separate class. The military occupation of the South and the Reconstruction régime, which was in part an effort to prevent this thwarting of the will of the victorious section, intensified the general bitterness and led to a stubborn opposition to many measures that might have met approval had they originated in a different source. The new constitutions made provision for a state system of schools. The financial burden was considerable, the public debt being heavy and the masses in poverty. The irritation was aggravated by the fact that the Negroes were the chief beneficiaries. The whites were bitterly opposed to the mixed schools, and little educational progress was made in the period prior to 1876.

There was a period of reaction as soon as Congress declared the reconstructed sections restored to regular relations with the United States government and withdrew the military forces. The new state governments began to restrict the political power of the blacks and to repeal laws passed during the Reconstruction period. The Negroes were removed from the white schools and separate schools were provided for them. As soon as the double system was established the schools for colored children passed into the hands of incompetent Negro teachers. The funds from local and state taxation were insufficient to maintain adequate school systems for both races and the expenditure for Negro education was reduced to the minimum. This was in harmony with the determination to keep the Negro "in his place." For twenty years the outlook for any real public education for the Negro was not promising.

At the present time there is gross inequality in the provisions for the education of the children of the two races.

In practically all the southern states the state school funds are distributed among the counties on the basis of total population. The apportionment, between the schools for Negro and white children, of these funds as well as of those raised by local taxation is made by the County Boards of Education. The amount that goes for the education of colored children is almost entirely dependent upon the racial sentiment of these white boards. That the sentiment is not everywhere favorable to equal educational opportunity may be seen in Table 25-1, adapted from *The Negro Year Book,* showing the annual expenditure by races for public school purposes in different states.

It is clear from these figures that the comparative educational opportunities of the Negro children are very unequal in the various states. In the District of Columbia, the distribution of funds is approximately the same as the distribution of the races; in Delaware the distribution favors the Negroes. In Kentucky, West Virginia, and Missouri, the annual expenditures for education are not greatly weighted against the Negro children. In some other states, notably Alabama, Florida, Louisiana, and Mississippi, the Negro children get only a minor fraction of their proportionate share of the school funds.

The actual per capita expenditures for white and Negro children also reveal something of the inequality in the educational opportunities open to white and colored children. For the fifteen southern states and the Dis-

Table 25-1: DISTRIBUTION OF SCHOOL FUNDS BY RACES, 1923–1924

States	Per Cent of Population		Per Cent of Expenditures	
	White	Negro	White	Negro
Alabama	61.6	38.4	89.9	10.1
Arkansas	73.0	27.0	82.0	18.0
Delaware	86.4	13.6	85.0	15.0
District of Columbia	74.7	25.2	74.0	26.0
Florida	65.9	34.0	94.4	5.6
Georgia	58.3	41.7	86.0	14.0
Kentucky	90.2	9.2	92.0	8.0
Louisiana	61.0	38.9	87.9	12.1
Maryland	83.1	16.9	88.3	11.7
Mississippi	47.7	52.2	80.0	20.0
Missouri	94.7	5.2	96.1	3.9
North Carolina	69.7	29.8	87.4	12.6
Oklahoma	89.8	7.4	94.9	5.1
South Carolina	48.6	51.4	89.7	10.3
Tennessee	80.7	19.3	87.0	13.0
Texas	84.0	15.9	86.1	13.9
Virginia	70.1	29.9	89.0	11.0
West Virginia	94.1	5.9	95.0	5.0

trict of Columbia, on a per capita basis, the white child, in 1923–1924, received $10.32 and the Negro child $2.89. In 1930, the average expenditure was higher for each race and inequalities somewhat less. The expenditures per child for white and colored children in these states in 1930 were as follows:

Table 25-2: PER CAPITA EXPENDITURE FOR THE EDUCATION OF NEGRO AND WHITE CHILDREN, 1930

State	White Child	Colored Child
Alabama	$ 37.50	$ 7.16
Arkansas	26.91	17.06
Delaware	83.52	91.17
District of Columbia	112.79	96.31
Florida	78.25	10.57
Georgia	31.52	6.98
Kentucky	25.27	25.77
Louisiana	40.64	7.84
Maryland	69.42	43.34
Mississippi	31.33	5.94
Missouri	59.29	35.34
North Carolina	44.48	14.30
Oklahoma	42.58	20.83
South Carolina	52.89	5.20
Tennessee	46.52	31.54
Texas	46.71	39.66
Virginia	47.46	13.30
West Virginia	61.94	63.11

The table shows clearly that in most of these states the educational opportunities for the Negro and white children are far from equal. But there are some notable exceptions to the usual unequal treatment. In West Virginia and Delaware the expenditure was greater for the Negro than for the white child. The greatest difference is in South Carolina where the Negro child receives less than one-tenth his proportionate share of the school funds.

The investment in public school property is another indication of the comparative educational opportunities of the Negro and the white children. In Delaware, the investment in public school property is about $8,000,000 for the whites and about $2,000,000 for the Negroes though the percentage of Negroes is less than one-sixth of the population. At the other extreme, Mississippi has an investment of about $34,000,000 in white public school property and about $8,000,000 in school property for the Negro children. South Carolina has over $35,000,000 investment for white education and about $4,500,000 for Negroes though the two populations are in each state about equal.

The comparison by states of the investment in school property for the two racial groups is shown in the following table.

Table 25-3: AVERAGE VALUE OF PUBLIC SCHOOL
PROPERTY PER CHILD OF SCHOOL AGE

State	Whites	Negroes
District of Columbia	$289.33	$237.23
Florida	231.99	31.56
Delaware	175.09	296.77
Maryland	155.72	73.41
West Virginia	142.07	11.89
Louisiana	140.68	18.53
North Carolina	138.32	34.84
Texas	132.24	40.00
South Carolina	125.00	14.10
Oklahoma	114.99	69.25
Virginia	111.03	38.28
Mississippi	93.94	17.30
Tennessee	87.50	41.97
Alabama	86.36	15.40
Georgia	73.34	11.01
Kentucky	73.15	74.35
Arkansas	58.92	18.57

Still another indication of the racial inequality in the school opportunities appears in the expenditure for instruction. In 1916, the Bureau of Education found the appropriation for white teachers' salaries to be about four times that for Negro teachers compared on the basis of the number of children. The figures are as follows:

Table 25-4: ANNUAL APPROPRIATION FOR TEACHERS' SALARIES
PER CAPITA FOR WHITE AND NEGRO CHILDREN, 1916

States	White	Negro
Alabama	9.41	1.78
Arkansas	12.95	4.59
Delaware	12.61	7.68
Florida	11.50	2.64
Georgia	9.58	1.76
Kentucky	8.13	8.53
Louisiana	13.73	1.31
Maryland	13.59	6.38
Mississippi	10.60	2.26
North Carolina	5.27	2.02
Oklahoma	14.21	9.96
South Carolina	10.00	1.44
Tennessee	8.27	4.83
Texas	10.08	5.74
Virginia	9.64	2.74

The expenditure of money for teachers' salaries bears some relation to the educational opportunities afforded the children. The comparison is not a direct one for the reason that the wage scale is generally lower for Negroes than for whites, and for the further reason that school teaching is the chief professional opening for Negroes. In 1916, the average annual salary in the Negro public schools ranged from $110.54 in South Carolina to $310.05 in Kentucky. As a result of the salary scale the most untrained persons are drawn into the teaching group. About seventy per cent of the teachers of the Black Belt in 1916 had less than a sixth grade education and at present the teachers are generally inadequately trained.

Table 25-5 gives the comparative average expenditures for teachers' salaries per pupil enrolled.

In the country districts the public school facilities for Negro children are particularly inadequate. The schoolhouses are commonly one-room buildings and they are frequently in an extremely dilapidated condition. In many instances school buildings are not provided from the public funds; only the teachers' salaries are derived from that source. In these rural schools there is practically no class-room equipment. In some of the states, as Virginia, all maps, charts, globes, and like equipment must be furnished by the teachers. In the states of the Lower South the physical equipment of the Negro schools is not in general as good as in Virginia and the border states.

In addition to poor physical plant and equipment the schools are commonly over-crowded. The city schools, while generally superior to those in rural districts in buildings and equipment, are more over-crowded. In many places the Negro children must attend part-time schools because of

Table 25-5: AVERAGE EXPENDITURE FOR TEACHERS'
SALARIES PER PUPIL ENROLLED

Year	State	White	Negro
1929	Alabama	25.26	7.35
1928	Arkansas	20.02	8.86
1929	Delaware	47.81	34.66
1928	Florida	35.20	9.80
1929	District of Columbia	77.30	66.61
1928	Georgia	22.45	5.65
1929	Kentucky	24.66	25.44
1929	Louisiana	38.40	8.68
1929	Maryland	51.52	33.63
1929	Mississippi	29.80	6.70
1929	Missouri	46.56	32.57
1929	North Carolina	26.79	11.10
1928	Oklahoma	30.06	23.98
1929	South Carolina	35.70	5.89
1929	Tennessee	25.70	13.01
1928	Texas	36.38	14.61
1929	Virginia	29.17	12.68
1929	West Virginia	47.81	40.76
	Average	32.57	11.78

the congestion. The number of pupils per teacher and the length of the school terms show the inadequacy of the educational facilities as well as the racial differences in educational opportunity. These facts are shown in Table 26-1, which includes both Negro and white pupils.

THE FOUNDATIONS AND NEGRO EDUCATION

Various philanthropic agencies have made relatively large contributions in support of Negro education. The General Education Board has contributed chiefly to college and other types of advanced work rather than elementary education. The Board pays the salaries of state agents for Negro schools, assists counties in the employment of supervising industrial teachers, assists the county training schools for rural teachers, aids selected Negro schools in their building programs, and aids Negro medical education. The Board has appropriated over $20,000,000 to the support and advancement of Negro education. The Jeans, Slater, and Rosenwald Funds have given their chief support to Negro rural schools. The Jeans Fund maintains and assists in the maintenance of elementary schools for Negroes in the southern states and pays the salaries of some 300 supervising teachers for Negro rural schools. The Fund co-operates with the public school superintendents. The John F. Slater Fund is used in aiding Negro schools to maintain normal training and industrial departments. The Fund, originally small, was increased by a donation from the Peabody Fund and now

Table 26-1: THE LENGTH OF THE SCHOOL TERM IN DAYS AND THE AVERAGE
NUMBER OF PUPILS PER TEACHER IN THE NEGRO AND WHITE SCHOOLS

Year	State	Length of School Term		Pupils per Teacher	
		White	Negro	White	Negro
1929	Alabama	159	129	33	48
1928	Arkansas	150	132	36	47
1929	Delaware	184	185	29	33
1928	District of Columbia	181	180	29	32
1928	Florida	163	128	29	42
1928	Georgia	158	137	34	46
1929	Kentucky	160	146	35	33
1929	Louisiana	174	112	30	53
1929	Maryland	188	178	32	36
1929	Mississippi	141	130	30	53
1929	Missouri	168	161	27	31
1929	North Carolina	151	137	33	42
1928	Oklahoma	162	153	33	36
1929	South Carolina	173	114	28	51
1929	Tennessee	116	156	33	40
1928	Texas	152	147	28	47
1929	Virginia	174	151	31	40
1929	West Virginia	165	158	27	29
	Average	164	144	31	44

gives assistance to public and private schools on condition that they maintain normal and industrial departments. The Fund has also aided in establishing and equipping county training schools. The Phelps-Stokes Fund gives aid to Negro universities and promotes research work. The Carnegie Corporation has donated funds somewhat liberally for the erection of public libraries for Negroes as well as for Negro schools: Hampton, Tuskegee, and numerous Negro schools have received gifts from this source. The Daniel Hand Fund, the Peabody Educational Fund, and a number of other Foundations have contributed to Negro education. The Julius Rosenwald Fund has aided in the construction of Negro rural school buildings and in various other ways contributed to the advancement of Negro education.

These and other organizations have done much for the public education of the race. But no matter how much is expended the funds from private and philanthropic sources can do no more than supplement public education. The publicly supported schools are and will continue to be the basis of Negro education. Over ninety per cent of the children attending elementary schools are in the publicly supported schools.

SECONDARY EDUCATION

The facilities for the secondary education of Negro children have been generally inadequate and the number of students small. In the northern and western states the races commonly attend the same schools and the opportunities are at least nominally equal. There are also a good many separate schools in particular communities. But most of the Negroes are in the South and attend segregated schools.

There has been a very rapid increase in the number of public high schools for Negroes. In 1915, the number was 91; in 1921–1922 there were 179 schools with 11,000 teachers and over 40,000 students enrolled; in 1930 there were about 1,000 public high schools for Negro children. Of these about one in five were accredited high schools. In general, of the states maintaining a dual set of schools, the facilities for the secondary education of Negro children are poorest in the states with a large percentage of the population Negroes.

The public high schools for Negroes are supplemented by a considerable private provision for secondary education. The private high schools and academies number about 150 and enroll about 10,000 students of secondary rank. In practically all cases the schools are primarily elementary: only about one-third of the students are of high school advancement.

The majority of the so-called Negro colleges and universities are secondary schools, and have a considerable part of their student bodies doing secondary or elementary work. In the whole group of private universities and colleges, the high school and elementary students are nearly twice as numerous as the students of college rank. The college students are about one-third of the total enrollments of the universities and colleges. These colleges and universities provide schooling for perhaps 11,000 high school students.

The quality of the work in both public and private schools is in general far below that of the white secondary schools. They are poorly equipped, the teachers are poorly trained and poorly paid, and the instruction is generally of inferior quality. A chief aim of many of the so-called colleges is to prepare teachers for the elementary schools, but they are often ill-adapted for this task.

Comparative Rates of Illiteracy

After the foregoing review of the history of Negro schooling and of the facilities for the education of Negro children, it is not surprising to find that the percentage of Negro illiteracy is relatively high. It is surprising that the percentage is as low as is reported.

The percentage of illiterates in the different enumeration classes in the population is shown in Table 27-1 for the four enumerations from 1900 to 1930. Illiteracy is defined by the Census Bureau as the inability of persons ten years of age or over to read and write in any language.

The figures show the percentage of illiteracy of the Negroes to be higher than that in any other important population group at each enumer-

Table 27-1: PER CENT OF ILLITERATES IN THE POPULATION: 1900–1930

Classes of the Population	1900	1910	1920*	1930
All Classes	10.7	7.7	6.0	4.3
White	6.2	5.0	4.0	2.7
Negro	44.5	30.4	22.9	16.3
Native white	4.6	3.0	2.0	1.5
White of native parentage	5.7	3.7	2.5	1.8
White of foreign or mixed parentage	1.6	1.1	0.8	0.6
Foreign-born white	12.9	12.7	13.1	9.9

* Includes persons of unknown age

ation. They also show a rapid decline in all classes of the population with the exception of the foreign born. In this decline the Negroes have shared, though the decline was more rapid in the earlier than in the later decades. In 1870, 81 per cent of the Negroes were reported as illiterate; in 1880 the percentage illiterate was reported at 70, and in 1890 the per cent illiterate was 57.1. In the future decades the decline will doubtless go on but at a retarded rate inasmuch as the increase in school facilities does not affect in any appreciable degree the illiteracy of the adult population. The rate will decline as the group loses by death its older and more illiterate members. There are, of course, some Negroes who learn to read and write when beyond the school age, as is shown by the decline in the illiteracy of the same group from one enumeration to the next. The following table brings out this fact in a striking way: the numbers decline as the age

Table 27-2: NEGRO ILLITERATES BY CORRESPONDING
AGE-GROUPS, 1910–1930

Year of Enumeration	Age in Years	Number Illiterate	Per Cent Illiterate
1900	15–24	652,610	33.4
1910	25–34	380,742	24.6
1920	35–44	310,538	23.3
1910	15–24	460,720	22.0
1920	25–34	287,063	17.9
1930	35–44	264,541	16.8

group advances due to mortality during the decade, but the percentage of illiterates also declines. Since there is no reason to assume that the death rate is appreciably higher in the illiterate than in the literate group, the decline must be due to cultural change.

But the increase in school facilities reaches a comparatively small number of the adult population. The decline in illiteracy is chiefly in the younger age groups of the population. The following table shows the relative literacy of the younger and older age groups as well as the relative increase in literacy from one decade to the next.

Table 27-3: NEGRO ILLITERACY BY AGE PERIOD AND CENSUS YEAR: 1900–1930

		Per Cent Illiterate		
Age Period	1900	1910	1920	1930
10 years and over	44.5	30.4	22.9	16.3
10 to 14 years	30.1	18.9	11.4	5.3
15 to 19 years	31.8	20.3	14.1	8.9
20 to 24 years	35.1	23.9	17.0	12.2
25 to 34 years	39.3	24.6	17.9	13.0
35 to 44 years	52.0	32.3	23.3	16.8
45 to 54 years	68.1	47.0	34.1	24.2
55 to 64 years	78.4	63.0	49.4	34.4
65 years and over	85.4	74.5	68.3	55.7

The geographic factor stands out prominently in the figures of Negro literacy. It varies from state to state, the amount of illiteracy being roughly inversely proportional to the amount spent per capita for Negro education. In the South it is high; in the North and West it is comparatively low. In South Carolina, Alabama, Louisiana, and Mississippi, the states where the average annual expenditure for the education of the Negro child of school age is relatively low, the percentage of illiteracy is relatively high. In South Carolina and Alabama in 1930, over 25 per cent of the Negro population was reported illiterate. The percentage was only slightly lower in Louisiana and Mississippi, and the other educationally backward southern states all reported high illiteracy rates for both Negroes and whites. In the northern states where the Negro children have essentially the same educational opportunities as the white children their rate of illiteracy was comparatively low: in New York in 1930 it was 2.5 per cent; in Illinois in 1930 it was 3.6 per cent. Table 27-4, which allows comparison of the Negro and white illiteracy by states, seems to bear out the generalization that literacy varies directly with educational opportunity and quite independently of race. In 33 states the Negro rate of illiteracy is lower than that of the foreign-born white, and the Negro rate in some states is lower than that of the native whites in other states. The illiteracy of the native white population of Alabama and Louisiana, for example, is greater than the Negro rate in 34 of the states, while the Negro illiteracy rate in New York is lower than that of the native whites in most of the southern states.

In the decade 1920–1930, the percentage of illiteracy declined in all racial elements of the population and in practically all areas. The rates for

Table 27-4: PERCENTAGE OF NEGRO AND WHITE ILLITERACY
BY SELECTED STATES, 1930

State	Native White	Foreign-born White	Negro
Alabama	4.8	8.5	26.2
Arizona	0.5	3.6	4.0
California	0.3	5.7	3.1
Colorado	0.8	8.6	3.9
Georgia	3.3	4.0	19.9
Illinois	0.6	9.0	3.6
Kansas	0.5	5.9	5.9
Kentucky	5.7	5.8	15.4
Louisiana	7.3	19.2	23.3
Maryland	1.3	12.2	11.4
Massachusetts	0.4	10.7	5.4
Michigan	0.5	6.7	3.0
Mississippi	2.7	12.6	23.2
New York	0.5	10.8	2.5
Oklahoma	1.7	5.6	9.3
South Carolina	5.1	5.7	26.9
Texas	1.4	7.3	13.4
Virginia	4.8	7.4	19.2

the Negroes in certain states are shown in Table 27-5 (p. 270) for the enumerations of 1920 and 1930. The rate for the native white of native parentage is given for 1930 as a basis for comparison.

Among the Negroes, as among the whites, the proportion of illiterates is smaller in the urban than in the rural districts. The proportion has declined for all elements of the population in both rural and urban areas. In 1920, the percentage of illiteracy was 13.4 in the urban and 28.5 in the rural population; in 1930 the corresponding percentages were 9.2 and 22.4. There were corresponding declines in all sections and divisions for both the urban and rural population. In the decade 1910–1920, the illiteracy of the rural Negroes of the South decreased more rapidly than that of the urban Negroes owing, chiefly, to improvement of the rural school supervision, and the extension work of Hampton Tuskegee, and other similar schools. In the last decade the decrease in illiteracy has been greater in the urban than in the rural Negro population of the South.

SCHOOL ATTENDANCE OF NEGRO CHILDREN

At the 1930 census enumeration there were 4,128,998 Negro children between 5 and 20 years of age in the continental United States. Of this number 2,477,311 or 60.0 per cent were attending school. This percentage was somewhat lower than that of other groups in the population with the exception of the foreign born. The percentage of the white children at-

Table 27-5: PER CENT OF NEGRO POPULATION 10 YEARS OLD AND
OVER OF SELECTED STATES REPORTED ILLITERATE
IN 1920 AND 1930 AND OF THE NATIVE WHITE
OF NATIVE PARENTAGE IN 1930

State	Negro 1920	Negro 1930	Native White of Native Parentage 1930
Alabama	31.3	26.2	4.9
Arizona	4.6	4.0	0.5
California	4.7	3.1	0.3
Colorado	6.2	3.9	1.0
Georgia	29.1	19.9	3.4
Illinois	6.7	3.6	0.7
Kansas	8.8	5.9	0.5
Kentucky	21.0	15.4	5.9
Louisiana	38.5	23.3	7.8
Maryland	18.2	11.4	1.4
Massachusetts	6.8	5.4	0.3
Michigan	4.2	3.0	0.5
Mississippi	29.3	23.2	2.7
New York	2.9	2.5	0.6
Oklahoma	12.4	9.3	1.8
South Carolina	29.3	26.9	5.2
Texas	17.8	13.4	1.4
Virginia	23.5	19.2	5.0

tending school was 71.5. Comparable data for the different groups in the
population appear in the following table.

In the population of school age, those from 5 to 20 years of age, the
main body of students are in the elementary and high school years. In
1930, the Negroes had smaller percentages in the younger and older years,
in the primary and college groups, and a larger percentage in the grammar
school grades. The percentage distribution was for the whites 8.1 per cent

Table 28-1: SCHOOL ATTENDANCE BY POPULATION GROUPS
FOR THE UNITED STATES, 1930

Population Class	Per Cent Attending School	Per Cent Distribution Total Population	Per Cent Distribution Attending School
All Classes	22.8	100.0	100.0
Negro	21.5	9.7	9.1
White	22.9	88.7	89.4
Native white	25.6	77.8	87.5
Native parentage	25.5	57.1	64.1
Foreign or mixed parentage	25.8	20.7	23.4
Foreign born	3.8	10.9	1.8
Other races	20.8	1.6	1.5

under 7 years; 88.1 per cent from 7 to 20 years; and 3.8 per cent 21 years and over. The percentage distribution of the Negro students was 7.1 per cent under 7 years; 90.1 per cent from 7 to 20 years; and 2.8 per cent 21 years and over.

In all ages from 5 to 20 years, the percentage attending school is higher for the white than for the Negro. This has been true at all times; the differential has gradually decreased but is still marked. In 1930, for example, the percentage of Negro children attending school was lower than the percentage of white attendance in 1920. This was not only true of the totals but also of all age groups.

A comparison of the Negro and white school attendance for 1920 and 1930 by age periods is given in Table 28-2.

Table 28-2: PERCENTAGE OF NEGRO AND WHITE CHILDREN FROM 5 TO 20 YEARS OF AGE ATTENDING SCHOOL, 1920–1930

| | *Per Cent Attending School* | | | |
| | *Negro* | | *White* | |
Age Groups	*1920*	*1930*	*1920*	*1930*
5 to 20 years	53.5	60.0	65.7	71.5
5 to 6 years	27.7	31.8	42.7	45.1
7 to 13 years	76.5	87.3	92.5	96.6
14 to 15 years	68.7	78.1	81.5	90.4
16 to 17 years	39.2	46.3	43.4	58.9
18 to 20 years	10.8	13.3	15.2	22.6

The percentage gain in school attendance in the decade was about the same in the two racial groups, but quite sharply different in details. The chief gain in the Negro group was in the grade school, in the ages from 7 to 15, and a marked but lesser gain in the high school period. In the white group the chief gains were in the older age groups, from 14 to 20 years, representing for the most part high school and college education.

The attendance of children, both Negro and white, is lower in the southern divisions, particularly in the states with a very large Negro population, than elsewhere in the country. This, again, is a differential of long standing. In 1920, of the Negro children between the ages of 7 and 13 years, Louisiana had 61.0 per cent attending school, Alabama 69.2, Arkansas 69.9, Georgia 70.2, Tennessee 71.1, Mississippi 71.5, and Florida 73.1.

The school attendance by races in the different sections of the country is given in Table 28-3.

A comparison of school attendance by sections and by age groups shows relatively minor differences between the races in the North and West where both races attend the same schools. The chief inequalities are in the

Table 28-3: PER CENT OF NEGRO AND WHITE
CHILDREN FROM 5 TO 20 YEARS ATTENDING
SCHOOL, BY SECTIONS, 1930

	Per Cent Attending School	
Sections	Negro	White
United States	60.0	71.5
The South	58.5	66.9
The North	68.2	72.8
The West	75.1	76.9

older age groups, the senior high school and college years. But in the South there are marked differences in the percentage of attendance at all ages.

The differences are better seen in the comparison of small units. As mentioned before, there has been a gain in school attendance in the recent decades and these have removed in part the extreme differences in educational opportunity in different parts of the country. The relative attendance and gain in attendance are seen by the comparison of attendance as shown in the following table for the decades 1910–30 in selected northern and southern states with large Negro populations.

Table 28-4: SCHOOL ATTENDANCE OF NEGRO CHILDREN
7 TO 13 YEARS OF AGE IN SELECTED STATES,
1910, 1920, AND 1930

	Per Cent Attending		
States	1910	1920	1930
Massachusetts	95.8	95.9	97.4
New York	91.3	93.1	96.6
Ohio	91.8	95.8	97.1
Illinois	87.3	93.7	96.8
Virginia	64.2	78.1	86.8
South Carolina	60.4	82.3	79.7
Georgia	60.3	70.2	83.1
Alabama	53.4	69.2	80.7
Louisiana	40.7	61.0	83.1

The low school attendance in the South is at least in part due to the non-enforcement of the compulsory attendance laws in these regions. The degree of enforcement is indicated by the attendance at eleven years of age since at this age all the states require that all children, unless excused for specific reason, attend school. The Negro attendance for the states of the South in 1920 and 1930 was as shown in Table 28-5.

It should also be noted in the present connection that the length of school terms is shorter in the southern than in the northern states. In the North the school year is seldom less than 170 days. But in the South the

Table 28-5: SCHOOL ATTENDANCE OF 11-YEAR-OLD
NEGRO CHILDREN, 1920 AND 1930

	Per Cent Attendance	
States	*1920*	*1930*
District of Columbia	95.8	98.2
Delaware	95.5	96.5
West Virginia	92.8	96.6
Kentucky	91.0	93.6
Texas	90.6	94.6
Maryland	89.0	96.6
North Carolina	87.3	92.9
South Carolina	87.2	86.9
Virginia	84.7	92.5
Oklahoma	82.3	95.3
Florida	78.4	87.9
Mississippi	77.2	92.8
Alabama	76.8	88.0
Tennessee	76.1	93.1
Georgia	74.6	88.6
Arkansas	74.4	91.8
Louisiana	68.3	88.7

school year even for the white children is often below the minimum in the North. The average school years for Negro children in 1920 was 69 per cent of the average of the country. It has been calculated that on the basis of a standard school year of 180 days, with the provision for education in 1920, it would require a Negro child in Louisiana 22 years, a Negro child in Alabama 26 years, and a Negro child in South Carolina 33 years, to complete an elementary school course. In 1920, the length of the South Carolina school year in days was 156 for the white children and 78 for the Negro children; Louisiana had a 156-day school year for white children and a 94-day school year for the Negro children.

The average lengths of the school years for Negro children of the southern states about 1930 are given in Table 29-1.

The percentage of Negro children attending school is higher in the urban than in the rural areas. This is true of the entire school population and of each age group considered separately. When the rural population is subdivided into the farm and village groups, the school attendance of the village group is higher than that of the rural-farm group, but in the older age groups the rural-farm children have a higher rate of school attendance than the village children. Some part of the explanation lies in the greater accessibility of the village schools and the consequent increased attendance of children in the very young ages. In the seven to thirteen age group the school attendance of Negro children in 1930 was 87.3 for the United States, 94.2 for the urban areas and 83.8 for the rural areas. But the section of the country in which the child lives is of more importance

Table 29-1: AVERAGE LENGTH OF THE SCHOOL YEAR
IN DAYS FOR SOUTHERN STATES, ABOUT 1930

Year	State	White	Negro
1929	Alabama	159	129
1928	Arkansas	152	132
1929	Delaware	184	185
1928	District of Columbia	181	180
1928	Florida	163	128
1928	Georgia	158	137
1929	Kentucky	160	140
1929	Louisiana	174	112
1929	Maryland	188	178
1929	Mississippi	141	130
1929	Missouri	168	161
1929	North Carolina	151	137
1928	Oklahoma	162	153
1929	South Carolina	173	114
1929	Tennessee	166	156
1928	Texas	152	147
1929	Virginia	174	151
1929	West Virginia	165	158
	Average	164	144

in determining school attendance and education than is urban or rural residence. The rural Negro children in the North and West have a considerably higher school attendance rate than the urban Negro children in the southern divisions.

THE HIGHER EDUCATION OF NEGROES

Following the Civil War a number of colleges and universities for Negroes were founded in southern towns and cities. There was a desire on the part of the religious denominations to spread their sectarian teachings among the freedmen. The type of education offered by these schools was often so ill-adapted to the needs of the situation as to bring the whole idea of higher education of the Negro into disrepute and the educated Negro tended to be an object of popular ridicule. As the enthusiasm of the anti-slavery period declined many of the colleges were left as completely without funds as, in the absence of lower schools, they were without college students. Some of them were discontinued and others became elementary or secondary schools, often, however, without change of name.

At the present time there are nearly a hundred institutions for Negroes bearing the name of college or university. With very few exceptions, they are controlled by religious denominations, and are of inferior scholastic standing. Some of them are colleges in name only: they offer no college courses. In others only a part, usually a minor part, of the courses are of college rank; the major part of the work is of an elementary and secondary character. Of the 37,000 students enrolled in these schools in 1930, those taking college courses numbered 14,000. Only a very few of the Negro universities are equipped in staff and facilities to do high grade college work: none is prepared to do more than a very limited amount of university work.

In the earlier decades the administrators and most members of the instructional staffs of the Negro colleges were white men. But year by year white instructors become fewer in number as the racial separation increases and as competent Negro men and women can be found for the positions. The change has gone on so rapidly that the number of competent and trained Negroes is insufficient to satisfy the demand and many important positions are occupied by mediocre men. The present tendency is toward a complete manning of these schools by Negroes.

Fortunately, the Negroes are not entirely dependent upon their own schools for college education; most of the northern universities and colleges are open to them without gross administrative discrimination. The number of college graduates is, therefore, a better index of educational attainment than is the enrollment in the Negro institutions. In 1930, the bachelor degree in arts and science was conferred upon 2,071 Negro students. The total number of Negroes who have graduated from college is approximately 18,000.

The increasing number of persons completing college courses in reputable schools is one of the most encouraging facts in Negro education. It means a gradual improvement in the intelligence and efficiency of Negro leadership; at present, with only occasional exceptions, the teachers, preachers, and other leaders are uneducated men.

The number of men trained to serve the race professionally is wholly inadequate to the need, and provision for the training of professional men is limited. The Negro professional schools are few in number and small in size. In 1924, Howard University at Washington maintained a law department with 129 students enrolled. Two other law schools—the Central Law School of Louisville, Kentucky, and the Law Department of the Virginia Union University at Richmond, Virginia—enrolled, respectively, 12 and 15 students. The total number of law students was thus 156. In the same year there were 352 students of medicine in the three medical schools and departments of medicine maintained for Negroes. The number of dental students was 402, and the three schools of pharmacy enrolled a total of 178 students.

There has been no recent growth in Negro professional education. *The Negro Year Book* about 1930 reported 138 Negro students of law—75 enrolled at Howard, 14 at Virginia Union University, and 49 at Simmons University. There were 449 medical students, 235 at Howard, and 214 at

Meharry Medical College. There were 155 dental students, 69 at Howard University and 86 at Meharry College. In the two schools of pharmacy, there were 119 students—56 at Howard University and 63 at Meharry College.

SUMMARY

The earliest and most important means of education of the Negro slaves was the contact and association with the white people which resulted incidentally from the servile status. They learned the language and acquired informally but effectively much of the culture tradition. Because of unequally favorable opportunities, the education of some was more rapid than of others and great differences developed which were increased and perpetuated by the continued importation of raw Negroes long after many of the Negroes had assimilated the externals of the foreign culture.

The formal education was, to all intents and purposes, negligible. The ministers in some cases interested themselves in the Negroes but this was essentially a religious interest; such secular education as they gave was incidental. Certain masters made it possible for favored individuals, chiefly mixed-bloods, to acquire some literary education, in some cases because of sentimental reasons; in other cases it was for the purpose of increasing slave efficiency. There were a few Negroes of some literary training all through the slave period but so few as to be curiosities; there was none of real education. In 1860 nine-tenths of the Negroes were wholly illiterate while the remainder had a very trivial amount of education.

The enthusiasm of the anti-slavery, war, and reconstruction decades led to the extension of church and missionary schools. Except as a means of religious propaganda, the literary and classical type of education was a failure. It was ill-adapted to the needs of the situation and did much to bring the whole idea of Negro education into disrepute.

The present rise of industrial schools came in the effort to give the masses of the race some education along the lines of their life problems. The forceful personality of Booker T. Washington popularized this type of education among the Negroes and in the country generally. The South approved it as in harmony with the philosophy of the Negro as a worker and a servant; they had opposed the classical education on the ground that it spoiled otherwise valuable servants and laborers. The white North approved of the idea of industrial education as an effort to do something practical in what appeared to be a hopeless situation. It was opposed by the Negro intellectuals on the assumption that it was designed to keep the race in subjection, and it was frequently made ineffectual because of the opposition of organized labor. It is chiefly because of this trade union opposition that industrial training in both Negro and white schools has not developed more rapidly.

The public schools for Negroes have had a slow growth and at the present time are for the most part poorly housed, inadequately supported, and taught by incompetent teachers. They have reduced in a remarkable way the formal figures of illiteracy but it must be remembered that literacy does not imply real education. Latterly there has been some tendency to improve the educational facilities in the South. The effort to stop the migration of Negroes led to somewhat more liberal educational appropriations and to a racially more equitable distribution of funds.

The provisions for higher education, particularly secondary and normal education, are quite inadequate. The institutions of secondary, normal, and college grade, with but few exceptions, carry on work of inferior quality.

The outlook for Negro education is not wholly bright. The bulk of the race is and probably will remain in the South. The dual system of schools in that section of the country makes it improbable that the education of either race will compare favorably with that in other parts of the country. The Negro schools have improved but there is no evidence of a general disposition to give Negro children educational opportunities equal to those provided for white children. Moreover, the Negro schools are passing, more and more, into the hands of the Negroes. But the number of Negroes of genuine education is very small. It is more true of the higher than of the elementary education that separate schools for Negroes mean inferior schools for Negroes. It would be a far wiser educational and racial policy to use the funds that now support inferior Negro colleges to send Negro pupils of ability to the real colleges and universities of other sections of the country.

READINGS

Bond, H. M., *The Education of the Negro in the American Social Order*, 1937.

Bulletin, Bureau of Education, 1916, *A Study of the Private and Higher Schools for Colored People in the United States*, Vol. 1, p. 423; Vol. 2, p. 724.

Bulletin, Bureau of Education, 1928, *Survey of the Negro Colleges and Universities*.

Census Bureau, *Negro Population in the United States, 1790–1915*, "School Attendance," pp. 375–403; "Illiteracy," pp. 403–435.

——, *Negroes in the United States, 1920–1932*, "School Attendance," pp. 208–228; "Illiteracy," pp. 229–252.

Johnson, C. S., *The Negro in American Civilization*, "The Beginnings of Negro Education," pp. 224–298.

Jones, T. J., *Recent Progress in Negro Education*, Bureau of Education, Bulletin No. 27, 1919.

Leavell, U. W., *Philanthropy in Negro Education*.

Weatherford, W. D., and Johnson, C. S., *Race Relations*, "Problem of Education," pp. 239–366.

Woodson, C. G., *The Education of the Negro Prior to 1861*.

Woofter, T. J., *The Basis of Racial Adjustment*, "Education," pp. 269–298.

FURTHER READINGS

Ashmore, Harry S., *The Negro and the Schools*. Chapel Hill: University of North Carolina Press, 1954.

Broom, Leonard, and Glenn, Norval, *Transformation of the Negro American*, Ch. 5. New York: Harper & Row, 1965.

Bullock, Henry Allen, *A History of Negro Education in the South*. Cambridge, Mass.: Harvard University Press, 1967.

Coleman, James Samuel, et. al., *Equality of Educational Opportunity*. Washington, D.C.: Department of Health, Education, and Welfare, U.S. Office of Education, 1966.

Dentler, Robert A., "Barriers to Northern School Desegregation," *Daedalus* (Winter 1966), 45–63.

Educational Policies Commission, *Education and the Disadvantaged American*. Washington, D.C.: National Education Association, 1962.

"Education and Civil Rights in 1965," *Journal of Negro Education*, 34 (Summer 1965), 197–379.

Fischer, John H., "Race and Reconciliation: The Role of the School," *Daedalus* (Winter 1966), 24–44.

Harvard Educational Review Editorial Board, *The American Failure: Equal Educational Opportunity*. Cambridge, Mass.: Harvard University Press, 1969.

Humphrey, Hubert H., ed., *School Desegregation: Documents and Commentaries*. New York: Thomas Y. Crowell Company, 1964.

McGrath, Earl J., *The Predominantly Negro Colleges and Universities in Transition*. New York: Institute of Higher Education, Teachers College, Columbia University, 1965.

Muse, Benjamin, *Ten Years of Prelude: The Story of Integration Since the Supreme Court's 1954 Decision*. New York: Viking, 1964.

"Negro Education in the United States," *Harvard Educational Review*, 30:1 (Summer 1960).

Pierce, T. M., et al., *White and Negro Schools in the South*. Englewood Cliffs, N.J.: Prentice-Hall, 1955.

Silberman, Charles E., *Crisis in Black and White*, Ch. IX. New York: Random House, 1964.

Wiggins, Sam P., *Higher Education in the South*. Berkeley, Calif.: McCutchan Publishing Corp., 1966.

Williams, Robin M., Jr., and Ryan, Margaret W., eds., *Schools in Transition: Community Experiences in Desegregation*. Chapel Hill: University of North Carolina Press, 1954.

XIV

THE NEGRO IN LITERATURE
AND ART*

Measured by objective standards, the contributions of the American Negroes in the realm of literature and the fine arts, as in science and scholarship, have been small and comparatively unimportant. There are few pieces of work of first or even second rank, and few individuals of more than local and racial reputation have appeared.

The fact is subject to social explanation and the relatively barren record probably implies nothing in regard to future accomplishment. The historic status of the race is sufficient to explain the absence of achievement. The conditions of life in America have been such as to discourage artistic activity and accomplishment of high order in whites as well as Negroes. The run of attention has been on other things; the prizes of popular esteem and approval have gone to men of action rather than to men of thought and sensibility.

There are additional facts of special application to the Negroes. The bulk of the race is only a generation from slavery. At the time of their emancipation the Negroes were without education and had no cultural background. The period of freedom has not been sufficiently long for the cultural level of the race to rise to European standards. The number of individuals of education is very small and the great mass barely literate. Moreover, the bulk of the population is rural and pretty effectively isolated from cultural stimulation. The economic position of the majority of the members of the race is insecure. There has been no leisure class interested in culture or in acting as patron to talent appearing outside. The race has lacked the poise, confidence, and self-respect conducive, if not essential, to artistic endeavor.

* This chapter remains the same as in the second edition. An explanatory editorial note appears under Further Readings.

The Literary Treatment of the Negro

In America the Negroes have been creators of literature and subjects of literary treatment. White writers have made a minor use of Negro life and character as the theme of story. The treatment has varied with changes in literary taste and fashion and, inasmuch as literary art reflects the social thought of the time, with changes in Negro culture and race relations.

There is a frequent plaint that white writers have not given the Negro an adequate literary interpretation. It is claimed that he has not been treated seriously as literary material, that the treatment has sometimes been unsympathetic and unjust, that he has been made the clown or the villain of the piece. There is of course both truth and error in the usual complaint. There is no doubt that Negro life contains a wealth of tragedy and of comedy untouched by the literary artist; there is a mine of material unworked from the interpretative point of view. But the position that the race is seriously maligned in literature is true only in the sense that art is everywhere a distortion of reality. The rank and file of writers seize upon facts of journalistic interest, the unusual and spectacular, and the types thus defined may become symbolic of a whole group. The sentimental, comic, and grotesque side of Negro life and character have been exploited, possibly out of proportion. But a similar thing is true in regard to the Jew, the white Southerner, the American farmer, the business man, and numerous other types that have been made the object matter of literary treatment.

The first successful use of Negroes in fiction was in Harriet Beecher Stowe's *Uncle Tom's Cabin*. This novel, published in 1852, had to do with slave life and character. It was a sentimental tale of little merit but the temper of the time was such as to secure it a wide reading. For a very long period it influenced or defined the public idea of Negro character. Topsy and Uncle Tom became and remain today the most generally known of American literary characters.

In the post Civil War decades several competent literary craftsmen made use of Negro characters. The sentimental attitude remained and colored the type of literary production. But the Negro was recognized as a source of comedy: the happy, picturesque, and care-free type was introduced to the reading public. Thomas Nelson Page gave a series of sympathetic pictures of Negro life and character. George W. Cable in his *Old Creole Days* and elsewhere made an invaluable contribution to an appreciation of life and character in the nationally and culturally mixed populations of New Orleans and Mobile. Thomas Dixon in his widely read novels, *The Leopard Spots*, *The Clansman*, and elsewhere, introduced the reading public to a different and less pleasant phase of Negro life and character.

Stories of irresponsible and picturesque Negro characters became and continue to be popular. The various darky stories of Octavus Roy Cohen and other writers have made the comedy side of Negro character known to a very large public.

In the more recent period a number of white writers have undertaken novels of Negro life. In major part this came in the decade following the World War. The spectacular migration of southern Negroes to New York and elsewhere created in the northern urban centers a new and strange life that attracted wide attention. The Negro, particularly the bizarre and exotic aspects of Negro life and behavior, became a fad and literary slumming became the vogue.

Of the writers of this period, Carl Van Vechten was one of the first and most popular of those to exploit the Negro characters. His *Nigger Heaven* (1926), a presentation of certain colorful and sensational aspects of Negro life in Harlem, was a great literary success.

T. S. Stribling's novel *Birthright* was published in 1922 after being serialized in the *Century Magazine*. *Birthright* deals directly with Negroes. The account centers about a northern educated mulatto who, imbued with a missionary zeal to improve the lives of Negroes, returns to the South and gets an unsympathetic reception. The same type of Negro reappears in various rôles in the later trilogy—*The Forge* (1931), *The Store* (1932), a Pulitzer prize novel, and *Unfinished Cathedral* (1934). The novels are in the main protests against Negro status, race prejudice, lynchings, economic exploitation, and other problems created by the presence of the two races in the same area. Aside from any question of their literary merit, they received attention because of the popularity of the theme in the period at which they appeared.

Roark Bradford approached the Negro in the spirit of the pre-Civil War days. Negroes are "darkies" and he is interested in exhibiting the picturesque qualities of Negro life and character. *This Side of Jordan* (1929) and *John Henry* (1931) are the best known. Each deals with Negroes of the Mississippi region. Bradford is best known by *The Green Pastures* which was based upon his sketches.

Du Bose Heyward's novel *Porgy* appeared in 1925 at the height of the vogue for Negro art and literature. Two years later the dramatic version appeared and was widely popular. It is a novel of some real literary merit concerning low-class Negroes of the Charleston waterfront. *Mamba's Daughters* (1929) is similar in interest and point of view.

Julia Peterkin has written numerous stories dealing with the so-called Gullah Negroes of the South Carolina cotton plantations. The novel *Black April* (1927) was a literary success. It brought to popular attention her earlier work *Green Thursday* (1924), and it was followed by *Scarlet Sister Mary* (1928), which received the Pulitzer prize in 1929, and by

Bright Skin (1932) and *Roll, Jordan, Roll* (1933). Peterkin's point of view is in general objective, without the reform spirit of Stribling or the patronizing attitude of Bradford.

The continued literary interest in the Negro is indicated by the fact that L. M. Alexander's novel *Candy* received an award of $10,000 as late as 1934. The novel is an account of Negro life in Georgia and exploits the conflict between the attraction of the North and the pull of the old conventional life.

In the same period, Negro characters and themes had an extended dramatic vogue. Eugene O'Neill's play *The Emperor Jones* appeared in 1921, and was followed a little later by *All God's Chillun Got Wings*. Paul Green's Pulitzer prize drama, *In Abraham's Bosom*, was produced in 1927. Marc Connelly's *The Green Pastures*, a dramatic version of Roark Bradford's *Ol' Man Adam an' His Chillun*, appeared in 1928.

Other recent attempts to treat the Negro seriously as literary material are numerous. Unfortunately, most of these efforts do not rank high when evaluated as literature.

THE NEGRO FOLK STORIES

The folk rhymes and tales more or less current among the Negroes require only brief comment. The rhymes reflect a simple outlook upon life; they are often picturesque in imagery, and sometimes they approach rhythmic perfection. They are often vulgarly expressed.

The literary work of Joel Chandler Harris is chiefly responsible for the popular idea that the American Negroes have a singularly rich body of folk tales passed on from original African sources. These stories are a literary achievement. They give an admirable interpretation of ante-bellum Negro life and character, and they are the best record extant of the Negro dialect of the period. But they are in no real sense a record of Negro folklore. Harris did not record real Negro folk tales; he used the current scraps of stories as a basis for literature.

For the most part the stories of *Uncle Remus* are not of Negro origin. Many of them were current in certain parts of the Lower South and known to both Negroes and whites. They are local versions of stories told in many parts of the world and found in different languages. Many of them are close versions of tales of Hindu origin. This is true, for example, of "The Lion Hunts for Mr. Man," "Br'er Rabbit," and others. Some of these stories are thought to have crossed Asia to Europe, and to have come into English by way of the French and Spanish. So far as the American Negroes are concerned the stories are mainly of Spanish origin. Some of the Hindu tales were carried into Africa by the Arabs and may have been introduced into America by the Arabized slaves. The source of some of the stories has not been established and some may be of African origin; the "Tar Baby" story, for example, may be of African origin.

PERSONAL NARRATIVES

The contribution made by Negroes to American literature is slight and contains very little of any permanent value. It is only very recently that there has been any contribution at all. There were from time to time efforts in this direction which attracted popular attention. But the public interest was excited by the unexpected fact that a Negro could write a book rather than because the production had merit. The output was small and the quality low, but since nothing worth while was expected the early efforts often received lavish praise.

One of the main lines taken by Negro literary activity has been that of personal narrative. The first of these stories appears to be that of Gustavus Vassa, whose 350-page autobiography was published in 1789. It was the beginning of a long series of personal appeals capitalizing on the sentimental interest that the whites everywhere have in the Negroes. In the later decades of the anti-slavery agitation a large number of such stories picturing the life of the slave were written by or for Negroes. *The Memoirs of Archy Moore; Naratives of the Adventures and Escapes of Moses Roper; The Kidnapped and the Ransomed; The Narrative of Sojourner Truth;* and *The Autobiography of a Fugitive Slave* are typical examples. The best known though perhaps not the best of these slave stories is the autobiography of Frederick Douglass published under the title *My Bondage and Freedom.*

The interest in this type of writing did not end with the freedom of the slaves. There is a sentimental white public ready for the story of any Negro and these personal narratives continue to appear. In Booker T. Washington's autobiography, *Up From Slavery*, this form of writing reached its best expression. William Pickens' *The Heir of Slaves* and Robert R. Moton's *Finding a Way Out* are more recent though somewhat less successful attempts to capitalize the popular interest. The two volumes by W. E. B. DuBois, *The Souls of Black Folk* and *Darkwater*, classify with this group of personal narratives.

THE LITERATURE OF PROTEST

Closely allied to these personal documents is the considerable literature of protest that has carried on, in the later-day situation, the anti-slavery spirit and tradition. The Negroes were out of bondage but still not free. The period from the Civil War to the end of the century was one of legal freedom and of psychological slavery. The great body of polemic and controversial writing of the half century was a plea to be made the equal of the white man, a demand of the Negroes that something be done for them. This body of writing varied in temper from the plaintive and pathetic to the intemperate and abusive, but it always and inevitably embodied an attitude of inferiority. It was a plea for mercy; a cry for justice; a demand for rights; a begging for alms.

Out of this hysterical knocking at the white man's door there is gradually taking form a modified type of protest, an inspirational literature. In one aspect it is an expression of the developing race psychosis, a philosophical rationalization of the intellectual and social status. But it is everywhere subjective, shot through with the prejudice and passion of revolt. Treated as data, it contributes to an understanding of racial phenomena; as an analysis of present problems it is notably lacking. With perhaps a single exception, no Negro essayist to the present time has succeeded in making a calm objective statement of the race problem.

The major part of the historical writing of Negroes is properly to be classed with the body of personal and protest literature and to be treated as data by the student of social and psychological phenomena. A large number of individuals are industriously engaged in compiling racial facts and interpreting American history from a racial point of view. The movement is at once an apology for a somewhat culturally barren past and an effort to provide an historical background for the growing spirit of nationality. It is an effort to create a racial self-respect. In content this writing varies from efforts to prove that a major part of world accomplishment is Negroid in origin and that numerous historic characters were men of African descent, to a dogged and systematic effort to introduce a black racial bias into the popular idea of American history. Just as the white American school child is taught American history from the point of view of the American chauvinist, the Negro school child is to see it from the point of view of the black racialist. The racial, as the patriotic, bias is of course incompatible with modern historiographic standards. It may be very valuable for certain purposes but much of it is not history.

The Negro Literature

It was not until near the end of the last century that Negroes made any contribution to American poetry. Prior to that time a few scraps of verse said to be composed by slaves found their way into print. There was a little verse composed by Jupiter Hammond, a Connecticut Negro, during the latter part of the eighteenth century. Just before the American Revolution a little collection of verse composed by a slave woman, Phillis Wheatley, was printed under the title *Poems on Various Subjects, Religious and Moral*. In 1829 a little group of poems composed by an illiterate Negro slave in North Carolina was printed under the title *The Hope of Freedom*. And there were other occasional bits of verse that found their way into print but there was nothing of literary merit.

The first Negro to gain distinction as a poet was Paul Laurence Dunbar. The enthusiastic introduction given the *Lyrics of a Lowly Life* by William Dean Howells brought the poetry of Dunbar into great vogue. At its best it is characterized by a simple blending of humor and pathos expressed in a homely Negro dialect. It is often compared with the poetry of James Whitcomb Riley and sometimes with that of Robert Burns.

Current Negro poetry had its beginning in the second decade of the present century, in the period when the Negro vogue made all art efforts of the Negro objects of immediate and favorable attention. Several versifiers of promise appeared and some few pieces of real merit have been published. Every effort in this direction is given great encouragement; many of the Negro papers and journals have poetry departments and print much verse. The assurance of immediate recognition awaiting even mediocre work promises to bring to expression whatever poetic genius the race may possess. But to the present, the volume of competent work is very slight. Chief among the Negro writers of verse who received great attention in the past decade are Stanley Braithwaite, Countee Cullen, Claude McKay, Langston Hughes, Jean Toomer, and James Weldon Johnson. To the present, however, there has been no poetic output to justify the enthusiasm of their reception.

In fiction no American Negro has as yet accomplished anything not surpassed by hundreds of other writers. Most of the efforts have been imitative rather than attempts to express racial life. Success in this field depends solely upon merit. There is no prejudice, no discrimination. There is a public eagerly awaiting any work of merit, and any competent craftsman is assured of immediate success. But a novel of importance by a Negro is as yet to be written.

Prior to the recent decades, the only fiction worthy of mention written by Negroes is perhaps that of Charles W. Chesnutt. *The Conjure Woman, The Marrow of Tradition, The Colonel's Dream*, and other semi-realistic stories and sketches of the South had a considerable vogue. The prose works of Paul Laurence Dunbar—*The Uncalled, The Sport of the Gods, The Strength of Gideon and Other Stories*, etc.—were not productions of particular merit.

The recent Negro fiction has been concerned in large measure with the problems of the race. Walter White's *The Fire in the Flint* is concerned with the details of lynching; Langston Hughes' *Not Without Laughter* recounts, among other items, the burning of a Negro village and he returns to the same theme in *The Ways of White Folks;* Welbourn Kelly's *Inching Along* culminates in the lynching of an innocent Negro; Charles W. Chesnutt's story, *The Sheriff's Children*, and numerous other stories by Negroes have to do with the mixture of the races; Nella Larsen's *Passing*, Jessie Fauset's *Plum Bun*, and various others have used the "passing" of white Negroes as a theme. A few Negro writers, notably Countee Cullen in *One Way to Heaven,* Langston Hughes in parts of *Not Without Laughter,* and Claude McKay in *Home to Harlem* and elsewhere have endeavored to picture Negro life and avoid social and moral controversy. George Schuyler's *Black No More* is a satire on the efforts of certain Negroes to appear white.

FOLK SONGS OF AMERICAN NEGROES

The Negroes have been a more important factor in the development of American music. They have had a very marked indirect influence and their positive contributions have been not only large but unique. It is in this field that they have made their chief contribution to the higher cultural life of the society.

In the slave period they produced a body of song that stands as America's only indigenous music. Like all folk music these slave songs were closely connected with work and play and varied with the local conditions of life. They were an outgrowth of the daily plantation life and expressed the hopes and joys and fears of a primitive group in an alien environment. Song was almost the only means they had for expressing their emotions; they reflect the whole emotional life of the race in servitude.

The songs are so simple and rhythmical as to require a minimum of accompaniment. They are replete with childish imagery and monotonous with much repetition. They are generally cheerful, sometimes humorous, rarely sad. They express a spirit of resignation, sometimes with a touch of yearning. They are characterized by the use of minor mode and the common use of syncopated rhythm. A plaintive note of self-pity runs as a main theme through all Negro songs, yet the slave songs were rather rarely sorrow songs.

The majority of the slave songs were semi-religious in character and express the child-like faith of the people. The spirituals were peculiar monotonous hymns, rudimentary in phraseology and ideas, composed and sung under stress of religious excitement. In some cases they were interpretations of standard hymns. The shout songs so common to revivals and camp meetings grew out of and long remained closely related to the sensuous primitive religious dance. This body of religious song is still being added to wherever groups work themselves into a religious frenzy. Happy phrases, frequently without thought content, improvised at such times are remembered, repeated on other similar occasions, and pass into the body of folk song.

The work songs were employed wherever there was a desire to stimulate the laborers, or a need to synchronize their efforts. They are still employed for both purposes. They commonly consist of a single line, often connected with the work, and a meaningless chorus, the whole being repeated over and over, sometimes with and sometimes without variation. These work songs, like the religious songs, are being added to, for the Negro still works and sings.

Romantic love was seldom the theme of Negro song. The only exception was in Louisiana, the French Lower South, and there the songs were perhaps rather creole than Negro. The French-English musician Gottschalk made these creole airs known to the musical world.

The plantation music has at times been exalted beyond its true importance. It has been treated as something of unique artistic value. Writers have professed to see in the crude, half-articulate, slave songs a "tragic profundity of emotional experience." There have been some attempts to refine and modernize the crude music of the slaves into a sophisticated art form as well as efforts to take the bits of melody and give them an artistic expression. They have furnished themes from which some musical compositions have been evolved. Dvořák's "New World Symphony" is founded chiefly on these themes and they have been somewhat widely exploited elsewhere.

What it may be possible for musicians to do with the slave songs remains to be seen and is, of course, a thing quite apart from the songs themselves. It is a far cry from the rude slave song to the writing of modern music.

THE MINSTREL MUSIC

Through the minstrels the Negroes indirectly exerted their greatest influence on the development of American music. The minstrel acts were at first brief humorous skits introduced between other features of an entertainment. Later they were developed into a whole evening's performance.

The Negroes were themselves interesting; with their peculiarities exaggerated they became highly so. The ludicrous side of Negro character, being most obvious, was hit upon; song and impersonation was the vehicle of expression. During the long-continued popularity of the early minstrel entertainments a more or less distinct group of melodies developed. The early shows were patterned on the plantation "darky." The feeling toward this type always contained a large measure of sympathy. The demand of the minstrels for suitable songs brought out the compositions of Stephen C. Foster and many other ballads of like nature.

The minstrel shows later changed form. The plantation "darky" was replaced by the city "coon" and the show became a spectacle. The period of plantation melody was superseded by the "coon" songs. These were in quasi-Negro dialect and the music abounded in the peculiar syncopation found in the true Negro melodies. This presently became the popular music of the day. Once the minstrel shows ceased to travesty the real plantation Negro and turned to exploit the city type they lost in popular favor and presently disappeared. In the impersonation of the simple Negro there was always an element of love and sympathy in the midst of the caricature. The city "coon" was an object of ridicule, not of sympathetic interpretation.

The minstrel shows left behind a rich body of popular music—the "darky" ballads and the "coon" songs. The Negroes were the inspiration of this music but had little or no part in it as creators.

THE NEGRO AND THE POPULAR MUSIC

The present-day jazz, rag-time, blues, and other varieties of so-called Negro music may be passed without extended comment. This musical variant that for a time dominated the amusement life of America is primitive rather than African in origin. It has had a long history in America in the bawdy houses, saloons, and indecent dance halls. It came into its great popular vogue with the slump of moral and aesthetic standards incident to the European War. Its popularity was in part due to the general lack of musical taste, in part to the fact that it is a very effective device for breaking down the inhibitions of culture and refinement.

In this musical development the Negro musicians have had a prominent place both as performers and as composers.

A few artists, Negro and white, have attempted to sublimate its crass vulgarity without destroying the essential element of its appeal. The effort to develop it as an artistic form has so far met with very limited success.

MUSIC AND THE NEGRO

What the Negroes eventually will be able to achieve in music remains for the future to disclose. The slave songs are of course a worthy achievement but are no assurance of ability to use an art form. It was the conditions of plantation life, not the fact of race, that produced these songs.

The fact of cultural exclusion has stood in the way of artistic achievement. With increased opportunity for training in musical technique it is reasonable to anticipate a great increase in the number of high-class artists. In spite of the handicaps of poverty and isolation the race has produced a fair number of capable performers. Samuel Coleridge-Taylor, an English composer of some Negro blood, was the most capable artist so far produced. In this country Will Marian Cook and Rosamond J. Johnson became best known for their popular songs. Roland Hayes is one of the best of the present-day tenors. Paul Robeson has won international acclaim. Harry T. Burleigh became known both as a soloist and as a composer. Nathaniel Dett is a composer of ability. James Reese Europe was a band leader of national reputation. Marian Anderson and several other

Negro artists have shown ability that has brought them recognition outside of race circles, and there are many younger artists of great promise.

But in music the Negroes remain more a hope and a promise than a present reality. As suggested above, this probably is due to lack of technical education. Except as poverty leads to an absence of opportunity for training, the Negroes have no serious handicap in the field of music. Indeed there is a popular tradition that they have a peculiar musical ability which assures any Negro performer a sympathetic hearing. Moreover there is an influential group in musical circles ready to accept any individual of promise. The eagerness for the appearance of talented individuals who would justify the faith that the race is destined to great achievement in music has sometimes resulted in premature and exaggerated praise. But the public attitude is such that it will bring to expression any musical talent that the race may possess.

DRAMA, PAINTING, AND SCULPTURE

In the other arts—drama, painting, sculpture—there have been indications of artistic ability and a few individuals have made a marked success but the body of achievement is small.

In dramatic composition practically nothing has been done by Negroes. Much has been done in the interpretation and caricature of Negro character. The sentimental drama, *Uncle Tom's Cabin*, enjoyed a long and wide popularity and did much to determine the popular sympathetic attitude toward the simple Negro. In the minstrel shows the Negroes had little part as performers or composers.

In comedy Bert Williams, a West Indian mulatto, gained a national reputation as an artist of first rank. Charles Gilpin gave a notable performance as Emperor Jones. A series of musical comedies of the type of *Shuffle Along* are essentially minstrel shows presented by Negroes.

The Negroes have accomplished little in the presentation of serious drama. A large white audience is awaiting any real talent that appears. The acting of Charles Gilpin in O'Neill's play, *Emperor Jones*, as previously mentioned, was outstanding. Paul Robeson and Charles Harrison are also widely and favorably known. But the amount of really high class artistic work by Negroes is not large.

In painting few Negroes have gained any prominence and in sculpture none. A longer period of freedom and the development of a culture tradition are necessary before much work of art value may be anticipated.

THE ARTISTIC FUTURE OF THE NEGROES

There is a general belief that the Negro people are, by racial nature, artistic. When free to select pursuits without economic or other pressure, they seem to show a tendency toward artistic rather than toward professional or business careers.

Of more significance than a possible temperamental bias is the social stimulation to accomplishment. The Negro child is socially conditioned to the arts. The Negro individuals who have won distinction in America have with few exceptions done so in music, literature, or some related field. The accomplishments of these men are known to all the children of the race. They are individuals of whom the race is justly proud; they are examples of black men who have succeeded. They exemplify the possibilities of success. It is inevitable that the aspirations of the ambitious individuals should be directed along similar lines, that they should look toward an artistic rather than toward a professional or business career. The tendency is reinforced in other ways. The general belief that the race is peculiarly gifted in artistic ways while lacking in the usual capacity for the mechanical and practical arts is shared by the Negroes and operates to encourage effort in certain lines and to discourage it in others. The question of prejudice enters. In the artistic field the fact of color is not a handicap, it may even be an asset. There is an enthusiastic white audience ready to welcome any Negro of special talent. The racial interest in literary and artistic endeavor, and the consequent stimulation to effort along these lines, is indicated by the fact that the race supports a number of magazines of general literature and others devoted exclusively to music. In addition to these the great majority of the newspapers of the race have departments to encourage Negro poets and writers. The general interest in the various forms of artistic work, and the stimulation that the general interest and unlimited opportunity give, makes it certain that whatever talent exists will be developed and get expression and recognition.

While it remains true that the body of artistic accomplishments to date is small and, for the most part, not of high order, there is reason to believe that the volume will increase and the quality improve.

Braithwaite, W. S., "The Negro in American Literature," A. Locke, ed., *The New Negro*, pp. 29–44.

Brown, W. N., "Hindu Stories in American Negro Folklore," *Asia*, 21(1921), 703–707.

Cullen, Countee, *Caroling Dusk, An Anthology of Verse by Negro Poets*.

Calverton, V. F., ed., *Anthology of American Negro Literature*.

Cable, G. W., "Creole Slave Songs," *Century*, 31(1886), 807–828.

DeArmond, F., "The Sociology of Negro Literature," *Opportunity*, 3(1925), 369–371.

Detweiler, F. G., *The Negro Press in the United States*.

DuBois, W. E. B., *The Souls of Black Folk*.

Gerber, A., "Uncle Remus Traced to the Old World," *Journal of American Folklore*, 6(1893), 245–257.

Handy, W. C., ed., *Blues: An Anthology*.

Higginson, T. W., "Negro Spirituals," *Atlantic Monthly*, 19(1867), 685–694.

Johnson, F. W., ed., *American Negro Poetry*.

Kerlin, R. G., *Negro Poets and Their Poems*.

Kirby, P. R., "Study of Negro Harmony," *Musical Quarterly*, 16(1930), 404–414.

Krehbiel, H. E., *Afro-American Folk Songs*.

Laubenstein, P. F., "Race Values in Aframerican Music," *Musical Quarterly*, 16(1930), 378–403.

Locke, Alain, and Gregory, Montgomery, *Plays of Negro Life*.

Loggins, Vernon, *The Negro Author*.

Matthews, B., "The Rise and Fall of Negro Minstrelsy," *Scribner's Magazine*, 57(1915), 754–760.

Nelson, John Herbert, *The Negro Character in American Fiction*.

"Negro Music and Negro Minstrelsy," *American History and Encyclopedia of Music*, 8:47–70.

Rollins, H. E., "The Negro in the Southern Short Story," *Sewanee Review*, 24(1916), 42–60.

Sampson, J. M., "The Negro in Anglo-Saxon Literature," *Opportunity*, 2(1924), 168–171.

Talley, T. W., *Negro Folk Rhymes*.

Upton, G. P., *The Song: Its Birth, Evolution, and Function*, "Negro Minstrelsy," pp. 111–119.

White, N. I., *American Negro Folk Songs*.

——, and Johnson, W. C., *An Anthology of Verse by American Negroes*.

FURTHER READINGS

Since Professor Reuter completed this chapter enormous developments have occurred in literature and art. For example, Leontyne Price has regularly sung at the Metropolitan Opera, as have other Negro vocalists on a less frequent basis. Negro actors have performed on the stage, in television, and in the movies, and Negro playwrights have had their works produced on Broadway. Negro painters and sculptors have achieved greater recognition through one-man shows and the inclusion of their works in major collections.

As a sociologist, the present editor does not feel competent to judge the achievements of these artists nor those of the growing number of novelists, poets, playwrights, essayists, and other writers who have appeared on the scene. The appraisal of the literary achievements of these writers should be left to the literary critics—of all races—who regularly pass judgment on these matters.

Among the group of writers attracting considerable attention since Professor Reuter's work was completed, one could mention novelists Richard Wright, Ralph Ellison, and James Baldwin. Lorraine Hansberry's play, *A Raisin in the Sun*, won the New York Drama Critics' Circle Award. LeRoi Jones is both a versatile and prolific writer—poet, playwright, novelist, and essayist. Other leading poets include Gwendolyn Brooks, Robert E. Hayden, and Margaret Walker. This list is by no means exhaustive but is merely meant as suggestive. "Further Readings" does not include book-length works of these writers, but it does list various anthologies that contain their bibliographies.

Bontemps, Arna Wendell, "The Negro Contribution to American Letters," in Davis, John P., ed., *The American Negro Reference Book*, Ch. 25. Englewood Cliffs, N.J.: Prentice-Hall, 1966.

Brown, Marion E., "The Negro in the Fine Arts," in Davis, John P., ed., *The American Negro Reference Book*, Ch. 22. Englewood Cliffs, N.J.: Prentice-Hall, 1966.

Brown, Sterling A., *Negro Poetry and Drama*. Washington, D.C.: Associates in Negro Folk Education, 1937.

Chapman, Abraham, ed., *Black Voices: An Anthology of Afro-American Literature*. New York: New American Library, 1968.

Cruse, Harold, *The Crisis of the Negro Intellectual*. New York: William Morrow, 1967.

Dorson, Richard M., ed., *American Negro Folktales*. Greenwich, Conn.: Fawcett, 1967.

Dover, Cedric, *American Negro Art*. Greenwich, Conn.: New York Graphic Society, 1960, reprinted 1965.

Emanuel, James A., and Gross, Theodore L., *Dark Symphony: Negro Literature In America*. New York: Free Press, 1968.

Geismar, Maxwell, "Introduction," in Cleaver, Eldridge, *Soul On Ice*. New York: Dell, 1968.

George, Zelma, "Negro Music in American Life," in Davis, John P., ed., *The American Negro Reference Book*, Ch. 20. Englewood Cliffs, N.J.: Prentice-Hall, 1966.

Jones, LeRoi, *Blues People: Negro Music in White America*. New York: William Morrow, 1963.

———, "Myth of a Negro Literature," *Saturday Review*, 46(April 20, 1963), 20-21.

Killens, John O., et al., *The American Negro Writer and His Roots.* New
York: American Society of African Culture, 1960.
"The Negro in Literature: The Current Scene," *Phylon,* 11(Winter 1950),
297-394.

X V

THE CHURCH AND RELIGIOUS LIFE
OF THE NEGRO

Religion plays and seems always to have played an important rôle in the life of the Negro people. Expressing as it does both the fears and aspirations of men, it is in some form characteristic of all human groups: there is no people without some practices and beliefs that may be brought within a definition of religion. But the complex is of particular importance in the earlier culture stages where it tends to be incorporated as an integral part of the fundamental social organization.

The religion of the African was, basically, a crude and simple demonology. It began and ended in a belief in spirits and in the practices designed to court their favor and to avoid the consequences of their displeasure. There was a lack of unity and system resulting from the decentralization and absence of unity in the political and social life. But as among most other peoples of primitive culture, the religious beliefs and practices formed an integral part of the fundamental social organization. The religious did not exist apart or readily separable from other elements of the culture; it was woven into the economic, social, and political life; the whole institutional life was affected by the belief in and the practices toward the supernatural powers. Nassau, an intelligent missionary of long residence among the African tribes, speaking of the West Coast peoples, stated that "Religion is intimately mixed with every one of these sociological aspects of family, rights of property, authority, tribal organization, judicial trials, punishments, intertribal relations and commerce." It is a generally accepted position that it is not possible to understand the Africans nor their social organization apart from the religious practices and beliefs that so intimately condition them.

Fear was the basic element in the religious complex of the Negroes. In the conditions of primitive existence in the African environment it could not well have been otherwise. The life of the native was never safe. Personal danger was the universal fact of life. There was an almost complete lack of control of natural forces. The forests and rivers were full of dangerous animals, and dangerous human enemies were always close at hand. The insect pests and the tropical diseases made the conditions of life hard and its duration brief. To the real dangers were added an abundance of malignant spirits. An ever present fear of the natural and supernatural enemies was the normal condition of daily life and protection was the ever present need. These facts everywhere found expression in the religious and magical beliefs and practices.

The state of religious development varied considerably with tribal groups. In some tribes nature worship was elaborated to the point where definite supernatural powers had been differentiated to preside over definite spheres of life. In other groups the basic fetishism was modified by and combined with a worship of nature. In certain of the more politically advanced groups ancestor worship was an important element in the religious complex. But everywhere the practices were directly designed to placate or coerce the malignant and insure the co-operation of the beneficent powers. Since it was the nature of the latter to aid, the cultus procedure in their case was less important and was quite commonly neglected. Magic, both sympathetic and imitative, was practiced by private individuals as well as by professional magicians. Sickness, accident, injury, death, and other misfortunes were attributed to evil influences exercised by or through some person, and the effort to find the persons guilty of exercising evil influence lay at the basis of the witch trials and the other bloody religious sacrifices of the African peoples.

In some sections the Negroes had been somewhat influenced by foreign religious contacts.

THE BEGINNINGS OF NEGRO CHRISTIANITY

The first Negroes brought to America were slaves who accompanied the Spanish explorers. They came from the slave population of the Peninsula and were at least nominally Christians. This continued to be the case for a considerable period after the discovery; the Spanish rulers insisted that only baptized African slaves be sent to the West Indies. The captive Negroes were taken to Spain and Christianized before being reshipped to the colonies. This policy was abandoned only when the Colonial labor demand became too great to be supplied from the servile population of the home country.

But the great majority of the Negroes had had no contact with Christian civilization prior to their importation. Consequently they brought to America a whole body of primitive religious beliefs and attitudes which the planters did not understand and for which they frequently offered no substitute. In general the Negroes clung to their supernatural conceptions and magical ideas with more tenacity than to any other element of their tribal culture. The practice of the pagan rites was in general suppressed but the beliefs frequently spread and continued in many places for long periods after the Negroes had taken on the forms of Christian worship. The white man's religious forms were often made to contain a strange content. Even at the present time in certain places in the West Indies and elsewhere primitive rites are occasionally practiced, sometimes according to the ritualistic forms of the Catholic Church. In the United States it was not until after the Civil War that the Negro church service became at all generally Christian in content.

In many cases the slaves, where the numbers were small, attended the church services as members of the master's family and became familiar with the white religious practices. But as the number of Negroes increased, special provisions had to be made for their attendance. In some cases the white churches provided galleries to accommodate the Negroes; in other churches the Negroes were allowed to occupy the back rows of seats. Some churches held special services for the Negroes in the church building at an hour that did not interfere with the worship of the whites. In other cases the services for the Negroes were held in the basement of the churches or some other separated place of worship was provided. Sometimes the Negroes were assembled in the church yard and heard as much of the service as drifted through the open doors and windows. In many cases the slaves rather quickly acquired some rudimentary conception of the white man's religion as well as some familiarity with his practices. The matter of their religious instruction was under the control of the slave owners and practice in regard to it differed from master to master. Some owners looked upon the religious conversion of their slaves as a moral duty and made definite provision for their systematic instruction. Other masters were indifferent and, beyond efforts to suppress the practice of witchcraft and other outcroppings of African religion, made no effort to bring the Negroes within the church. Still other masters, fearing that religion would create unrest in the slave population, opposed all efforts to instruct them. As early as 1623, four years after the coming of the first slaves, there appear to have been Negro church members in the Jamestown settlement. The religious contacts of these individuals before 1619 are, of course, not known. The slaves in the small households and the family and house servants most quickly acquired the religious beliefs as they did other elements of the white culture. The numbers were few and their contacts relatively numerous. On the plantations the process was much retarded; the number of slaves was large and their contacts relatively few, and there was a continued importation of raw Negroes from abroad. As the old African stock died out the grosser customs tended to disappear; the native-born Negroes were more susceptible to the religion of the whites.

The conversion of the slaves to the Christian forms was at first a frequent cause of embarrassment. Their paganism was the basis of their slave status. To many persons it appeared impious to hold Christians in bondage, and the rapid conversion of the Negroes seemed for a time to threaten the permanence of the slave institution. The uncertainty tended in certain places to retard missionary efforts; masters sometimes refused to allow their slaves to be baptized for fear of losing their services. In some cases they were given religious instruction but were not baptized. The problem became acute and various Colonial legislative bodies found it necessary to declare that slaves might become Christians without in any way altering the civil status. In 1667 the Virginia Assembly enacted a law declaring that "Baptisme doth not alter the condition of the person as to his bondage or freedom, in order that diverse masters freed from this doubt may more carefully endeavor to propagation of Christianity." It was not until 1729 that all doubt on the subject was put to rest by a Crown declaration that baptism in no way changed the status of the slaves.

The Beginnings of the Negro Church

The conversion of Negroes very early gave rise to questions in regard to their church status. In general the first converts became members of white church congregations. But this disposition met with a good deal of opposition; the association was too close to please the whites and too restricted to satisfy the Negroes. The Negroes were tolerated rather than welcomed as members of the white churches. As the number increased the white congregations were generally willing and sometimes anxious to be rid of their Negro members. The belief was very generally held that the gospel could not be presented successfully to the two races together. In many places the arrangement gave rise to administrative difficulties. In New England, for example, where the church and the state were closely connected, membership in the church granted political as well as religious equality and the disposition to Christianize the slaves was opposed by the desire to exclude them from the political organization.

If they were to be converted the alternative to accepting them as members of white congregations was to provide separate accommodations for their worship. The sentiment in favor of separation grew rapidly. The opportunity for separation came in many places as a result of population growth and the increase in the number of Negro converts. When it became necessary for congregations to divide, because the church buildings were too small to accommodate the growing membership, race and color seemed to be the obvious and natural line of division and separate buildings were provided for the Negro part of the membership.

This separation was usually welcomed by the Negroes. In the white churches they were in an inferior position and commonly had no voice in the church affairs; the control was in the hands of the whites and the Negroes were given special seats apart from the white members. Even at this early date there were some beginnings of a desire for self-determination. In some cases the free Negro members, with the consent and assistance of the white members, withdrew and established their own churches. The separate service gave more freedom of expression, and the separate buildings gave them in many cases not only a place of worship but also a center for their social life.

The early Negro congregations, however, were only nominally separated from the whites, the special churches being for Negroes rather than being Negro churches. They were under white control and supervision and in general white preachers ministered to their needs. They had the same doctrine as the white congregation and used the same literature. In a few cases there were Negro preachers for the Negro groups. This was rarely the case in the South where, for reasons to be indicated presently, the whites retained a fairly close and complete control. In the North a few Negro preachers appeared even before the Revolutionary War. The whites came presently to look upon the separated local Negro part of the congregation as a necessary but undesirable adjunct and often took little account of it.

In the South before the Emancipation, the Negroes, both slave and free, had to be content with such religious privileges as were granted them by the whites. So far as the slaves were concerned, the privilege of church attendance depended upon the will of the master and a number of considerations led to the regulation and restriction of their religious development. Many of the southern masters were sincere in the belief that the system of domestic slavery afforded the only sane and natural method of elevating the Negroes. They recognized the moral injury that came to the slave as a result of participation in religious excitement and imposed various restrictions to guard against their demoralization. The so-called camp meetings were usually forbidden as were in general all night meetings of Negroes. The religious activities of the free Negroes were also restricted. There were a few independent Negro congregations but the evils of these were notorious and so much disorder cloaked itself under the name of religion and the independent churches were so often the center of disorganizing forces that their formation was generally forbidden. This was partly on the ground of public safety: the assembly of any considerable body of Negroes for any purpose tended to be disorderly and contained or was believed to contain elements of public danger. The fear of servile insurrections led to various legislative and police prohibitions on the assembly of Negroes and these became more stringent as certain abortive rebellions called attention to the dangers. The Negro meetings were frequently disorderly and complaints of the disturbance of the peace of the community led to many police restrictions. The Negro church meetings, when they ceased to be a curiosity, became a public nuisance and were suppressed like other disorderly meetings of the Negroes. To make religious worship an amusement and an amusing spectacle was offensive to many pious persons and their shocked sensibilities were an element in the opposition to independent Negro churches. Negro preachers were generally discouraged or suppressed. In nearly all cases they were grossly ignorant and incompetent persons and their preaching often morally injurious to the Negro listeners. There was also always the possibility of irresponsible Negroes abusing the opportunity and endangering the peace of the community. They became especially unpopular as the whites realized the opportunities they had to incite trouble. Nat Turner, the leader of a Negro insurrection in Virginia, operated as a preacher. However, there were Negro churches and Negro preachers in the South. In many places they were allowed to exist undisturbed if they had the sanction of the white minister. In other places no prohibition was placed upon Negro churches, or the prohibitions were not enforced as long as they did not offend against public peace and decency. In some places there was little opposition to the black preachers who were known not to be trouble makers engaged in stirring up the Negroes to oppose the social order. The restrictions upon the extravagant behavior of the Negroes continued in some places even after the Civil War; Mississippi, for a time after the Emancipation, prohibited these meetings in the interests of social order.

Separate, and presently independent, Negro church organizations grew and multiplied whenever the restrictions were removed. The Negroes were nowhere enthusiastically welcomed as members of white congregations; at best they were tolerated and when opportunity arose they had the co-operation of the whites in the establishment of separate churches. The separate meetings afforded the Negroes an opportunity to escape the restraints imposed by the whites and to enjoy their religious emotions to the full. Restrictions on this natural segregation tendency were imposed in various places in the interests of law and order and to prevent the demoralization and moral evils that frequently resulted.

THE SEPARATION AND GROWTH OF THE NEGRO CHURCH

A few separate local churches grew up among the free Negroes in the latter quarter of the eighteenth century and separate church organizations were formed during the first half of the nineteenth century. At the time of emancipation there were perhaps 700,000 Negro church members most of whom held their membership in white churches. Approximately one-half of the number were Baptists and four-fifths of the remainder were Methodists. After the Civil War the Negro churches entered upon a new period of development. Separate churches sprang up everywhere and the Negro members rapidly withdrew from white churches and joined those of their own race.

In 1890, the time of the first census of Negro churches, there were over 23,000 separate organizations. At the second enumeration in 1906 the number of organizations had increased to nearly 37,000. At the enumeration in 1916, there were over 39,000 separate organizations; in 1926 the number had increased to 42,585; and in 1936—the last year the Bureau of the Census conducted such an enumeration—there were 38,303 Negro churches. The church membership increased from more than 2,500,000 in 1890 to 5,660,618 in 1936.* The figures reported at the various enumerations are given in the following table.

Table 30-1: NEGRO CHURCHES AND CHURCH
MEMBERSHIP, 1890–1936

Enumeration Date	Number of Organizations	Membership Reported
1890	23,462	2,676,539
1906	36,563	3,691,844
1916	39,592	4,602,805
1926	42,585	5,203,487
1936	38,303	5,660,618

During this period there was a similar increase in the amount and value of church property. In 1890 the church buildings numbered about 24,000. The number increased to nearly 35,000 in 1906 and to 37,000 in 1916. In 1926 the number was reported as 37,347, and in 1936 there were 34,896. The value of church property increased from approximately $26,500,000 in 1890, to roughly $56,500,000 in 1906, and to nearly $87,000,000 in 1916. In 1926 it was reported as $205,782,628, and in 1936 as $164,531,531. The debt on this church property increased from approximately $5,000,000 in 1906 to approximately $8,000,000 in 1916, and to $22,178,581 in 1926, but declined to $19,224,858 in 1936. Figures in regard to church debt were not secured at the first enumeration. The exact figures for churches and

* Since 1936 the *Statistical Abstract of the United States* has included a minimum of data on religion, obtained largely from the National Council of the Churches of Christ in the United States of America. Nonwhite church membership—including groups other than the Negro—was reported as 11,972,000 in 1957.

church property as reported at each enumeration are given in the following table.

Table 30-2: NEGRO CHURCHES AND CHURCH
PROPERTY, 1890–1936

Enumeration Date	Number of Churches	Value of Church Property
1890	23,770	$ 26,626,448
1906	34,648	56,636,159
1916	37,083	86,809,970
1926	37,347	205,782,628
1936	34,896	164,531,531

The figures here given include about ninety per cent of the churches; in 1916, the percentage of churches reported was 93.7; in 1926 it was 87.7; and in 1936 it was 91.1. The average value of the church edifices was $1,635 in 1906, $2,341 in 1916, $5,510 in 926, and $4,804 in 1936.

Until the decade ending in 1926, there was a similar growth in the Sunday schools and in the attendance at the Sunday schools maintained by these churches. In the ten-year period from 1906 to 1916 there was an increase of about 3,000 in the number of such schools. During the same decade there was an increase of over 4,000 in the number of students enrolled in the schools. In the next decade there was a slight decrease in the number of the schools and in the students enrolled: the number of schools decreased by about 4,000 and the number of students enrolled by about 9,000. While there was a decline in the number of Sunday schools reported in 1936, there was an increase of slightly more than 280,000 in the number of students enrolled. The exact figures reported at the enumerations from 1906 to 1936 are given in Table 30-3.

The figures relate only to the Sunday schools reported by the individual churches and do not include undenominational Sunday schools. Also, they do not include the parochial and weekday schools that are maintained by a number of religious organizations such as the Roman Catholic Church and certain of the Lutheran bodies.

The great majority of the Negro church members belong to one of the

Table 30-3: NEGRO SUNDAY SCHOOLS AND SUNDAY
SCHOOL ENROLLMENT, 1906, 1916, 1926, 1936

Enumeration Date	Churches Reporting Sunday Schools	Enrollment Reported
1906	33,538	1,740,099
1916	36,797	2,153,843
1926	36,378	2,144,553
1936	35,021	2,424,800

Baptist or Methodist bodies. In 1936 the membership of the Negro Baptists was almost 4,000,000; the four Negro Methodist bodies reported a membership of slightly under 1,500,000; the Roman Catholic churches reported 137,684 members; and the Protestant Episcopal church, a little over 30,000. The sex distribution in the membership in these congregations favors the women: as far as the facts may be known, the sexes in 1936 were in the ratio of 60.5 men to 100 women. In 1926 the churches and church membership were also largely rural, with approximately seventy-five per cent of the Negro churches and about sixty per cent of the membership being rural. While there were more rural than urban churches in 1936, the number of urban members was larger. Approximately fifty-two per cent of the membership was urban. At the first three enumeration dates there was a sharp rural-urban division in churches: the Baptist and Methodist groups were predominantly rural; the Roman Catholic and Episcopal groups were predominantly urban. In 1936, however, probably as a result of growing urban migration, both the Baptist and Methodist groups had slightly more urban than rural members, while Roman Catholics and Episcopal groups continued as predominantly urban.

The Negro church divides into two main groups—those which are exclusively Negro in membership and control, and those organizations which are parts of white denominations. Of the thirty-three recognized independent Negro denominations in the United States in 1936 only a few were important from the point of view of membership and property. In Table 31-1 comparable statistical facts of significance are given for the larger Negro churches.

Table 31-1: THE MORE IMPORTANT INDEPENDENT
NEGRO DENOMINATIONS, 1936

Denominations	Number of Churches	Church Membership
Negro Baptists	23,093	3,782,464
African Methodist Episcopal Church	4,578	493,357
African Methodist Episcopal Zion Church	2,252	414,244
Colored Methodist Episcopal Church	2,063	269,915
All Others	3,347	219,709
Total	35,339	5,179,689

In addition to the independent Negro denominations there are some twenty-six white denominations composed in part of Negro organizations. There were about 4,000 such Negro organizations in 1890; the number increased to about 5,000 in 1906, and in the following decade declined slightly. In 1926 there were 6,080 such organizations, but they had declined to 2,964 by 1936. The membership increased slowly during the first three and a half decades covered by the figures—from about 330,000 in

1890 to nearly 500,000 in 1906, to over 530,000 in 1916, to 644,692 in 1926—but declined to 480,929 in 1936. The value of property owned by these organizations increased from $6,000,000 in 1890 to $12,000,000 in 1906, to approximately $16,500,000 in 1916, and to $37,489,276 in 1926, and declined to $21,951,386 in 1936. This group of church organizations conducted 2,379 Sunday schools enrolling 163,873 pupils in 1936.

With a single exception these organizations are small, and in many cases very small. In the following table comparable statistical facts of significance are given for each of the organizations reporting 100 or more church congregations in 1936.

Table 31-2: WHITE CHURCH DENOMINATIONS WITH IMPORTANT NEGRO BRANCHES, 1936

Denominations	Number of Churches	Church Membership
Methodist Episcopal Church	1,730	193,761
Congregational and Christian Churches	233	20,437
Disciples of Christ	189	21,950
Roman Catholic	178	137,684
Protestant Episcopal Church	145	29,738
Church of God (Headquarters, Anderson, Indiana)	117	4,310
Other Denominations	372	73,049
Total	2,964	480,929

There are throughout the United States a few thousand individual Negroes who hold membership in white churches.

NEGRO DENOMINATIONS AND CHURCH MEMBERSHIP

It is evident from the foregoing summary of growth and membership that the Negroes not only tend to join the independent denominations but that they also gravitate to a limited number of them.

It is commonly asserted, possibly with some measure of truth, that this denominational distribution is an expression of racial temperament. There is said to be something peculiarly racial in religion and its expression. The logical philosophical speculation that appeals to the Oriental does not satisfy Western peoples, who seem to find satisfaction in more concrete expression of religious belief, and the conversion of individuals of one group to the religion of the other seems often to result in a change of form without a corresponding change of fundamental content.

But any organized body of culture facts undergoes an unavoidable and real change in transmission from group to group quite independent of temperamental differences. Normally a people select elements from a foreign culture complex and incorporate the abstracted elements in a more or less disguised form into their system. Where the opposite is the case, where one group takes over bodily the culture system of another, the elements of the adopted system are understood in terms of the body of similar doctrine already possessed by the group. The full significance that the system has for the people who evolved it to serve their peculiar needs is not understood by the people who adopt it and, in the new hands, it is modified and, from the point of view of its originators, corrupted in the foreign usage. Language undergoes profound changes in its transmission to foreign groups and in being adapted to their needs. The labor of missionaries has not infrequently resulted in the transmission of a ritualistic ceremonial according to which the natives thereafter practiced their heathen rites. The external culture form has a content as variable as the situation and the need to which it is adapted.

The Negroes took over the church forms and religious beliefs of the white men. In so doing, they understood and interpreted the forms and beliefs in terms of their existing body of philosophic thought and employed the forms to express their social and temperamental needs. Unconsciously and unintentionally perhaps but none the less truly, they modified the religion given them by their white teachers. These early conceptions were passed on to the children and were gradually corrected with the advance in the culture of the group. It was slowly and by degrees only that the Negroes came fully into the religious heritage of the white people.

The denominational affiliation of the Negroes was determined in part by the general attitude of the white organizations. Some of the church groups not only welcomed a Negro membership but systematically proselyted the Negroes; others made no special effort to attract them and sometimes even discouraged their membership. The character of the church service operated in the same direction. The Catholic church maintained schools and missions but the service did not greatly attract the Negroes. The sects with a free, informal, and spectacular form of worship made a greater appeal to the Negro than did those with a more dignified, formal, and ritualistic service. The attitude of the church and the nature of the service operating in the same direction resulted in the concentration of the Negroes in relatively few evangelical denominations. As of 1936, nearly two-thirds of the Negro church members belonged to Baptist organizations and one-quarter to the Methodist organizations.

THE CHURCHES AND CHURCH PROPERTY

Owing largely to the fact that so many avenues of expression have been closed to them, the Negroes have put a great amount of energy, money, and enthusiasm into their church life. It has been almost the only institution that they could really call their own; in it at the present time they are more completely independent than in any other important social relation.

To its support they probably give more, in proportion to their wealth, than any other group.

But the race is poor and the typical congregation is small. Consequently, the individual churches, in spite of frequent and liberal contributions from friendly whites, are generally without adequate financial support. The average value of the Negro rural churches in 1926 was given as $2,115 and in 1936 as $1,990, with an average indebtedness of over $500 in 1926 and of $115 in 1936. (If one used only churches with indebtedness to compute the average indebtedness, the 1936 average debt was $715.)

The typical Negro country church is a small rectangular frame building of rough and simple structure. It is generally located at some crossroads. The exterior is frequently unpainted and the furnishings limited to rude benches facing a platform and pulpit. The congregation is frequently very small—the 1936 average was 109 members. The people are poor, ignorant, and widely scattered. In these circumstances it is difficult to obtain educated ministers. The congregation is frequently unable to support a resident pastor. In some cases they are served by a farmer or laborer who preaches on Sunday. In other cases they are served by a pastor from a near-by town at such hours as do not conflict with his regular duties. In still other cases one preacher divides his time and ministers in a partial way to two or more rural congregations. In many cases church services are held but once or twice a month or whenever a minister can be secured. Prayer meetings and Sunday schools are held at regular intervals. There are, of course, notable exceptions but in general the rural Negro church is backward and neglected.

While the village and small town churches do not differ essentially from those in the rural districts, they are in a very much stronger position. The membership is larger—the 1936 average of the urban congregation was 219—and less scattered; they generally support a resident pastor and hold regular services.

The more wealthy congregations in the larger towns and cities often have large and well-built churches that conform in architecture and furnishings to the conventional church standards.

The church congregations, where the community undertakes the support of more than one church, very generally parallel the prevailing class and caste distinctions. The educated, well-bred, prosperous, and light-colored individuals compose a large percentage of certain congregations while other congregations are made up almost in their entirety of the dark-skinned and ignorant manual laborers. The denominational separation frequently follows similar lines: the aristocratic congregations are frequently Presbyterian, Congregationalist, or Episcopalian; the Baptist and Methodist congregations in a much larger percentage of cases are made up of the poor, ignorant, and simple people. This segregation in so far as it is economic, shows unmistakably in the proportional distribution of church property owned by denominations.

THE NEGRO MINISTERS

During the period of slavery the white religious organizations supplied the Negro congregations with the majority of the preachers. In these churches Negro exhorters were sometimes allowed to speak from the floor though seldom if ever from the pulpit. A few congregations had preachers of their own race and several of these individuals gained some notoriety through the effectiveness of their work. But there was no real opportunity so long as the churches remained under white control; it was not until after the Emancipation, when the ministry passed into the hands of the race, that the Negro preachers became a factor of importance in the church and religious life.

In the early days of freedom the educational equipment of the Negro ministers was very meager. There was a dearth of trained men. Moreover, the ministry of the independent churches was open to any individual who felt the "call to preach," regardless of intellectual, educational, moral qualifications, and often the pulpits were filled by men who were profoundly ignorant and in other ways ill-fitted to assume the moral leadership of a backward people. Many of these men had a certain natural eloquence—the easy flow of words that so often accompanies an absence of thought—and the masses of the race were at a culture stage where they reacted to the sound of the sermon rather than to its content. Ignorance therefore, was not a serious handicap to successful preaching. Any man who could deliver a "rousement" sermon became an outstanding character and a religious leader of the people.

Even at the present time the standards are low. The great majority of the ministers are men of mediocre ability and of limited education; there is little prospect of an early improvement. The number of specially trained men is entirely inadequate to supply the congregations. The schools for the training of these men are, with few exceptions, of inferior grade, poorly endowed, and poorly attended and the graduates are by no means all men of merit. The ministry is in disrepute—as among the whites; it is often looked upon as at best a necessary nuisance. Partly because of the inferior quality of the personnel, few capable young men aspire to make the ministry their life work and the theological classes are quite generally composed of students who lack the native capacity to meet the more rigorous standards maintained in academic and professional fields. The standards are sometimes low in other than intellectual ways. "It is often charged against him, that even among the elect, a high standard of morality does not accompany emotional fervor, and that even gross immorality is frequent, and too frequently condoned." Because of his position the preacher has a very great influence on the tone of the community life: Negro writers have frequently explained the low moral standards of the race as a whole as due at least in part to the low ideals of those holding influential positions in religious affairs. The incentive to an educated ministry is absent: training is not necessary in order to be licensed, preferment does not depend upon it, congregations do not in general demand it.

There are, of course, many educated and capable men in the ministry. In spite of the liberal standards for admission there are many in the Baptist and Methodist fraternities, and Presbyterian and Congregational ministers are usually well trained. But the organizations with high standards and orderly service have a relatively small membership. The intellectual preacher does not appeal to the average church-going Negro who desires an emotional, not a reasoned, type of sermon. It is the "hallelujah" type of sermon that makes him "feel good" and the preacher who follows this traditional line of preaching is most often the one who fills the church with hearers.

The intelligent Negro religious leader is in a peculiarly difficult position. He must deal with various problems that ministers of white congregations may take for granted. Problems of church finance always exist. Money must be raised to meet the payments on the church debt, to pay the minister's salary, to support the denominational schools, and to meet the other regular and special church expenses. The preacher's ability to raise money is often a more important consideration than his piety, morality, or intelligence. To raise money it is essential that he attract and hold the crowd. He can hold them only by meeting their demands. This requires that he preach the traditional type of sensational sermon that the uneducated "enjoy" and that he stress the spectacular elements of the church service—communion, baptism, and the like—rather than expound what lies behind the forms. He also faces a dilemma on the question of discipline. The best paying members are sometimes individuals of questionable character and occupation. They must not be offended; many ministers even find it necessary to cater to them, thus endorsing or seeming to endorse the separation of religion and practical morality and reducing the stimulus that religious instruction might be to better living. Ministers of the better type are often forced to abandon their standards in order to hold the membership; they must preach "effective" sermons rather than test the truth of propositions; they must make the congregation "feel good" before they can impress moral or religious truth. Even in the upper circles of Negro life the intellectual preacher cannot always compete with the emotional exhorter; the present cultural level of the mass of the congregations penalizes the minister with high intellectual and personal standards.

The Nature of the Religious Service

Because of the great variation in practice, it is difficult accurately to describe in brief space the nature of the church service. The behavior differs, as it does in the white churches, with the ceremonial practices that characterize the organization. In some sects and denominations the procedure is orderly, dignified, formal, ritualistic; in others there is less of uniformity and more of freedom and spontaneity. Practice also differs with the individual congregations of the same denomination: some are quiet and reserved, others emotional and noisy. And within the same congregation the behavior differs with the occasion: the group that is orderly and dignified at one time may be demonstrative and disorderly at another.

Among the more uneducated classes, the religion is a form of group expression and it affords frequently the only opportunity for individual recognition. Music is perhaps the outstanding feature; the services ordinarily begin with the congregational singing of hymns. Frequently no fixed program is adhered to and there is occasional confusion; any member may start a hymn in which all presently join. There is a pronounced minor chord and the singing takes on a character between a dirge and a chant, the psychological effect of which is marked and definite. The effect is deepened by the sermon which is nearly always weak on the intellectual side. There are long, extemporaneous prayers by the lay members. The ignorant Negro is frequently eloquent in prayer, the halting and less expert are stimulated and encouraged by the "amens," "praise the Lord," and other shouts of encouragement and approval from the congregation. Prayer and testifying sometimes assume a competitive character. As the service progresses it becomes animated and the emotional tone rises. Even the ordinary service tends to be a highly emotional demonstration. By songs, prayers, preaching, shouting, and testimony individuals are stimulated to crowd frenzy and the service is punctuated by the hoarse, inarticulate cries of the emotionally disturbed. The physical accompaniments of religious hysteria—leaping, falling, frothing, jerking, and the like—are frequent. The services sometimes last for hours, the demonstration gradually subsiding with the physical exhaustion of the participants.

Religious excitement reaches its greatest development in the "revivals" of the Baptists and the "camp meetings" of the Methodists. These have always had a great appeal for the ignorant Negroes as they have for the ignorant whites. Both are types of religious orgy ostensibly for the purpose of recruiting membership. They are still in vogue among both the whites and Negroes in various sections of the country that are out of contact with the modern currents of thought. At the present time the camp meetings are largely confined to the southern sections of the country where they tend to take on the character of an annual picnic with a re-

ligious element. They are generally held in the autumn when the harvest
season is well over and are looked forward to for months before they
occur. They are often in the nature of reunions; families come from far
and wide and remain camped for days or weeks in the vicinity of the
preaching. It is an occasion for reunions, feasting, visiting, love-making,
and gossip as well as for preaching and prayer. These camp meetings are
commonly held under the auspices of the local clergy and congregations
but special exhorters are brought in for the occasion. There is much singing and prayer. The preaching is commonly of a lurid and exaggerated
type. "Experience" meetings and "testifying" are more or less continuous.
It is a time of great emotional excitement—all come with the expectation
that something spectacular will happen. The strange surroundings and
crowd excitement increase the tension. The ignorant Negro is peculiarly
susceptible and easily succumbs to the "jerks" and other physical exercises which are interpreted as expressions of the "spirit." These camp
meetings are sometimes the scenes of gross immorality. The "revival
meetings" featured by the Baptists are of a nature similar to the camp
meetings. They are scenes of wild excitement in which susceptible individuals often fall helpless and semi-conscious, see strange visions, and later
utter prophecies.

Religion and the Moral Life

The emotional type of church worship has very little influence on the
practical affairs of life; it is, indeed, rather to be understood as a method
of escape from the repressions of daily existence. The praying, shouting,
singing, and exhortation often have no definite connection with individual
morality. The Negroes came late into the religious system and, because
of their church isolation, they have had no part in and have not kept pace
with the modern movement that has tended to make Christianity a system
of moral practices and ethical ideals instead of a body of supernatural
beliefs. Division between the churches is not theological, and ministers
seldom preach denominational sermons. The ordinary church-going Negro accepts any doctrine without questioning and remains religious; the
modern church has tended to become ethical. The church has probably
been an influence in uplifting the race but it has been so because of the
social nature of the institution rather than because of its religious services
and teachings. Its moral influence is often weak and stumbling.

Many individuals of the younger generation of educated Negroes have
become ashamed of the primitive religious practices and avoid the emotional types of religion. In the cities especially, they conduct a quiet,
reserved, and orderly service that differs in no essential respect from the
type of service to be observed in the better white churches of the same
denominations.

THE NEGRO CHURCH AS A SOCIAL CENTER

The Negro church is much more than merely an institution of worship. The strictly religious meetings are a small part of the weekly program of the ordinary church. It tends to be a center around which a great part of the social and public life of the people revolves.

This has always been the case. Before the Emancipation, meetings for any other purpose were commonly forbidden and the church, especially where there was a separate building and an exclusively Negro congregation, was the center of all activities. After the Emancipation the machinery came into the hands of the race and the church, developing in accord with the racial standards and needs, assumed the functions normally belonging to other institutions which had not yet developed or had been suppressed. It was for a very long time the only institution in which the Negroes were free and which they could really call their own. In it all the social interests and aspirations of the people found expression.

It is still the center of the racial life. This is particularly the case in the villages and rural districts where the church building is the place of assembly for all public purposes. There are no club houses, theaters, parks, or other places of assembly or amusement and the church serves in the place of all. It reaches all conditions of life. A large percentage of the Negroes are members; most of those not members are more or less regular in their attendance. It is the center of information for the community; it functions as a newspaper. It is a place to see friends, hear the neighborhood gossip, meet strangers, carry on flirtations and courtship. Politicians and business and professional men depend upon their church membership, attendance, and activity to extend their acquaintance and increase their prestige. The pastor and his wife are often social leaders whose good will must be courted by the social climbers. For those individuals who desire to rule, the church affords the best opportunity and it gives also the best chance for expression and public display. Funerals and weddings are held in the churches. Aside from the regular services the churches are generally open more than one and sometimes every night of the week. They are often in use in the afternoons and every holiday is the occasion for some special entertainment. There are many minor social or semi-religious organizations connected with the church. It acts either directly or through one of its groups as a welfare agency and charity bureau to help the unfortunate, care for the sick, and bury the dead. It encourages musical and dramatic performances. It is the center of the organized hedonistic activities: social gatherings, suppers, picnics, and entertainments of all kinds take place in the church or are sponsored by it. Lectures and political meetings are held in the church and it is the place where all sorts of fakirs get a hearing.

It is however losing ground. This is to some extent a part of the general decline of religion resulting from the development of science and the spread of knowledge; the Negroes are being influenced to some extent by the spread of modern ideas. But there are other and more important reasons, chief of which is the development of new avenues of expression and amusement. In the larger towns the churches no longer have a monopoly on social resources. There is better music to be heard outside of the church. Other men are better trained than the ministers and individuals no longer turn to the churchmen for information and instruction. Places of amusement are developing and with them the churches cannot compete. The fraternal and secret orders take much time formerly devoted to the church and they satisfy certain exhibitionist tendencies even better than the church activity. There is a growing distrust of the ministers and their motives even among the masses of the race and a growing tendency to restrict the sphere of their influence to religious affairs and so reduce the power of the church in racial life.

THE FUTURE OF THE NEGRO CHURCH

On the whole the church has probably been a factor in the advancement of the race and at present, in spite of its character, is probably on the whole a power for good. The co-operative work on the group of problems centering about the building, financing, and management of the churches and the organization and management of the subsidiary organizations makes for racial unity and has a socializing and civilizing influence quite independent of the value of the churches themselves.

The importance of religion in Negro life will of course decrease as the race advances in education. The influence of religious beliefs and practices is at its maximum among people of simple culture. They live in the midst of phenomena which they can control but imperfectly or not at all, and the varied facts of life and nature, incomprehensible to the untutored mind, are interpreted in terms of immediate experience—that is, in subjective terms. They thus create a philosophy, however crude and simple, in the effort to make intelligible the world of reality and people the world of nature with a host of beneficent and malignant powers. The dangers which surround their existence, exaggerated by the imaginative constructions resulting from lack of control and inability to comprehend in natural terms, inspire fear and so create the need, more or less vaguely realized, for protection and guidance. The need generates the belief in protecting and guiding powers: everywhere men have created beneficent powers with which they have peopled nature. These beneficent and malignant demons with which the simple mind peoples nature are very real —that is, psychologically real—and exert a profound influence on personal behavior and group development. The simple man moves in an animistic world and gives much time and effort to the coercion and propitiation of the demon children of ignorance and fear. The importance of this type of activity will decline as the Negroes increase in education. The direct and simple demonology becomes enriched and modified with the increase of knowledge, the character of the supernatural powers change with the needs of their creators, and magical practices play a decreasing rôle as the accumulating body of culture facts gives an increasing control over the destructive forces and as science provides explanation and makes possible the manipulation of forces not previously understood. Religion and magic decline as science and knowledge advance.

Other elements are woven into the philosophical complex; the aspirations of men frequently become an integral part of the structure. The conditions of life are everywhere hard; human existence at its best is disappointing and unsatisfactory. The fundamental human wishes may be but partially and imperfectly realized. Unwilling or unable to accept the finality of objective reality, simple man is impelled to the creation of another world order and another reality free from the hardships and disappointments, the compulsions and repressions, of the crudely organized social life he knows. So long as the conditions of Negro life remain as they are, the masses will have resort to a realm of organized phantasy in which they may realize vicariously and in the full the wishes thwarted by the imperfections of the social order. The tendency to escape reality remains so long as individual experience is restricted, and is powerful in proportion to the depth and extent of the unsatisfied needs.

Religion and the church will doubtless continue in the immediate future to play an important rôle in Negro life. The masses of the race are uneducated and the majority grossly ignorant and backward. So long as this condition prevails the continuance of magical forms of thought is inevitable. The hardships and restrictions of everyday life make it certain that the masses will continue to find solace in picturing a future existence free from the real and imaginary shortcomings of the present order. But as the race advances in education and larger numbers come into the modern culture, the crude primitivity of belief and practice of the popular churches will tend to pass. The organizations elaborated in the service of the supernatural powers will, of course, remain as important instruments for achieving individual ends and as means of group expression long after the factors instrumental in their origin have passed out of the group philosophy.

Bennett, J., "A Revival Sermon at Little St. John's," *Atlantic Monthly*, 98(1906), 256–268.

Bruce, P. A., *The Plantation Negro as a Freeman*, "Religion," pp. 93–110; "Superstition," pp. 111–125.

Census Bureau, *Religious Bodies*, 1916, "Summary of Statistics of Negro Church Organization," pp. 129–139.

———, *Religious Bodies*, 1926, "The Negro Church," pp. 69–90.

———, *Negroes in the United States, 1920–1932*, "Religious Bodies," pp. 530–554.

Daniel, W. A., *The Education of Negro Ministers*.

Evans, M. S., *Black and White in the Southern States*, "Negro Organization—Church and Lodge," pp. 114–122.

Mays, B. E., and Nicholson, J. W., *The Negro's Church*.

Negro Year Book, 1931–1932, "The Church Among Negroes," pp. 254–278.

Woodson, C. G., *The History of the Negro Church*.

Woofter, T. J., *The Basis of Racial Adjustment*, "Religious Development," pp. 212–234.

FURTHER READINGS

Drake, St. Clair, and Cayton, Horace, *Black Metropolis*. New York: Harcourt, Brace, 1945.

Essien-Udom, E. U., *Black Nationalism: A Search for Identity in America*. Chicago: University of Chicago Press, 1962.

Fauset, Arthur H., *Black Gods of the Metropolis*. Philadelphia: University of Pennsylvania Press, 1963.

Fichter, Joseph H., "American Religion and the Negro," *Daedalus* (Fall 1965), 1085–1106.

Frazier, E. Franklin, *The Negro Church in America*. New York: Schocken Books, 1963.

Herskovits, Melville J., *The Myth of the Negro Past*. New York: Harper, 1941.

Johnson, Charles S., *Growing Up in the Black Belt*. Washington, D.C.: American Council on Education, 1941.

Lincoln, C. Eric, *The Black Muslims in America*. Boston: Beacon, 1961.

Washington, Joseph R., Jr., *Black Religion: The Negro and Christianity in the United States*. Boston: Beacon, 1964.

XVI

DELINQUENCY AND CRIME

Under the slave régime the Negroes were for the most part subject to the direct control of the owner and all minor offenses committed by the slaves were dealt with by the slave overseer or the master without reference to the courts. In some of the states the laws specifically delegated to the masters an absolute authority over their Negro slaves. In North Carolina, for example, they were empowered by statute to try all manner of offenses committed by slaves. Where such power was not specifically delegated, it was commonly assumed by the masters. Limitations were placed at various times on the authority of the owners but in general these had to do with such matters as the freeing or educating of slaves rather than with the master's control of delinquent behavior. In the case of major crimes the practice varied somewhat with different states, but in general murder, rioting, insurrection, and rape were dealt with by the courts rather than by the masters.

The frequency of slave crimes is not in general a matter of record. But the scattered evidence indicates a considerable amount of criminality. The records of South Carolina, which provided a special court of two justices of the peace and three freeholders to act in the case of Negro crimes, show many slave executions. Virginia provided that the masters of all slaves convicted of crime should be reimbursed for the loss of the slave's labor. The records show 1,418 slave convictions between 1780 and 1864. Of these 105 were for rape or attempted rape. In Louisiana, where at least a partial record of criminal court precedures was kept, slave crimes were somewhat frequent. In 1860, there were 83 slave prisoners serving life sentences in the Louisiana state prison. Such figures, taken in connection with the fact that only a fraction of slave offenses came before the courts or were made a matter of record, seem to show that the number of slave

315

crimes was relatively large. No exact or reasonably reliable information is to be had.

SLAVE EMANCIPATION AND NEGRO CRIME

The general behavior of the Negro people, following the Civil War and the Emancipation, was as admirable as could be expected of any people in the circumstances; they were an unusually law-abiding group. But it was inevitable that many individuals should abuse their new freedom, and there was a sudden and great increase in the amount of Negro delinquency. The transition to the new status took place in the period of profound economic and social disorganization resulting from the war and political chaos incident to the Reconstruction policies. As a natural reaction from forced labor and because of the disorganized state of economic organization, the Negroes in large numbers were idle and tended to be vagrant. As a result of habits formed in slavery, the freedmen committed innumerable petty thefts and other offenses. Both things brought them into contact with the criminal law administered in general, after the Reconstruction régime, by unfriendly courts. In the decades following the Emancipation there is no measure of the amount nor of the relative amount of Negro delinquency, but there was a rapid increase as the Negroes outgrew the restraining habits of servitude.

The amount of Negro crime in the decades following the Emancipation, as shown by the number of prisoners, was greatest in the northern states where they lived for the most part in cities and where law and public sentiment were less tolerant of minor offenses committed by them. The amount of delinquency increased more rapidly in the North and in the cities as the migratory wanderings brought the freedmen into the new and strange surroundings. In 1870 there were 2,025 Negro prisoners in the northern states and 6,031 in the southern states. A decade later the number had increased to 3,774 in the northern states and 12,973 in the southern states. In 1890 the number in the northern states was reported as 5,635; the number in the southern states as 19,244. The relative excess of Negro prisoners in the North is appreciated only when the Negro population of the two sections is taken into account. For each 100,000 of the Negro population in 1870 there were in the northern states 372 Negro prisoners and in the southern states 136. Ten years later the number of Negro prisoners per 100,000 population was 515 in the northern and 221 in the southern states; in 1890 the corresponding number had increased to 773 in the northern and 284 in the southern states.

THE CRIMINAL STATISTICS

The only general data with regard to crime rates in the United States come from the periodic figures of the Census Bureau. From time to time the Bureau has collected and published the statistics of the prison population and given figures in regard to the annual number of commitments. In 1910 the data covered some 3,271 institutions: 3 federal penitentiaries, 58 state prisons, 20 reformatories for adults or for adults and juveniles, 100 reformatories for juveniles only, 2,502 county jails, workhouses, and similar institutions, and 588 municipal jails or workhouses. These statistics include data in regard to the sex, age, race, nativity, marital condition of prisoners, illiteracy, occupation before commitment, offense for which convicted, and sentence.

It must be noted that these data are in regard to commitments to prisons and in regard to prison populations. They are therefore comparative statements of the number of each race convicted of crime, not a measure of crime itself. In only a minor fraction of cases where crimes are committed in the United States are the criminals apprehended and the great majority of those arrested fail to be convicted. Consequently such figures as those of the Census Bureau must not be taken as a measure either of the number of crimes committed or of the relative amount of crime of different racial groups; they must be taken only for what they purport to be—prison commitments and prison population.

As an additional warning against accepting the figures of Negro crime as indicating more than they probably do indicate, the caution of the Census Bureau may be cited.

While these figures and those given in tables following will probably be generally accepted as indicating that there is more criminality and law breaking among Negroes than among whites and while that conclusion is probably justified by the facts, it should be borne in mind that the difference between the two races in this respect may very well be less than the ratios based on the number of commitments to prison or jail would indicate. It is a question whether the difference shown by the ratios may not be to some extent the result of discrimination in the treatment of white and Negro offenders on the part of the community and the courts. An offense committed by a Negro is perhaps more likely to be punished than the same offense committed by a white man, especially if the victim of the offense committed by the Negro is white, while in the other case the victim is Negro. It is probable that as compared with the white man the Negro when brought on trial on a criminal charge is in fewer instances able to employ expert counsel to defend his case and assist him in taking advantage of any technicalities in the law which may be in his favor. Moreover, in the case of those offenses for which the penalty may be a fine with imprisonment as the alternative if the fine is not paid, it is probable that the Negro is more often unable to pay the fine than the white man and is therefore more likely to be sent to jail; but of course this consideration has little weight in connection with the more serious offenses which are seldom penalized by fines only. On the other hand, it is not improbable that many of the minor offenses committed by Negroes and not directly affecting white people are more likely to be disregarded by the officers of the law than are the same offenses committed by the whites. Although these are questions on which no statistical data can be presented and in regard to which opinions may differ, it seems proper to call attention to them as representing possibilities which ought to be considered before accepting the record of prison commitments as an accurate measure of the difference between the two races in respect to criminality. It must always be borne in mind that the amount of crime punished in different classes or communities may not bear a fixed or unvarying ratio to the amount of crime committed.

THE NEGRO PRISON POPULATION

The census data relating to crime are based upon the reports received by the various prison officials and are incomplete in character. They do not cover the entire field of imprisonment and not all prison officials respond with the information asked for on the schedules. The variation in the number of prisons covered at the prison enumerations makes it impossible to give comparable crime rates at different dates.

In 1904, the enumeration covered 1,337 prisons, including 81 penitentiaries and reformatories, and a total of nearly 77,000 prisoners. The enumeration of 1910 covered 3,198 prisons including 181 penitentiaries and reformatories, and gave a total prison population of over 111,000 prisoners. In 1923, the enumeration covered 2,341 prisons, including 102 penitentiaries and reformatories, and reported a total of 109,085 prisoners. The distribution by race of the prisoners enumerated at these dates is given in Table 32-1.

Table 32-1: ENUMERATED PRISON POPULATION
OF THE UNITED STATES BY RACE,
1904, 1910, 1923

Date	Institutions	Prisoners	
		White	Colored
1904	1,337	50,111	26,661
1910	3,198	72,797	38,701
1923	2,341	73,549	35,526

On the first day of January, 1910, the total prison population of the United States, prisoners and juvenile delinquents, was reported as 136,472; of this number 93,841 were reported as white and 41,729 as Negroes. The Negro prisoners constituted 30.6 per cent of the total prison population though on that day they constituted only 10.7 per cent of the general population. The ratio of prisoners per 100,000 of the total population was 148.4; for the white population it was 114.8; for the Negro population it was 424.6.

The percentage of Negroes among prisoners and juvenile delinquents

Table 32-2: INMATES OF FEDERAL, STATE, AND LOCAL PENAL
INSTITUTIONS, BY SEX, RACE, AND NATIVITY, 1960*

Prisons and Reformatories		Negro	Other Races	Native White	Foreign-born White	Total
Total:	Number	82,935	3,644	137,053	2,712	226,344
	Per Cent	36.6	1.6	60.6	1.2	100.0
Male:	Number	78,670	3,510	132,986	2,640	217,806
	Per Cent	36.1	1.6	61.1	1.2	100.0
Female:	Number	4,265	134	4,067	72	8,538
	Per Cent	49.9	1.6	47.7	0.8	100.0
Federal						
Total:	Number	6,736	773	16,840	671	25,020
	Per Cent	26.9	3.1	67.3	2.7	100.0
Male:	Number	6,321	741	16,442	662	24,166
	Per Cent	26.2	3.1	68.0	2.7	100.0
Female:	Number	415	32	398	9	854
	Per Cent	48.6	3.7	46.6	1.1	100.0
State						
Total:	Number	76,199	2,871	120,213	2,041	201,324
	Per Cent	37.8	1.4	59.7	1.1	100.0
Male:	Number	72,349	2,769	116,544	1,978	193,640
	Per Cent	37.4	1.4	60.2	1.0	100.0
Female:	Number	3,850	102	3,669	63	7,684
	Per Cent	50.1	1.3	47.8	0.8	100.0
Local Jails and Workhouses						
Total:	Number	42,174	3,450	72,097	1,950	119,671
	Per Cent	35.2	2.9	60.3	1.6	100.0
Male:	Number	38,773	3,032	68,216	1,845	111,866
	Per Cent	34.7	2.7	61.0	1.6	100.0
Female:	Number	3,401	418	3,881	105	7,805
	Per Cent	43.6	5.4	49.7	1.3	100.0

* Source: *U.S. Census of Population: 1960*, "Inmates of Institutions," PC(2)-8A, Table 25

was relatively large. This was true in all parts of the country. The fact that the percentages were higher among prisoners and juvenile delinquents than for the commitments for the year indicates that the term of imprisonment for Negroes was above the average for all prisoners. A comparison of the percentage of Negroes in the prison population in 1910 and the percentage of commitments during the year is given in Table 32-3.

In every section of the country the percentage of Negroes among prisoners and juvenile delinquents was much higher than their percentage in the general population. For the country as a whole the Negroes constituted 10.7 per cent of the total population, while they constituted 30.6 per cent the prison population. In the South they made up 29.8 per

Table 32-3: PERCENTAGE OF NEGROES IN THE PRISON POPULATION: 1910

Section and Division	In Total Population	Among Prisoners and Juvenile Delinquents	
		Enumerated Jan. 1	Committed During Year
United States	10.7	30.6	21.9
The South	29.8	70.1	58.9
South Atlantic	33.7	72.0	61.6
East South Central	31.5	73.1	63.6
West South Central	22.6	62.4	46.0
The North	1.8	13.1	9.6
New England	1.0	4.6	2.6
Middle Atlantic	2.2	12.8	9.4
East North Central	1.6	14.7	11.0
West North Central	2.1	20.8	14.4
The West	0.7	5.9	3.2
Mountain	0.8	7.8	4.4
Pacific	0.7	4.6	2.5
U.S. Penitentiaries	....	31.3	24.6

cent of the population and 70.1 per cent of the prisoners; in the North they were 1.8 per cent of the population and 13.1 per cent of the prisoners; in the West, 0.7 per cent of the population and 5.9 per cent of the prisoners were Negroes.

The percentage of Negro prisoners and juvenile delinquents was greater than that of the whites in all of the age groups except the higher ones. Of the total prison and juvenile delinquent population from 15 to 25 years of age, the Negroes composed about one-third; of those in the age group from 25 to 35 years, they composed about one-eighth; while in the age groups over 45 years, they composed somewhat less than one-twelfth. This decrease in the older age groups appears to be accounted for in large part by the fact that a majority of the total number of commitments in the older age groups are for drunkenness, vagrancy and disorderly conduct, while the percentage of Negroes committed for these offenses is below the average for the population.

In the age groups under 15 years about one-fifth of the prisoners were Negroes. This was much smaller than the proportion in the age groups from 15 to 34 years. This smaller proportion among the Negro juvenile delinquents seems to be due to the fact that Negroes in larger proportion than whites lived in communities where there are no juvenile reformatories. In the absence of such institutions, juvenile offenders are more likely to be allowed to remain at large. The establishment of such institutions tends to increase the number of commitments since they provide care for offenders considered too young to justify a jail or prison sentence.

Another fact of importance in the same connection is that a large percentage of juvenile cases are truancy cases. But this offense does not exist in the absence of compulsory school attendance laws. In the communities where the larger percentage of the Negroes live there was an absence of compulsory school laws and so the offense of truancy did not exist.

In the distribution of the prison population by sex there was a preponderance of males: the percentage of females is relatively low for each race. The total number of prisoners and juvenile delinquents enumerated was 136,472, of whom 124,424 were males and 12,048 were females. Of the total enumeration 93,841 were white, of whom 85,218 were males and 8,623 were females. Of the total of 41,729 Negroes enumerated, 38,346 were male and 3,383 were females. The percentage of female prisoners was thus slightly higher in the case of white than of Negro women. In the total prison and juvenile delinquent population enumerated there were 91.2 males and 8.8 females in each 100. In each 100 white prisoners enumerated, 90.8 were male and 9.2 were female; in each 100 Negro prisoners enumerated 91.9 were male and 8.1 were female. Of each 100 prisoners in the total prison population 68.8 were white and 30.6 were Negroes. Of the male population enumerated 68.5 per cent were white and 30.8 were Negro; of the female population enumerated 71.6 were white and 28.1 were Negroes.

NEGRO COMMITMENTS TO PRISON

The statistical data available for the period approximately one-quarter of a century later than the figures just given show a similar though less pronounced disproportion between the races.

The 1933 report on the *County and City Jails* lists the sentenced prisoners in jails and other penal institutions under county and municipal jurisdiction. The relative numbers were much higher for the Negroes than for the whites. The distribution is shown in the following table.

Table 32-4: SENTENCED PRISONERS PRESENT,
COUNTY AND CITY JAILS, JANUARY 1, 1933

Race	Number	Number per 100,000 of 1930 Population 15 Years Old and Over of Same Race	Per Cent Distribution
Total	41,261	47.6	100.0
Native White	24,646	38.3	59.7
Negro	10,334	128.5	25.0

The Department of Justice figures for commitments to federal institutions—federal penitentiaries, reformatories, and camps—show a disproportionate number of Negroes. The commitments during the year 1950 are given in the following table for the native-born whites and the Negroes.

Table 32-5: COMMITMENTS TO FEDERAL
INSTITUTIONS, 1930–1936*

Year	Native-born White	Negro
1930–31	7,693	1,138
1931–32	8,037	1,114
1932–33	6,726	906
1933–34	6,038	736
1934–35	8,106	1,378
1935–36	8,237	1,797
1938	8,000	2,306
1942	7,621	2,549
1943	7,162	2,028
1945	7,321	2,761
1946	7,997	3,107
1949	6,660	2,465
1950	6,671	3,030

* Source: 1938–50 data, Dept. of Justice, Bureau of Prisons, *National Prisoner Statistics*, Table 3. Data for 1938–50 refer only to male felons. The number of females is so small that data are unavailable for most years

During the year 1935, there were 65,723 prisoners received at the federal civil prisons, reformatories, and prison camps and at all the state prisons and reformatories except those of Georgia, Alabama, and Mississippi. Of the total 48,582 or 73.9 per cent were white, 16,362 or 24.9 per cent were Negro, and 779 or 1.2 per cent were of other races. These ratios indicate that in proportion to population the Negro commitments were over three times those of the whites.

The rate of Negro criminality, as measured by the commitment figures, is higher than the white in all sections of the country. The rates show extreme fluctuation from state to state: in general the Negro rates are higher in the northern than in the southern states; they are higher in general in the states where the Negroes constitute a relatively minor part of the total population.

The following table gives a rough comparison. It shows the percentage that the Negroes compose of the total population of selected states for 1930 and 1950, and the percentage of Negroes among the prisoners committed to prison from each of these states.

Several factors enter into any attempt to explain the differences reported. In the northern and western sections of the country a very high percentage of the Negro population lives in cities; a somewhat larger proportion of the Negroes are in the age-groups where the crime tendency is greatest; they are perhaps less well adjusted to the economic and

Table 32-6: NEGRO PERCENTAGE OF STATE POPULATIONS AND NEGRO
PERCENTAGE OF PRISONERS COMMITTED TO STATE AND FEDERAL
PRISONS, 1930–1950

States	Negro Percentage of Total Population		Negro Percentage of Prisoners Committed to Prison	
	1930	1950	1930	1950
Mississippi	50.2	45.2	70.9	70.4
South Carolina	45.6	38.8	36.1	30.3
Louisiana	39.9	32.9	65.1	55.4
Florida	29.4	21.8	53.2	40.9
North Carolina	29.0	25.8	40.4	49.4
Virginia	26.8	22.1	56.6	54.0
Arkansas	25.8	22.4	41.7	41.0
Tennessee	18.3	16.1	41.4	32.6
Maryland	16.9	16.5	54.8	59.9
Texas	14.7	12.7	31.8	28.9
Kentucky	8.6	6.9	30.8	20.3
Oklahoma	7.2	6.5	21.6	17.7
West Virginia	6.6	5.7	14.3	13.2
Missouri	6.2	7.5	28.7	26.7
New Jersey	5.2	6.6	26.9	35.0
Ohio	4.7	6.4	23.8	34.8
Pennsylvania	4.5	6.1	21.7	34.5
Illinois	4.3	7.4	23.1	34.2
Indiana	3.5	4.4	15.6	16.7
Kansas	3.5	3.8	13.0	16.9
Michigan	3.5	6.9	12.4	N.A.
New York	3.3	6.2	15.7	36.3
Arizona	2.5	3.5	9.2	13.5
Connecticut	1.8	2.6	7.9	24.7
California	1.4	4.4	6.1	19.1
Rhode Island	1.4	1.8	6.1	13.3
Massachusetts	1.2	1.6	6.1	8.2
Colorado	1.1	1.5	3.5	5.7
Nebraska	1.0	1.4	6.0	5.9

social conditions of the northern urban environment. In various southern areas, the whites often protect Negroes who humbly accept inferior status in plantation and other economic and social systems, especially when the Negroes are guilty of minor offenses.

THE CRIMINAL OFFENSES OF NEGROES

Examination of the statistics shows some differences between the Negroes and whites in the incidence of specific criminal offenses. Not only is the percentage of Negroes among offenders sentenced in excess of their relative number in the population, but it is also higher for each of the major offenses except embezzlement and fraud. The rate is particularly high for homicide and crimes of violence.

Table 33–1 gives a classification of crimes for which commitments were made to state and Federal Prisons and Reformatories in 1930–1964.

Reference to the table shows that in 1930 of each 100 prisoners received between one-fifth and one-fourth were Negroes. At this date the Negroes composed slightly less than one-tenth of the total population. Of the prisoners sentenced for homicide almost one-half were Negroes; of those sentenced for assault, the number of Negroes exceeded the number of the whites. The difference between the races is less marked in cases of stolen property, forgery, violation of liquor laws, and of sex offenses; and in case of embezzlement and fraud the Negro rate is below that of the white. A generation later (1964), for each 100 prisoners received from courts roughly 36 were Negroes. At this time Negroes constituted about eleven per cent of the total population. Among them homicide and assault continued to be high. In 1930 about one out of four drug-law violators were Negroes but in 1964 one out of two were Negroes. It is also interesting to note that almost one out of three auto thefts in 1964 were committed by Negroes.

Table 33-1: PER CENT OF PRISONERS RECEIVED FROM THE COURTS, BY RACE AND OFFENSE, 1930–1964*

| | 1930 | | 1943[a] | | 1950[b] | | 1964[c] | |
| | | | | | | | Non- | |
Offense	Negro	White	Negro	White	Negro	White	white	White
All offenses	22.4	74.7	30.8	63.7	29.8	67.3	37.0	63.0
Homicide	46.4	49.8	52.3	46.2	54.6	44.1	56.2	43.8
Robbery	21.1	77.5	42.2	57.3	34.8	64.7	49.6	50.4
Assault	48.3	47.7	53.7	44.6	53.6	44.7	56.2	43.8
Burglary	28.1	69.4	35.1	63.9	30.0	68.7	34.7	65.3
Auto theft	....	....	13.8	85.3	14.6	83.6	32.6	67.4
Other larceny	22.2	75.3	33.1	66.0	31.4	67.3	37.4	62.6
Embezzlement and fraud	6.9	92.0	10.6	88.8	12.9	86.2 ⎱	17.7	82.3
Forgery	11.0	86.3	13.6	84.9	18.3	80.4 ⎰		
Stolen property	14.6	84.8	40.9	58.8	26.9	72.1	N.A.	N.A.
Rape	16.1	80.6	23.5	74.1	24.8	73.2 ⎫		
Other sex offenses (inc. commercialized vice)	12.8	85.5	13.3	85.3	15.2	83.7 ⎭	31.5	68.5
Violating drug laws	23.5	65.7	27.4	63.5	46.1	51.4	50.6	49.4
Violating liquor laws	13.9	82.1	30.9	67.5	36.6	63.2	N.A.	N.A.
Other offenses	16.4	80.3	13.6	85.2	24.5	74.0	31.7	68.3

* Source: Dept. of Justice, Bureau of Prisons, *National Prisoner Statistics*
[a] Data for 1943 refer to male felony prisoners received from courts
[b] Data for 1950 refer to male felony prisoners received from courts
[c] Data for 1964 refer to male felony prisoners received for state institutions

There is a very widespread belief that the Negro people are peculiarly prone to commit sex offenses—there has even come to be a very general idea that this crime is, if not peculiar to the Negro, at least more characteristic of this group than of others.

In 1910 there was a total of 1,480 persons committed for rape in the United States. Of these 380 or 25.7 per cent were Negroes. This percentage is between two and three times their percentage in the total population, not greatly above their percentage of commitments for all crimes, 21.9, and much below their percentage of conviction for other offenses: for grave homicide, 56.0; for lesser homicide, 49.0; for assault, 41.1; for robbery, 33.3; for burglary, 30.5. For a number of other offenses their percentage of the total convictions was in excess of their commitments for rape. In the South 247 of a total of 372 commitments for rape were Negroes. This was 66.4 per cent of those committed. This was higher but not markedly higher than the percentage of Negroes in commitments for all offenses in the South—58.9. It was lower than the percentage of Negroes in commitments in the South for grave homicide, 77.4; lesser homicide, 67.6; assault, 76.2; robbery, 71.8; burglary, 68.8; and larceny, 72.5. In the North the total commitments for rape numbered 955. Of these 122 or 12.8 per cent were Negroes. Here again the percentage of Negroes among the number committed was below their percentage in the groups convicted of half a dozen other serious crimes. In the West, of a total of 144 commitments for rape, six were Negroes—4.2 per cent of the total. And here again their percentage was higher among the commitments for other serious crimes than for the crime of rape.

The commitment figures for later years show similar ratios. In 1930, the total commitments for rape were 1,876. Of these 302 were Negroes, 1,512 were white, and 62 were men of other races. The Negro rate for this crime was below their rate for most other crimes.

That the Negroes are excessively prone to the commission of offenses of this order is not indicated by the available data. Of those committed to prison in 1904 for major offenses, the percentage committed for rape was, for different nationalities, as follows:

In 1935, a total of 1,584 male prisoners received by the state and federal prisons and reformatories were sentenced for rape. Of the total 1,137 were native white, 108 were foreign-born white, 289 were Negroes, and 50 were of other racial groups.

In 1943 there was a total of 1,687 male felony prisoners committed for rape in the United States. Of these 397, or 23.5 per cent, were Negroes; in 1950, 24.8 per cent of prisoners committed for rape were Negroes. This was below their percentage of convictions for homicide, robbery, assault, burglary, larceny (except auto theft), stolen property, and violations of drug and liquor laws, and only higher than their percentages for four

Table 33-2: PERCENTAGES OF COMMITMENTS
FOR RAPE IN THE MAJOR OFFENSES, 1904

Race	Percentage of Commitments
Colored	1.9
White	2.3
Foreign White	2.6
Irish	1.3
German	1.8
Polish	2.1
Mexican	2.7
Canadian	3.0
Russian	3.0
French	3.1
Austrian	4.2
Italian	4.4
Hungarian	4.7

other major offenses—auto theft, embezzlement and fraud, forgery, and sex offenses other than rape.

Other evidence seems to be fairly in keeping with the facts here shown. So far as the available statistical evidence goes it gives no support for the general idea that the Negro people are peculiarly prone to commit crimes of this nature. It is by no means the most important in the list of Negro crimes. It must, however, be remembered that offenses of this nature when the victim is a Negro woman are little likely to come before the courts.

THE LENGTH OF PRISON SENTENCES

It seems generally to have been true that the punishment meted out to Negro offenders has been more severe than that given white offenders for similar crimes. They have been committed to prison more frequently and on the average received longer sentences for similar offenses.

In 1910 there were 130 offenders sentenced to death in the United States. Of this number 49 or 37.7 per cent were Negroes. Between 1930 and 1967, of the 3,859 persons executed under civil authority in the United States 1,751 were white and 2,066 were Negro. The percentage of Negroes who received prison sentences of over one year was about three times as high as the percentage of the white commitments. In 1900 approximately one-third of all Negroes committed to prison received sentences of one year or more; of the white commitments for the same year less than ten per cent received sentences of one year or more. The percentage distribution of Negro and white commitments under sentence of imprisonment only, for the year 1910, appears in Table 34-1.

Of the total number of persons sentenced for one year or longer 40.9 per cent were Negroes, while of those sentenced to terms of less than one

Table 34-1: COMPARISON OF PRISON SENTENCES
BY TERM OF COMMITMENTS, 1910

Length of Sentence	Percentage Distribution Negro	White
Total	100.0	100.0
Life	1.7	0.2
One year and over	28.3	8.2
Less than one year	58.8	74.3
During minority	4.5	5.6
Indeterminate	5.9	11.2
Not reported	0.7	0.4

year only 13.4 per cent were Negroes. This difference was in part sectional rather than racial. In the South where the bulk of the Negroes reside the proportion of long prison sentences for both races was greater than in the North. This, however, does not explain the entire difference, for within the same section and state the percentage of Negroes among those committed for long terms was greater than among those sentenced for short terms, and the percentage of Negroes increases as the length of the term of imprisonment increases.

The same tendency toward greater severity in the treatment of the Negro offender appeared in cases punished by fine or by fine and imprisonment. In 1910 the sentence of fine and imprisonment was imposed upon eleven per cent of the Negro offenders and upon 7.8 per cent of the white offenders. A smaller per cent of Negroes than of whites are convicted of minor offenses. If a fine without prison sentence was imposed the Negroes, because of lower economic status, were less frequently able to pay the fine, so more frequently committed to jail. In 1910, the percentage of Negroes imprisoned for non-payment of fine comprised 62.7 per cent of the total number of Negro commitments as against 54.6 per cent of the total number of white commitments. This high rate of imprisonment for non-payment of fine reflected southern conditions, such court practice being more common there than elsewhere for both races.

The approximate average length of sentence in months for Negro and white prisoners and juvenile delinquents sentenced for definite terms in 1910 was as shown in Table 34-2.

In later and current practice the racial differences in prison sentences are considerably reduced: in some cases they seem to have been entirely removed. The average length of definite sentence in 1931 was 42.1 months for Negroes, 39.7 months for the native white prisoners, and 44.7 months for the persons of foreign birth. For certain offenses—homicide, robbery, assault, forgery, and larceny—the Negro sentences averaged lower than those of the native white and the foreign-born whites; for other offenses —rape, burglary, sex offenses other than rape, and violation of drug laws—

Table 34-2: AVERAGE LENGTH OF SENTENCE
IN MONTHS OF NEGRO AND WHITE
COMMITMENTS, 1910

Divisions	Negro	White
United States	17.4	5.2
The South		
South Atlantic	15.4	9.6
East South Central	31.7	16.2
West South Central	29.7	25.3
The North		
New England	4.7	3.5
Middle Atlantic	4.9	3.3
East North Central	17.7	4.8
West North Central	9.1	4.5
The West		
Mountain	5.1	6.2
Pacific	11.8	6.5

the Negro definite sentences were longer than the average sentences of the whites.

In 1930, there were 112 prisoners committed to state and federal prisons under sentence of death. Twenty-two were Negroes, 82 were white, and 8 were of other races. During the same year, 155 prisoners in the state and federal prisons were executed. Of these 65 were Negroes, 85 were whites and 5 of other races. In 1960, 56 prisoners were executed under civil authority in the United States: 21 were white and 35, Negro.

NEGRO CRIMINALITY BY SEX

The percentage of women in the commitments of prisoners and juvenile delinquents has been much higher among Negroes than among whites. This is a condition of long standing. Table 34-4 (p. 330) shows the number of commitments by race and sex for the year 1900.

Of the total number of commitments 90.2 per cent were males and 9.8 per cent were females. Of the total number of Negroes committed 80.9 per cent were males and 19.1 per cent were females. Of the total white commitments 92.8 per cent were males and 7.2 per cent were females. In the case of white commitments the ratio of men to women was approximately 13 to 1; in the case of Negroes the ratio of men to women was about 4 to 1. In the total commitments for the year 77.3 per cent were whites and 21.9 per cent were Negroes. But of the total number of commitments of males 79.6 per cent were white and 19.7 per cent were Negroes, while of the total number of commitments of women only 57.0 were white and 42.6 per cent were Negroes.

Of the total sentenced in 1910 the sex ratio was approximately four men

Table 34-3: MEDIAN LENGTH OF SENTENCE IN MONTHS
OF NEGRO AND WHITE COMMITMENTS
TO STATE INSTITUTIONS, 1953*

Region and Offense	Time Served in Months	
	Negro	White
United States	24	22
Murder	85	98
Robbery	39	36
Aggravated assault	20	20
Burglary	25	22
Rape	39	35
Northwest	27	23
Murder	129	189
Robbery	41	37
Aggravated assault	25	24
Burglary	30	25
Rape	43	33
North Central	26	22
Murder	130	199
Robbery	38	38
Aggravated assault	24	22
Burglary	26	24
Rape	36	33
South	21	18
Murder	77	70
Robbery	40	36
Aggravated assault	17	15
Burglary	24	19
Rape	40	35
West	27	23
Murder	95	84
Robbery	36	34
Aggravated assault	25	24
Burglary	27	21
Rape	49	36

* Source: Dept. of Justice, Bureau of Prisons, *National Prisoner Statistics*, Table 7B

to one woman; in the case of the whites 7.2 per cent of the commitments
were of women, a ratio of about 13 to 1. In the total of female commitments, the proportion of Negroes was relatively high; in 1910 of the total
of female commitments, 42.6 per cent were Negroes; of the total number
of male commitments, the Negroes constituted 19.7 per cent. A similar,
though less marked, contrast existed in the prison population. The higher
percentage of colored women in the prison commitments was true at all
ages though it was more pronounced in the younger ages, particularly in
the ages from 18 to 24. In that age-group the Negro male rate was three

Table 34-4: COMMITMENTS TO PRISON BY RACE AND SEX, 1900

	Total	Negro	White
Both sexes	493,934	108,268	382,052
Male	445,368	87,598	354,367
Female	48,566	20,670	27,685

to four times that of the white while in the female group the Negro rate was from eleven to sixteen times that of the white.

The differences in the race and sex ratios in prison commitments and in the prison population were probably in large part the outcome of variation in the average term of imprisonment: the average time was greater for Negro males than for white males but less for colored than for white women. It would thus appear that the Negro women were on the average guilty of less grave offenses than were the white women and more given to petty offenses. Eleven times as many Negro as white women were committed for larceny; for the more serious offense of assault the number was over thirty times as great. This was sharply contrasted to the male distribution: the proportion of major offenders was greater among the Negro than among the white, owing in part, probably, to the fact that it was easier to convict a Negro than a white person of a serious offense. The absence of reformatories for Negro women was doubtless a factor of importance in accounting for race differences; the relative number committed to reformatories was considerably larger for whites than for Negroes.

The population of the city and county jails in 1933 showed an excess number of Negro women; of the total female population of 2,325, the white numbered 1,111 and the Negro 1,001. The percentage distribution by race and sex is shown in the following tabulation.

Table 34-5: PRISONERS, BY RACE AND SEX,
IN COUNTY AND CITY JAILS, JANUARY 1, 1933

Race	Number per 100,000 of 1930 Population 15 Years and Over of Same Race and Sex		Per Cent Distribution	
	Male	Female	Male	Female
Total	88.7	5.4	100.0	100.0
Native White	73.1	3.5	60.4	47.8
Negro	236.8	24.4	20.0	41.1

A similar disproportion appears in the figures for female offenders sentenced to the state and federal prisons and reformatories. Of the 3,056 female prisoners received in 1930, the whites numbered 2,153 and the Negroes 863. Reduced to the basis of 100,000 female population fifteen years old and over of the same race, the total rate was 7.4, the white rate was 5.8 and the Negro rate was 25.2.

The distribution of female offenders according to the offenses for which they were committed shows the number of Negroes to be particularly large in the case of homicide and assault and comparatively small for forgery and embezzlement and fraud. The distribution by type of offense is given in the following table.

Table 34-6: FEMALE PRISONERS RECEIVED IN STATE
AND FEDERAL PRISONS AND REFORMATORIES,
BY RACE AND OFFENSE, 1930

Offense	Negro	White
All offenses	863	2,153
Homicide	181	63
Robbery	36	42
Assault	96	35
Burglary	44	52
Larceny	125	193
Embezzlement of funds	5	31
Stolen property	21	36
Forgery	19	136
Sex offenses	87	521
Violating drug laws	50	132
Violating liquor laws	63	260
Other offenses	136	652

THE EXCESS OF NEGRO CRIMINALITY

From every angle, the general statistics seem to indicate a greater amount of criminality on the part of the Negro than of the white element of the population. Their ratio of commitments to prisons and penal and reformatory institutions is out of proportion to their ratio in the general population. They likewise constitute a disproportionately large part of the prison population, and the excess is especially great in the group incarcerated for major offenses. The general opinion that the Negroes are a highly criminal element of the population would thus appear to be proven by the statistics of criminality.

There are, however, several important facts of a qualifying nature that must be taken into account. The statistical information is very misleading; it reflects a good deal of the bias of popular opinion.

Rightly or wrongly, the race in America is believed to be highly criminal and this general belief functions to increase both the number of offenses and the appearance of excessive criminality. Because of the belief there is a tendency to exaggerate whatever basis of fact may exist in support of the belief. The popular idea is fostered by the white press. Crime always has a news value. It is to be expected that news items which coincide with traditional beliefs will get into print; the news value of a crime story is enhanced by the fact that the criminal is a Negro, and it receives additional space and prominence because of the fact. In giving publicity to crimes, the fact of race is exploited for its news value just as is the fact of nationality when the criminal happens to be of foreign birth or parentage, and as is the fact of sex in case the offender is a woman, and as is age when the offender is very young or very old. These details add to the news value of the story. There is always a tendency to assume and believe the familiar and the expected. The reporters, usually with the same beliefs and prejudices as the newspaper public, see and report facts of race, and the display of the facts in news items serves to reinforce the popular idea that Negroes are peculiarly criminal. The impression is further fixed by the fact that so few other Negro activities get into the white papers. It is probably true, also, that the number of articles on Negro crime in the daily press is greater, relatively, for the Negroes than for other groups in the population; because of the popular belief, they have, other things equal, greater news value and so are more likely to be featured. The press thus caters to the general belief and the general belief is in turn reinforced by the stories in the press. There is in consequence a vicious circle: a tradition of Negro crime, the deliberate or unintentional selection of news, the confirmation of the popular belief.

The diametrically opposite news situation appears in the Negro press. Crimes committed by white men especially where Negroes are the victims are featured; they have great news value. Their publication confirms the beliefs already held by the readers and increases the news value of other such crimes.

Some part of the apparent excessive criminality of the Negro people finds its explanation in police discrimination. The police and police officers charged with the duty of preventing crime and apprehending criminals are in nearly all cases white men who share in the general idea that the Negroes are highly criminal. As a consequence they are very frequently arrested on suspicion and they are more frequently held on slender evidence. This is especially true in the case of Negro women; there is little danger of disagreeable consequences if mistakes are made. This attitude on the part of the police power tends to swell the number of arrests and, through humiliating the victims and destroying their self-respect, to increase the amount of crime. Such police discriminations are more general in the northern than in the southern communities where petty offenses on the part of the Negroes are expected and often tolerated rather than punished.

The Negro offenders meet the same bias when they appear for trial. The judge, the jurors, the court officials, and others who deal with the accused in the various stages from the arrest to the final conviction or acquittal are white men and in general share in the prevailing conception of the Negro people. That there is such a bias is not always recognized and its existence is sometimes catgorically denied. Where the existence of bias is not recognized and systematically discounted, the idea of an impartial trial is little more than a legal fiction.

It generally requires less evidence to convict a Negro than to convict a white man accused of the same crime. This differential treatment before the courts is a constant factor tending to increase the number of Negro convicts and it is an important factor in explanation of the fact that the excess of Negroes is greatest in the group of more serious crimes.

That justice is not meted out alike to black and white in the courts is rather freely and generally admitted. The only question is concerning the amount of injustice that the Negroes suffer in this respect. General statement is difficult because of the variation in different situations. When the population is nearly all white the Negro offender is likely to receive scant consideration; he is likely to receive a severe penalty for a relatively trivial offense. In the sections where the population is largely white there is generally some approximation to an evenhanded justice unless the interests of the white and black are in conflict.

In the regions where the Negroes are a large part of the population they are likely to get more just treatment from the court, while white men ordinarily escape punishment for offenses in proportion to their family connections, business standing, or political influence. The situation also varies with the specific local situation; judges are elected for short terms and are subservient to the opinion of the electorate.

THE CAUSES OF NEGRO CRIMINALITY

Aside from the question of the excess of criminality on the part of Negroes as compared with the whites—the question of whether the disproportionate number of commitments indicates greater criminality or merely discrimination and differential treatment—is that of the cause of such criminality as the group actually erupts. Whether or not the amount of crime is excessive, as compared with other groups in the population, its causal explanation lies in the social situation and this must needs be understood if any approximately adequate means of control are to be evolved. The Negro population is very unevenly distributed and offenses are in large degree determined by local conditions.

Some part of the explanation of the crime rate shown by the statistics lies without doubt in the social traits of the Negro people themselves. In very considerable part they are still ill-adjusted to the impersonal and highly individualistic nature of present-day American life. Their relatively recent status of servitude with the degradation of personality incident thereto is reflected in the crime rates as in other social phenomena characteristic of the group. Neither the attitudes of mind nor the type of personality developed under a régime of repression fit the person for free life. The group still shows a deplorable lack of thrift. Ideas of private property are frequently loose; there is a great amount of petty pilfering. The percentage of individuals who are unreliable in any capacity is very high. The bonds of family life among large numbers of the race are weak and sexual looseness is very common. All of these things and others, understandable in terms of previous condition and present status, result in bringing numbers of the race afoul of the criminal law.

The very general assumption that the Negro is criminal by nature and particularly inclined to crimes of violence is probably without basis in fact. There are of course numerous Negro criminals, probably Negroes who are criminals in the sense of being especially predisposed to certain behavior and conspicuously lacking in a normal power of inhibition. It is possible that the percentage of Negro individuals with defects likely to bring them into conflict with the criminal law may be higher than the percentage of such individuals in other groups, but there is no body of evidence adequate to justify such an hypothesis. Aside from defective individuals, who may be more numerous than in other groups, there is no reason to believe that the Negro people are peculiarly predisposed to criminal behavior. Criminally inclined individuals are a very small part of the race, in spite of the fact that in the conception of many persons the Negro criminal is the typical Negro. Such publicity has been given to crimes committed by certain Negroes that the race is credited with them and regarded as being composed chiefly of criminals. The intense fear that so many white women have of all Negroes frequently leads to wrong accusations, and accident or ignorance on the part of Negroes is sometimes distorted into offenses of criminal intent.

A fact that accounts for a considerable item of Negro criminality is the Negro's fear of the white man. Rightly or wrongly, there is a very general belief among the Negro people that the Negro accused of crime cannot hope to receive fair treatment from the police or the courts. In certain sections he is denied all the political rights and feels that he has no adequate protection either in law or custom. The attempt to enforce a double standard of justice gives rise to an attitude of resentment. The existence of such social attitudes gives certain assurance to the criminal Negro that he will be shielded by his fellows whenever it is possible for them to do so. In the situation, the person who dares to violate the laws made and enforced by the white man is often looked upon as representing the spirit of racial protest and aggressiveness, and becomes a romantic figure warring against the white man's society.

The convict lease system, a modified form of slavery elsewhere described, operates to increase the Negro's skeptical attitude toward the white man's justice. Prison labor is sold to private persons who work the convicts for profit. The punishment for criminal acts is thus a means to public and private revenue rather than a social effort to reform criminals or prevent crime. The Negroes look upon the system as an additional type of oppression and exploitation devised by the dominant race for its own purposes. Peonage and debt slavery are means of securing cheap labor; the system operates to an increase in criminality. A sentence to the chain gang makes the Negro victim a hardened offender and increases the fear and resentment of the Negroes.

It is frequently asserted that the continued agitation for Negro rights carried on by many individuals and organizations is responsible for much Negro crime. This is probably true. Certain individuals in lodges, churches, and other groups foment strife between the Negroes and their white neighbors. Others operating through the press and by means of pamphlets preach a doctrine of hate and talk of appeals to force. It is not possible to state how much effect the preaching of racial antagonism has upon the volume of Negro crime but certainly its influence is not negligible. It sometimes results in exaggerated ideas of personal rights. It makes for restlessness and discontent, increases dissatisfaction with existing economic and social conditions, adds to the suspiciousness in regard to the honesty of the dominant race, and makes for a certain solidarity of race. All of this may very well incite individuals to lawless acts and cause other persons to sympathize and protect violators of the law. But it differs in no essential respect from agitation and protest on the part of other groups and concerning other evils and reflects in part the general American attitude of lawlessness. If agitation is a cause of criminality the situation lies easily within the control of any community; agitation can flourish only in the presence of evils that call for removal.

There is nowhere any adequate provision made for the segregation and proper care of feeble-minded and otherwise defective Negroes. In the United States there are only a few hundred feeble-minded Negro children in special institutions. In general it is only the helpless and idiotic who are turned over to the public authorities; the great majority of the mentally defective remain at large. This failure adequately to restrain and segregate the defectives explains many crimes committed by members of the race. The absence of institutions for the care and training of neglected children allows numberless young persons to become habituated to vicious surroundings and drift into a life of crime.

Some part of Negro criminality is a more or less direct outgrowth of the racial prejudice of the whites. The Negroes are debarred from many occupations, denied the right to live outside certain restricted areas, and not allowed to participate freely in the civic and social life. The method of enforcing this caste system is often such as to break down the morale and destroy the self-respect of the Negro people. It is assumed and expected that they will be vicious and criminal. So long as the Negroes feel that their guaranteed rights and privileges are not recognized nor respected, and so long as they are publicly and privately discriminated against because of race and color, they will be discontented and resentful.

Where race prejudice enters the industrial field it contributes to Negro criminality by debarring them from opportunity to earn an honest living. This factor is of greater importance in the North than in the South. They are commonly excluded from the labor unions. Employers rarely consider them for any except unskilled labor. Even the Negro of education often finds difficulty in securing employment as a skilled workman. The effect of these restrictions is to force the Negroes into underpaid and undesirable occupations, and to increase the competition and lower the wage in these limited fields. The poverty, low wages, and lack of accumulated property contribute to crime. The direct relation is indicated for example by the fact that there was a decrease in the Negro crime rate in Chicago during the prosperity of the war period. To the extent that race prejudice keeps the Negro men from lucrative employment, the women are forced into work away from home and their children left without oversight. Almost half of the bread winners of the race are women. An inevitable result is that colored children, being neglected, swell the number of juvenile delinquents. The race prejudice and discrimination as well as the highly social disposition of the Negroes results in segregating them in one part of the city. As a result of their poverty this is always an undesirable section. Their housing conditions are poor, crowded, and insanitary. Their surroundings are usually vicious; the houses of prostitution are in most cases either in or adjacent to the Negro settlement. On the principle that an individual is profoundly affected by his immediate environment it follows that some part of the criminality of the Negro is a more or less direct result of the color prejudice.

Negro illiteracy is probably a contributing factor in Negro crime. The great ignorance of the adults makes anything like proper control and training of children impossible. There is no reason to believe that Negro children are more criminal in inclination than other children, but the lack of home training and the lack of parental control are conducive to delinquency and crime. The untrained parents do not understand how properly to govern the child and in many instances are too ignorant to recognize or impart any clear distinction between right and wrong in the ordinary affairs of life. As a result children grow up without training in self-control and without any intelligent appreciation of the prevailing moral values. The Negro writers frequently emphasize the general ignorance of the group in explanation of the excessive amount of delinquency and complain of the whites for encouraging ignorance and subserviency instead of intelligence, ambition, and independence.

Crime is certainly as much a matter of delinquent communities as of individual perversity. Whether of white or Negro, of juvenile or adult, it is a form of community disease. The neglect to provide adequate and proper facilities for the care and training of the young is, of course, the community dereliction that explains most crime, and the degree of that dereliction is reflected in comparative crime rates. The same forces are at work among the Negroes. But in many cases at least the causes are more active among them than among the other groups, especially the native elements of our population. Their education and training is less; their poverty is greater and consequently their housing and living conditions are more deplorable; there is less provision made for caring for colored defectives; they are in a more or less unstable condition because they have been but lately given freedom and many of them, especially in the cities and in the North, are in a new and strange environment; they are discriminated against socially and industrially; they are often abused by the police; and sometimes, at least, not fairly treated by the courts.

Breerley, H. C., "Homicide in South Carolina: a Regional Study," *Social Forces*, 9(1930), 218–221.

Cable, G. W., *The Silent South*, "The Convict Lease System in the Southern States," pp. 115–182.

Chicago Commission on Race Relations, *The Negro in Chicago*, "Crime and Vicious Environment," pp. 327–356.

Census Bureau, *Negro Population in the United States, 1790–1915*, "The Delinquent, Defective, and Dependent Classes," pp. 436–447.

———, *Negroes in the United States, 1920–1932*, "Prisoners in State and Federal Prisons and Reformatories," pp. 555–567.

———, *Census of Prisoners, 1923*.

———, *County and City Jails, 1933*.

———, *Prisoners, 1935*.

Department of Justice, *Federal Prisoners, 1935–1936*.

Johnson, C. S., *The Negro in American Civilization*, "Law Observance and Administration," pp. 311–329, "Juvenile Delinquency," pp. 330–336.

McCord, C. H., *The American Negro as a Dependent, Defective, and Delinquent*.

Sellin, T., "Race Prejudice in the Administration of Justice," *American Journal of Sociology*, 41(1935), 212–217.

———, "The Negro Criminal," *Annals, American Academy of Political and Social Science*, 140(1928), 52–64.

———, "The Negro and the Problem of Law Observance and Administration in the Light of Social Research," in C. S. Johnson, *The Negro in American Civilization*, pp. 443–452.

Stephenson, G. T., *Race Distinction in American Law*.

Sutherland, E. H., *Criminology*, "Composition of the Criminal Population—The Negro," pp. 102–106.

Tannenbaum, F., *Darker Phases of the South*, "Southern Prisons," pp. 74–115.

Thompson, Anna J., "A Survey of Crime Among Negroes in Philadelphia," *Opportunity*, 4(1926), 251–254.

Weatherford, W. D., and Johnson, C. S., *Race Relations*, "Negro Crime and Treatment of Criminals," pp. 424–440.

Wembridge, E. R., "Negroes in Custody," *American Mercury*, 21(1930), 76–83.

White, Walter, "The Negro and the Supreme Court," *Harper's Magazine*, 162(1931), 238–246.

Woofter, T. J., *The Basis of Racial Adjustment*, "Law and Order," pp. 125–148.

FURTHER READINGS

Cavan, Ruth Shonley, "Negro Family Disorganization and Juvenile Delinquency," *Journal of Negro Education*, 28(Summer 1959), 230–239.

Clark, Kenneth B., "Color, Class Personality, and Juvenile Delinquency," *Journal of Negro Education*, 28(Summer 1959), 230–251.

Clinard, Marshall B., *Sociology of Deviant Behavior*, 3rd ed., Ch. 8. New York: Holt, Rinehart and Winston, 1968.

Frazier, E. Franklin, *The Negro in the United States*, rev. ed., Ch. XXV. New York: Macmillan, 1947.

Glueck, Sheldon and Eleanor, *Unraveling Juvenile Delinquency*. New York: Commonwealth Fund, 1950.

Henry, A. F., and Short, J. F., *Suicide and Homicide*. Glencoe, Ill.: Free Press, 1954.

Johnson, Guy, "The Negro and Crime," *The Annals*, 217(September 1941), 93–104.

Kephart, William M., *Racial Factors and Urban Law Enforcement*. Philadelphia: University of Pennsylvania Press, 1957.

Langberg, Robert, *Homicide in the United States, 1950–1964*. Washington, D.C.: U.S. National Center for Health Statistics, 1967.

Myrdal, Gunnar, *An American Dilemma*, Vol. 2, pp. 966–79. New York: Harper, 1944.

The President's Commission on Law Enforcement and Administration of Justice, *The Challenge of Crime in a Free Society*. Washington, D.C.: U.S. Government Printing Office, 1967.

Van Hentig, Hans, "The Criminality of the Negro," *Journal of Criminal Law and Criminology*, XXX(January 1940), 662–80.

X V I I

CRIMES AGAINST THE NEGRO*

Any treatment of Negro criminality would be incomplete which did not comprehend some discussion of the criminal activity of which the Negro is made the victim. In other connections attention is called to the denial, by formal legal or informal extra-legal means, of the exercise of the franchise; to the public acquiescence in measures which provide inferior educational facilities for the Negro children and so retard individuals in their efforts to acquire the essentials of Western culture; to the restrictions placed by state law, municipal ordinance, or mob rule upon the Negro's choice of residence; to the public or quasi-public interference with or restriction upon his freedom of mobility; to the public toleration of legal or extra-legal devices by which his industrial efficiency is hampered and his vital power economically exploited; and to the denial of various other personal, social, and civil rights specifically guaranteed by the constitution and federal laws or plainly implied in any adequate conception of a democratic social order. Some of these things clearly fall within the concept of crime, even in the narrow legalistic definition of crime as an act in violation of the law, and their discussion might with propriety be included in the present chapter. But the criminal aspect of a differential racial treatment in civil and social activities is incidental to such conditions and discussion from that point of view frequently obscures and always gives an inadequate comprehension of the problems involved and of the conditions necessary to their resolution. They have, therefore, been given treatment in connection with the fundamental social and economic conditions to which they are incident and the present chapter restricted to a consideration of individual and mass behavior directed against the person or property of unprotected and defenseless individuals and groups. This behavior,

* This chapter remains the same as in the second edition except for minor additions to two tables.

of course, like the discriminatory treatment in civic affairs, is a function of the racial situation and a symptom of profound social disorders and might, likewise, be treated incidentally. But the phenomena are sufficiently distinct and unified, and sufficiently notorious and menacing, to call for and justify separate treatment. The phenomena of inter-racial conflict, which falls without the realm of ordinary police control and assumes the aspect of racial warfare, is treated in a subsequent chapter.

THE NUMBER OF LYNCHINGS IN THE UNITED STATES

The number of persons done to death in the United States each year by mobs and self-appointed discipline committees can be stated with only approximate accuracy. The statistics are based chiefly upon newspaper reports and it cannot be known how many such occurrences escape the news gatherers or, if known to the reporters, fail of publication. Certainly some illegal killings escape publicity in the press. And of such happenings reported, we may not be certain that all come to the attention of the students of such statistics. The collectors of lynching statistics, as a Negro editor rather shrewdly pointed out, have generally been "more interested in the race problem than in historical accuracy" and have given chief attention to securing a complete tabulation of such crimes against the Negro and in the South. Similar crimes in other sections and against persons of other races are perhaps somewhat less completely reported. It is quite certain that the statistics understate and possibly very greatly understate the number of lynchings.

There have been three chief sources of lynching statistics. Since 1885 a Chicago newspaper has kept a record of such killings as have been reported in its news columns. Beginning at a little later date, Tuskegee Institute has made a systematic collection and tabulation of similar data. Since 1912 the National Association for the Advancement of Colored People has kept an independent record of lynchings. There is great discrepancy in the figures as given by these organizations. In 1914, for example, Tuskegee Institute reported 52 lynchings for the year, the *Chicago Tribune* reported 54, and the *Crisis*, the official organ of the National Association for the Advancement of Colored People, gave the number as 74. The variation is due in part to different conceptions of what constitutes a lynching, but the possibility of minor inaccuracy in the figures themselves must be recognized.

According to the records of the newspaper mentioned, the total number of lynchings in the forty-year period 1885–1929 was something over 4,000. According to the figures published by the National Association for the Advancement of Colored People, approximately 3,600 persons have been killed by lynching mobs since 1889, exclusive of the victims of the Atlanta, Georgia, the East St. Louis, Illinois, and other race riots. The

Table 35-1: PERSONS LYNCHED IN THE UNITED STATES,
1885–1930

Year	Whites	Negroes	Total
1885	106	78	184
1886	67	71	138
1887	42	80	122
1888	47	95	142
1889	81	95	176
1890	37	90	127
1891	71	121	192
1892	100	155	255
1893	46	154	200
1894	56	134	190
1895	59	112	171
1896	51	80	131
1897	44	122	166
1898	25	102	127
1899	23	84	107
1900	8	107	115
1901	28	107	135
1902	10	86	96
1903	18	86	104
1904	4	83	87
1905	5	61	66
1906	8	64	72
1907	3	60	63
1908	7	93	100
1909	14	73	87
1910	9	65	74
1911	8	63	71
1912	4	60	64
1913	1	51	52
1914	3	49	52
1915	13	54	67
1916	4	50	54
1917	2	36	38
1918	4	60	64
1919	7	76	83
1920	8	53	61
1921	5	59	64
1922	6	51	57
1923	4	29	33
1924	..	16	16
1925	0	17	17
1926	7	23	30
1927	0	16	16
1928	1	10	11
1929	3	7	10
1930	1	20	21
Total	1,375	3,386	4,761

number reported by Tuskegee for 1885–1930 is given by years and by the race of the victim in Table 35-1. Lynching statistics for 1931–55 are given in Table 35-2.

Table 35-2: PERSONS LYNCHED IN THE UNITED STATES, 1931–1955*

Year	Whites	Negroes	Total
1931	1	12	13
1932	2	6	8
1933	4	24	28
1934	..	15	15
1935	2	18	20
1936	..	8	8
1937	..	8	8
1938	..	6	6
1939	1	2	3
1940	1	4	5
1941	..	4	4
1942	..	6	6
1943	..	3	3
1944	..	2	2
1945	..	1	1
1946	..	6	6
1947	..	1	1
1948	1	1	2
1949	..	3	3
1950	1	1	2
1951	..	1	1
1952–54	..	..	..
1955	..	3	3
Total	13	135	148

* Source: *Historical Statistics of the United States: Colonial Times to 1957*, Table H 452–454

Women and girls as well as men and boys have been the victims of lynching mobs. Of the 702 white persons lynched in the thirty-year period 1889–1918, there were 11 women and 691 men. Of the 2,522 Negroes lynched during the same period, 50 were women and 2,472 were men. There were 61 women lynched during this period, 11 of whom were white and 50 colored. With the exception of one white woman killed in Nebraska, all the women lynched were the victims of southern mobs.

During the period covered by the statistics there has been a fairly regular decrease in the annual number of mob killings. In the decade 1885 to 1894 there were 1,723 persons lynched in the United States, a yearly average of over 172. In the following decade the total was 1,239; in the decade ending in 1914 the total was 702; and in the decade 1921–1930 the number was 275. The decrease by five-year periods is shown in Table 35-3.

The decrease in the lynching practice has been characteristic of all sections of the country but it has been more marked and rapid in the northern and western than in the southern sections of the country. There has also been a more marked decline in lynching of white men than in the lynching of Negroes.

Table 35-3: LYNCHINGS BY FIVE-YEAR PERIODS,
1885–1934*

Years	Total Number	Yearly Average
1885–89	758	151.6
1890–94	965	193.0
1895–99	702	140.4
1900–04	537	107.4
1905–09	389	77.8
1910–14	313	62.6
1915–19	306	61.2
1920–24	231	46.2
1925–29	84	16.8
1930–34	78	15.6
1935–39	45	9.0
1940–44	20	4.0
1945–49	13	2.6
1950–54	3	0.6

* Source: 1935–1954 data computed from *Historical Statistics of the United States: Colonial Times to 1957*, Table H 452–454

The lynching of white men was in large part a phenomenon of the frontier and declined coincidentally with the passing of the frontier. The lynching of Negroes, on the other hand, represents an effort on the part of a racial majority to perpetuate a traditional body of relationships in a rapidly changing order. The number of white lynchings before the beginning of the present century was a rough measure of the efficiency of the police and courts in the control of criminal activity. The number of Negro lynchings is an index of the accommodation of the races rather than an indication of the amount of Negro criminality.

Chart 35-3A shows separately the Negro and white lynchings, so far as they are a matter of record, during the past half century.

THE GEOGRAPHIC DISTRIBUTION OF LYNCHINGS

In the recent decades the great majority of the lynchings in the United States have been in the states of the South. It is possible that the statistics bearing upon this sectional distribution are somewhat biased because of the wider newspaper publicity given to mob violence in the South and to the more complete records, but the regional contrast is too great and too

LYNCHINGS IN THE UNITED STATES

BY RACE OF VICTIM 1882-1936

LIGHT LINE - WHITE LYNCHINGS
HEAVY LINE - NEGRO LYNCHINGS

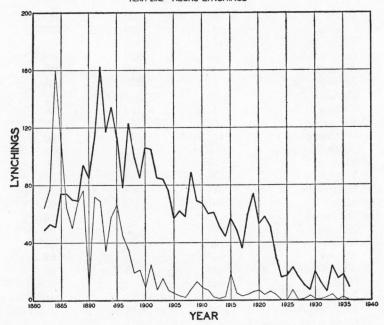

consistently maintained to leave any doubt concerning the general fact. In 1921, for example, there were sixty-four persons lynched in the United States. Of this number sixty-three, all except one, were in the South. In the list Mississippi led with fourteen; Georgia was second with eleven; Texas was third with seven; Arkansas and Florida each had six; South Carolina and Louisiana had five each; North Carolina had four; Alabama had two; and Tennessee, Virginia, and Missouri each had one. The total lynchings reported from 1882 through 1930 are shown by states in Table 35-4.

LYNCHINGS BY THE CAUSES ASCRIBED

Any classification of Negro lynchings which attempts to assign specific causes is of necessity superficial. In practice such classification seems in general to be the result of efforts to shift the responsibility for the lynching crime from the criminals to the victims of the mob. Such procedure also involves a grave error of method but one which is common to most social statistics. As will be pointed out more adequately presently the spe-

Table 35-4: LYNCHINGS IN THE UNITED STATES,
BY STATES, 1882–1930

State	Whites	Negroes	Total
Mississippi	45	500	545
Georgia	34	474	508
Texas	143	349	492
Louisiana	60	328	388
Alabama	46	296	342
Arkansas	64	230	294
Florida	25	241	266
Tennessee	44	196	240
Kentucky	62	151	213
Oklahoma	116	44	160
South Carolina	5	154	159
Missouri	53	63	116
Virginia	16	88	104
North Carolina	14	85	99
Montana	91	2	93
Colorado	70	6	76
Nebraska	55	5	60
Indiana	33	19	52
Kansas	34	18	52
West Virginia	15	35	50
California	42	4	46
Wyoming	38	7	45
New Mexico	39	4	43
Arizona	35	1	36
South Dakota	34	0	34
Illinois	15	16	31
Maryland	3	27	30
Washington	30	0	30
Oregon	22	3	25
Idaho	16	6	22
Ohio	9	13	22
Iowa	19	1	20
North Dakota	12	2	14
Nevada	12	0	12
Minnesota	6	3	9
Utah	6	3	9
Michigan	4	4	8
Pennsylvania	1	5	6
Wisconsin	6	0	6
New York	1	1	2
Delaware	0	1	1
New Jersey	0	1	1
Totals	1,375	3,386	4,761

cific offense of which the person is accused or guilty is the occasion rather than the cause of the mob action. It is at most a single element in the causal complex, never in itself an efficient cause. Consequently, any tabulation in terms of reason assigned, while it may have some value as an indication of the frequency of certain offenses, gives no real explanation of the killings.

The list of causes assigned in justification or explanation of lynchings includes everything from major crimes to trivial offenses. In many cases no offense at all can be cited. In 1921, for example, five whites were lynched, four for murder and one for rape. Two Negro women were lynched the same year, one charged with assisting in the escape of a criminal, the other with inciting racial trouble. Of the fifty-seven Negro men lynched during the year, eleven were charged with murder and three with attempted murder, fifteen with rape and three with attempted rape; four with being guilty of killing men in altercation; four with wounding men; two with furnishing ammunition to a man resisting arrest; and two with being leaders in a race clash. One was lynched for assisting an accused criminal to escape; one victim was accused of having made improper remarks to a woman; one for having threatened to kill another; one for having entered a young woman's room; one for insulting a woman; one for writing a note to a woman; and one for having attacked a man and woman. In three cases there was no charge reported against the victims.

Among the list of offenses of which white men have been guilty or accused and for which they have suffered at the hands of lynching mobs are the following: miscegenation, seduction, incest, elopement, wife beating, cruelty, kidnapping, disorderly conduct, being a disreputable character, prospective elopement, saloon keeping, being obnoxious, illicit distilling, being a revenue informer, swindling, turning state's evidence, refusing to turn state's evidence, protecting a Negro, fraud, arousing political prejudice, arousing mob indignation, arresting a miner, aiding in the escape of a murderer, being suspected of killing cattle.

The list of offenses charged against Negroes who have been lynched include jilting a girl, insulting women, writing a letter to a white woman, asking a white woman in marriage, eloping with a white girl, paying attention to a white girl, grave robbery, slander, wife beating, circulating scandals, voodooism, conjuring, self-defense, resisting assault, resisting arrest, threatening political exposures to prevent giving evidence, refusing to give evidence, testifying for one of his own race, cutting levees, poisoning wells, poisoning stock, poisoning horses, writing insulting letters, insults, supposed offense, slapping a child, being disreputable, incendiary language, quarreling, making threats, being troublesome, conspiracy, giving information, shooting an officer, swindling, gambling, drunkenness, fraud, passing counterfeit money, violation of contract, keeping a gambling house, quarreling over profit sharing, lawlessness, throwing stones, concealing a criminal, felony, forcing white boy to commit crime, rioting, strike rioting, turning state's evidence, political troubles, unpopularity, bad reputation, criminal abortion, enticing servant away, introducing smallpox, running quarantine, disobeying ferry regulation, inflammatory language, kidnapping, colonizing Negroes, suing whites, testifying against whites, wrong man lynched.

Obviously attempts at the classification of any such miscellaneous array of alleged offenses will show considerable variation. There is first a difficulty in choosing a satisfactory and reasonably limited set of categories for classification and, once the categories are decided upon, the further difficulty of determining where any particular alleged offense should appear in the scheme. The classification used by the Tuskegee Institute is a seven-fold grouping into homicide, felonious assault, rape, attempted rape, robbery and theft, insult to white persons, and all other causes. On this basis of classification the lynchings known to the Institute are classified in Table 35-5 for each year since 1889. The table includes both the white and the Negro victims.

In the list of offenses most frequently cited in explanation of the mob action, murder stands first. When the figures for this offense are combined with those given under the caption "felonious assaults" over one-third of the cases are included.

Second in importance from the point of view of the number of cases is rape. But the figures give very little support to the popular belief that lynchings are a manifestation of popular fury resulting from attacks upon women. Such attacks are, of course, a frequent occasion for mob action but they are not the only nor the most usual reason assigned for the killings. Of the sixteen lynchings reported in 1924, seven were for assaults on women; in the previous year seven of the thirty-three victims of the mob were charged with rape or attempted rape. In the total number of cases from 1889 to 1930 the number charged with rape or attempted rape is reported as 871, about one-sixth of the entire number. It is a more usual cause in the lynching of Negroes than in the lynching of whites. In the period 1885–1930 there were 894 persons lynched on the charge of rape or attempted rape. Of these, 60 were white persons and 834 were Negroes. In some cases the persons lynched are guilty of both rape and murder. It is possible that in some of the cases where murder is assigned as the cause of the mob action rape may also have been committed or attempted and the popular action be as fairly assignable to the one act as to the other. It is probable that the figures somewhat understate the importance of attacks on women as a cause of lynchings. Cutler, however, could not discover that more than thirty-four per cent of the Negroes lynched in the South in the twenty-two years covered by his investigation had either attempted or been accused of this offense.

Table 35-5: LYNCHING IN THE UNITED STATES
BY CAUSES, 1889–1930

Year	Homicide	Felonious Assault	Rape	Attempted Rape	Robbery and Theft	Insult to White Persons	All Other Causes
1889	51	5	34	4	19	..	63
1890	25	2	26	2	5	..	67
1891	52	2	38	2	28	..	70
1892	88	4	37	12	38	2	74
1893	56	2	34	4	10	2	92
1894	73	2	42	10	16	6	41
1895	71	1	29	13	20	1	36
1896	42	9	29	6	14	..	31
1897	68	5	25	9	23	2	34
1898	74	5	11	7	8	2	20
1899	56	..	5	6	6	..	34
1900	43	10	18	13	7	..	24
1901	48	9	21	8	21	1	27
1902	43	7	19	11	1	..	15
1903	53	8	16	7	..	1	19
1904	36	4	14	6	1	2	24
1905	34	4	15	4	2	..	7
1906	24	7	16	14	1	1	9
1907	20	7	13	11	4	1	7
1908	50	10	14	6	4	3	32
1909	28	12	3	18	1	3	5
1910	38	6	16	8	2	2	2
1911	37	4	9	6	1	4	10
1912	37	6	10	2	1	3	5
1913	20	11	5	5	2	1	8
1914	30	8	6	1	1	..	6
1915	26	10	11	..	9	3	8
1916	20	7	3	9	8	2	5
1917	6	2	7	5	2	2	14
1918	28	2	10	6	2	..	16
1919	28	3	9	10	1	6	26
1920	22	9	15	3	..	3	9
1921	19	7	16	3	..	3	16
1922	15	5	14	5	4	2	12
1923	5	5	6	1	1	1	14
1924	4	2	5	2	..	3	..
1925	8	1	4	2	..	1	1
1926	13	3	2	3	1	1	7
1927	7	2	2	3	..	..	2
1928	5	3	2	..	..	..	1
1929	1	3	3	..	..	2	1
1930	5	..	8	2	3	..	3
Total	1,399	214	622	249	267	66	897

Lynchings ascribed to other causes than murder and felonious assault or to rape and attacks upon women are of small numerical importance, and this is notably the case since the passing of the frontier. Where other causes are given in explanation of the mob action, it is commonly safe to assume that the victim was put to death for some reason other than the particular offense mentioned.

THE METHODS OF LYNCHING MOBS

In the majority of lynchings the victims have been put to death by hanging or by shooting or by both. But other methods, sometimes of a most brutal nature, are employed, and where death finally results from hanging or shooting the victims have frequently been subjected to most barbarous treatment before being killed. In some cases barbarously refined methods of torture have been employed.

Of the sixty-four persons lynched in 1921, for example, four were burned to death and the bodies of three others were burned after they had been killed. In the following year, eighteen were hanged, sixteen were shot to death, eight were burned alive, two were shot and burned, two were tortured and drowned, one was hanged and burned, one was drowned, and one was beaten to death. The manner in which eleven others died was not reported. These years are typical of the recent decades.

But as the practice of lynching continues there is some evidence that the methods employed by the mobs tend to become more brutal and the torture of the victim before death to be more usual.

There appears to be no relation between the crime of which the person is accused or of which he is guilty and the method of killing selected by the mobs. Of the four persons burned to death in 1921, two were charged with murder and two were charged with rape.

EXPLANATIONS AND APOLOGIES

The popular reaction to the lynching of Negroes runs the whole gamut from bitter denunciation of the practice and abusive indictments of whole populations of regions where such crimes occur to ingenious defense of the practice and blatant justification of the criminal mobs and of the community conditions which generate them.

The explanations offered in excuse and apology are numerous and more or less conflicting. The general tenor of such explanations is an effort to shift the responsibility from the mob and the community conditions which give rise to mob action to the victim on whom the mob members vent their fear and hate. The practice is said to be necessary in order to control the vicious elements of the race. Many persons are apparently sincere in the belief that Negroes can be controlled only by fear; that periodic lynchings terrorize them, so are effective as a means of control.

This view, in spite of its general acceptance, has little evidence in its support. Lynchings probably operate to increase rather than to decrease crime; the mob spectacles give wide publicity to crimes committed, so act suggestively to incite others to similar types of behavior. They increase the bitterness and hatred of the race whose members are the victims of mob action and lead to the concealment of offenders and to reprisals when opportunity offers. On the other side the lawlessness tends to spread: lynching for one offense leads to lynching for others, and the practice of killing Negroes is presently extended to include other persons feared or disliked.

The claim is frequently made that lynching mobs are composed of the ignorant and socially depressed classes of the community or that they are formed from the irresponsible elements of the society and that they do not represent community sentiment. It does not appear possible, however, to discover any such relation. There is no relation, for example, between the amount of illiteracy and the number of lynchings when comparison is made between counties in the South; they are not confined to the backward regions so far as illiteracy is a measure of backwardness. The opposite statement, frequently made by Negro writers, that lynch law is administered by responsible and comparatively prominent men is equally incapable of proof.

Another familiar apologetic explanation of lynchings is that they are due at least in part to the slow administration of justice and to the possibilities of delay and appeal, and to the danger of administrative clemency and pardon in case conviction is secured. At an earlier time and in a frontier condition such facts did obtain and this explanation had some basis in fact. But at the present time, and particularly in the South where such mob crimes are most frequent, the explanation does not explain: there are no such delays and no such dangers.

A closely related type of explanation is that there is difficulty in securing conviction and that this accounts for the action of mobs. There is danger that the person accused will be freed, will not receive a sentence commensurate with the seriousness of the crime as it appears to the popular mind. A special circumstance of similar import appears when the offender is accused of attack upon a white woman. In such cases a legal trial and conviction would involve a humiliating ordeal for the woman; to avoid the necessity of such ordeal, the mob visits summary punishment upon the criminal.

This order of explanation is not convincing in regard to serious crimes committed by Negroes in the South. The law and the administration of the law are in the hands of the whites and may be made as severe and be administered with as much dispatch as desired. The trial judge is white as are also the prosecution, the jury, and probably the defense attorney. That

there will in these circumstances be a miscarriage of justice because of un-
due clemency is a possibility too remote for consideration. The idea that
the criminal mob is motivated by a fastidiously chivalric attitude toward
woman is a thing that does not fall, and may not be brought within the
orbit of serious discussion.

Another position is to the effect that certain crimes are abhorrent to all
persons and provoke characteristic reactions. The common assertion that
lynchings, especially of Negroes in the South, are provoked by crimes
against women is the typical form of this explanation. Such crimes, when
white women are the object of attack by Negro men, arouse great popular
indignation; the mob behavior is the effort of an outraged community to
punish by extra-legal means the person guilty of an atrocious crime. In an
outburst of passion the community brushes aside the technicalities and
delays of the law but carries out the law's intent. Lynching apologists, on
the basis of such interpretation, have defended the practice as a vindica-
tion of justice and as a protection of civilization.

There is some element of truth in explanation of this type. Some mob
killings in this and other countries are best and perhaps only to be understood as the more or less spontaneous reaction of an outraged community.
But the practice of lynching cannot be accounted for in these terms nor
can any considerable number of individual cases. The position, which tac-
itly assumes that attacks upon women are the chief or only cause of lynchings, loses its chief element of plausibility when it is brought against the
fact that in the great majority of lynchings the victim is not guilty of or
even accused of offenses against white women. The explanation appears
to be an unwarranted generalization from a few isolated and relatively
exceptional cases.

It would not be profitable to continue the detailed investigation of explanations of the lynching practice. The defense of the practice and the
apologies that undertake to explain the practice and shift the responsibility
by pointing the criminality of the Negro miss the point as do also the press
denunciations which follow such events. Neither defense nor denunciation
is of value in understanding the phenomena and so are without value from
the point of view of control.

THE HISTORY OF LYNCHING IN THE UNITED STATES

In the early history of the country there was a vast amount of lawlessness and a frequent resort to summary and extra-legal methods of control.
The settlers, especially in the back country, made use of any measures that
seemed to them expedient in dealing with the Indians, and public sentiment
was such that white persons were not punished for murder or other crimes
when the victims were Indians. Summary measures were employed in dealing with criminals and other undesirable characters. The absence of ade-

quate and efficient legal machinery as well as the difficulty, expense, and delays involved in bringing criminals from remote settlements for trial encouraged the frontiersmen to take the law into their own hands. In some places organized and more or less permanent bodies grew up and assumed responsibility for the suppression of crime; robbers, horse thieves, and other criminals generally were commonly dealt with by committees and groups of citizens banded together for the protection of the community. Summary measures were also used to suppress behavior contrary to the code of the border country but not recognized as criminal by the law: individuals were sometimes disciplined for failure to pay debts, for starting law suits, and other behavior deemed unnecessary and socially injurious. These summary methods were carried westward as the frontier advanced.

The punishment administered by the vigilance committees commonly took the form of flogging, sometimes with great severity, and banishment from the community. Killing was unusual except in the case of Indians guilty of offenses against the whites and of outlaws guilty of major crimes.

In the Revolutionary period the social conditions were such as to encourage the frequent resort to extra-legal methods of redressing grievances. It was a period of great popular excitement in which the civil authorities lost the respect and support of the people. Tories, British sympathizers, persons not in sympathy with the American cause, tea commissioners and consigners, customs informers, importers of British goods, and various other persons in popular disfavor were frequently made the objects of popular discipline. The use of tar and feathers came to be a characteristic popular punishment considered peculiarly appropriate for Tories and others who aroused popular indignation by expressing sentiments deemed injurious to the American cause. But other kinds of punishment were also employed, particularly flogging and banishment, and capital punishment was sometimes inflicted by citizen committees.

After the Revolution, summary punishment of offenders fell into disuse in the older settled regions. But the weakness of the civil government and the general inadequacy of civil regulations on the frontier made the border country a retreat for horse thieves, counterfeiters, robbers, and other lawless persons. The presence of these persons, in the weakness of civil regulations, gave an excuse and a justification for lynch law; it was necessary to curb the vicious and the lawless. Summary measures were commonly taken in particular emergencies though in some places there were more or less permanently organized committees prepared to act when any emergency should arise. In various of the back country settlements infested with lawless persons and where the civil authorities were weak and could not be relied upon to apprehend criminals and bring them to justice the frontier type of summary justice continued to the end of the century and was justified or condoned on the ground of necessity.

During most of the period Negroes were seldom lynched or otherwise disciplined by the community. The slaves were under the control of their owners and all ordinary discipline of unruly individuals was at the discretion of the masters. Runaway and other unruly Negroes were sometimes whipped by the authorities but there was a powerful economic force operating to protect the life and vital force of the slaves. Those who came into contact with the community disciplinary committees were chiefly the free Negroes and mulattoes who were numerous in some of the colonies and who were in some cases idle, vicious, and disorderly persons.

In the period of anti-slavery agitation there was a revival of lynching and a spread of the practice throughout the country; from a temporary expedient of border communities inadequately protected by the civil authorities, it became a common practice in regions where the civil authority was adequate to cope with the lawless element. The society was undergoing rapid reorganization and the social and political disorder of the time was conducive to the spread of violence. The spirit of the times favored it. Some part of the apparent increase was no doubt due to improved communication and more complete newspaper report; much lawlessness of earlier periods did not come to general attention. But there was also a real increase in lawlessness and a more frequent resort to lynch law. With the revival there was also a change in the character of the practice; whipping and expulsion from the community were frequently supplemented or replaced by capital punishment of the offenders.

The abortive slave insurrection led by Nat Turner was an item of some importance in the revival of lynch law in the older settled regions. It was the first important instance of open rebellion among the slaves in the United States and was marked by the indiscriminate massacre of all white persons who came within the reach of the revolting Negroes. The rebellion was promptly suppressed and with severity not less frightful than the atrocities committed by the slaves.

The whole country was thrown into a state of panic. Especially in the South, popular fears were roused to such a point that quite innocuous behavior came to be looked upon as a major offense. If the law did not reach such behavior that in itself became a reason for and justification of summary procedure. The fears aroused did not subside: the danger of slave insurrections and the massacre of the whites became an obsession of the southern mind. The flood of incendiary publications let loose by the anti-slavery agitators increased the fears of the southern whites and made for increased lawlessness. No punishment was severe enough for an abolitionist. Anyone suspected of tampering with the slaves, inducing them to run away, or guilty of distributing "incendiary tracts" was whipped or tarred and feathered, sometimes both, and driven out of the community. Crimes committed by Negroes were visited with great severity; the illegal execution of Negroes became common. In a number of cases Negro criminals were burned. Those suspected of conspiracy to raise insurrections were caught up and summarily punished, sometimes by death. White persons leagued with the Negroes or engaged or believed to be engaged in organizing the blacks suffered a like treatment. Other unpopular individuals were subjected to lawless discipline.

While occasionally victimized by lynch law, the mob killing of slave Negroes was not a common practice and they did not make up any considerable percentage of the persons lynched. They were valuable pieces of property; the death of an able-bodied slave was a considerable economic loss. Consequently they were killed only in case of real or supposed conspiracy against the whites or for participating in insurrection. In general the Negroes who were guilty of the murder of their masters, mistresses, or overseers or guilty of assault on white women were dealt with by legal means. In the following decade there was an increase in the use of summary methods: in the ten-year period 1850–1860 twenty-five slaves were legally executed and thirty-eight killed by mobs. Twenty of the legal killings were for the crime of murder and five for attacks on white women. Of the thirty-eight illegal executions twenty-six were for murder and twelve for attacks on white women. Two of those killed by mobs were women and twelve of the thirty-eight were burned to death. The sentiment of the South was favorable to lynching; the generality of southern newspapers of the time either excused or openly advocated the practice.

After the Civil War the South was over-run by discharged soldiers—a great body of men thoroughly demoralized as a result of army life. The economic, social, and political life was disorganized and the freed Negroes were often idle and sometimes disorderly. There was a long period of disorder and lawlessness in which Ku Klux Klan had a prominent part. The habit of summary treatment of Negroes remained after the disappearance of these lawless bands and the restoration of the civil government. But the annual number of mob murders has been on the decline during the past fifty years.

FACTORS INVOLVED IN THE LYNCHING PRACTICE

The foregoing sketch makes it apparent that lynchings fall into three fairly distinct groups.

The visitation of summary and extra-legal punishment on persons guilty or thought to be guilty of behavior contrary to the traditions and mores of the group is found among all peoples and in all times. Brutal, revolting, and unusual crimes occasionally arouse the passions of law-observing citizens to the point of mob action resulting in the injury or death of the offender. Among all peoples, offenses against the security of the group, treason, frequently leads to the administration of popular punishment. The violation of white women, rape, in recent times in the countries of white European civilization, often incites the populace to run amuck. The particular behavior that arouses the passions of men is not the same in all times and places, but given a condition of popular excitement mobs form and occasionally destroy offending individuals. There are also sporadic cases of punishment by mobs of persons for whose punishment under the law little tangible evidence can be adduced, and of persons whose offenses are of such a nature that legal penalties are inapplicable.

Another type of popular justice administered by extra-legal means makes its appearance in situations where the social organization is incomplete or disorganized and the processes of law are, in consequence, uncertain and subject to unreasonable delay. In the frontier type of society where civil government is weak and inefficient, citizens have often had resort to rough and ready modes of police control and mob administered justice as a means of protection against lawlessness and criminality. With the disappearance of the frontier conditions and the growth of efficient civil government able to apprehend criminals and protect property and maintain peace, and with the establishment of criminal courts effective in the execution of the law, the need for extra-legal means of protection disappears and popular justice gives way to civil and legal processes.

At the present time most lynchings do not fall into either of the foregoing groups. They are not manifestations of border law; they are acts in violation of law rather than efforts to establish or preserve order. They occur in old settled regions where the law is established and the machinery for its administration adequate and where both the administration and the execution of the law are in the hands of the groups guilty of its violation. Nor are they sporadic and spontaneous outbursts of popular passion in the presence of atrocious and revolting crimes. As previously pointed out, the offense of the victim carries no explanation of and frequently bears no discoverable relation to the criminal behavior of the mob. They are peculiar to America and chiefly restricted to the South; in no other non-barbarous country do people carry on man hunts to take criminals from jails or from officers of the law to administer mob punishment.

The practice reflects a social situation comprehending two imperfectly accommodated racial groups and a characteristically American conception of law and order. Any adequate explanation of lynching must take into account the two distinct and separately derived groups of social factors— the American attitude toward law and the white Southerner's racial attitude—operating in a bi-racial situation.

In the American South there is a deep-seated and all-pervading fear of the Negro. One source of this fear is the treatment that the Negro has received at the hands of the whites. The slavery of the Negro, his economic and industrial exploitation, his moral degradation, and other historic facts of the modern situation are fundamentally repugnant to civilized moral standards. The members of the dominant racial group are more or less conscious of the injustice that the Negro has suffered at their hands. There is in consequence an uneasy sense of moral guilt, as may be seen reflected in the rationalized justifications of the historic treatment and of the existing social situation as well as in the naïve apologies for behavior not defensible on accepted moral standards. By a familiar psychological process, sentiments and attitudes that non-socially trained persons imagine that they would have had they been subjected to similar treatment, are imputed to the Negro; the Negro thereby becomes possessed of behavior tendencies menacing to the white man, to his domination of the social situation, and to the culture he represents. This fear complex, having a taproot in a treatment of the defenseless group that cannot be made to square with the civilized moral code, functions to create an external image which objectifies the psychological state; the Negro becomes the objective symbol of that subjective state rather than an objective social reality.

Fears having their origin in the misuse of the subordinate group are reinforced by others of a somewhat more direct and immediate nature whose source and origin roots in the shifting economic relations of the races. Habituated to the Negro in the capacity of a menial, and dependent upon his labor to insure a satisfaction of the fundamental human wish for security as well as to provide a milieu conducive to a satisfaction of the wish for recognition, the members of the dominant race are stirred by grave fears of personal and social disaster as the economic and industrial development of the Negroes tends to bring profound changes in the traditional status of the racial groups. Such changes seem to foretell a situation in which the Negro will be a competitor instead of a servant of the white man. Such a development would mean a profound change in the social order established by the white man and operated for his comfort and profit. Any threatened disturbance in a prevailing social order generates uneasiness and fear; the unknown is always a source of real or possible danger. But in the racial situation of the South, change is fraught with special danger and the popular fear reactions are correspondingly intense. There are many individuals who fear that the economic advance of the Negroes would disturb profoundly the customary economic adjustments of the races. The general economic advance of the Negroes and the disappearance of the caste order based on skin color would inevitably increase individual economic competition in which the competent would tend to rise and the incompetent would tend to fall quite regardless of color of skin or previous social status.

To these more or less vague, unanalyzed, and inarticulate fears which provide a background for much of the southern rationalizing on race relations, must be added more specific and concrete fears fostered by politicians and other persons who stand to profit by an intense and active racial animosity. The incendiary propaganda carried on by various Negro nationalistic groups further localizes the racial fear and gives it a tangible and concrete basis.

An inevitable corollary and necessary consequence of the chronic fear tension is a hatred of the Negro. Fear is painful and the persistence of the painful state generates a wish to destroy the fear object. Moreover, the presence of a misused person is a perpetual reminder of conduct in violation of the customary moral standards: the presence of the misused person is a constant irritant and becomes an object of aversion and hatred. It is not meant to imply that the psychological process is recognized in an honest and objective way. On the contrary, the mental processes operate to conceal the psychological facts and justify the aversion. Crime, dirt, vice, and the like are unlovely things, and they are things that it is easily possible to associate with and accept as characteristic of Negroes. And it is easy, perhaps inevitable, that an aversion for the Negro having its real explanation in other facts should be explained and justified in terms of alleged Negro characteristics.

This fear-hate complex is supported by a group of social attitudes commonly included under the phrase race prejudice. As previously pointed out, race prejudice is chiefly a matter of status. The Negro as an inferior and docile person is accepted and in individual cases may even be the recipient of some degree of genuine affection, but in any relation other than that of conspicuous inferiority the Negro becomes an object of active hostility.

This complex of racial attitudes lies at the basis of all crimes against the Negro. The particular offense of the Negro is not a matter of consequence; the racial antagonism is always ready to express itself in overt activity. The occasion calling out the expression is a matter of accident.

But racial prejudice not unlike that prevailing in the American South exists in other places where divergent races and contrasted cultures are brought together in the same political situation. Since the lynching is limited to the one environment it is obvious that racial prejudice alone is not an adequate explanation of the practice.

The second factor necessary in a causal explanation is the general American attitude toward law and legal control. There is here an absence of reverence and respect for law and legal procedure such as exists in many European countries where the statute law is in major part the articulate and formal expression of established custom and ancient folk practice. It is administered with a dignity unknown to American procedure and by officials whose individuality is largely sunk in their representative capacity and who are not directly answerable to the community in which they administer the law. Moreover, there is a uniform enforcement of the law throughout the country; an enforcement that is not immediately controlled by political considerations. In the American conception law is merely a device for arriving at certain objectives. There is no reverence for the law as such and little or no respect for the law as such. It is a thing to be used when its use may be employed for personal ends, a thing to be observed when observation is less personally expensive than violation, and a thing to be violated or defied when violation is personally profitable. To circumvent the law is not only not offensive, it is the most lucrative form of professional service. Violation of law is more usual than law observance, and is not infrequently a source of distinction. An unpopular law is commonly violated with impunity and the degree of enforcement of any law varies with public sentiment and local political expediency. The people consider themselves above the law; they make laws and break them, and they elect judicial and administrative officers who enforce the law when it is considered politically expedient to do so.

The co-existence of the two groups of attitudes gives a situation in which lynching can flourish. The racial attitudes, in appropriate situations, tend to express themselves in violence against the Negro. Such behavior is normally inhibited by a complex of co-existing attitudes which comprehend respect for law and fear of legal consequences. In the absence of a group of attitudes inhibiting lawless action the logical consequences of the racial attitudes appear. The practice of lynching Negroes is thus to be understood as a result of racial antagonism in the absence of a controlling law-abiding attitude.

EFFORTS TO CONTROL LYNCHING

In many of the states at the present time the public sentiment against mob law is such that racial hatred rarely expresses itself in mob action. That some effort is being made to create a similar sentiment against the practice in other states is evident from the number of formal resolutions adopted by religious, educational, and other bodies representing the responsible, intelligent, and self-respecting elements of the population, as well as from the general tenor of editorials on mob killings.

The general sentiment is well reflected in the debate and discussion relative to federal legislation on the subject. The Dyer anti-lynching bill was introduced in the Congress of 1912. It provided a heavy fine or imprisonment for officers of the law proven negligent in their duty of protecting prisoners and long terms of imprisonment for members of criminal mobs as well as a heavy forfeit from the county or counties in which lynchings occur. The bill has continued to be a matter of debate and jockeying in following Congresses. Several states have passed laws defining punishment for individuals participating in lynchings. The Kentucky Legislature passed such a law in 1920 providing not only for the punishment of individuals participating in mob activity but for the removal from office of officers permitting a prisoner to be lynched or injured by a mob. In the following year laws with similar intent were passed in North Carolina, West Virginia, and Minnesota. The South Carolina law made the county in which a lynching occurred liable for damages. Anti-lynching laws were passed by the New Jersey and Pennsylvania Legislatures in 1923, by Nebraska in 1927, and Virginia in 1928. Similar legislation has been recommended by the governors or introduced into the Legislatures of Missouri, Arkansas, Texas, Georgia, Mississippi, North Dakota, and South Carolina without, however, being enacted into law.*

Such laws, while they indicate the drift of public sentiment, are in general without great influence on the practice itself. When the sentiment of a community favors lynching the laws are difficult or impossible of enforcement. It is often impossible to indict since the grand juries make little sincere effort to discover evidence even though the identity of criminals may be known and acknowledged. When facts upon which action may be based are discovered, conviction is generally impossible; individuals are acquitted in spite of conclusive evidence of guilt.

Measures designed to penalize the communities in which lynchings occur promise to be far more effective in limiting the practice than are the laws designed to punish mob members or the officers negligent in the protection of prisoners; they tend to put the responsibility where it properly belongs. If there are persons and groups in a society ready to commit such acts of violence it is because the society makes or tolerates conditions that produce such persons; their ideas, prejudices, and criminal tendencies are the result of the environmental training and education that the society provides. The society is responsible for the individual or group acts of violence that are an expression of the social conditions and the social creed.

If the efforts to prevent crimes against the Negroes are to rise above the level of the police methods commonly advocated, they must bring about a change in the general racial attitude. Whatever operates to lessen the prejudice of the white people or to develop a law-abiding attitude will decrease the abuse of the Negroes and the frequency of mob action. Lynchings will also decrease with an increase in the ability and disposition of the Negroes to protect themselves from mob violence.

* In 1969 states with anti-lynching laws included: Alabama, California, Georgia, Illinois, Indiana, Kansas, Kentucky, Minnesota, Nebraska, New Jersey, New York, North Carolina, Ohio, Pennsylvania, South Carolina, Tennessee, Texas, Virginia, and West Virginia.

Bancroft, H. H., *Popular Tribunals*, 2 Vols.

Bye, R. T., *Capital Punishment in the United States*, "Lynching," pp. 62–73.

Census Bureau, *Negro Population in the United States, 1790–1950*, "The Delinquent, Defective, and Dependent Classes," pp. 436–458.

Chicago Commission on Race Relations, *The Negro in Chicago*, "Crime and Vicious Environment," pp. 327–356.

Coker, F. W., "Lynching," *Encyclopaedia of the Social Sciences*.

Collins, W. H., *The Truth About Lynching and the Negro in the South*.

Cutler, J. E., *Lynch-Law: An Investigation into the History of Lynching in the United States*.

Negro Year Book, 1931–1932, "The Lynching of Negroes," pp. 293–299.

Phillips, U. B., *American Negro Slavery*, "Slave Crime," pp. 454–488; "The Force of the Law," pp. 489–514.

Raper, Arthur, *The Tragedy of Lynching*.

White, Walter, *Rope and Fagot*.

FURTHER READINGS

Ames, Jessie D., *The Changing Character of Lynching: Review of Lynching, 1931–1941, with a Discussion of Recent Developments in this Field*. Atlanta, Ga.: Commission on Interracial Cooperation, 1942.

Cantril, Hadley, *The Psychology of Social Movements*, Ch. 4. New York: John Wiley and Sons, 1941.

Cox, Oliver C., "Lynching and the Status Quo," *Journal of Negro Education*, XIV(Autumn 1945), 576–88.

Greenberg, Jack, *Race Relations and American Law*. New York: Columbia University Press, 1959.

Meltzer, Milton, ed., *In Their Own Words: A History of the American Negro*, 3 vols. New York: Thomas Y. Crowell Company, 1964–67.

Myrdal, Gunnar, *An American Dilemma*, Ch. 27. New York: Harper, 1944.

National Advisory Commission on Civil Disorders, *Report of National Advisory Commission on Civil Disorders*. New York: Bantam, 1968.

XVIII

THE GROWTH OF
RACE CONSCIOUSNESS*

An outstanding fact in the recent social evolution of the American Negro people has been the tendency toward segregation and the formation of more or less compact groups. The residential and institutional separations are expressions as well as causes of the more fundamental sentimental unity that has been slowly evolving during the period of freedom. Even before the Emancipation there was some vague feeling of group unity resulting from the similarity of race and status as well as from association and common interests. In freedom, reacting to the social policies and practices of the dominant white group and to a vigorous and persistent propaganda, the race-conscious attitude gradually developed and came presently to dominate the thinking of a considerable segment of the group. The use made of the Negroes in the European War, particularly their organization into separate units under Negro officers, gave a new impetus to the movement. In the post-war period, under the stimulation of race-conscious Negro leaders the masses have become in a measure imbued with the spirit and have tended to take on the form of an oppressed nationality.

An oppressed nationality psychosis is perhaps an inevitable expression of the social situation in which the race has been placed. Any natural group that is isolated, regardless of the nature or the cause of the isolation, tends to develop a provincial unity in the struggle for recognition and self-respect. If discrimination, repression, or persecution be added to the fact of separateness, the solidarity of the group is strengthened; it becomes self-conscious and compensates for inferior status by unconsciously exaggerating the significance of whatever cultural elements it may possess. The exclusion of the group may result in the first instance from its

* This chapter remains the same as in the second edition.

cultural retardation. But the militantly self-conscious group is wholly incapable of an objective evaluation of its comparative cultural worth. The grievances which such a group comes to cherish may be and indeed frequently are partly or wholly imaginary, and when real may be a consequence of the behavior resulting from the persecution psychosis rather than its immediate cause.

The members of such a group, in the presence of real or fancied discrimination, become hypersensitive. Their comprehension of the social situation is partial and their definition biased. The balking of the fundamental desire for recognition centers attention upon themselves and the indifferent, secondary, and impersonal contacts of daily life are translated into personal terms. There is a chip always on the shoulder. The body of social opinion becomes negative, frequently a mere reversal of the prevailing consensus. Reacting to real or imaginary hostility, individuals become violent and abusive or withdraw from contacts, retire within their own group and endeavor to make it self-sufficient. In either case an elaborate body of compensatory doctrine is fabricated in the effort to achieve self-respect; unsupported opinions and beliefs come to be held with the greatest emotional certitude. The group becomes impervious to facts conflicting with this emotional complex; it tends to react negatively to all suggestions having their origin in the dominant group. In the situation many of the behavior reactions of the nationalistic folk become unintelligible in terms of the social psychology of normal groups.

The limitations which the social situation places upon personal behavior thwart, in numerous cases, a normal expression of the fundamental wishes and generate a restlessness that frequently gets expression in diverse and fantastic ways. From the restraints of daily life and the restrictions of status there is a swing to the opposite extreme; from servility there is, with a removal of restrictions, a swing to exaggerated and bumptious self-assertion. There is a tendency to compensate for the lack of power and prestige by oratory and other forms of exhibitionism. The black Christ and Madonna of the Garvey movement, the fabrication of racial history, the simulated contempt for white civilization, and other like phenomena presently to be discussed are efforts to achieve a self-respect and a basis for racial pride. The racial myths and the endless organizations and societies with their grandiose titles and glittering regalia are in large part a means of escape from reality through the fabrication of a world of dreams.

The appearance of such a nationalistic psychosis among the Negroes is a relatively recent phenomenon. Historically they have been a rather highly accommodated group. Their prevailing psychology has been that of inferiority and of the acceptance of inferiority. Throughout the period of life in America they have lived in the midst of a larger population possessed of a superior culture. It was inevitable that the white standard and the white beliefs should be the ones accepted by the minority group. From infancy to old age, they were impressed on every hand with the idea of their innate racial inferiority, and in the large they accepted the doctrine as one of the obvious facts of nature. They had no part in the culture system and never escaped the implication of their race and status.

As a result the ambitious and superior individuals generally manifested a pathetic desire to be like the white man, to be identified with the race in which effort, ability, and personal worth were recognized and rewarded. The Negroes discounted their own personal and racial worth. Color was or was believed to be a barrier to advancement. The ideal of worth, beauty, and accomplishment lay outside the racial group and dissatisfaction with the conditions of life expressed itself in efforts to conform at least outwardly to the white model.

THE VOLUNTARY SEGREGATION OF THE NEGROES

In America the Negroes have always been in some degree a group apart. The physical differences between the races are so great as generally to make intimate association mutually repugnant. The cultural differences have at all times been wide. The whites have generally refused to fraternize with the Negroes and, when free to do so, the great majority of the Negroes have lived in separate settlements as a matter of choice. Other things equal, they seek and prefer the association of persons of their own race and color. By the mass of the Negro people, separation as such has not been looked upon as a hardship but rather as a simple, natural fact in accord with their wishes.

In the slave order the opportunity of the slaves to associate with each other was usually very limited. The economic interdependence of the races was such as to prevent any general expression of the natural tendency toward segregation. In some of the community relations of life they were allowed to segregate themselves but in most respects no free expression of the natural tendency was possible. In the decade immediately following the Civil War, the breach between the races widened. The ex-slaves, forced to depend upon their own efforts, gradually built up a more or less independent and characteristic set of institutions and a sense of racial unity began gradually to appear.

But the difficulties in the way of a race conscious Negro population were apparently insuperable. The Negroes were economically and culturally dependent upon the more numerous white group. They were without ancestral pride or family tradition. They had no distinctive language or religion. These, like their folkways and moral customs, were but recently acquired from the whites and furnished no nucleus for a racial unity. The group was without even a tradition of historic unity or of racial achievement. There were no historic names, no great achievements, no body of literature, no artistic productions. The whole record of the race was one of servile or barbarian status apparently without a point about which a sentimental complex could form. The one distinctive fact of the race was a characteristic physical appearance. But color was everywhere associated with servile status and backward culture; it was a fact of which the rising members of the group were ashamed and from which they desired to escape; it was not a fact of which they were proud.

It was not until after the scheme for giving the freedmen a classical education had failed and given place to the movement for industrial education that a real racial unity was possible. This new educational program, resulting as it did in a body of trained persons useful in the situation, gave an increasing number of independent and self-respecting men. It gave the beginnings of a middle-class group with a pride of accomplishment and a self-respect born of independent endeavor. As this group increased in numbers it formed a locus about which the Negroes tended gradually to unite. With its development came also some realization of the great opportunities before the race and a growing determination to use the opportunities. There was in consequence an increased tendency to withdraw from dependence upon the whites and engage in co-operative effort to advance the racial interests. The sentimental preference for the familiar which gave some natural basis for a degree of unity was thus reinforced by the apparent self-interest of the group.

Discrimination and Enforced Segregation

The conditions of life that the Negroes have faced in America during the period of their freedom have been conducive in the highest degree to the growth of a nationalistic spirit. At every point in their social evolution they have met opposition and been reminded by persistent discrimination that they form a group apart. They have been denied full participation in the cultural life and ambitious individuals, striving to escape the inferior status, have been forced back upon their own group. At every turn the Negroes have been made to realize that they will be tolerated only in the capacity of menials.

This white policy has been characteristically undiscriminating. The assimilation of the white culture by the Negro has not changed the general attitude; no exception is made of the individuals of education and refinement. Indeed, the advance of Negroes has in general tended to intensify prejudice and increase discrimination. The changed attitudes and individual desires of the Negroes which come with higher standards of life and education clash with the conservative desire of the whites to perpetuate the traditional relation of superiority and subordination. The efforts of the educated and partly educated Negroes to escape the racial isolation and participate in new capacities in the cultural life have generally aroused an intense prejudice on the part of the whites, and this emotional attitude has expressed itself in various more or less conscious and deliberate efforts to prevent the rise of the Negroes, to control the type of racial contacts, and to maintain the caste distinction. The popular white policy and practice have been to treat all Negroes categorically, to refuse to accept even the most exceptional persons on the basis of personality and individual worth.

Not only has the discrimination tended to include all individuals of the race, it has extended to every phase of the racial life and isolated them as completely as possible from all social and cultural contacts. They have in general been excluded from white residential areas and forced to live in segregated and generally in neglected and undesirable sections. Their children have been forced into separate and inferior schools. The intermarriage of the races has been forbidden, and by various means, often grossly humiliating, all other contacts that might even indirectly imply social equality have been prevented. The Negroes have been made to realize that regardless of individual worth and refinement they may not aspire to a social and personal relation with the whites.

Everywhere they have met unequal treatment before the law, and unequal protection from the law. The police have generally been undiscriminating and the courts severe. In times of racial disorder the police and military power of the state has often been used to suppress the Negroes rather than to restore or maintain order. Their women have generally been outside the protection of the law. More frequently than others, they have been the victims of lynching mobs. Various self-appointed disciplinary bodies have made them the victims in programs of violence. They have lived always in an atmosphere of fear and seldom if ever wholly free from the possibility of personal mistreatment.

By force and fraud they have for the most part been denied the franchise and made an issue rather than a factor in the political life of the nation. Campaigns repeatedly have been made to turn, regardless of the issues involved, upon the racial attitudes of the candidates. In the economic and industrial life they have been an exploited group and their helplessness has been the greater because they have generally been denied membership in the labor organizations. In civil life discrimination has been equally general and galling. They have been excluded from hotels and restaurants, made unwelcome in public parks and playgrounds, assigned to separate sections in theaters and places of amusements, tolerated rather than welcomed by the colleges and universities. On trains and street cars and in depots and public places generally throughout the South they have been provided separate accommodations and denied the use of facilities provided for the general public. The larger retail establishments have frequently denied them service or discouraged their patronage. And in innumerable other ways they have met inconveniences and restrictions, frequently of an intentionally humiliating type.

Thus throughout the country and at all periods, and in every department of life, the Negroes have been set apart; they have not been allowed to participate fully in the civilization. They have been denied all personal and social relations with the whites, they have met discrimination in public as well as in civil life. Continually they have been reminded of the fact that they are a peculiar race and they have been treated as inferior regardless of individual attainment and personal worth.

RACIAL SEPARATION AND NEGRO LEADERS

The two forces—the natural disposition of the Negroes to associate with and live near others of their race, and the exclusion policy of the arrogant white group—operated to the same end. Each tended to create a Negro group independent of and separated from the surrounding whites. The separation of the racial groups gradually increased and extended to more and more departments of life. With the separation and consequent self-dependence there developed a new self-confidence and an increased sense of racial unity. The Negroes became increasingly open to the propaganda of organizations engaged in combating the discriminatory practices of the whites and more disposed to accept the doctrine that the race should develop its own independent culture.

Certain advantages inherent in racial unity were presently recognized. The segregation and exclusion of the group made a place and provided a function for racial leaders. The separation of the group created a need for business and professional men and the growing unity of the group made it possible for them to survive and prosper. Merchants who could not offer a type of service that would enable them to survive in a free competition with the more experienced and better equipped white rivals found the key to business success in a racial solidarity that assured them a patronage that their service could not otherwise command. In a similar way, Negro physicians, dentists, entertainers, and other professional men were able to thrive when racial sentiment over-balanced the difference in skill between themselves and the competing white practitioners.

The patronage of the race enabled Negro business men to live, to gain experience, and to improve their service. Their success was often assured by the action of the whites; in some cases by encouraging the Negro establishments with their patronage, and in other cases by the refusal of white business men to take trade from the competing Negro establishment. More than one Negro bank owes its initial success to the fact that with its establishment the white bankers required their Negro depositors to close their accounts and transact their business through the Negro institution. The refusal of white physicians to accept Negro patients when a physician of the race opened an office assured many Negro physicians a practice from the start. The success of the early professional men was thus made possible by the attitude of the white business and professional men and by the growing racial unity, and as the type of service given by the Negroes improved there was a natural growth. Success often depended upon a racial separation and sentimental unity that gave a virtual monopoly; the greater the sentimental unity the less there was of white competition.

The success of the first venturesome individuals, due largely to an absence of keen competition, stimulated other ambitious persons to secure the education or training necessary to a professional or business career. The racial solidarity thus operated to the advantage of various individuals.

THE ADVOCACY OF BI-RACIAL INSTITUTIONS

A realization of the great immediate advantage inherent in race unity and solidarity led to an active propaganda in favor of a bi-racial organization. Individuals of both races and of widely divergent interests and motives advocated racial solidarity and made every effort possible to bring the masses of the race to a realization of its importance.

Business and professional men exploited the sentiment and stimulated its growth. As the sentiment grew the business men appealed for patronage more and more on the ground of racial loyalty. These Negro business concerns were generally small, their standards low, and their service poor. They could seldom offer the inducement of superior goods, lower prices, or better service. Instead, the appeal for patronage was presented as an obligation that individuals were under to support the enterprises conducted by members of the race. The interests of the group were made to appear identical with those of individuals who profited immediately and directly from the success of the business undertaking. There came to be much criticism and personal abuse of individuals who allowed economic rather than sentimental considerations to decide the establishment from which they purchased goods. It was argued that the race could advance through co-operative unity only and that individuals who allowed their self-interest and personal convenience to outweigh their racial obligations were traitors: their behavior tended to weaken or destroy the unity and integrity of the group. The men who for one reason or another did not support race institutions or did not favor the growth of the nationalistic spirit were treated as enemies within the race.

The Negro newspapers almost without exception became ardent advocates of racial unity. Some part of this is to be understood in terms of self-interest. As news vehicles they did not rank high, their circulation was dependent upon the existence of a racial spirit that would support them in spite of their imperfections. Like the generality of white papers they were published in the interests of business men or were dependent upon business advertising for support; they reflected the interests of the advertising classes. But the attitude of the papers was not wholly a calculating one; the convictions of the editors were pretty uniformly in harmony with the circulation interests; they were generally sincere in the belief that the welfare of the group was furthered by the existence of a race-conscious unity.

Many racial leaders came to accept the position that the prejudice and discrimination of the whites was an advantage to the race. If the white people, it was argued, allowed Negroes to attend their churches there would be no Negro congregations, so no possibility of a Negro ministry; if the Negroes were not excluded from or discriminated against in white establishments there would be no place for or possibility of Negro restaurants, hotels, barber shops, or other places of business; if Negroes were not denied membership in white organizations there would be no possibility of Negro secret societies and fraternal organizations; if it were not for the disinclination of white professional men to serve a Negro clientele there would be no possibility of a Negro professional group; if it were not for segregated schools there would be no place for Negro teachers. So in other activities of life; the place of the Negro leader was made possible by a group solidarity that resulted chiefly from the prejudice of the whites and the exclusion of Negroes from white groups.

The advocates of the nationalistic movement have cited a wide variety of evidence in its support and defense. The arguments advanced are frequently partly or wholly contradictory.

Many of the supporters of the bi-racial system have held the belief that such an arrangement would lessen the friction between the races. Aside from any moral judgment in regard to it, racial prejudice is a fact. It is most intense in the ignorant classes and becomes particularly active in the event of obvious economic competition. By keeping the masses of the two races apart in many or most of their activities, thus avoiding individual competition and occasions for friction, it was believed that harmonious and friendly relations could be more easily maintained. Other persons, chiefly Negroes, have advocated a racial solidarity and stimulated its growth as the most effective means for opposing the discrimination of the whites. They look forward to conflict between the races as inevitable and when it comes a high degree of solidarity will be racially advantageous. Again, it is believed by many who do not anticipate a racial war that a self-conscious racial unity will make it possible for the race to present a united front in the struggle against discrimination and injustice. Acting as a group they will be able to exert a political and moral power and get a degree of consideration not obtainable by the individuals acting in their several capacities. Police protection, political recognition, economic equal-

ity, housing reform, sanitary measures and the like may be secured if at
all only by group action. The size and complexity of modern society is
such as to make impossible the participation of the great number of individuals as individuals; they must participate, if at all, in the general affairs
of the city, state, and nation through the deliberations of local, occupational, or racial groups. Only by separate racial organization and unity of
action is it possible for them to make their influence felt in the determination of national policies and practices.

Many advocates of the bi-racial arrangement anticipate as a result of
racial unity and self-consciousness that the Negro people will be able to
make a distinctive contribution to American and world culture. They are
frequently exhorted by both Negro and white men of prominence to
develop a culture of their own. They are advised to be the best possible
black men rather than imitations of white men. They are told to publish
their own papers, write their own books, preach their own sermons, teach
their own children, organize their own societies, and otherwise develop
an independent culture complex. The underlying thought seems to be
that the Negroes have special racial needs and capacities; instead of assimilating and sharing the culture facts of white American life they should
produce new culture facts, values of independent Negro invention.

Of a slightly different nature is the prevalent idea that the backward
group has or, because of temperamental characteristics, may develop some
unique culture elements which would be lost to civilization by the rapid
enlightenment of the group. As the Italian immigrant to America brings
a musical heritage the incorporation of which would greatly enrich American culture and which would be incorporated if the process of Italian
assimilation went on slowly but is lost to the group and to America in the
course of rapid assimilation, so the characteristic elements of Negro culture may be preserved to enrich American civilization provided the group
maintains a separate and independent status.

EXPRESSIONS OF RACIAL SOLIDARITY

In the present day a race-conscious Negro group is largely an accomplished fact. Its expression is, or is rapidly coming to be, as general as the
activities and contacts of the race. There is to be sure a bitter internal
strife among the factions striving for ascendancy, and the group is torn
by endless class prejudices and personal jealousies. But back of the petty
political maneuvering of individuals, factions, and classes is a fundamental
trend of sentiment which may be observed in widely separated fields and
in otherwise unrelated activities.

The rapid fabrication of a Negro history and culture tradition is a
major expression of an actively self-conscious group. A tradition of historic greatness is an invaluable aid, if not an absolute prerequisite, to na-

tionality. But the American Negroes are without such a background. The major part of the period of residence in this country was spent in slavery, and in freedom they have been a culturally backward and excluded group. The race as a whole has no history; even the few rude cultural beginnings that ethnological research uncovers are in most cases not indigenous. But the obstacle that this paucity of historic accomplishment offers to the development of racial pride is rapidly disappearing. There are various achievements of men of Negro blood that are a source of racial pride. These are being continually retold and embellished. Recently there has been a marked tendency to emphasize early African civilization and to exploit the part that Negroes have had in the building of other cultures. The fact that the historic structure thus being woven is largely one of myth and fiction in no way lessens its importance; it is adequate for the purposes of a nationalistic movement. The thing essential for nationalistic unity is belief; historic accuracy is a point of negligible concern. So, regardless of the historic accuracy of this body of material it has an historic significance: it serves to crystallize Negro opinion and to foster the belief that the race has a past of which it may be proud, that Negro culture and achievement are things of historic importance. This rapidly increasing body of material is an expression of the striving of a repressed group for self-respect at the same time that it is a basis for a pride of race.

The increasing number of racial organizations of national scope is another expression of the growing race consciousness. The Negro church and religious organizations are in nearly all cases separate. The number of benevolent and secret societies of national scope is over half a hundred. During the present century there have been created a very large number of national organizations for professional and political advancement, for general and civic improvement, for economic development, for advancing the interests of Negro women, and for a wide variety of other purposes. The number and prosperity of these organizations indicate the trend of development and the extent of racial separation. The race supports numerous newspapers and periodicals, several with a national circulation.

The so-called back to Africa movement was at once an expression of a nationalistic spirit and an evidence of its wide spread among the masses of the group. The Universal Negro Improvement Association was established in 1917 by Marcus Garvey, an immigrant Negro from the West Indies. The avowed purposes of the Association were to improve the commercial status of the Negro peoples throughout the world and to restore Africa to the Africans. The founder desired to prove to the world the political, social, and industrial ability of the Negro peoples and to establish a Negro nation, that the Negroes might be accepted by other races on an equal footing. By accident or design Garvey raised the most delicate issue in Negro politics—the question of color. For support he appealed directly to the black and ignorant masses of the race, ignoring the light-colored classes and later attacking them on the ground that they were out of touch and sympathy with the masses. The result was the arousal of the most bitter opposition of the mulatto leadership and a correspondingly increased enthusiasm on the part of the black and ignorant classes. Membership in the organization increased rapidly; before the collapse of the movement with the arrest and imprisonment of Garvey, over a million Negroes had contributed funds to its support and the claim was made that the followers numbered one-third to one-half of the American Negro population. The whole movement from any standpoint—political, economic, financial, social—was farcical but it was a dramatic demonstration of the social unrest of the inarticulate masses.

Extreme sensitiveness is increasingly characteristic of the race in America. There is everywhere manifest a spirit of resentment of any and all things that imply disrespect. The use of the various descriptive terms and epithets—darky, coon, pickaninny, and the like—is almost universally resented and there is continued discussion concerning even the race name Negro as against "colored people," "Afro-Americans," and the like. To write the name of the race without capitalizing the initial N, as has been the convention, is resented as a discourtesy. The displaying of "for white only," "for colored only," or other similar legends is the object of vigorous attack. Almost invariably the reaction of the Negro press to news reports of and editorial comments on race friction appearing in the white newspapers is that these news items are intentionally biased and the editorial utterances meant to excuse the whites and exaggerate the offenses of the Negroes. There is an increasing tendency to boycott firms treating Negroes unfairly or discourteously. More and more the Negroes are showing a disposition to defend themselves against white mobs, and to move away from communities where lynchings have occurred. There is an increasing confidence in Negro leadership. In some quarters there is a disposition to reject all things white, even the Christian religion. Negro dolls have to a large extent replaced white dolls as toys for Negro children. There is a large and increasing interest in race literature, music, and other artistic expressions and a disposition to exploit them as focuses of racial pride. Various other items of behavior and opinion might easily be cited as expressions of a growing nationalistic spirit. The tendency is manifest in every field of Negro activity and is spreading rapidly among the peasant and laboring groups.

CONSEQUENCES OF A NATIONALISTIC COMPLEX

The significance to the race of a high degree of solidarity is not always clearly understood by many of its advocates, its disadvantages are frequently overlooked and its advantages sometimes grossly exaggerated.

From the point of view of the inclusive group, a militantly nationalistic spirit is fraught with consequences that seem not always to come within the orbit of thought of the bi-racial advocates.

In the initial stages of the culture development the advantages that result from a strong sentimental unity seem to overshadow the disadvantages. By destroying or lessening competition with better equipped and better trained men, it gives a virtual monopoly on the patronage of the race. The consequent success of a few enterprising men in these circumstances is a stimulus to other active-minded and ambitious individuals to essay business careers or to prepare themselves for professional service.

But there are obvious limits on the extent to which this process is racially advantageous. Temporarily it is of great value to the struggling business and professional men; ultimately it must react disastrously upon the group and upon the very classes that at first profit by it. To the extent that these classes secure a monopoly on the patronage of the race, they are under no strong economic compulsion to maintain a high grade of service, and lower business and professional standards tend to prevail. Inferior service is a price which any group pays for the indulgence of a racial sentiment. Professional men lack the stimulation and example of outside groups and the standards of training and skill decline or fail to advance as rapidly as in less isolated groups. It is possible to succeed on the basis of low standards and inferior men gain a footing in the professions. The group pays the price in the inferior service it receives.

To the extent that the Negroes develop peculiar and exclusive institutions, they are to that degree isolated from the only culture they may hope to acquire. The creation of a distinctive Negro culture in the midst of an advanced and highly complex civilization is manifestly impossible. If, because of distinctive temperamental traits, the Negro group has the capacity to enrich modern culture by a distinctive racial contribution, it can be done by the incorporation of the group rather than by its exclusion. There is no trace of African culture surviving in the American group. The only culture values within the Negro heritage are those common to the regions in which they live. The language, religion, technology, customs, moral standards, and so through the list of culture values are European and not African. Into this culture heritage the Negroes have but recently come and they do not in all cases measure up to its standards. Their cultural standards are retarded but not peculiar. In the situation the problem of the Negro, as of any other backward group, is to master the existing culture. Just as the first need of the child is education, a knowledge of what has been done and a training that will give him a workmanlike control of the tools of culture, so the Negroes need to be assimilated to the existing culture and measure up to the standards of European civilization. To refuse to be assimilated into the existing culture and master the body of knowledge of that culture can result in nothing except the retardation of the rate at which the group advances.

Cultural progress comes by invention and the incorporation of the new into the previously existing cultural complex. In the modern world this social change is rapid. The large size of modern groups makes frequent the appearance of individuals capable of making cultural contributions, and the highly developed means of communication in the Western world enables society at large to profit from the inventions of the superior. The modern peoples are thus not dependent for cultural advance upon the accidental and unpredictable appearance of extraordinary men within the group; they profit equally by the superiority appearing in other groups at a similar stage of cultural advance. The necessity of cultural contact increases as the size and culture of the group decline. The smaller the numbers the less likelihood of the appearance of superior persons and the greater its dependence upon superiority appearing in other groups. In the case of a culturally retarded group the necessity of cultural contact increases since the probability of native superiority appearing is less and the need greater.

Any degree of exclusion results in cultural retardation since no group however talented may hope to produce a galaxy of genius that would enable it to progress at a rate comparable with others not limited for copy to their own inventive genius. The cause or type of isolation does not alter the end result; illiteracy is not less significant than physical isolation; the sentiment of nationality isolates as definitely as does physical separation.

Various nationalistic groups retard their advance by a sentimental determination to persist in the use of their own objectively inferior culture elements—as the Polish refusal to accept the German language, or the Irish refusal to accept a Protestant religion—because the alternative and superior forms originated with or are in the hands of groups toward which their nationalistic antipathy is directed. To the extent that the Negro people develop a nationalistic complex, to that extent they are isolated from the contacts necessary to their cultural advance. There is created a sentimental barrier that hinders their acceptance of invention that comes from the antipathetic source; there is an emotional refusal to accept and incorporate culture facts superior to existing elements. A sentimental complex, a nationalistic psychosis, isolates a group as effectively as a linguistic insularity. The Negro has all to lose and nothing to gain by the growth of such a nationalistic sentiment.

The existence of a race-conscious attitude operates to retard racial development by stimulating the growth of separate institutions and by centering attention upon inferior models. The institutions developed by the Negroes are more or less faithful copies of corresponding white institutions but, in the nature of the social process, they will be inferior to the originals. Separate Negro churches are a source of pride and they afford an opportunity for a Negro ministry and in a measure serve a peculiar need, but they also prevent the attendance of the Negroes on more valuable services. The separate Negro schools provide a livelihood for teachers who otherwise would be forced into less congenial occupations but they also mean inferior school facilities for Negro children. Separate institutions are inferior institutions. They are manned by persons incompletely assimilated to modern culture and, in the present development of the race, they cannot be adequately supported. They make possible the development of individuals and allow many, unable to survive in competition with the whites, to secure a more or less genteel living but they retard the development of the mass.

The attention of the race-conscious Negro tends to be upon inferior models. To the extent that the Negro reads "race literature" to the exclusion of literature he is deprived of an important culture contact. It makes a market for writing of too little merit otherwise to find its way into print. To the extent that he reads "Negro history" instead of history his knowledge is perverted and his degree of approximation to modern cultural standards is lessened. It enables the "race historian" to market his wares but at the cost of retarding the enlightenment of the group. The emphasis upon "race music" operates to retard the musical appreciation of the people. The similar thing is true of "Negro art," "Negro drama" and other things "Negro." They occupy the attention of persons and they take the place of other available forms; they thus function to retard the intellectual freedom and the cultural advance of the race. In various ways the race-conscious attitude among the Negroes as among other groups leads to the use of inferior in the presence of superior models.

A race-conscious attitude on the part of the Negro group is freighted with other consequences which are unfortunate from the point of view of the inclusive social group as well as from that of the Negro people. The isolation and solidarity of the group tends to lessen individual competition between Negro and white persons. It tends to the creation of an occupational segregation on racial lines; the competition consequently becomes that of racial groups. The emphasis is placed upon the group rather than upon the members of the group.

As has been pointed out, the solidarity of the group increases its power and may lead locally and temporarily to conspicuous success. The success of individuals of the race is to be expected and is a matter of indifference. The advance of individual Negroes is tolerated and may even be encouraged by the dominant group. It is not a phenomenon that attracts the attention or arouses the fears of the whites. But the advance of the group and their increasing unity and power are things that attract attention and excite fear. On the part of many white individuals and groups there is a very real fear that the Negro may become the equal or even come to dominate. This latent fear becomes active in the presence of group solidarity and aggressiveness. The Negroes cannot develop a social solidarity without stimulating a reciprocal attitude on the part of competing white groups.

In such a situation—two race-conscious groups with mutually hostile attitudes—the more numerous and politically powerful group will take measures to suppress and repress the numerically weaker group and protect its own race interests whenever competition becomes dangerous. In the presence of a more numerous hostile group, the unity that has apparently been of advantage in their rise is a thing that puts them in a position where repressive measures are easy to enforce. At this point there is in operation a vicious circle. Race-conscious solidarity on the part of the Negroes leads to their voluntary segregation and to a certain type of success in racial competition; this arouses the fear and leads to the solidarity of the whites and to measures of repression, so to increased solidarity and segregation of the minority, and to an increase in repressive measures. At this stage race consciousness has defeated its own ends.

Once the process reaches this stage, the individuals of the minority group are virtually helpless: an isolated minority has a limited range of choice in such situation. They may accept the limitations and handicaps that the superior group sees fit to impose—accept the inevitable and become accommodated to an inferior status. This in the great majority of cases they must do. In the case of a few individuals, escape is possible through a change in racial status. But of the Negro group only the mulattoes with a negligible amount of Negro blood can pass as white. The number is very limited and those able to do so with success leave the race in any event. Relief through emigration is equally limited. To go to other sections of the country in numbers gives rise to similar restrictive measures long before the emigration becomes large enough to afford relief. Emigration of the Negroes to other countries is not a present possibility. To oppose discrimination and repression by armed struggle is suicidal. Such a nationalistic conflict could result only in defeat and the imposition of more severely restrictive measures. To fight through formal legal means is futile; the success of litigation depends, in the long run, upon mass sentiment.

RACE CONFLICTS

The numerous race riots that have occurred, particularly in the postwar decade, are both evidence and expression of a militant race-conscious attitude developed in the presence of a fixed and powerful prejudice of race.

Until recent years the racial attitudes in the United States have been such as to make group conflicts infrequent. As previously pointed out, the prejudice of race and caste is an element of the American social heritage. Habituated to the Negroes as social inferiors, the whites had a sentimentally tolerant attitude toward them and their shortcomings as menials. But in any other capacity they were not tolerated. There was on the part of most Americans an emotional repulsion to any sort of relationship that implied equality. For purposes of race relations this attitude may be taken as a fundamental datum. It is a constant factor in the causal complex of every racial conflict of which there is any adequate report. But race prejudice alone is not the cause of conflict. The races were reasonably well accommodated on the basis of white superiority and Negro subordination. The Negroes were an excluded group with a slave psychology; they were repressed and inferior and they accepted their status.

It is only after a repressed group has evolved internal bonds of unity that there is a possibility of mobilizing its strength for group action. The unity may come from a sense of solidarity arising in the sentimental and personal contacts of the primary group situation, or it may be some sense of a community of interest conceived to be peculiar to the members and opposed to the interests of other groups. If the initial solidarity arises through the secondary stimulation of external circumstance, it comes presently to be reinforced by the emotional attitudes arising from the personal contacts incident to the interest association. If the group unity arises from the fact of primary association, the sentimental bonds are presently supplemented by the bonds arising from the community of interest peculiar, or thought to be peculiar, to the group. In either case the subjective side of group solidarity is a complex of rational and emotional attitudes that make possible a concerted type of activity of indefinite duration. Until such time as an oppressed group evolves the internal bonds of unity there is little likelihood of concerted behavior. Individuals may protest and struggle against abuse and mistreatment, there may even be simultaneous revolt of many persons against persecution, but the phenomena remain essentially individual. It is only when the group has developed a sense of solidarity that it tends to respond as a group in the presence of behavior injurious to the group or insulting to its members.

The social order imposed after the Civil War period obviously could not endure. Had it been designed to that end, it could not have been better adapted to bring about discontent and friction. This white racial program involved an inherent contradiction: it provided on the one hand for the general education and enlightenment of the race and for its economic and social advance; on the other hand it denied satisfaction to practically every desire and aspiration created by the cultural enlightenment. The constitution and the laws guaranteed the Negroes equal rights and privileges with other men at the same time that customary practice forbade the exercise of the rights that were legally granted and assured.

As the Negroes outgrew the grosser forms of their slave psychology they developed an oppression psychosis and chafed against the racial status as defined in custom. As wealth and literacy increased they grew more and more restless. They became increasingly resentful of abuse, more unwilling passively to submit to discrimination, more disposed to protest against mistreatment, and more disposed to insist upon their legal rights. They became increasingly conscious of a common problem and a group interest. As group solidarity developed, in the presence of a popular determination to maintain the customary status, racial tension increased. The necessary background of racial strife existed and the trend of events was clearly in that direction. The situation was most advanced in the cities and especially in the northern cities. There the Negroes were less abused, terrorized, and browbeaten than in the South and the rural districts. They had more legal and police protection. In general they were more literate, better informed as to their legal rights, and more highly race conscious, their leadership was more militant, doctrinaire, and incendiary. They were more resentful of discourtesy and more rebellious in cases of discrimination. Moreover, they were keenly aware of the divided sentiment within the white group, aware of the fact that many persons and groups looked upon Negroes as individuals and desired to see them treated on the basis of personal worth.

The war, in a number of places, brought the inter-racial situation to a premature climax. The increased mobility, the improved economic position, and the army experience of the Negroes stimulated the development of a race-conscious solidarity. On the part of the whites an increased hatred of race was an integral part of the war-time intolerance. There were a number of armed conflicts resulting in bloodshed and the destruction of property. Even more frequent were the occasions where riots were narrowly averted or were suppressed before they assumed the proportion or duration of racial wars. In the year 1919 serious riots occurred in seven cities: Chicago, Illinois; Elaine, Arkansas; Charleston, South Carolina; Knoxville, Tennessee; Longview, Texas; Omaha, Nebraska; and Washington, D.C. In the following year similar riots took place at Duluth, Minnesota; Independence, Kansas; and Ococe, Florida. In 1921 there were riots of serious proportions at Springfield, Ohio, and Tulsa, Oklahoma. Other serious race conflicts occurred at Coatesville, Pennsylvania; Springfield, Illinois; Chester, Pennsylvania; Rosewood, Florida; Johnstown, Pennsylvania; and East St. Louis, Illinois.

The various racial clashes that have so far occurred in America have differed in detail only, chiefly in the external conditions that provided the setting for and the incidents that led to the expression of racial hatred.

The migration of Negroes into northern cities made additional living quarters necessary. The consequent invasion of neighborhoods previously white was a frequent point of friction. The suddenly increased economic competition of the races in many northern communities roused the latent prejudice of race. It has so frequently happened that racial conflicts have been associated with labor troubles that some writers have mistaken the fundamental element and argued that race riots are merely economic and labor wars. But this is to confuse an inciting incident or a contributory fact with the basic cause. There is no doubt that the rude and offensive behavior of certain migrant Negroes, over-compensating for their recent repression in the new and strange freedom of northern cities, was a factor contributing to racial hatred and strife. The newspapers of both races inflamed the passions of their readers by playing up sensational incidents and rumors. The immediate incidents resulting in mob behavior bear no necessary relation to the racial strife. In East St. Louis the inciting incident was apparently the irresponsible behavior of a group of drunken revellers. In Elaine the incident seems to have been the action of a sheriff seeking, in sport, to frighten a group of Negroes. In Chicago the rioting started from the quarrelling of rowdies at a public bathing beach. With the proper background of prejudice and sentiment any incident may precipitate a racial war.

THE FUTURE OF THE RACIAL PSYCHOSIS

The continued growth of a Negro nationalistic spirit in America is perhaps inevitable. It arises naturally out of the social situation which comprises two races of marked and obvious physical differences and on different levels of cultural evolution. In such a situation, the great majority of individuals of the backward group form their primary associations with others of the same caste, and color prejudice inevitably appears, enforces proscriptive regulations, and operates to reinforce the natural solidarity of the lower caste.

Certain obvious advantages immediately appear as a result of racial unity. It seems to stimulate ambitious individuals to enter business and professional and artistic pursuits by virtually insuring them successful careers through guaranteeing patronage. The solidarity of the group gives a certain political power that is less obvious when individuals act separately, and the group is in consequence able to demand a recognition and consideration not otherwise obtainable. There is a certain protection that comes with combination and the consequent ability to present a united front. The isolation of the group that comes as a result of the race-concious attitude decreases interracial contacts and so decreases the amount and opportunity for racial friction.

But in any long time view, the development of a nationalistic unity operates to the disadvantage of the Negro and so to the disadvantage of the whole community. It places attention upon the group rather than upon the person and thereby restricts individual freedom. It holds the attention of the members of the race upon inferior patterns and habituates them to inferior institutions thereby retarding the cultural advance. It arouses the fears and intensifies the prejudices of certain white persons, thus increasing the difficulty of establishing and maintaining just and amicable inter-race relations.

It would be to the advantage of the Negroes and to the advantage of the white people to remove all handicaps imposed by caste and other prejudice. They retard the cultural advance of the Negroes and to that extent the advance of the community. The result is the same whether the Negroes are handicapped in their individual freedom directly by discriminatory acts of the whites or indirectly by the existence of a sentimental race complex. The latter arises as a consequence of the former and so long as discrimination and exclusion are general it is folly to oppose the growth of nationality.

Chicago Commission on Race Relations, *The Negro in Chicago*, "The Chicago Riot," pp. 1–52; "Other Outbreaks in Illinois," pp. 52–78.

Detweiler, F. G., "The Rise of Modern Race Antagonisms," *American Journal of Sociology*, 37(1932), 738–747.

DuBois, W. E. B., "Negro Nation Within the Nation," *Current History*, 42(1935), 265–270.

Faris, Ellsworth, *The Nature of Human Nature*, "Racial Attitudes and Sentiments," pp. 317–328.

Frazier, E. F., "American Negroes' New Leaders," *Current History*, 28(1928), 56–59.

Garvey, Amy J., *The Philosophy and Opinions of Marcus Garvey*.

Kerlin, R. T., *The Voice of the Negro*.

Miller, H. A., *Races, Nations, and Classes*, "The Oppression Psychosis," pp. 32–38; "The New Negro," pp. 146–158.

Reuter, E. B., "The Possibility of a Distinctive Culture Contribution from the American Negro," in *Social Attitudes*, Kimball Young, ed., pp. 347–356.

———, *The Mulatto in the United States*, "Present Tendencies," pp. 375–397.

Robinson, G. T., "Racial Minorities," H. T. Stearns, *Civilization in the United States*.

Seligman, H. J., "Menace of Race Hatred," *Harper's Magazine*, 140(1920), 537–543.

Standing, T. G., "Nationalism in Negro Leadership," *American Journal of Sociology*, 40(1934), 180–192.

Stolberg, B., "Black Chauvinism," *Nation*, 140(1935), 570–571.

Stuart, G. A., "New Negro Hokum," *Social Forces*, 6(1928), 438–445.

Weatherford, W. D., and Johnson, C. S., *Race Relations*, "The Changing Attitude of the Negro," pp. 534–542; "Can There Be a Separate Negro Culture?" pp. 543–554.

FURTHER READINGS

Baldwin, James, *The Fire Next Time*. New York: Dial, 1963.

Brink, William, and Harris, Louis, *The Negro Revolution in America*. New York: Simon & Schuster, 1964.

Broom, Leonard, and Glenn, Norval, *Transformation of the Negro American*. New York: Harper & Row, 1965.

Essien-Udom, E. U., *Black Nationalism*. Chicago: University of Chicago Press, 1962.

Etzkowitz, Henry, and Schaflander, Gerald M., *Ghetto Crisis: Riots or Reconciliation?* Boston: Little, Brown, 1969.

Kardiner, Abram, and Ovesey, Lionel, *The Mark of Oppression*. Cleveland: World, 1962.

Killian, Lewis, and Smith, Charles U., "Negro Protest Leaders in a Southern Community," *Social Forces,* XXXVIII(March 1960), 253–257.

King, Martin Luther, Jr., *Stride Toward Freedom: The Montgomery Story.* New York: Harper, 1958.

Lincoln, C. Eric, *The Black Muslims in America.* Boston: Beacon, 1961.

Lomax, Louis E., *The Negro Revolt.* New York: Harper & Row, 1962.

Meltzer, Milton, ed., *In Their Own Words: A History of the American Negro, 1916–1966.* New York: Thomas Y. Crowell Company, 1967.

Schuchter, Arnold, *White Power/Black Freedom: Planning the Future of Urban America.* Boston: Beacon, 1968.

Silberman, Charles E., *Crisis in Black and White.* New York: Random House, 1964.

Taeuber, Karl E. and Alma F., *Negroes in Cities.* Chicago: Aldine, 1965.

Thompson, Daniel C., "The Rise of the Negro Protest," *The Annals* (January 1965), 18–29.

Wagstaff, Thomas, ed., *Black Power: The Radical Response to White America.* Beverly Hills, Calif.: Glencoe Press, 1969.

Woodward, C. Vann, *The Strange Career of Jim Crow.* New York: Galaxy, 1957.

Young, Whitney M., Jr., *To Be Equal.* New York: McGraw-Hill, 1964.

XIX

THE PRESENT AND THE FUTURE*

Persons interested in the American race problem in its so-called practical aspects have from time to time proposed and advocated numerous "solutions." These proposals differ with time and place as well as with the information and point of view of the individual reformers. Those advanced by the reformers of one race seldom receive even the qualified approval of the racially opposed group of reformers.

A persistent popular idea prevails to the effect that the problem is in the way of solving itself through the disappearance of the Negro people. It is thought that they are biologically incapable of adaptation to the American climatic conditions and will, through the operation of the selective forces of nature, presently become extinct. So far as this idea is anything more than the rationalization of a pious wish, it seems always to be based upon certain immature deductions from inadequate and partly analyzed statistical data. The opposite belief—that the Negroes are a rapidly increasing group—is equally the result of an inadequate comprehension of population phenomena.

A deportation scheme arose very early and had a convinced and enthusiastic following. In spite of the manifest impossibility of carrying any such plan into execution as well as the very questionable desirability of doing so if it were possible, it has even at the present time a great many advocates. Some of the persons who sponsor this type of solution would force all Negroes to migrate to Africa or elsewhere; others would colonize them in some American state or in some territory adjacent to the United States. Another numerically important group of persons believes that Christianity is the only solvent of racial problems but they are sometimes vague as to the practical details of the program. It would not be profitable to discuss at length the numerous proposals of which deportation, colonization, and Christianity are typical.

* This chapter remains the same as in the second edition.

On somewhat more intelligent levels white opinion is not formed. A certain highly articulate group advocates the immediate admission of the Negroes to full social and public equality with the whites and their treatment as individuals on the basis of their personal worth. Others seem to desire their independent but somewhat separate development in order that the culture may profit by any unique contributions that they, because of their racial temperament, may be able to make. Still others are willing to grant equal civic and intellectual equality but would place restrictions upon intermarriage and other personal and social activity. The general body of southern opinion leans to the side of repression, to the plan of excluding the race from all participation in public life. Certain extremists would gladly see the restoration of a slave régime. The more moderate view would keep the Negroes as laborers and menials, permitting such development as promised to be conducive to the comfort and convenience of the whites. Certain individuals and groups see a solution of the problem in a manual and industrial education of the Negroes, an education that would make them more efficient laborers without creating discontent with an inferior racial status. The solution through popular education has in general the same reservation: it is designed, fundamentally, to make of the Negroes a greater convenience to white men than they are as illiterates; there is no intention on the part of the advocates of popular education for the Negroes, nor on the part of the philanthropic men who have contributed so generously to the elementary instruction of the race, that they shall be given equal or sufficient education to jeopardize the existing racial order. There is difference of opinion as to the type and amount of training to be provided but no radical difference of opinion as to the desirability of racial inequality in educational opportunity. A very popular present-day solution of the race problem is the interracial commission. Here there is apparently an acceptance of the essential political soundness of a biracial organization and the assumption that satisfactory relations may be maintained between competing nationalistic groups within the same political unit by diplomatic mediation.

There are three or four fairly well-defined racial programs with numerically respectable followings in the articulate Negro world.

Under the masterly political leadership of Booker T. Washington a solution was sought in terms of the economic and educational advance of the Negro masses. The emphasis was upon decent living, school attendance, better health, home owning, improved farming, and other concrete and homely things designed to create individual and racial self-respect. There was a conscious effort to avoid friction by conciliation and to maintain friendly and co-operative relations between the races. It was, at least on the surface, an effort to face a real situation and make a common-sense adjustment, without whining, in terms of reality. As it stood in the mind of Washington, the industrial education movement was a method rather than an end. The white world would be more disposed to grant equal political and public treatment when the Negro masses more nearly approached the moral, economic, and educational standards of the dominant race; and the Negroes would be in a position effectively to insist upon the establishment of a democratic social order and their equal participation therein when and only when they measured up to the cultural standards of the time. The death of Washington left this movement without competent leadership and without a spokesman and in the past decade there has been a marked decline in its relative importance in Negro thought on the race problem.

A second approach to the practical problem is by way of publicity, propaganda, and legal action—an open fight to secure for Negroes the full and complete enjoyment of constitutionally guaranteed rights. The National Association for the Advancement of Colored People has been the chief organization sponsoring this type of solution. This has been an aggressive and militant organization of bi-racial membership that has brought to the present-day situation the spirit and methods of the abolition societies of an earlier generation. It has engaged in systematic and persistent agitation and protest against all forms of inequality in racial treatment, engaged in numerous legal struggles to stop discriminatory treatment, and lobbied extensively for legislation favorable to the interests of Negroes. The tacit assumption is that the race problem is a political problem, or at least a problem that may be solved by political means. It is only recently that this school of Negro thought gained any considerable following. The National Association for the Advancement of Colored People had a small membership during the first two decades of its existence. In 1916 it claimed a membership of only 9,500. After the death of Booker T. Washington and the virtual, if temporary, collapse of the movement to raise the masses through common school and industrial education, the militant groups came, for a time, to be the chief forces molding Negro opinion on race problems.

The Garvey Movement, so-called from its founder, Marcus Garvey, an immigrant Negro from the West Indies, was an attempt to solve the race problem by perfecting a world organization of Negroes into a provisional African empire that would force the recognition and respect of the white world.

CONSTANT FACTORS IN RACE RELATIONS

The various methods advocated by individuals and organizations as solutions of the race problem may be dismissed with brief comment. There is no solution.

But the recognition of this fact does not lessen the importance of racial opinions and racial movements. Nothing is to be gained by ignoring unpleasant elements of the situation nor by denying or minimizing their importance. Any reasonably satisfactory working arrangement between the racial groups will have to be made on the basis of the significant facts. And there is no more important body of fact in the racial situation than the opinions of men in regard to it. It is their beliefs and opinions, their sentiments and attitudes, their antipathies and prejudices, their prepossessions and biases that create and define the racial problem. If men, black and white, were rational creatures these facts would not enter and the race problem as commonly understood would not exist. But in the world of reality they are the significant facts, the primary data, in terms of which racial adjustments must be made.

It must at the same time be recognized that the sentiments and attitudes of men undergo change and that the change is in some measure the result of an increase of information. A summary restatement of certain facts elsewhere discussed in detail should contribute to this end.

THE GROWTH OF THE NEGRO POPULATION

The first source of persistent wrong thinking in the practical world is the current body of misinformation in regard to the relative rate of increase of the Negro element of the population. The most contradictory statements are made and accepted. On the one hand it is believed that the race has an excessively high birth rate and rate of natural increase; on the other hand it is confidentially asserted that the race in the American environment is dying out.

At the beginning of American national life there was one Negro to four white persons in the population. In the following decades the proportion of whites increased; in 1930 there were approximately nine whites to each Negro. Each race increased rapidly in number and the rate of increase of each race steadily declined. The decennial increase of the white element of the population has been markedly higher than that of the Negro element for each census decade. This discrepancy between the rates of increase has been taken often as a measure of relative racial fertility and the declining importance, numerically, of the Negroes predicted. But the natural increase of the whites has been supplemented by the population of territorial additions to the national domain and by a steady flow of European immigrants, while the increase of the Negro stock has been due, almost exclusively, to the excess of births over deaths. It is immediately evident that the gross ratios of racial increase are not comparable. When we compute the natural increase of the native white stock it is found that there has been no very significant difference in the racial rates of increase. "In the nineteenth century the native Negro stock increased 663.3 per cent, while the native white stock increased 693.3 per cent."

There is no present reason to assume that the rough parallelism between the racial rates of natural increase characteristic of the past century will cease in the present. The two races seem to respond in the same way and in approximately the same degree to the increasing pace and complexity of modern life. To the extent that the population is maintained and increased by natural growth there is no convincing reason for believing that the present proportion of Negroes will not remain fairly constant.

But the immigration policy is, of course, an unknown factor that makes any attempt to predict the proportion of Negroes in the population at the end of the century or other future time an idle exercise.

THE MENTAL CAPACITY OF THE NEGRO PEOPLE

A second fact that should be recognized and taken into account in any program of racial adjustment is the essential equality in mental ability of different racial groups.

The popular idea that the Negroes lack the inherent mental capacity necessary for cultural achievement is a direct inference from the retarded culture and the absence of historic achievement. It is perhaps inevitable that such beliefs should arise and persist. The cultural and historic facts are patent, and common sense operates on the basis of gross phenomena. Moreover, the popular logic has had the support of much scholarly writing. Until very recently there has been no attempt at a scientific analysis and study of the social and cultural processes. Indeed, the mere existence of such processes was until recently not recognized. The result was a tendency to build an explanatory structure from the materials of physical and biological science. The inadequacy of this procedure became increasingly apparent as a scientific sociology developed and the relative independence of the social processes was demonstrated. But many persons find it inconvenient or difficult to evacuate a position once occupied and others are uninformed as to recent developments in social theory. One result is the frequent restatement of a point of view that scholarship has shown to be untenable. But the older position is in accord with popular sentiments and its repetition is in consequence most frequent in the semi-scientific books and journals seeking general circulation. This type of writing is a chief source to which the publicist turns for information on scientific subjects and its point of view transmitted through editorial and news channels to the general public reinforces the traditional and common-sense opinions.

This is, of course, aside from the various problems of mental life and ability that occupy the attention of scholars. There is perhaps no competent student who would assert unequivocally the complete mental equality of races. Differences probably do exist but they are not of such nature as to have present significance for political and public policy. A genuine racial program, one based upon the findings of modern social science, will assume essential equality in the mental ability of races.

RACIAL DIFFERENCES

The third group of facts which a successful program will frankly recognize is the contrast in physical appearance, cultural status, and historic background of the races.

The distinctive appearance of the Negroes sets them apart, gives objective definition to the group. The resulting categorical treatment makes it difficult or impossible for individuals to escape the racial status, to function as individuals. However desirable or convenient it might be to ignore this fact it may not be done in an interracial plan that is to be workable. It is within the limits imposed by the cultural advance of the group as a whole that the great majority of individuals must confine their activity. But it goes beyond this. The race includes a great variety of physical types ranging from the West African to those just unable to pass as Europeans. This mixture of blood has been made the basis of a differential treatment that has determined cultural advance; the mixed-blood segment of the race is a generation or more in advance of the dark-skinned masses. Within the race, as between the races, color is a physical fact that automatically classifies. Its presence or absence determines eligibility in innumerable ways: it is a chief basis for class distinctions, it is an important factor in marriage selection, it is a declining element in determining an individual's fitness for positions of distinction and leadership. Neither the physical facts nor the extreme sensitiveness in respect to them may be ignored in any racial adjustment that is to be other than superficial.

The practical situation also involves a recognition of the present educational, economic, and general cultural status of the race. The mass of the Negroes are very backward and the educated group is very small. The separation between the groups is wide and it is complicated by the class and color prejudices just mentioned. Discussion typically ignores the one group or the other. The solutions and programs that come out of the white South generally have no place for the individuals of education; those that come from the intellectual Negro group are sometimes equally provincial in point of view.

In historic experience and social heritage the races differ as profoundly as they do in physical appearance. The resulting differences in mental pattern may not be ignored in framing a practical program.

THE PREJUDICE OF RACE AND CASTE

The existing prejudice of race and caste must be accepted as a relatively fixed factor in the racial situation.

This does not express nor imply any moral approval or disapproval of racial attitudes. It simply recognizes that prejudices do exist and that there is no evidence whatever to justify an assumption that they will be less important in the future than they are in the present and have been in the past.

It is possible to defend and more or less justify the existing prejudice and to do so from more than one point of view. Its effects are not all bad. It has been pointed out, for example, that the prejudice of the white man was an important element in developing the independence and self-respect of Negro groups, that, for better or worse, it has retarded racial amalgamation, that it provided economic and other opportunities for success and leadership, that it created a sense of racial unity, that it made for public peace by an enforced separation, and in other ways brought results believed by many persons to be socially desirable. On the other hand it is possible to elaborate upon the undesirable consequences. Race prejudice and the resulting isolation of the Negroes has blinded the whites to their virtues, retarded their cultural assimilation, restricted their opportunities, perverted the democratic political institutions, prevented the economic and educational advance of the South, and in various other ways operated to the injury of both racial elements in the population.

It is possible to show the origin and trace the development of the racial attitudes, to show the way in which they change, and to show how changes may be brought about. But dealing with the fundamental factors operative in a social situation does not come within the region commonly described as practical; it does not provide tangible and immediate results, and it does not eventuate in political programs.

What it is meant to emphasize here is, on the one hand, the futility of the numerous romantic programs that either do not see prejudice as a reality or assume that it will disappear in the presence of sentimentality and, on the other hand, the positive disutility of the militant programs and solutions depending for success upon the overriding of such prejudices or their destruction by direct frontal attack. Prejudice is a reality in the racial situation. It is not less real and probably not less permanent than the physical marks of race. A practical program must accept it as a primary datum.

THE RACIAL PSYCHOSIS

One other and increasingly important factor in race relations may be emphasized—the sense of Negro nationality.

A sense of race solidarity was inevitable as the Negroes advanced culturally in the presence of the white exclusion policy. There was, of course, some natural basis for separation and unity. Social contacts with individuals of a strange race are characterized by a vague, undefined feeling of discontent; there is a natural, or early acquired, preference for the familiar, a spontaneous tendency toward a separate racial life. As independent Negro institutions developed there was a growth in self-confidence, a feeling of independence, and a pride of accomplishment. The intolerant attitudes and discriminatory practices of the whites provided external conditions conducive to internal organization. There was a common enemy. It was the growing fear and hatred of the white that made possible a race-conscious solidarity in spite of the almost endless amount of internal jealousy and discord.

This nationalistic spirit is still in process of becoming. The course of its development and its rôle in the interracial situation will be determined by the racial policies of the dominant white group. But it is and will continue to be an important element to consider in interracial programs.

THE FUTURE

The foregoing partial enumeration of facts and conditions is sufficient to show that the problem of races is not a thing that may be removed by political and administrative measures. It is a relatively permanent fact of American life and one that will increase in importance.

The general objective of one important school of thought is full equality of public treatment and acceptance of individuals, regardless of racial connections, on the basis of personal worth. In the various programs designed to realize this objective is the basic assumption that it is possible to remove or override prejudice of race. But this appears to be a vain assumption so long as there are distinguishable physical marks of race or social marks of caste. There is reason to anticipate an increased tolerance in intellectual and cosmopolitan circles but little reason to anticipate it elsewhere.

The trend of events is in the opposite direction. It is possible that adjustment may be made by an increased exclusion of the Negroes and their organization and perpetuation as an inferior caste. This arrangement has behind it the force of long tradition as well as certain deep-seated human tendencies. A relatively new factor operating in this direction is the industrial development of the South. As this increases, and its increase threatens to be rapid, the status of the Negroes will change but there is no reason to believe that it will improve. At present the whole force of the educational system is pitted, superficially at least, against a caste solution. But this is a slender barrier since the institution is the creature of the public will and by relatively minor changes it could be changed from an opponent into a powerful ally of the caste order.

As a result of intermixture the Negroes as such ultimately will disappear from the population and the race problem will be solved. But in the meanwhile there will be the problem of defining relations in terms tolerable to the members of each racial group.

Bailey, T. P., *Race Orthodoxy in the South.*

Beals, C., and Plenn, O., "Louisiana's Black Utopia," *Nation,* 141(1935), 503–505.

Bond, H. M., "The Negro Looks at his South," *Harper's Magazine,* 163(1931), 98–108.

Chicago Commission on Race Relations, *The Negro in Chicago,* "Public Opinion and the Negro," pp. 436–594.

Detweiler, F. G., *The Negro Press in the United States,* "Other Solutions of the Race Problem," pp. 165–202.

Holmes, S. J., *The Negro's Struggle for Survival.*

Hussey, L. M., "Homo Africanus," *American Mercury,* 4(1925), 83–89.

Herskovits, M. J., "Race Relations," *American Journal of Sociology,* 35(1930), 1052–1062.

——, "The Racial Hysteria," *Opportunity,* 2(1924), 166–168.

Kerlin, R. T., *The Voice of the Negro.*

Park, R. E., "Education in Its Relation to the Conflict and Fusion of Cultures," *Publications, American Sociological Society,* 13(1918), 38–63.

Ratliff, B. A., "Mississippi: Heart of Dixie," *Nation,* 114(1922), 587–590.

——, "Mississippi Replies," *Nation,* 115(1922), 124–126.

Schuyler, G. S., "The Negro Looks Ahead," *American Mercury,* 19(1930), 212–220.

Stephenson, G. T., *Race Distinctions in American Law,* "Race Distinctions *versus* Race Discriminations," pp. 348–362.

Weatherford, W. D., and Johnson, C. S., *Race Relations,* "Programs Looking Toward the Solution or Amelioration of Race Relations," pp. 519–532.

Wood, C., "Alabama, A Study in Ultra-Violet," *Nation,* 116(1923), 33–35.

FURTHER READINGS

Carter, Wilmoth A., *The New Negro of the South.* New York: Exposition Press, 1967.

Cronon, Edmund D., *Black Moses: The Story of Marcus Garvey and the Universal Negro Improvement Association.* Madison, Wisc.: University of Wisconsin Press, 1955.

Essien-Udom, E. U., *Black Nationalism: A Search for Identity in America.* New York: Dell, 1964.

Etzkowitz, Henry, and Schaflander, Gerald M., *Ghetto Crisis: Riots or Reconciliation?* Boston: Little, Brown, 1969.

Grier, William H., and Cobbs, Price M., *Black Rage.* New York: Basic Books, 1968.

Himes, Joseph S., "The Functions of Racial Conflict," *Social Forces,* 45:1 (September 1966), 1–10.

Killian, Lewis W., and Grigg, Charles M., *Racial Crisis in America: Leadership in Conflict*. Englewood Cliffs, N.J.: Prentice-Hall, 1964.

Lincoln, C. Eric, *My Face is Black*. Boston: Beacon, 1964.

Lomax, Louis E., *The Negro Revolt*. New York: Harper & Row, 1962.

Parsons, Talcott, and Clark, Kenneth B., eds., *The Negro American*. Boston: Houghton Mifflin, 1966.

Powledge, Fred, *Black Power, White Resistance*. Cleveland: World, 1967.

"Report from Black America," *Newsweek* (June 30, 1969), 16–35.

Wagstaff, Thomas, *Black Power: The Radical Response to White America*. Beverly Hills, Calif.: Glencoe Press, 1969.

APPENDIX: THE NATURAL HISTORY
OF RACE RELATIONS*

The race relations cycle, the natural history of race relations, and similar verbal formulae conceptualize the theoretical position that inter-racial behavior is something more than arbitrary arrangements dictated by expediency, and that changes in race relations are not brought about by incantations or determined exclusively by fortuitous circumstances. The expressions imply the hypothesis that racial behavior shows some of the characteristics of a natural process, that racial status and its changes are, in some measure, the consequence of factors of more general incidence than the historical accidents of particular local areas. In the contact and association of racially and culturally divergent peoples, there seem to be certain invariable characteristics; these common facts seem to stand in sequence and to reappear in all areas of racial contact.

This hypothesis that race relations are natural phenomena seems to be a necessary idea in the intellectual climate in which we live. The discoveries of the physical and biological sciences have given some understanding of the nature of the universe and some genuine knowledge of the mechanisms and processes of the physical reality. This knowledge has given man an appreciable measure of control over the external physical environment. Translated into the productive arts and technologies, it has revolutionized transportation and communication, multiplied the means of subsistence in a niggardly world, trebled the length of human life, and in numerous other ways has operated to satisfy in some measure a major segment of human needs. In some measure scientific knowledge has been misused as in war, misappropriated as in economic exploitation, or stupidly used as in radio and motion pictures. But the knowledge is genuine. In spite of its occasional misuse it is the basic factor in civilization: there is no respect in which the modern differs from the medieval world that does not trace back to science and its applications.

It is perhaps inevitable that the achievements in the physical and biological realms should have led to the belief that equally significant gains are possible in the world of human relations, and that there should be a corresponding loss of faith in the old formulae and procedures traditional in these areas. At any rate it is true that there has developed a belief, amounting to a profound and

* Paper read at Music Festival, Fisk University, 1945.

widespread faith, in the possibility of so controlling the forces of external nature and of so directing the economic, social, and political relations of peoples
as to mitigate or eliminate the intolerable misery that has characterized the
life of all but a few men throughout the period of human existence. Peoples
and groups no longer accept the traditional doctrine that catastrophes are acts
of God that must be passively endured; they no longer believe that ill-health,
poverty, illiteracy, exploitation, cultural exclusion, and the like are inevitable
results of uncontrollable forces of physical and animal nature. In increasing
numbers, the peoples of the Western world are committed to the position that
the conditions of the past and present are the results of human ignorance and
greed, and they are engaged in efforts to control to human ends the conditions
of human life. The struggle against existing racial patterns is but one expression of the general human rebellion against unnecessary factors that frustrate
and enslave the masses of men.

But the achievements in technology and the practical arts that impress the
man in the street are secondary phenomena—the utilization in concrete and
immediately practical problems of bits of information made available by the
preceding abstract research into the mechanisms and process of the physical
universe. By the application of scientific knowledge, the technician is able to
exercise a measure of control in the concrete realm. Knowing the nature, that
is, the behavior and normal sequence of events, the technician, by the introduction of other factors, may be able to retard or accelerate the normal process or
to change it into a different process operating to other ends. Scientific knowledge of social reality should make possible the replacement of good intentions
by economic and effective procedures.

The facts are simple and clear but, since they are not generally understood
and are often ignored, a brief concrete illustration may not be wholly amiss.
The physician, a professional technologist, is called to minister to the needs of
a sick person. He may find from the symptoms and the tests that the person is
suffering from a particular type of pneumonia. From his scientific training, the
physician knows that the normal sequence of steps in the disease, to mention
only a few, is an increasing congestion of the lungs, a consequent disturbance
of the circulatory system, and finally the death of the patient from heart failure. Knowing such facts, he is able to interfere at any point in the normal sequence—by the use of drugs, by supplying the patient with oxygen-enriched
air, by the use of digitalis or other heart stimulants—and change the normal sequence and the usual result. His ability to control the concrete situation derives
from the abstract sciences of chemistry and biology.

In social reality we seek a similar or analogous power to control; we wish to
direct human relations toward constructive instead of destructive ends. To the
present, such efforts have not been conspicuously successful, as the existing relations among nations, peoples, and races testify. When a given program has
achieved a measure of success, the factors that determined the outcome generally are not understood and the same or similar procedures used in other situations often give indifferent or negative results.

Apparently our ability to achieve a measure of control in social relations will
become effective only when we come to understand human behavior as a
natural process and base our political procedures and other action programs on
such knowledge. Until such scientific knowledge is available and utilized by
competent technicians, social efforts will largely remain, as at present, at a blind
trial and error stage: they will continue to be a treatment of symptoms—an ad-

ministration of aspirin rather than an effort to control the natural sequence—and a waste of energy in efforts to do the impossible.

The natural history of race relations implies an effort to understand human and social processes in naturalistic terms, to understand social reality as we do physical and biological reality, and thus provide a basis for effective control. If human and social behavior are natural phenomena, and no other assumption seems possible in the world in which we live, there is no insuperable reason why the processes should not be discovered and defined and the behavior be brought within the orbit of human control. If human and social behavior are not natural phenomena, they lie in the realm of the supernatural, hence they are outside the orbit of human comprehension, and are amenable to control only by appeals that influence—or by magical formulae that coerce—the demon world. In this case, the action programs of the practical workers and the scientific research of the students are equally futile and meaningless. But any such assumption runs counter to the thought processes of the modern world; the modern faith is in science and in the techniques of control.

But there is no general consensus on the position here sketched. And the grounds for anti-scientific attitudes are varied and numerous. In general the literary and humanistic cults, interested in emotional exaltation rather than in intellectual clarity, are actively anti-scientific: they prefer a return to the medieval thought processes to effective adjustments in the modern world. There are other individuals who seek to avoid the implications of the position they profess to occupy: accepting the logic and procedures of science as the only source of positive knowledge, they nevertheless retain some mental, emotional, or mystical reservations in the area of human and social behavior. There are those who oppose the development of a genuine social science because of a fear that its findings may not parallel their personal interests or sentiments. Still others, not too clear concerning the relations of social science and social engineering, are irritated by the objective attitude of the research students and their detachment from pressing current social problems. They are impatient to do something now. Some impatiently ask, "Science for what?"; others take a generally anti-scientific attitude and insist that social science is a political, i.e., immediately practical study. One former university president, now the manager of a leading publishing company, measures the importance of research by the salability of manuscripts. The recent exodus of academic and research students from the colleges to technological and social engineering jobs has resulted in some efforts to rationalize the change of status. At another level, an anti-scientific attitude rests on the basis of simple illusion. Race relations are facts of familiar experience. Acquaintance and habitudinal adjustments give the non-critical person the feeling that he "understands" the phenomena. The more provincial the person and the more limited his experience the more profound is his conviction. A case in point is the familiar dogma of the old South that the Negro is the southerner's problem, that only the white southerner is able to understand and competent to deal with the race problem.

Aside from these and other divergent views and misunderstandings, the students proceed with their efforts to analyze social reality in naturalistic terms and thereby provide a scientific structure that will direct human efforts into channels that will produce effective results. They work on the hypothesis that race relations are of a single basic pattern, that the same steps are repeated, with endless variations according to local conditions, in all areas of conduct.

THE HISTORICAL SEQUENCE

In the long perspective, historical and other data seem to establish the fact that the contacts of peoples have been accompanied and followed by racial and cultural phenomena of relatively uniform pattern. The sequence is apparently the same for all the historical peoples. The movement of man from the simple and direct modes of primitive existence to the complex and secondary types of civilized life seems to be a result of biological processes and a function of social and cultural contact. In this long historical view, one is able to see that the present is not an era of anarchy but a passing stage in the ceaseless process of social change. The processes are clear and distinct but their coexistence in time and place has often led to misunderstanding and to misinterpretations of the causal sequence.

If one may treat the Biblical story of the Garden of Eden as an ethnological document, it becomes a paradigm of general application. Stripped of its literary excellence and metaphorical language, it becomes the proposition of Malthus and other population scholars. In a limited area of abundance, the population increased; plenty gave way to scarcity; threatened starvation forced dispersion and a search for new means of life. The legends of all tribal groups seem to account for their origin in a similar way—in terms of a migration of their ancestors from some far-off land. The increase in numbers in time and areas of abundance leads to over-population, the resultant hardships lead to migration and the formation of new settlements; the gradual adaptation to the new climatic conditions brings a present repetition of the growth-starvation-migration cycle.

As the more inhabitable areas were occupied a new condition arose. The migrating bands came with increasing frequency into contact with previous migrants who were now settled groups. The immediate events and subsequent relations seem to have been indefinitely variable. In some cases the migrating bands were welcomed as desirable additions to the population; in other cases the invaders overpowered the local people and imposed themselves as rulers or co-residents of the area; in still other cases the migrants were captured and enslaved by the settled peoples. The details are matters of indifference; the significant fact is that migration in a settled world results in the contact and association of previously isolated peoples.

The contacts, whether initially friendly or hostile, seem everywhere to have been followed by the same type of phenomena. Invariably they have resulted in the present biological fusion of the racial or biological stocks and in the formation of new peoples variously marked by the heritable traits of the ancestral groups. On the other hand, the contacts seem always to have led to a selective blending of the social heritages and the present emergence of an enriched culture. The details vary with time and place and people but the historical sequence remains unchanged.

THE NATURAL PROCESS

The student of racial realities is interested in something more than the sequence of historical events. He seeks to define a developmental sequence, a growth process in which each event is a maturation of the factors present in the preceding stage and their emergence in a new form in the present; he seeks to define a sequence in which the full cycle is nascent in the original fact, as the oak tree is said to exist in the acorn. As the florist knows when he plants his seeds that they will germinate and pass through a definite life cycle, so the social scientist wishes to know the life cycle of the process initiated by racial contacts.

It is obvious, of course, that the sociologist is here concerned with an ideal rather than a historical reality. He is not even concerned with a typical cycle such as conceivably may be stated in terms of common, general, and recurring historical phenomena. He seeks, rather, to know what would go on if there were no complicating factors. From the multiplicity of historical sequences, contemporary studies, and other relevant data he seeks to abstract and generalize a natural process, an ideal construct, from the confused mass of concrete reality.

One need not be unduly concerned by the fact that an abstract statement never corresponds with the concrete reality. It is not intended to do so. It describes what would happen in carefully defined conditions; it gives the pattern to which all such behavior would correspond if there were no distortions by fortuitous events. In the light of the abstraction it is possible to examine and understand the deviate behavior. The physicist knows that no body ever falls at the accelerated rate stated in the law of gravitation; so long as air offers resistance to moving bodies no object ever will. The florist is fully aware that the development of his plants will be conditioned by moisture, sunshine, and other variables and that they may be destroyed by accidents or pests and never complete the cycle of growth. The physician knows that no disease ever exists in isolation, that there is always a person who suffers from the disease, and that its course is always modified by the coexisting facts. But a knowledge of the abstract process, a knowledge of what goes on in the test tube, is at the basis of his diagnosis and treatment of the specific case. In a similar way, the sociologist knows that race relations coexist with economic, political, and other relations —that they are a part of the concrete complex reality of observation and experience. But he is also convinced that if race relations are to be understood they must be isolated, statistically or otherwise, from coexisting relations that condition the racial process as such.

It is not the intention here to elaborate the natural history of race relations or to attempt any detailed analysis of the processes. Some steps in this direction have been made and the literature is readily available. There is need for further analysis and for numerous empirical studies to expand and correct the body of theory. The purpose here is to emphasize the importance of the concept of a means of promoting profitable types of racial research and as a means of integrating racial studies into a more or less coherent, meaningful, and socially useful body of knowledge.

All race relations have their origin in invasion. Like other scientific concepts, this is an abstract and morally colorless term symbolizing the entrance of foreign persons into an occupied territory or the introduction of strange tools, ideas, or processes into a culture area or complex. The forms are numerous and diverse; conquest, immigration, the importation of laborers, the coming of missionaries, are random examples. The historical phenomena are often of wide popular interest but the events are of no importance in themselves; the significance of invasion lies in the fact that it initiates contacts and leads to interaction between previously separated peoples and cultures—it puts in train a sequence of steps that ultimately leads to a new social order.

The contact and interaction of peoples and heritages, resulting from the invasion of a territory or a culture, initiates a period of change marked by confusion and disorder. The relations of the people, whether friendly or hostile, are matters of historical detail and of great popular interest but they are not matters of scientific concern: they do not determine the course of events. The factors common to the various areas of contact are a decline in the population of the simpler group, a disorganization of the native culture, and a demoralization of the native people. The inevitable competition between the contrasted ways of life presently results in the elimination of the less efficient.

In time the state of disorder gives way to a system of status arrangements and working relations between or among the groups. The development of customs and reciprocal habits adjusts the groups to each other and to the conditions that they cannot change. In the mutual living together of more or less accommodated groups, there is a gradual acculturation of the subordinated group, a progressive adoption of the more efficient economy and ways of life, a continuous decline in the native economy, and an increasing dependence upon the invaders for the means of life. In varying degrees the members of the subordinated group come to conform, psychologically and socially, to the thought and behavior patterns of the ruling group.

Status and accommodation gradually evolve into a stage of race relations in which the major characteristic is a struggle for status. The assimilated and partly assimilated individuals of the excluded group seek to invade and participate in the culture of the dominant group. If their aspirations are frustrated, the struggle presently takes on the form of a social movement which, in turn, creates or strengthens an obverse counter movement.

In the area of practical affairs, there is a very real need for organizing principles and a body of integrating theory. As concrete observational phenomena, the relations of racial groups appear as peculiarly intricate and difficult areas of social reality. The failure to reach mutually satisfactory adjustments, or to maintain harmonious relations once they have been established, are phenomena of wide incidence. Europe and Asia as well as America and Africa have chronic or recurring racial problems, and these problems take many patterns. Some are of long standing, others are of recent origin; the details vary with time, places, and circumstance. In some areas racial tensions, chronic friction, and recurring periods of overt conflict seem to be accepted as expected phenomena; in other areas of contact divergent racial groups carry on a common life with little or no show of antagonism. The gross surface phenomena are so diverse that they create an illusion that each area of racial contact is a separate thing—a unique and accidental concatenation of factors.

The literature on, or tangent to, the facts of race and the relations of races and peoples gives much the same impression. It is diverse and confused, expresses different interests, points of view, objectives, and procedures. The terms are commonly undefined and loosely used; the term race is used to refer to minorities, nationalities, neighborhoods, religious sects, and so on—to almost anything from biological varieties to linguistic groups; the word relations is used to connote any and all forms of personal and group interaction from the primary and sacred behavior of intimates to the secular and exploitive activities of war and commerce. The discussions are largely polemic, reflecting varied interests and embodying contradictory sentiments. History gives a recital of various unique and spectacular items of the past few thousand years. This is supplemented by romance, song, and story, which elaborate the biographical and anecdotal aspects of myth and history.

On the basis of his limited personal experience and reading, the layman, as the social practitioner, reacts according to his personal attitudes and objectives. The current general disposition is to attribute objectionable characteristics to members of the other group and justify one's own behavior in terms of these characteristics. To the Jew, the problem of relations has its roots in the characteristics and behavior of the non-Jews; to the non-Jews, the problem has its locus in the offensive characteristics of Jews. The white man endows the Negroes with all the characteristics that occur to him as offensive; the Negro, in turn, endows the white man with a different but equally damning complement of characteristics. All this provides a basis for friction and conflict but it contributes nothing to understanding or constructive action. Some people deplore friction and violence, and plead and struggle for cooperation and harmony; others recognize the facts but deny that anything of consequence can be done to change them. Still others participate in programs to remove or perpetuate inequalities in race relations.

To deal with the concrete and immediately practical problems, programs of action are necessary and desirable. But their success or failure depends upon the soundness of the underlying assumptions and the validity of the data. Here abstract theory is the one indispensable guide. It encourages the worker to substitute objective and realistic attitudes for the sentimental and moralistic approach, it gives a basis for separating significant problems from isolated and special problems, it enables him to distinguish meaningful facts from symptoms, and it enables him to substitute systematic programs for programs of opportunistic expediency.

In an integrated program there is of course no conflict between theoretical and empirical procedures; they are simply different aspects of the same thing. Theory is simply a conceptual organization of knowledge that comes from valid empirical investigation. On the other hand, genuine and profitable research is always related to the existing body of theory; research problems are never set by the immediately practical concerns of concrete reality; research problems are defined by the abstract theory to which the empirical research seeks to make a contribution. The concrete social scene, the area of social engineering and political action, becomes meaningful and intelligible in the light of social theory and research. The concept of the racial cycle gives a frame of reference for evaluating and interpreting racial activities and investigations and for indicating the types of research needed if the practical action programs are to become progressively more efficient.

INDEX
